Washington, D.C.

A Turn-of-the-Century Treasury

Edited by
Frank Oppel
&
Tony Meisel

CASTLE

Washington, D.C.
A Turn-of the Century Treasury

A division of Book Sales, Inc.
110 Enterprise Avenue
Secaucus, NJ 07094

Manufactured in the United States of America.
ISBN: 1-55521-226-3

Contents

Historic Houses of Washington (1893)

HISTORIC HOUSES OF WASHINGTON.

By Teunis S. Hamlin.

TO most visitors Washington is only the seat of government, and interesting merely because of the department buildings, the White House, and the Capitol. Having seen these, with the National Museum and the Smithsonian Institution, tourists go away content. They do not pause to think that nearly all the great men of the nation have, at one time or another, had homes at the capital, and have here done a very large share of the work that has made them famous. Yet so true is this that no other city on this continent is so rich in historical associations, and these associations are in the homes of the capital. They cluster around houses that have sheltered the makers of the republic, and are involved with those personal incidents that are the most fascinating part of history. Some of these spots are remote from the portions of the city now frequented by visitors. Georgetown, which flourished before Washington was laid out even on paper, and whose older inhabitants still look down on all the region east of Rock Creek with placid scorn, has a large number of fine old dwellings, several of them richly stored with relics of the revolutionary period. Capitol Hill, at the other extremity of the city, is justly proud of the fact that General Washington designed it to be the site of the great metropolis that should bear his name ; that the Capitol faces eastward ; that every President at his inauguration takes the oath of office looking toward the dignified old part of the city and not toward the pretentious new part, of which Capitol Hill feels an ill-disguised jealousy. There is a block of houses at I and Second Streets which few visitors to Washington ever see, yet which are connected with several of the greatest names in our history. No. 201 was built by Stephen A. Douglas when he confidently expected to be President. In its great ball-room he gave splendid entertainments that he believed were promoting his political fortunes. In the reception-room at the right of the hall, he received, in April, 1860, the news that the Charleston Convention had adjourned to meet at Baltimore, and he instantly declared, "That means disunion." After Douglas's lamented death this house was sold to Justice Joseph P. Bradley, of the Supreme Court, and its great ball-room became his library. The next house in this block was given by New York friends to General Grant, and here he had his home until he moved to the White House, when it became, through a similar act of generosity, the home of General Sherman.

The region about the Court House is also full of interest. At the corner of D and Sixth Streets lived Salmon P. Chase, whose beautiful and brilliant daughter made his home socially famous. Just around the corner on D Street, Webster had his last Washington home ; and from the steps of what is now the Webster Law Building he made his memorable midnight speech, when, in 1852, Scott had captured from him the Presidential nomination, and he realized that his political career was closed.

But though there are many such fascinating homes in unvisited places, yet no part of the city is so rich in historic interest as Lafayette Park. From the beginning of the government at Washington to this hour it has been the haunt of many of our greatest men. In Corcoran House Webster lived while Secretary of State, and over his sumptuous dinner-table the Ashburton Treaty was discussed and practically concluded. At the northwest corner of H Street and Vermont Avenue, Sumner had his home ; and here, surrounded with books, in an aristocratic semi-seclusion, he did his work and nursed his vanity. Northward on the same square lived Reverdy Johnson, whose house, with others of historic interest, was demolished two or three years ago to make room for the new portion of the Arlington Hotel.

At 17 Madison Place have lived two of the greatest statesmen that America has produced—William H. Seward and James G. Blaine. The site of this house was once owned by Henry Clay, who is said to have traded a Kentucky mule for it. Commodore Rodgers built the house, and it has seen very varied fortunes. In the southwest room of the third story, Seward was attacked by the assassin Payne, on the fatal 14th of April, 1865, and received wounds that he carried to the grave. In the same room Mr. Blaine slowly sunk to rest after the brilliant successes and the bitter disappointments of his splendid career.

There are, however, houses that may be called historic in a fuller sense even than these, and that are still more likely to be passed by unknown by the stranger and even the resident; for many residents are quite unaware of the facts that give interest to the buildings with which they are most familiar. I shall seek to recall some of the heroic and graceful figures that have made these places memorable, and thus to suggest how rich in ennobling associations is this city, known at present chiefly or only for its modern beauty.

When the Congress, sitting at Philadelphia, in 1790, determined to locate the seat of the general government on the banks of the Potomac, the site chosen was very sparsely settled, and but little of it was under cultivation. Most of the territory covered by the present city was primeval forest. The owners of the land were Daniel Carroll, Notley Young, Samuel Davidson, and David Burns. Of their original homes only one remains, the cottage of Burns. He owned most of what is now the northwest section of the city. He was a hard-headed, close-fisted Scotchman, not at all willing to surrender a foot of his land without being roundly paid for it. The commissioners appointed by the Congress to lay out the Federal city could do nothing with him. Again and again General Washington rode up from Mount Vernon, and sitting on a rough bench before the cottage, discussed the matter with "obstinate Mr. Burns." At length he said: "Had not the Federal city been laid out here you would have died a poor tobacco-planter." "Ay, mon," retorted Burns; "an' hed ye no married the Widder Custis, wi' a' her nagurs, ye'd ha'e been a land-surveyor the noo, an' a mighty poor ane at that." Finally General Washington assured Mr. Burns that the Government must and would have his land. Once convinced of this, the wily owner hastened to make favorable terms; and in the end, seeing how vastly he was profiting, even became quite generous. He gave his apple-orchard, which is now the superb Lafayette Square.

Thus David Burns, recently widowed, became the first rich man of the capital, and his only child, Marcia, a prospective heiress. She was extremely lovely in both person and character. Her father's cottage, from having been the resort of neighboring farmers who gathered around his fire on winter evenings to discuss the crops and drink apple-jack, became the gathering place of the greatest men and women that the Government brought to the new capital. Washington, Jefferson, Hamilton, and Burr were frequent visitors. Tom Moore was entertained here, and from this cottage wrote to his friend, Thomas Hume:

> "Thus let us meet, and mingle converse dear
> By Thames at home, or by Potowmac here!
> O'er lakes and marsh, through fevers and through fog,
> 'Midst bears and Yankees, democrats and frogs,
> Thy foot shall follow me; thy heart and eyes
> With me shall wonder, and with me despise."

From many suitors Marcia Burns chose the handsome and courtly John P. Van Ness, then a member of Congress from New York, "well-fed, well-bred, and well-read." They were married on May 9, 1802. She was then twenty years of age, and her father had died but a short time before. After several years' residence at the cottage an elegant mansion was built near it, Latrobe being the architect, at a cost of over $75,000, an immense sum for that day. It stands in a large enclosed park, then beautifully kept. Two fine lodges of stone are at the entrance. The vestibule is supported by massive columns. The second floor (it is an English basement) has two sumptuous parlors and a dining-room to correspond. The view from the chambers of the third story across the Potomac and to the Virginian hills is enchanting. In luxuriousness of appointments it had no equal in this country at the time it was built. It was the first house in which cold and hot water was carried to all the floors. The wine vaults were very extensive. It was in them that the conspirators intended to hide President Lincoln in 1865, when it was their purpose to kidnap instead of to assassinate him. The drawing-rooms were adorned with mantels of Italian marble by Thorwaldsen. Two of these were removed by Governor Swann, of Maryland (who came into possession of the Van Ness property, and whose heirs still own it), to beautify his house in Fifteenth Street.

The Van Ness house at once became the centre of elegant and liberal hospitality. All the great Americans of that period were numbered among its guests. But its mistress never lost her love for the humble cottage. She delighted in showing it to her most eminent visitors, and recounting the scenes that it recalled of her happy girlhood. Since her death, on September 9, 1832, and especially since her husband's death, on March 7, 1847, the estate has fallen into sad neglect. The house has been put to disreputable uses, having at one time been the haunt of a gang of negroes who terrorized the whole neighborhood. In the cottage silk-worms were kept for some time, and from their cocoons a bridal-dress was made for one of the daughters of Colonel John Tayloe. The house was so well built that it is still in very good preservation; but the cottage is now rapidly crumbling to pieces and will hardly endure the storms of another winter.

The war of 1812 left the capital with many helpless and dependent children of soldiers, and Mrs. Van Ness conceived the idea of founding an asylum for them. This idea bore fruit in a meeting held in the hall of the House of Representatives, October 10, 1815. Mrs. Madison was made first directress and Mrs. Van Ness second. On Mrs. Madison's leaving the city in 1817, her successor at the White House, Mrs. Monroe, was chosen first directress; but she declined to serve and the choice fell on Mrs. Van Ness. For fifteen years thereafter she gave the most sedulous attention to this work. Her interest was deepened by the sad death of her only child, Ann Elbertine, highly educated, beautiful, and brilliant, who only two years before had married Arthur Middleton, of South Carolina. Mrs. Van Ness gave a lot on H Street, near Ninth (on which stood her family mausoleum, now in the Oak Hill Cemetery), where the asylum had its first permanent home. Her devotion to the poor and suffering was incessant, and her nursing of the victims of cholera caused her own death of the same disease. She was the first and only woman in private station to be honored with a public funeral at the capital.

At the northeast corner of New York Avenue and Eighteenth Street stands the Octagon, one of the oldest houses in the city, still in very good preservation. It was begun by Colonel John Tayloe in 1798, and occupied in 1801, the year following that in which the Government removed from Philadelphia to Washington. It had been his intention to build a winter residence in the former city, and he changed his plans at the earnest request of General Washington, who took the greatest interest in the progress of the building. Colonel Tayloe was the richest Virginian of his day. At Mount Airy he had the largest landed estate in the Old Dominion, and occupied the most elegant mansion, which had been built by his father in 1758. Among his five hundred slaves were artisans of every class. His hospitality was lavish, his guests the most eminent men of the time. All this magnificence was transferred to his town house during the winters, and for the first quarter of this century the Octagon was the centre of all that was most brilliant and refined in unofficial society.

For a brief period it was also the official centre. On August 24, 1814, the British burned the Capitol and the Executive Mansion. The President had left two days before to join the army under General Winder. Mrs. Madison had been meanwhile ready for flight with such state papers as she could carry. At the last moment she insisted on securing the picture of Washington, which now hangs in the East Room. By her orders the frame was broken and the canvas removed. She then made her escape across the Potomac into Virginia, where she was joined late the same evening by the President.

Returning two days later to find the White House in ashes, the President was offered the use of various houses, and finally rented the Octagon. It was worthy of such occupants. The circular hall, marble-tiled, was heated by two picturesque stoves placed in small recesses in the wall. Another hall beyond opened into a large and lovely garden surrounded by a high brick wall after the English fashion. To the right was a handsome drawing-room with a fine mantel, still well preserved. To the left was the dining-room, of equal size and beauty. A circular room over the hall, with windows to the floor and a handsome fireplace, was President Madison's office. Here, on February 18, 1815, he signed the proclamation of the Treaty of Ghent, formally closing the war with England. The treaty had been unanimously approved by the Senate on the 16th.

This part of Washington has long since fallen into disfavor. It was thought to be malarial, and no doubt was so before the filling and improvement of the flats to the southward. Few visitors to the city probably ever go nearer to it than the State, War, and Navy Building. But its fortunes seem to be reviving. Excavations are now (July, 1893) in progress between the Van Ness house and the Octagon for the magnificent new Corcoran Art Gallery. And some men of wealth and taste with the historic spirit may yet restore the social fortunes of these famous houses.

Colonel Tayloe's second son, Benjamin Ogle, was born at the residence of his maternal grandfather, Governor Ogle, at Annapolis, Md., May 21, 1796. From his youth he was accustomed to the society of such men as Hamilton, Jay, Marshall, and Pinckney. He was educated at the Phillips Academy, Exeter, N. H., and at Harvard University in the class of 1815. He studied law in the office of the Hon. Richard Rush, then Attorney-General; and in 1817, when President Monroe made Mr. Rush minister to England, Mr. Tayloe accompanied him as private secretary. At London, Paris, Brussels, Rome — indeed, wherever he went, he was warmly and intimately received by the best people of the day.

On November 8, 1824, Mr. Tayloe married Miss Julia Maria Dickinson, of Troy, N. Y., intending to pursue the life of a country gentleman on his estate at Windsor, Va. But this life was not so congenial to his wife as to himself. She desired a town house, and he accordingly built the elegant and spacious residence, now No. 21 Madison Place, Lafayette Square, and occupied it in 1829. For nearly forty years, until his death on February 25, 1868, this house was the scene of the most generous and refined hospitality. Marshall, Webster, Calhoun, Clay, Cass, Edward Livingston, Robert C. Winthrop, Scott, Everett, Seward, Irving, Prescott, and Bancroft; Presidents John Quincy Adams, Jackson, William Henry Harrison, Taylor, Fillmore, and Buchanan; Lords Napier, Ashburton, Lyons, and Radstock were a few of his intimate friends. Remaining steadfastly in private life, against many solicitations to accept office, he still had a powerful influence in national affairs. Few men have better understood the bearing of social relations on political questions or employed it more skilfully.*

Mrs. Madison was unquestionably the most popular woman that has ever presided over the social life of the Executive Mansion. She was extremely beautiful in person and gentle and courteous in manner. Consummate tact made good her lack of liberal education. Madison first met her when he was a member of Congress at Philadel-

*Mrs. Tayloe died July 4, 1846, and on April 27, 1849, Mr. Tayloe married Miss Phœbe Warren, also of Troy, N. Y.

phia, and, with Aaron Burr, boarded at the house of her father, Mr. Payne. She was then the Widow Todd. The future President promptly fell in love with her. But having some doubts about her mental qualities, he one day handed her a book to read and asked her to give him her opinion of it. She gave the book to Burr with the request that he would write a letter for her to copy. This he did with his usual brilliance; and Madison, on receiving the note, was fully convinced that his lady-love's intellect was equal to her beauty. He at once offered himself and was accepted.

As a social leader, however, Mrs. Madison was her husband's superior, although he was a well-bred and hospitable man. She was phenomenal in several ways. She never forgot a face or a name. At one time a gentleman approached her whom she had not seen for twenty-six years and said: "Mrs. Madison, I am confident you do not remember me." But she instantly mentioned his name and the time and place of their former meeting. She always gave her special attention to the diffident and embarrassed among her guests. Once a tall, awkward backwoodsman came to a reception at the White House. After standing painfully in a corner for an hour or more, he at last summoned courage to take a cup of the coffee that was being handed around. Mrs. Madison had been trying to reach him, and at this moment approached and addressed him. He was so frightened that he dropped the saucer from his trembling left hand and thrust the cup into his trousers' pocket with his right. Mrs. Madison quietly said: "The crowd is so great here that one cannot avoid being jostled. I will see that you have another cup of coffee. How is your excellent mother? I once knew her very well." With such homely talk she soon beguiled him from his bashfulness and enabled him to forget his mortification. It is not wonderful that when she retired from the Executive Mansion on March 4, 1817, she left behind a multitude of regretful friends.

Madison survived the close of his public life for nineteen years, passed in dignified comfort and happiness at his estate of Montpelier, Va., where he died on June 28, 1836. He left his widow what would have been a comfortable fortune had she not spent most of it to pay the debts of her drinking and gambling son, Payne Todd. A part of the estate was the fine house at the southeast corner of Madison Place and H Street, now the home of the "Cosmos," the largest scientific club in the world. It had been built about 1825 by Richard Cutts, the brother-in-law of Mrs. Madison.*

It came into the ex-President's possession the year before his death, in settlement of a debt. But Mrs. Madison was too poor to occupy it, and rented it successively to Attorney-General Crittenden, to the Hon. William C. Preston, of South Carolina, and to James I. Roosevelt, member of Congress from New York. On March 3, 1837, an act of Congress was approved by President Jackson, appropriating $30,000 to purchase Madison's diary of the debates and events connected with the framing of the Federal Constitution.† This money enabled Mrs. Madison to live in her city house; and the same year she very gladly returned to the capital, which she had always tenderly loved. Her return was a renewal in private life of all her social triumphs from 1801 to 1817, for eight years as the wife of Jefferson's Secretary of State, and for another eight years as the wife of the President. But it was a new generation that crowded to do her honor. Looking over the company on the occasion of her first reception, she said to an old friend at her side: "What a difference twenty years make in the face of society! Here are young men and women not born when I left the capital, whose names are familiar, but whose faces are

* Nepotism seems to have been known, and charged upon women as well as men, even in those simple-hearted days. When Mrs. Madison fled from the city in 1814, taking only this family of relatives with her, these lines were published:

"My sister Cutts, and Cutts, and I,
And Cutts's children three,
Will fill the coach; so you must ride
On horseback after we."

† These papers were published in three volumes in 1840. On May 31, 1848, $25,000 was appropriated for the purchase of Madison's unpublished papers, then owned by his widow; and they were given to the public in 1856.

unknown to me." At sixty-five, however, she retained all the fascination of her girlhood and young womanhood. She was heartily interested in both the old and the young. Her kindness of heart and gentleness of manner were unfailing. Her home fairly rivalled the White House as a social centre. On New Year's days the same distinguished crowd that paid their respects to the President hastened across the square to greet Mrs. Madison with all good wishes. On every Fourth of July her parlors were thronged.

Four months before her death, in her seventy-eighth year, the young sister of Admiral Dahlgren called upon her, and rising to leave, said: "Mrs. Madison, I have a new autograph album, and I must have you write in it before any-one else." Throwing her arms about her young friend, Mrs. Madison said: "Well, you darling little flatterer, if you will get me a good quill, I will do it. I cannot write with these new-fangled steel pens." So Miss Dahlgren sent her the best quill pen to be found and received her album with the beautifully written autograph of which the following is a fac-simile.

For Miss Dahlgren.

—"Deliberate on all things, with thy friend;
But since friends grow not thick on every bough,
First, on thy friend, deliberate with thyself;
Pause, ponder, sift; not eager in the choice
Nor jealous of the chosen; fixing, fix
Judge before friendship, then confide till death"

D P Madison

Washington Feby 14th 1849.

After Mrs. Madison's death this house was sold to Admiral Wilkes, who occupied it until the civil war. In 1862 it was the head-quarters of General McClellan, who was accustomed to leave it in great splendor to review the armies across the Potomac, attended by his distinguished staff, which included the Prince de Joinville, the Duc de Chartres, and the Comte de Paris. The interior is now much changed. In Mrs. Madison's day the entrance was on Lafayette Square, but otherwise its external appearance has been preserved.

Besides the Executive Mansion, no building was erected on Lafayette Square until the close of the War of 1812, when St. John's Church was built. The first private house was that of Commodore Stephen Decatur, at the southwest corner of H Street and Jackson Place. It was built in 1819, the architect being Latrobe, the master-mind of our unequalled Capitol. It remains to this day substantially unchanged, and is one of the most elegant interiors in the city. The exterior is extremely plain. The grounds are spacious and entirely enclosed.

Decatur was brave and patriotic. His famous toast was characteristic: "My country: may she be always in the right; but right or wrong — my country." He distinguished himself on many memorable occasions. On February 16, 1804, off Tripoli, he boarded the Philadelphia, set her on fire, and escaped with his crew amid a

DRAWN BY FRANCIS C. JONES.

The David Burns Cottage.

ENGRAVED BY VAN NESS.

The Van Ness House.

rain of shot from one hundred and forty-one guns. Admiral Nelson pronounced this "the most daring act of the age." Decatur had his full share in the War of 1812, and at its close completely and finally humbled the Barbary States, for which he had the gratitude of all Europe; and President Madison, in his Annual Message to the Congress, December, 1815, said: "The high character of the American commander was brilliantly sustained on this occasion."

When Decatur came to reside in Washington he had all the fame and fascination that always attach to the hero of battles and of victories. These were supplemented by the unusual attractiveness of his wife. She was beautiful and highly educated, and despite the shadow of her birth, had been the reigning belle of Norfolk. She had elegant manners and splendid conversational powers. Jerome Bonaparte offered himself to her, but she refused him, on the advice of her friend, the Hon. Robert G. Harper, who assured her that the Emperor Napoleon would never recognize such a marriage. His judgment was shown to be correct when Jerome afterward married Miss Patterson, of Baltimore. The Decaturs at once became social leaders, but for only a single season.

Early in March, 1820, at a dinner given by Decatur, the conversation turned on the late war, and he spoke very severely of Commodore Barron for not returning from Europe to bear his part in that struggle. One of the guests reported this to Commodore Jesse Duncan Elliott, and he to Commodore Barron. Ill feeling between Decatur and Barron dated back to 1808, when the former was a member of a court-martial to try the latter for surrendering the Chesapeake to the British man-of-war Leopard. Barron was convicted and suspended from rank and pay for five years. He also believed that Decatur's influence had availed to keep him on land when he desired active sea-service as a means of restoring his reputation. He was therefore ready to take fire at Decatur's dinner-table talk. Angry letters passed between them. Elliott probably fermented the strife. He had a grudge against Decatur, who held in his hands letters from Commodore Perry reflecting severely on Elliott. Commodore

Dale did his best to effect an adjustment, assuring Decatur that Barron was a man of honor, undeserving of the severe remarks made about him over the wine. But a challenge had been given and accepted, and according to the standards of honor at that day, retreat was impossible. Commodore Morris was asked by Decatur to be his second; he declined, saying the duel was entirely needless; that peace ought to be made, and offering his services in that interest. They were refusea and preparations went forward as secretly as possible.

On Saturday evening, March 19th, Decatur gave a very handsome party to Mrs. Gouverneur, the newly married daughter of President Monroe. Several of the guests observed in their host an unusual solemnity of manner. He was exceptionally devoted to his wife, and when she sang, accompanying herself upon the harp, he stood in the centre of the semi-circle about her, brilliant in his full uniform, but absorbed and melancholy. During the evening he said to his next friend, Commodore Porter, who was to give a similar entertainment for Mrs. Gouverneur the following week, "I may spoil your party."

Ogle Tayloe records that he met Decatur early in the day preceding the duel, and that he looked ill and seemed abstracted; that he met him again late in the afternoon of the same day and was greatly impressed by his solemn manner. On this occasion he saw Decatur accost Commodore Macdonough, take his arm and pace the pavement with him for some time. Macdonough afterward said: "I knew nothing of the contemplated duel or I would have prevented it." Commodore Stewart said the same in regard to himself.

On Wednesday morning, March 22d, Decatur quietly left his house at daybreak, walked to Beale's Hotel, near the Capitol, took breakfast with his second, Commodore Bainbridge, and reached the duelling ground at Bladensburgh about nine o'clock. Barron was already there with his second, Commodore Elliott. Barron was wounded in the hip, where Decatur, who was an unfailing shot, had declared beforehand that he should hit him. Decatur's wound was in the abdomen, and was at once seen to be mortal. As they lay bleeding, Decatur asked: "Why did you not return to America when the war broke out?" "I had not the means," replied Barron. "Why did you not inform me of your situation?" asked Decatur; "I would gladly have furnished you with the requisite funds." When reproached for not having made this explanation before and thus secured an apology from Decatur, Barron replied: "I would explain nothing while under his insult."

Mantel by Thorwaldsen in the Van Ness House.

Decatur was carried home about noon and placed on a couch in the library at the left of the hall on the first floor. His wife said she was too stricken to see him. He died during the evening. At his funeral on Saturday, the 25th, attended by vast numbers of citizens and by almost the whole Congress, John Randolph, of

DRAWN BY FRANCIS C. JONES.

ENGRAVED BY E. H. DEL'ORME.

Entrance to Grounds of Van Ness House.

Roanoke, then much demented, made himself very conspicuous by talking about how he would resent an insult in the same fashion. Decatur's body was placed in the family vault at Kalorama, at the head of Twenty-first Street.

Public feeling at first ran very high against Barron, President Monroe and his Cabinet leading it. But the tide soon turned, and Decatur was very generally condemned as having pursued Barron relentlessly.

Room in the Octagon where President Madison signed the Proclamation of the Treaty of Ghent.

For some months Mrs. Decatur lived in seclusion. She then removed to Kalorama, to the fine house built in 1805 by Joel Barlow, and some time ago obliterated. Here she lived in great style, giving weekly dinners of the most splendid and costly sort. Her name was freely connected with that of Mr. Stratford Canning, then British Minister here, and with that of the aged Charles Carroll, of Carrollton, both of whom no doubt greatly admired her. But she never remarried. Late in life she entered the Roman Catholic Church, and she died in the convent at Georgetown in 1855.

Hall of the Octagon.

On leaving her house on Lafayette Square, Mrs. Decatur leased it to Baron Tuyl, the newly arrived Russian Minister. He was an epicure and a martyr to the gout. He gave no large entertainments, but many superb dinners. He said: "Washington, with its venison, wild turkeys, canvas-back ducks, oysters, and terrapin, furnishes better viands than Paris, and needs only cooks."

Baron Tuyl left Washington early in 1825; and Henry Clay, Secretary of State to John Quincy Adams, took the Decatur house. He furnished it very elegantly and lived in the style befitting his position. Aside from this house Clay had no home at the capital, but lived at the National Hotel, in room No. 32, in which he died on June 29, 1857. This room was for a long time afterward occupied by Alexander H. Stephens. With equal credit lived his successor in both office and home, Martin Van Buren. Upon his leaving the Cabinet, after two years of service, Edward Livingston, of Louisiana, succeeded him, and for an equal period made this now famous house one of the most attractive in the city. He was of mild and genial temper, the soul of gayety and good-humor,

Doorway of the Octagon—corner New York Avenue and Eighteenth Street.

with an inexhaustible fund of stories that he acted out with a contagious glee. He was, withal, an inveterate punster, though he said that the only good one that he ever made came to him in his sleep. He dreamed of being in a church at the ceremony of the taking of the veil by a nun named Mary Fish. To the question who should be her patron saint, he awoke himself by replying aloud, "Why, St. Poly Carp, to be sure."

Mrs. Livingston was equally as attractive as her husband. She was very beautiful and brilliant. A native of San Domingo, and an exile from that island, she had been a reigning belle in New Orleans as a widow, Mme Moreau. Her romantic midnight marriage to Livingston in the chapel of the Ursuline Convent did not forbode the leisurely repentance that often follows such events. She made him a model wife. Under date of August 10,

DRAWN BY FRANCIS C. JONES. ENGRAVED BY VARLEY.

The Tayloe House, No. 21 Lafayette Square.

Dolly Madison's House, corner of H Street and Madison Place.

(Now the home of the Cosmos Club.)

1805, he wrote to his sister, Mrs. Tillotson: "I have again a home, and a wife who gives it all the charms that talents, good temper, and affection can afford." She managed all the household affairs and relieved him from every private care. She had learned English from the classics, and spoke it with great purity, but with a marked though graceful accent. The daughter, Cora, was as brilliant and fascinating as the mother. She married Thomas Barton, afterward Secretary of Legation with Mr. Livingston at Paris. Mrs. Barton returned to the capital for a visit, in 1871, and was received with great affection and reverence.

After the brilliant occupancy of these three successive Secretaries of State, the Decatur house again became the home of two foreign ministers, Sir Charles Vaughan and Baron Hyde de Neuville. The former, though refined, highly educated, and a Fellow of Oxford, seemed to think he must resort to slang, and even to profanity, to show himself at home in a republic. His first appearance in society was at a small evening reception at Mrs. Kuhn's. His hostess graciously expressed her regret that the weather was so warm. "Warm, madam," he said; "it is as hot as hell!" Then turning to Percy Doyle, his secretary: "Percy, you little rascal, come here and be presented to Mrs. Kuhn." On his leaving the country a farewell ball was given him, at which General Van Ness gave this toast: "Sir Charles Vaughan, H. B. M.'s minister near the court of Washington."

The French Minister, de Neuville, had all the grace and elegance of his nation. He had been an *émigré* during the French Revolution, and lived on the Raritan, in New Jersey, much esteemed and beloved by all his neighbors. He was intimate with Louis XVIII., who made him his minister to the United States. The baroness spoke English with an engaging French accent, and not always accurately. Her uniform salutation to her guests was: "I am charming to see you."

After having thus sheltered three Secretaries of State and the representatives of three of the greatest nations of Europe — Russia, England, and France — this house was occupied by John Gadsby, proprietor of the National Hotel; by Joseph Gales, one of the owners of the *National Intelligencer;* by Howell Cobb, John A. and James G. King, and William Appleton, all of whom maintained with credit its social prestige. The latter was especially noted for his benevolence. One winter his butler told him that his wood, which was piled on the sidewalk, was rapidly disappearing. "I think," he said, "it had better not be put away while the weather remains so cold." Its last tenant before the civil war was Judah P. Benjamin, then Senator from Louisiana, afterward Attorney-General, then Secretary of War, and finally, Secretary of State to the Confederacy. His name, combined with his advocacy of the legal claims of slavery, drew from Benjamin Wade the characterization of him as "a Hebrew with Egyptian principles." He fitted up the Decatur house magnificently, bringing much furniture of Louis Philippe from the Tuileries, and intended to maintain its leading position in society. But political events made this impossible.

During the civil war this house was rented by the Government and used for offices. At the close of the war General Edward Fitzgerald Beale bought it, but still rented it to the Government, not moving into it until early in President Grant's second term, in 1873. In 1876 he went as Minister to Austria, and on his return the next year his house became the centre of all that was best in Washington society. He was a grandson of Commodore Truxton, under whom Decatur, the builder of this house, had served as a midshipman.

Drawing-room of the House of the Late General E. F. Beale.

(Built in 1819 and occupied by Commodore Decatur.)

In all respects, General Beale was a worthy successor of Decatur. Equally brave, patriotic, and talented, he rendered his country quite as conspicuous service. In the navy, the army, and civil life his career was highly brilliant and successful. His home is filled with mementos of his service by sea and land, many of them of the most rare and precious sort. He was scholarly and refined, very modest, seldom speaking of his achievements except to his most intimate friends.

On June 27, 1849, General Beale married Mary E., daughter of the Hon. Samuel Edwards. With fine talents, elegant culture, and a hospitable disposition, she has fully sustained the reputation of the long line of brilliant women that have made this home so

Mantel in Room 32, National Hotel.
(In this room Henry Clay died, June 29, 1857.)

Hall and Stairs in the Beale House.

(On the left, entrance to the room in which Commodore Decatur died.)

famous. General Beale died on April 22d of this year, and thus the doors that have opened to nearly every President from Madison to Cleveland, and to all the greatest men and most beautiful women of America and Europe for three-quarters of a century, are for the present closed to the public.

Washington, Our Beautiful Capital: Its Seamy Side (1908)

WASHINGTON, OUR BEAUTIFUL CAPITAL—ITS SEAMY SIDE

BY JUDSON C. WELLIVER

VISITORS to the American capital have so long and so uniformly agreed in characterizing Washington as the best-ordered city in the United States that he who would suggest that there is a seamy side to the picture undertakes an ungracious task. Residents, however, know only too well that there are other aspects than those which impress the tourist who "sees Washington" from the front seat of a "rubber wagon"—aspects which this cursory observer doesn't want to see, and which the voluble guide doesn't feel it worth while to display.

In a peculiar way, Washington is the national city. No other of the world's capitals is this in quite the same way. In most cases, the capital is also the metropolis. London, Paris, Berlin, St. Petersburg, Peking, Rio de Janeiro, Buenos Ayres, and so on, are the great cities of their respective countries; their political status is more or less incidental. Washington, on the other hand, is simply and almost exclusively the capital. Not only was it founded expressly to be the capital, but it was named for the Father of His Country, and its location, on the dividing line of the two sections, was determined as part of the great compromise between the Federalists and the Democrats which was necessitated by factional differences at the very beginning of constitutional government in the United States.

Still more than this, the national government, recognizing its peculiar relation to its political headquarters, generously contributes from the Federal treasury one-half the total expense of the city government. For every dollar that the citizens of Washington pay in taxes, Uncle Sam goes into his pocket for another dollar. Therefore, the people of the whole country have a financial as well as a sentimental interest in knowing the truth about their capital; in seeing its blemishes as well as its beauties; in learning whether it is economically and properly administered.

A CITY UNDER ALIEN GOVERNMENT

Furthermore, the people of the United States owe a peculiar duty to Washington and to the people of Washington. They are bound to give the capital a good government, because they have taken away from it the right to govern itself. Washington is in this regard an anomaly among American cities. Congress is its town council. The President might have added to his title that of "King of Washington." Congress being the municipal legislature, the President is the real executive; for in him is vested the power to appoint the three commissioners of the District of Columbia, who administer the laws passed by Congress.

Washington, therefore, has an alien government. It is subjected to taxation without representation. The citizen with a grievance can't get out on the corner and denounce the aldermen. He gets no chance to appear at the polls on election day and "work against" the offending functionary. He can't draw up a platform of protest and announce himself as an opposition candidate. All he can do, if he is convinced that his town council isn't running the town properly, is to appeal to the people of Tombstone and Kalamazoo, of Pontiac and El Paso, of Tallahassee and Seattle, of Portland, Maine, and Portland, Oregon, and all the rest of these eighty-five million patriotic Americans who want Washington to be a model city, and beg them to elect a council that will be intelligent enough and disinterested enough to do better.

It is quite apparent that the protest of a comparatively small city of three hundred thousand people, spread all over this big country, and competing with the national interest in multifarious national issues, is likely to have very little effect. That is why Washington has rather got discouraged and benumbed. "What's the use?" it asks helplessly.

Washington has some very real and very concrete grievances, and the editor of MUNSEY'S MAGAZINE having opened the way for a brief statement of these grievances, it is proposed here to make use of the opportunity. There is no purpose of calamitous lament. It is recognized that the whole nation is anxious to deal more than fairly with Washington, and that in many ways it is generous with its ward. It is proud of Washington, and wants to feel that its pride is justified.

Washington is not entered in competition for the pitiful distinction of being the worst-governed city in the country; but it is about the most expensively governed, and the results do not justify the cost. Everybody's business is notoriously nobody's business; and in a most literal way, Washington's government is everybody's business.

THE SEAMY SIDE OF WASHINGTON

One fundamental difficulty with the government of Washington by Congress has been the disposition of our legislators to manage the city too much for the nation and too little for the people living in it. Splendid sweeps of asphalt avenues lined with glorious trees — for Washington has more trees than Paris, and vastly finer ones — constitute the front view which everybody admires; in the rear, too often, are squalid alleys in which insanitary hovels serve as the miserable shelter of wretched families. This is the seamy side—a side which the casual visitor does not take the trouble to see.

In these unsightly and unhealthy surroundings, packed together in their poverty-breeding poverty, live the unfortunates who, falling easy victims to consumption and typhoid and pneumonia, make Washington's record of deaths by these diseases one of the worst in the land, and a standing reproach to the government which veneers the front of things and doesn't look behind the veneer.

To this the unsatisfactory answer may be given that all large towns seem fated to have their slums. Perhaps; though nowadays the war on the slum is being waged relentlessly in cities where conditions are far more inherently difficult than in Washington, and the total extinction of the slum is no longer a dream of senseless idealism. And until the national pride in our capital shall have remedied existing conditions, the responsible powers have no right to point with pride to the municipal administration of Washington as a model for other cities.

Again, the condition of the public schools in Washington must make effective appeal to the average American who regards it as a first duty to every village, town, or city to establish the very best system of education that the community can afford.

Washington's public schools have been in turmoil for years. The laws have been changed so often and so fundamentally that no one organization gets its bearings worn down to the point of smooth working before a new scheme is legislated into being—and a new form of turbulence and disorganization results. There is always the most frank and cheering willingness to admit that things are wrong; but the remedy is likely to be worse than the disease. When the patient needs rest, he gets medicine. So the schools go on and on, costing enough to justify expectation that they should be the best, but failing sadly to realize that expectation.

How does it strike the self-satisfied American who is sure that his capital is a well-ordered city to know that when the public schools opened last year, there was overcrowding to the point of danger in many buildings, and to the extent of making good work impossible in more? In some cases it was necessary to go outside and rent structures erected for other purposes, in order to accommodate the pupils at all. In the last ten years the appropriations for erecting school-houses have been two million dollars less than the amount for which the school authorities have asked to meet their requirements.

A POLICY OF MISTAKEN ECONOMY

This suggests a niggardly policy at the point where economy should last be contemplated. Yet this, even, is not quite fair. The point is that Congress has utterly failed to take a comprehensive view of the situation. In other cities, where the government is close to the people and responsive to them, the budgets for current expenses and extraordinary charges are carefully separated; here there is no such wise and proper distinction. Congress seemingly feels that the veneer must be kept fresh and attractive, because Washington is a national show town; if to keep it thus takes too much money, why, something else must be lopped off to make the account balance.

In another city, bonds would be issued to meet extraordinary expenditures, such as buying a park which posterity will enjoy, and for which it may fairly be expected to help to pay. Washington doesn't issue bonds, which is right; with the United States behind it, bonds ought not to be needed. Washington pays cash, and is retiring the small amount of bonds issued under a former dispensation as fast as possible.

But there is one advantage about issuing bonds in such cases. It enforces a differentiation between current and extraordinary expenditures. It guards against borrowing from the current expense pocket in order to pay into a depleted extraordinary expense pocket. The fact that the city needs two million dollars' worth of new school-buildings is not an argument that the new city hall should not have been built, or that Congress, last session, should not have appropriated two millions and a half to buy land for an extension of the Mall; but it is an argument in favor of a system under which a lopping off of the current expense fund will not be made to pay for any special increase in extraordinary expenses.

The reorganization in this regard of the financial system of the city has been repeatedly urged upon Congress by the commissioners of the District of Columbia; but without results. Congress, apparently, feels that if it pays half the expense of running things, and is reasonably liberal, and if it keeps up the polish on the nickel-plated front, so that visitors will exclaim about the beauties of Washington—why, the slums, and the death-rate, and the lack of school-buildings can be looked after some other time.

Right here is illustrated the weakness of the Washington system of government. Congress proposes to conduct its little experiment in city government in quite the right way—no bonds, no vague and dangerous floating debts, and so forth. The thing looks exceeding well. But the time comes when a few millions are wanted for some permanent investment—to buy a park, or to develop the system of boulevards connecting the parks, or to install a filtration plant for the city water. What happens?

Too frequently the disposition of Congress has been to keep the annual total of appropriations down to something like a traditional average. That means that to provide for these special expenditures the demands for current administration must be pruned down; that necessities of the schools, of the penal system, or of the sanitary establishment must await consideration till some later time.

Back in 1900, at the time of the centenary of the founding of Washington, the Senate Park Commission scheme for the development and beautification of Washington was tentatively adopted. In truth, it was simply bringing together the best things in the plans of Washington and of L'Enfant, the great French engineer who made the first plat of the city. It involved a magnificent mall from the Capitol to the White House, the Washington Monument, and the State, War, and Navy Building; the completion of the system of great parks around the city, and their connection by parkway boulevards; the improvement of the Anacostia River basin — whose present condition is another reproach to Washington which the sightseer doesn't investigate; and the extension of Rock Creek Park from Washington down to the mouth of the beautiful Rock Creek, at Georgetown.

The commissioners of the District have ever since clung as closely as possible to this ideal in making their recommendations to Congress. It was impossible that so magnificent and expensive a scheme should be adopted at one stroke of the legislative pen; but the administrative authorities have worked persistently to secure the essentials of the scheme by piecemeal. They have made progress, too.

SPECIAL FAVORS TO THE RAILROADS

Part of the project involved the removal of the Pennsylvania station from land which the railroad never owned, in the Mall. Congress gave the company fifteen hundred thousand dollars to leave that land and join in the erection of the splendid new Union Station. There has been bitter criticism of that legislation. The Baltimore and Ohio demanded equally liberal terms for evacuating the public ground its terminal occupied, and got them. Thus three million dollars was voted away, one-quarter of which was contributed by the taxpayers of Washington, to pay, as has been charged, for that which the railroads never owned.

There are strange stories of the devious methods by which this legislation was passed; still stranger ones of the means by which, many years before, after the Pennsylvania was permitted to lay tracks in the Mall subject to the will of Congress, clauses were clandestinely inserted into enactments giving color to the railroad's claim of legal title to the privilege. These stories are characteristic. Washington people believe there has been all too much of kindly consideration for favored interests, the favors being ultimately charged against the capital city in its account with the public treasury and with its own tax-payers. They believe that Congress has thoughtlessly and good-naturedly — and sometimes, as to some influential members, corruptly—permitted special interests to exploit Washington and the national treasury, to their own enrichment, but to the grave disadvantage of the city and to the despoilment of Uncle Sam's treasure-chest.

Washington is expected to take what it gets without complaint, because Uncle Sam pays half the bills. But let's see about this. France—not Paris, with its millions of people and its immense commercial interests — has paid to make Paris what it is, the gayest and most delightful capital of Europe. Germany —not the huge population of Berlin, eight times as great as Washington's— foots the bills that represent the cost of making Berlin a true imperial city. Russia—not alone the property owners of St. Petersburg—has contributed most lavishly to make the seat of the Czars what it is. And so with others of the national cities. After all, the United States is only doing what other nations are doing for their capitals—vastly less than some of them do.

In Washington, things must be done on a national scale. The streets must be wide; there must be numerous parks, large and small; trees from all parts of the world must be brought and coaxed to grow here; every possibility of natural beauty must be developed; every blemish with which nature marred the prospect must be removed. All this, that the American citizen who on his bridal trip or his anniversary tour includes Washington in his itinerary, may feel a due thrill of admiration and pride. National feeling demands all this. It must and ought to be done. But in frescoing the front of a noble building, there should not be neglect of the interior. The people who live in Washington ought to have the necessaries and the utilities, as well as the adornments and the luxuries.

What does this allusion to the necessaries mean? Well, a city of three hundred thousand people must have street-car service. Washington has it. It has a street-car system controlled by several companies. On the authority of a gentleman who made a careful computation for publication, which has never been questioned, it is stated that the aggregate capitalization of these lines is something over thirty millions of dollars—which is more than two-thirds of a million per mile of double-track line. Compared with other cities of the size and class of Washington, these are exceedingly high figures. Yet Washington is saddled with the necessity of paying returns on this huge sum. It would be impossible here to go into the marvels of finance by which these lines have been organized and reorganized into their present condition of inflated capitalization. Suffice it to say that that condition is a monument to the laxity of Congress — to its easy willingness to acquiesce in the purposes of prominent citizens who have "little bills" which would be "a good thing" for them.

THE GAS SCANDAL

Again, take the case of the Washington Gas Company. It started more than half a century ago, with an authorized capitalization of fifty thousand dollars. That limit has been raised from time to time till the company now has outstanding $2,600,000 of stock, an equal amount of certificates of indebtedness, and $600,000 of bonds. The stock is worth about three dollars to one of its face value; and now the company is in court with a proceeding, under color of a law of 1896, to double or treble its capital. If permitted, the increase will simply mean that for all future time the gas-users of the city must pay returns on so much more capital. It is a repetition of the easy process of stock-watering by stock dividend. In a good many cities which regard themselves as none too well governed, that sort of performance is frowned upon, and in recent years it has been forbidden by law in many States.

The law of 1896, under which authority is claimed for this inflation, was forced through Congress in return for a reduction in the price of gas, then conceded to be excessive. The price was fixed at one dollar per thousand feet, with twenty-five cents penalty if bills be not paid within the first ten days of the month. To-day the dollar price is excessive by from twenty-five to fifty per cent, if comparison be made with other cities of Washington's size and circumstances.

Something like a year ago, the gas interest set about to have the courts make a valuation of its property, announcing its purpose, under the terms of the 1896 statute, to increase its capital issue up to the limit which a judicial valuation would fix on its property. The court took the procedure in hand, and it is still pending there, on an appeal to the Supreme Court of the United States.

To understand what this inflation process means, it is necessary to explain that the original capital of fifty thousand dollars was never paid up in cash. Part of it was actually put into the company's treasury; then the earnings paid not only extremely profitable dividends—one hundred per cent in one year, and repeated dividends of fifteen to fifty per cent—but also the cost of extending the plant and keeping step with the city's requirements. The issue of $2,600,000 of certificates of indebtedness was simply a device, of doubtful legality, to increase the nominal capital. The certificates were distributed *pro rata,* free of charge, to stockholders. They draw six per cent interest.

But the earnings have continued to grow until another huge increase of capital is necessary to hide their exorbitant character; wherefore the movement to expand the company's capital by five or ten millions of dollars.

AN APPEAL TO CONGRESS

When the gas company filed its petition reciting the law of 1896, and asking that the court make a valuation, the commissioners of the District of Columbia protested, and instructed the corporation counsel to oppose the proceeding. Then, while the motion was still pending, the commissioners earnestly petitioned Congress to repeal the inflation act and to stop the scheme of injecting water by which to float the present excessive price of gas.

The consideration of this measure in Congress illustrates just what is the matter with Washington's government. The commissioners asked two things—that the inflation law be repealed, and that the price of gas be reduced from one dollar to seventy-five cents per thousand feet.

There was a long and hard fight over these propositions in the House Committee on the District of Columbia. The civic organizations of the city unanimously indorsed both proposals. Three of the four daily newspapers of Washington strongly advocated them; the fourth is owned by the president of the gas company, and is recognized as the organ of that corporation.

The fight over these two simple and manifestly reasonable proposals occupied the attention of the committee during most of the last session of Congress. The Senate and House Committees on the District of Columbia are the real legislative bodies for the city of Washington; for Congress commonly indorses whatever the committees recommend. So it early became apparent, as the contest had centered in the House committee, that if that body would only report the bills, they would in all probability pass.

The session wore away, with the people and the unfettered press clamoring for the proposed legislation. Experts were produced who demonstrated, to the confusion of the gas company's agents, that the terms of the bills were reasonable and fair. President Roosevelt himself took a hand to the extent of sending for at least one member of the House committee, and asking him to investigate and to do what he could for the two bills.

At length the committee voted on the bills, and ordered them reported to the House. It looked as if victory had been won; but here there arose an unforeseen obstacle.

THE GAS BILLS AND CHAIRMAN SMITH

When a committee has ordered a bill reported, the chairman must report it to the House and call it up for consideration. Samuel W. Smith, Congressman from the sixth district of Michigan, is chairman of the House Committee on the District of Columbia; and as such, under the procedure of the House, he was still the guardian and custodian of the gas bills. He flatly declined to call them up.

From the beginning, Mr. Smith had been opposed to the gas legislation. He had thrown every possible obstacle in the way of the two bills. He didn't want to interfere with "vested rights." Apparently he had never heard that vested wrongs sometimes need correction, quite as much as vested rights require protection. He was angry and disgusted when, over his head and against his protest, his committee instructed him to report the bills.

So Chairman Smith declined to call up the bills on the floor of the house. He invented various excuses, and finally settled down to the allegation that Speaker Cannon would not recognize him to call them up; there was too much business of greater importance.

Speaker Cannon was seen in the interest of the bills. He declared flatly that Mr. Smith would be recognized to call them up. Mr. Smith was told what the Speaker had said. The membership of the House was almost unanimous in favor of them. The newspapers had aired the situation thoroughly, and Congress recognized that they ought to pass. In the case of the bill repealing the inflation act, it was of pressing necessity to secure immediate action. Failure might result in the courts sustaining the old law, allowing the inflation, and authorizing the issue of millions of watered stock. Once issued, and in the hands of "innocent" purchasers, it would be beyond attack.

Nevertheless, Mr. Smith stood firm against his committee, against the House, against the people of Washington—and in favor of the gas company. He was still standing firm when Congress adjourned at the end of May—the bills still in his inside pocket, the price of gas still exorbitant, and the inflation procedure merrily moving toward consummation in the courts.

Unfortunately, Samuel W. Smith is a typical example of the men who get into positions where, as legislators, they have to choose between the public and the private interest in Washington affairs. Out in his Michigan district they say that he is a stupendous success at getting garden-seeds and pensions; that he is an excellent letter-writer, and an admirable "mixer." He has been in Congress for nearly twenty years. So far as is recorded, he never served any especial purpose there, aside from his seed-distribution and pension-procuring functions, till he became chairman of the House Committee on the District of Columbia. In that capacity he has served the purposes of the Washington Gas Company—and also the purpose of illustrating for this article, "What's the matter with Washington?"

The people of Mr. Smith's district would defeat him at the polls in November if they knew and appreciated his attitude toward the franchised and privileged monopolies of Washington. They would do it because they would want to rid themselves of the discredit of furnishing a Representative willing to rivet the shackles of monopoly on a community defenseless against an alien government; they would do it, especially, because they would be moved by the same pride in the national capital which has inspired so many millions of loyal Americans who have seen the veneer but not the inside.

Mr. Smith should certainly be defeated. All Congressmen and Congressional candidates of his class should be defeated.

The Site of the National Capital (1870)

THE SITE OF THE NATIONAL CAPITAL.

VIEW FROM THE CAPITOL GROUNDS.

OLD residents of Washington, when spoken to about the efforts making to remove the Seat of Government, say, "Oh, that is nothing; we are used to it; we have heard that all our lives." A review of the struggle does show that it dates back to the foundation of the city. Its phases are, moreover, full of interest as local history, and from the glimpses which they give of the character and anticipations of our forefathers.

In the Convention which framed the present Constitution of the United States, at Philadelphia, on Wednesday, 5th September, 1787, Mr. Briarly, from the committee of eleven, made a report, a part of which reads as follows:

"4. Immediately after the last clause of Section 1, Article 7, insert, 'To exercise exclusive legislation in all cases whatsoever over such district not exceeding ten miles square, as may, by cession of particular States, and the acceptance of the Legislature, become the seat of the Government of the United States; and to exercise like authority over all places purchased for the erection of forts, magazines, arsenals, dock-yards, and other needful buildings.'"

The foregoing quotation is from the notes of Mr. Madison, who states further: "So much of the fourth clause as related to the seat of Government was adopted, *nem. con.*"—no one contradicting, or without debate. It accordingly became part of the eighth section of the first article of the Constitution, and is all which that instrument contains upon the subject. Hence in this shape it passed to the first Congress, which met at New York city, on the 4th of March, 1789.

The Legislatures of Pennsylvania, Maryland, and Virginia, which States comprised the entire area within which it was thought the Capital could be located, had each meanwhile passed laws transferring to the United States exclusive jurisdiction over any district within their respective States which Congress might choose for the seat of Government.

On the 3d of September, in the House of Representatives, Mr. Scott, of Pennsylvania, moved:

"That a permanent residence ought to be fixed for the General Government of the United States at some convenient place, as near the centre of wealth, population, and extent of territory as may be consistent with convenience to the navigation of the Atlantic Ocean, and having due regard to the particular situation of the Western country."

The House at once went into Committee of the Whole upon this motion. Mr. Goodhue, of Massachusetts, introduced the following:

"*Resolved*, That the permanent seat of the General Government ought to be in some convenient place on the east bank of the river Susquehanna, in the State of Pennsylvania; and that until the necessary buildings be erected for the purpose, the seat of Government ought to continue at the city of New York."

Mr. Lee, of Virginia, introduced the following:

"*Resolved*, That a place, as nearly central as a convenient communication with the Atlantic Ocean, and an easy access to the Western territory will permit, ought to be selected and established as the permanent seat of the Government of the United States."

This "place as nearly central" meant upon the banks of the Potomac; and it was so understood, and pitted against the former proposition for the Susquehanna. The Eastern members of the House were agreed on the Susquehanna; the Southern members were agreed on the Potomac. The two localities were rivals for the second choice of the remaining members, whose first choice would perhaps have been for Philadelphia. The debate was vigorous and interesting.

Mr. Sedgwick, of Massachusetts, declared "It is the opinion of all the Eastern States that the climate of the Potomac is not only unhealthy, but destructive to Northern constitutions." He thought "the centre and influence of government ought to incline to Northern interests and a poor soil, because such parts are the nurseries of soldiers and sailors, and the sources of that energy which is the best security of the Government."

Mr. Wadsworth, of Connecticut, "did not dare to go to the Potomac. He feared that the whole of New England would consider the Union as destroyed."

Mr. Ames, of Massachusetts, said: "The Susquehanna is the centre of common convenience......West of the Ohio is almost an unmeasurable wilderness. Gentlemen will pardon me if I think it perfectly romantic to make this decision depend upon that circumstance ......It would give me no uneasiness to think that a hundred years hence it would be liable to be removed."

Mr. Vining, of Delaware, said: "I declare that I look on the Western territory from an awful and striking point of view. To that region the unpolished sons of the earth are flowing from all quarters; men to whom the protection of the laws and the controlling force of the Government are equally necessary. From this great consideration, I conclude that the banks of the Potomac is the proper station."

Mr. Stone, of Maryland, said: "Now the Potomac, as I am informed, connects with the Youghiogheny, a river less rapid than the Alleghany, and is itself communicable with the Atlantic. In that case the Potomac will be the highway for such vast quantities of wealth as to give every superiority......It may be the more necessary as *we ought to keep the boundary line distinct between the Spaniards and savages.*"

Mr. Lee, of Virginia, said: "If it should be found that the Northern States did consult their partial interests, and form combinations to support them, the faith of all south of the Potomac would be shaken."

Mr. Madison, of Virginia, said: "If a prophet had risen in that body," the Convention of Virginia, "and brought the declarations and proceedings of this day into view, I as firmly believe Virginia might not have been a part of the Union at this moment."

Mr. Scott, of Pennsylvania, said: "If it were possible to promulgate our laws by some instantaneous process, it would be of less consequence where the Government might be placed."

Mr. Clymer, of Pennsylvania, said: "There was a communication by the Juniata, with a road actually laid out of about forty miles; hence you descend the Kiskiminetas to the

Alleghany, and thence to Pittsburg is thirty miles."

Mr. Lee moved to strike out "the east bank of the river Susquehanna," and insert "the north bank of the river Potomac," which was lost; and after several days' controversy, and numerous attempts to change its tenor, the original Susquehanna resolution passed the House by a vote of 31 to 17, and was so sent to the Senate.

On the 26th of September the bill came back from the Senate, where it had been, without recorded debate, amended to read: "A district of ten miles square, bounded on the south by a line running parallel at one mile's distance from the city of Philadelphia."

Thereon a good deal of wrath was expended in the House, which refused to concur in the amendment, and the matter dropped for the session. The action of the Senate was determined, after a tie vote in that body, by the casting vote of the Vice-President, Mr. Adams, but for whom the Capitol of the United States would now stand "on the banks of the Susquehanna," probably at Wrightsville, in York County, opposite Columbia.

On the 31st of May, 1790, a bill was introduced in the Senate by Mr. Butler, of South Carolina, "to determine the permanent seat of Congress and of the Government of the United States." This bill passed the Senate on the 1st of July, providing "that a district on the river Potomac, at some place between the mouths of the Eastern Branch and Conococheague, be and the same is hereby accepted for the permanent seat of the Government of the United States." This was by a vote of 14 to 12, and, as before, without recorded debate. The bill further provided that the temporary seat of Government should be at Philadelphia until the year 1800, buildings meanwhile to be prepared on the Potomac. Efforts were made to keep it at New York till 1800, till 1794, till 1792, but all without avail.

The President was also directed to appoint commissioners, who, under his direction, should survey and purchase lands within the District for the capital, and provide the necessary buildings. He was also, for defraying the expense of "such purchases and buildings," "authorized and requested to accept grants of money."

The acceptance referred to in the bill related not only to the phraseology of the Constitution, but also to the act of cession by the Legislature of the State of Maryland. The Maryland Legislature also granted $72,000, and the Virginia Legislature $120,000, in pursuance of the suggestion contained in the bill. So the bill went to the House.

Mr. Sherman, of Connecticut, at once moved to strike out the Potomac and insert "a district to include the town of Baltimore."

Mr. Burke, of South Carolina, preferred Baltimore. "There was no political necessity for removing from New York to Philadelphia. The measure would excite the most turbulent passions in the minds of the citizens of New York." He spoke in handsome terms of the State of Pennsylvania. "He had as high an opinion of the people of that State as any man whatever; but he was afraid of their influence. A Quaker State was a bad neighborhood for the South Carolinians."

Mr. Lawrence, of New York, "adverted to the *funding business*, and very strongly intimated that these and other important matters which remain to be decided on were to be determined according to the fate of this bill."

Mr. Madison, of Virginia, said: "It is not in our power to guard against a repeal. Our acts are not, like those of the Medes and Persians, unalterable. A repeal is a thing against which no provision can be made. I am not under apprehensions of repeal; but if danger of repeal does exist, it is of that kind against which we can not guard."

Mr. Gerry, of Connecticut, said: "It appears pretty evident the advocates of the bill are sure of a majority; it is very evident that it has had a very pernicious influence on the great business of funding the public debt." He ridiculed the idea of fixing the Government at Conococheague (just where it is now). "He did not think there was any serious intention of ever going to that Indian place. He considered the whole business as a mere manœuvre."

Mr. Hartley defended the Quakers, "remarkable for their moral laws, for the plainness of their manners, and their benevolence. Nay, should the gentleman go to Philadelphia, he will find that these people will treat him as well as any other society."

Mr. Page, of Virginia, with primitive credulity, remarked: "There is not a city in the world in which I would sooner trust myself and Congress than in New York; for it is superior to any place I know for the orderly and decent behavior of its inhabitants."

Mr. Gerry, of Connecticut, continued: "That taking so southern a situation [*i. e.*, as the Potomac] would amount to a disqualification of many of the Northern members, who would forego their election rather than attend the national Legislature on that river."

But the "determined majority" of which he spoke had their way nevertheless; and on the 8th of July, 1790, by a vote of 32 to 29, the bill became a law. Whence the majority came from is a curious piece of semi-private history.

The references to the "Assumption Bill" are full of meaning. In the compilation of Hamilton's writings it is stated that, "it being ascertained that in a certain contingency there was a majority in favor of the Assumption in the other House, a bill finally passed the Senate providing that the seat of Government should remain at Philadelphia until the year 1800; and that it should be permanently established, after that time, near the Potomac—a decision in which regard to the personal wishes of Washington had weight."

This may be true, but not such weight as the

"contingency," however. Mr. Monroe wrote from Virginia to Mr. Madison: "The Assumption will be disliked here under any shape it can assume. I believe, however, a satisfactory adjustment of the other business [the Potomac] would make this [the Assumption] more palatable here." But for a full explanation we must hear Mr. Jefferson:

"This game was over, and another was on the carpet at the moment of my arrival [from France to become Secretary of State]; and to this I was most ignorantly and innocently made to hold the candle. This fiscal measure was known by the name of the Assumption. Independently of the debts of Congress the States had, during the war, contracted separate and heavy debts. This money, whether wisely or foolishly spent, was pretended to have been spent for general purposes, and ought therefore to be paid from the general purse. This measure produced the most bitter and angry contest ever known in Congress before or since the Union of the States. I arrived in the midst of it. But, a stranger to the ground, a stranger to the actors in it—so long absent as to have lost all familiarity with the subject, and as yet unaware of its object—I took no concern in it. The great and trying question, however, was lost in the House of Representatives. So high were the feuds excited by this subject that on its rejection business was suspended. Congress met and adjourned from day to day without doing any thing, the parties being too much out of temper to do business together. The Eastern members particularly, who, with Smith of South Carolina, were the principal gamblers in these scenes, threatened a secession and dissolution. Hamilton was in despair. As I was going to the President one day I met him in the street. He walked me backward and forward before the President's door for half an hour. He painted pathetically the temper into which the Legislature had been wrought, the disgust of those who were called the creditor States, the danger of the secession of their members, and the separation of the States. He observed that the members of the Administration ought to act in concert; that, though the question was not of my department, yet a common duty should make it a common concern; that the President was the centre on which all administrative questions ultimately rested, and that all of us should rally around him, and support with joint efforts measures approved by him; and that the question having been lost by a small majority only, it was probable that an appeal from me to the judgment and discretion of some of my friends might effect a change in the vote, and the machine of government, now suspended, might be again set in motion. I told him that I was really a stranger to the whole subject; that, not having yet informed myself of the system of finances adopted, I knew not how far this was a necessary sequence; that, undoubtedly, if its rejection endangered a dissolution of our Union at this incipient stage, I should deem that the most unfortunate of all consequences, to avert which all partial and temporary evils should be yielded. I proposed to him, however, to dine with me the next day, and I would invite another friend or two, bring them into conference together, and I thought it impossible that reasonable men, consulting together coolly, could fail by some mutual sacrifices of opinion to form a compromise which was to save the Union. The discussion took place. I could take no part in it but an exhortatory one, because I was a stranger to the circumstances which should govern it. But it was finally agreed that, whatever importance had been attached to the rejection of this proposition, the preservation of the Union and of concord among the States was more important, and that therefore it would be better that the vote of rejection should be rescinded, to effect which some members should change their votes. But it was observed that this measure would be particularly bitter to the Southern States, and that some concomitant measure should be adopted to sweeten it a little to them. There had before been propositions to fix the seat of Government either at Philadelphia or at Georgetown on the Potomac; and it was thought that by giving it to Philadelphia for ten years, and to Georgetown permanently afterward, this might, as an anodyne, calm in some degree the ferment which might be excited by the other measure alone. So two of the Potomac members (White and Lee, but White with a revulsion of stomach almost convulsive) agreed to change their votes, and Hamilton undertook to carry the other point. In doing this, the influence he had established over the Eastern members, with the agency of Robert Morris with those of the Middle States, effected his side of the engagement." So "twenty millions of stock were divided among favored States," and the Capital went to the Potomac.

The above is from Jefferson's diary. Later, in a letter to Washington, he adds: "I was duped by the Secretary of the Treasury, and made a tool for forwarding his schemes; and of all the errors of my political life, this has occasioned me the deepest regret."

A later law, at Washington's suggestion, so changed the boundaries as to include a portion of Virginia with the town of Alexandria.

How far Washington had engaged in this contest does not appear, although the project was at the time denounced as his "hobby-horse." It is said the spot attracted him during his early life while surveying, and that he afterward encamped there during Braddock's campaign against the Indians. It is certain that he entered on the work with vigor, and that he did not grow less sanguine. Commissioners were appointed, and in March, 1791, he writes to the Secretary of State:

"The terms entered into by me, on the part of the United States, with the landholders of Georgetown and Carrollsburgh are that all the land from Rock Creek along the river to the Eastern Branch, and so upward to or above the Ferry, including a breadth of about a mile and a half, the whole containing from three to five thousand acres, is ceded to the public on condition that, when the whole shall be surveyed and laid off as a city (which Major L'Enfant is now directed to do), the present proprietors shall retain every other lot; and for such part of the land as may be taken for public use, for squares, lots, etc., they shall be allowed at the rate of twenty-five pounds per acre, the public having the right to reserve such parts of the wood on the land as may be thought necessary for ornament; the landholders to have the use and profits of all the grounds until the city is laid off into lots, and sale is made of these lots, which by this agreement become public property. Nothing is to be allowed for the ground which may be occupied as streets and alleys. To these considerations all the principal landholders have agreed, and it is not doubted that the few who were not present will readily come into the measure, even the obstinate Mr. Burns."

The refractory personage last mentioned was appealed to by Washington, explaining to him the advantages he was resisting; to all which he replied: "I suppose you think people here are going to take every grist that comes from you as pure grain; but what would you have been if you hadn't married the widow Custis?"

The Father of his Country had no more to say. But the Maryland Legislature was in turn too much for Mr. Burns. The laws of Maryland were to have force within the District until Congress otherwise provided, so they went on to enact, that "whereas some of the proprietors of lots, as well as some of the proprietors of lands, have not, from imbecility and other causes, come into any [the above] agreement concerning their lands, therefore," the Commissioners were by law vested with the title to their lands on the same terms with the rest.

It does not appear that at this time Washington knew that the city would be called by his name. A few months later the Commissioners, Johnson, Stuart, and Carroll, wrote to Major L'Enfant, the French engineer who had been employed to lay out the city:

"GEORGETOWN, *September* 9, 1791.

"SIR,—We have agreed that the Federal District shall be called 'The Territory of Columbia,' and the Federal City 'The City of Washington;' the title of the map will therefore be, 'A Map of the City of Washington, in the Territory of Columbia.'"

In 1792 Washington writes: "It is with pleasure I add, as my opinion, that the roots of the permanent city are penetrating deep, and spreading far and wide. The Eastern States are not only getting more and more reconciled to the measure, but are beginning to view it in a more advantageous light, as it regards their policy and interests." In 1793 he writes: "The Federal City, in the year 1800, will become the seat of the General Government of the United States. It is increasing fast in buildings, and rising into consequence; and will, I have no doubt, from the advantages given to it by nature, and its proximity to a rich interior country and the Western territory, become the emporium of the United States."

Mention was made in the Senate of "fifteen years since the Government removed here, during the first six years of which period there prevailed, not only in this country, but all over Europe, a degree of enthusiasm bordering upon madness respecting the future destinies of this metropolis."

Difficulties, however, attended the whole undertaking, and calamitous disaster overtook it. The French engineer, L'Enfant, was found to be as touchy as he was thought to be talented, and was proportionately troublesome. At the first sale of lots the rumor was industriously spread that Congress never would remove to the Potomac, but would remain at Philadelphia. In 1792 Washington wrote to the Commissioners, that unless great activity prevailed, their whole previous labor might be lost. Later he was obliged to make residence on the spot a *sine qua non* with the Commissioners. The want of money was severely felt. The $200,000 subscribed by Virginia and Maryland was all expended. In 1796 Congress authorized and guaranteed a loan by the Commissioners of $300,000, but the money was not to be had. The State of Maryland, at Washington's personal request, took two-thirds of it; but required the Commissioners to add their individual guarantee to that of Congress. In 1798 Congress added $100,000; and in 1799 the State of Maryland lent $50,000. As a result of all these efforts, however, the public buildings made fair progress.

The private owners did not fare so well. Of the seven thousand acres which the map of Major L'Enfant represented, its extraordinary plan took about one-half for highways. A series of avenues, diverging from several centres, was overlaid by a series of parallel streets, with a result of innumerable angles and impracticable spaces, in addition to the twofold roadway to be built and kept in repair, and to distend and retard the city. To one-half of the remainder of the ground the United States was entitled under the agreement. It took at the assessed value, in addition, five hundred and eight acres. A part of this was subsequently given away to local institutions. In 1793 the Commissioners sold to Robert Morris and James Greenleaf 6000 lots at $80 each; but in 1795 these parties became insolvent, having accomplished very little. "Long rows of brick houses were commenced at other points between the Arsenal and Navy-yard, and for many years the chimneys remained standing as monuments of the frailty of human judgment." Large sums of money were invested on that side of Washington next Georgetown, at several times the few cents per square foot the vacant property is worth in 1869. It is current that the Hon. Daniel Carroll, one of the Commissioners, who owned most of Capitol Hill, about one-third of the city, refused an offer of $200,000 from Stephen Girard and others for every alternate lot, and demanded $1,000,000 for the same. Also, that he died insolvent, leaving the property vacant, and $13,000 unpaid city taxes. This is the old fable of the boy's hand in the jar; but still, "the main reason for its slow growth in the first forty years is to be found in the uncertainty which so long existed as to its being the permanent seat of Government."

In 1800, during the Presidency of the elder Adams, the transfer was effected, the executive offices being removed to Washington in June. It was not a very formidable transfer, so far as persons or materials were concerned. The "Oldest Inhabitant" assures me that a single "packet" sloop brought all the office furniture of the Departments, besides the "seven large boxes and four or five smaller ones" which contained the "Archives" of the Government. Fifty-four persons, comprising the President, Secretaries, and the clerical force, chose their own method of conveyance.*

THE CAPITOL, 1814.

The comfortable quarters and good living which Philadelphia afforded were not abandoned for the backwoods without severe discontent. On the 4th of July, the Secretary of the Treasury, Mr. Wolcott, gives his impressions in a letter to his wife:

"The Capitol is situated on an eminence, which I should suppose was near the centre of the immense country here called the city. There is one good tavern about forty rods from the Capitol, and several other houses are built and erecting; but I do not perceive how the members of Congress can possibly secure lodgings, unless they will consent to live like scholars in a college, or monks in a monastery, crowded ten or twenty in one house, and utterly secluded from society. The only resource for such as wish to live comfortably will, I think, be found in Georgetown, three miles distant, over as bad a road in winter as the clay grounds near Hartford.

"I have made every exertion to secure good lodgings near the office, but shall be compelled to take them at the distance of more than half a mile. There are, in fact, but few houses in any one place. and most of them small, miserable huts, which present an awful contrast to the public buildings. The people are poor, and, as far as I can judge, they live like fishes, by eating each other. All the ground for several miles around the city, being, in the opinion of the people, too valuable to be cultivated, remains unfenced."

President Adams arrived with his family in November. On the 25th Mrs. Adams wrote to her daughter, Mrs. Smith:

"I arrived here on Sunday last, and without

* This paper presents views of the National Capitol as it appeared at different periods. The corner-stone was laid by Washington, in 1793. Up to 1812 only the wings had been completed, and work was suspended during the war. After the destruction of the interior by the British, in 1814, a building was erected for a temporary Capitol. This building was used during the war of Secession as a prison, and was known as the Old Capitol Prison. It has received some alterations, and is now used as dwellings. The original Capitol was completed in 1825. The corner-stone of the extension, which constitutes the main portion of the present Capitol, was laid on the 4th of July, 1851, by President Fillmore, upon which occasion Daniel Webster delivered one of his most eloquent orations, and deposited under the corner-stone a document in his own handwriting, which reads:

"If, therefore, it shall hereafter be the will of God that this structure shall fall from its base, that its foundations shall be upturned, and the deposit beneath this stone brought to the eyes of men, be it then known that on this day the Union of the United States of America stands firm, that their Constitution still exists unimpaired, and with all its original usefulness and glory, growing every day stronger and stronger in the affections of the great body of the American people, and attracting more and more the admiration of the world. And all here assembled, whether belonging to public or to private life, with hearts devoutly thankful to Almighty God for the preservation of the liberty and happiness of the country, unite in sincere and fervent prayers that this deposit, and the walls and arches, the domes and towers, the columns and entablatures, now to be erected over it, may endure forever. God save the United States of America!"

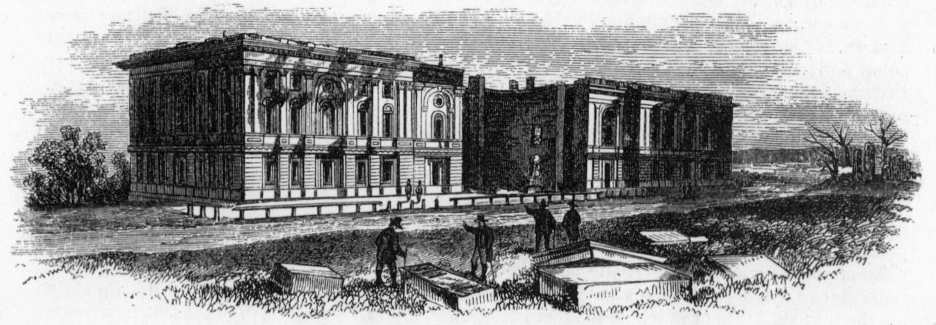

RUINS OF THE CAPITOL AFTER THE FIRE.

RUINS OF THE PRESIDENT'S HOUSE AFTER THE FIRE.

meeting with any accident worth noticing, except losing ourselves when we left Baltimore, and going eight or nine miles on the Frederick road, by which means we were obliged to go the other eight through the woods, where we wandered two hours without finding a guide or the path. Fortunately, a straggling black came up with us, and we engaged him as a guide to extricate us out of our difficulty; but woods are all you see from Baltimore until you reach *the city*, which is only so in name. Here and there is a small cot, without a glass window, interspersed among the forests, through which you travel miles without seeing any human being.

"In the city there are buildings enough, if they were compact and finished, to accommodate Congress and those attached to it; but as they are, and scattered as they are, I see no great comfort for them......

"If the twelve years in which this place has been considered as the future seat of Government had been improved, as they would have been in New England, very many of the present inconveniences would have been removed. It is a beautiful spot, capable of any improvement, and the more I view it the more I am delighted with it."

John Cotton Smith, a member from Connecticut, wrote also:

"Our approach to the city was accompanied with sensations not easily described. One wing of the Capitol only had been erected, which, with the President's house, a mile distant from it, both constructed with white sandstone, were shining objects in dismal contrast with the scene around them. Instead of recognizing the avenues and streets portrayed on the plan of the city, not one was visible, unless we except a road, with two buildings on each side of it, called the New Jersey Avenue. The Pennsylvania, leading, as laid down on paper, from the Capitol to the Presidential mansion, was then nearly the whole distance a deep morass covered with alder-bushes, which were cut through the width of the intended avenue during the then ensuing winter.

"Between the President's house and Georgetown a block of houses had been erected, which then bore, and may still bear, the name of the *Six Buildings*. There were also two other blocks, consisting of two or three dwelling-houses, in different directions, and now and then an insulated wooden habitation; the intervening spaces, and, indeed, the surface of the city generally, being covered with *shrub oak bushes* on the higher grounds, and on the marshy soil either trees or some sort of shrubbery. Nor was the desolate aspect of the place a little augmented by a number of unfinished edifices at *Greenleaf's Point*, and on an eminence a short distance from it, commenced by an individual whose name they bore, but the state of whose funds compelled him to abandon them, not only unfinished, but in a ruinous condition......

"One of the blocks of buildings already mentioned was situated on the east side of what was intended for the Capitol Square, and being chiefly occupied by an extensive and well-kept hotel, accommodated a goodly number of the members. Our little party took lodgings with a Mr. Peacock, in one of the houses on the New Jersey Avenue, with the

TEMPORARY CAPITOL, 1814.

THE CAPITOL, 1825.

addition of Senators Tracy, of Connecticut; and Chipman and Paine, of Vermont; and Representatives Thomas, of Maryland; and Dana, Edmond, and Griswold, of Connecticut. Speaker Sedgwick was allowed a room to himself; the rest of us in pairs. To my excellent friend Davenport and myself was allowed a spacious and decently furnished apartment, with separate beds, on the lower floor. Our diet was various, but always substantial, and we were attended by active and faithful servants. A large proportion of Southern members took lodgings at Georgetown, which, though of a superior order, were three miles distant from the Capitol, and of course rendered the daily employment of hackney coaches indispensable.

"Notwithstanding the unfavorable aspect which Washington presented on our arrival, I can not sufficiently express my admiration of its local position...... Whenever, during the six years of my connection with Congress, the question of removing the seat of Government to some other place was agitated—and the proposition was frequently made—I stood almost alone as a Northern man in giving my vote in the negative."

The death of Washington, in 1799, spared him a knowledge of this discontent. He had anticipated its direction if it should at any time exist. Perhaps his death also had checked the preparations. His memory may have also checked the agitation for removal, but in 1808 it was openly renewed by a bill for the temporary removal of the seat of Government to Baltimore, which Mr. Wright, of Maryland, introduced in the Senate, avowedly as a spur to the inhabitants of Washington, and Mr. Jackson, of Georgia, denounced as a "bill to frighten the women and children" of the city, and calculated to defeat the very purpose of the mover. Mr. Anderson, of Tennessee, was in favor of the bill, but allowed that "in such an event an obligation would arise to indemnify the proprietors for the losses they would thereby sustain." Mr. John Quincy Adams, of Massachusetts, considered the measure as inexpedient as it was unconstitutional. Mr. Dayton, of New Jersey, said if a removal took place, Congress was bound to indemnify the proprietors. Mr. Jackson said further: "The time would come, though he hoped to God neither his children nor his children's children would live to see it when the population on this side of the Mississippi would pass that river, and the seat of Government would be translated to its banks. Centuries would, however, elapse before that period arrived." Mr. Maclay, of Pennsylvania, contended that no constitutional obstacle did exist. Mr. Adams insisted further, that from the foundation of the Constitution until the removal of the Government to this place, but one sentiment had existed, which was that the seat of Government, once fixed under the Constitution, became the permanent seat. The preponderance of opinion was against Mr. Adams, but the bill was nevertheless lost by a vote of 19 to 9, and Congress resumed its migrations between Georgetown and the Capitol.

About this time Sir Augustus Foster, the Secretary of the British Minister, gave *his* view of the feelings by which the powers that be were actuated:

"The richer and more respectable members of Congress had, for the most part, always inclined to vote for returning to Philadelphia, or selecting some other town of practical importance; but every such proposal had been distasteful to the majority, it being in a great measure

THE CAPITOL. 1870.

composed of rough and unfashioned persons, to whom it is of consequence to be in a place where they could be attended to more than in a large city. This majority had usually found support in the Government, so long composed of Virginians, who naturally preferred Washington to any remoter situation; but the removal could hardly, he apprehends, have been avoided but for the determined personal opposition of Jefferson. This President alleged as his reason the danger of throwing open again a question so difficult and delicate as that of the choice of the seat of Government."

In 1814 there was trouble again. The city had been captured by a force less than half that which disgracefully fled, and the public buildings were all sacked and burned, with many private houses. Congress assembled in September. The situation of the city at that time is thus described: "Twelve or fifteen clusters of houses, at a considerable distance from each other, bringing to our recollection the appearance of a camp of nomad Arabs, which, however, if connected together, would make a very respectable town, not much inferior, perhaps, to the capital of Virginia, and here and there an insulated house; the whole of it, when seen from the ruins of our public edifices, looking more like the place where proud Washington once stood than where humble Washington now lies."

Mr. Fisk, of New York, introduced in the House a resolution of inquiry into the expediency of removal. The country, he said, was alarmed for the safety of Congress—it was necessary that some steps should be taken.

Mr. Lewis, of Virginia, hoped, by rejecting it, an end would be put to similar attempts hereafter, "and that the good people of this District would be permitted to continue their improvements here without the dread of being sacrificed."

Mr. Macon, of North Carolina, said that "if the seat of Government was once set on wheels there was no saying where it would stop."

Mr. Oakley, of New York, said it was true a removal might injure individuals, but he presumed no gentleman in the House would hesitate to make a fair and liberal compensation by way of indemnity to such sufferers.

Mr. Stockton, of New Jersey, relied on the fifth section of the Constitution to prove his position. It is there provided that "neither House shall, without the consent of the other, adjourn for more than three days, nor to any other place than that in which the two Houses shall be sitting." This, Mr. Stockton said, "expressly admits and regulates the general power of removal."

The debate continued several days; the old ground was gone over, the proposition negatived by a vote of 83 to 74, and the rebuilding set vigorously on foot.

The corporation of Alexandria, in 1846, memorialized the Legislature of Virginia, asking its consent to the retrocession of so much of the District as had been taken from that State. The Legislature at once, and by a unanimous vote, approved the proposition; and in May of that year a bill to that effect passed the House of Representatives, after an animated debate, in which the question of constitutional power was not seriously raised. In the Senate, however, the debate turned largely on that point. Mr. Haywood, of North Carolina, and Mr. Miller, of New Jersey, doubted the power of Congress in that particular. But Mr. Reverdy Johnson, Mr. Calhoun, and Mr. Hunter, of Virginia, having carefully examined the subject, were clear that there was nothing in all of the proceedings relative to the establishment of the seat of Government to prohibit the retrocession of the ten-mile square to the States from which it was taken, or any portion thereof. Mr. Calhoun, in particular, considered the right to remove the seat of Government incontestable. He, however, stated that it happened at the Memphis Convention, a body composed of six hundred members, possessed of great intelligence, and representing almost exclusively the interests of those who lived upon the soil, a resolution was offered recommending a change of the seat of the General Government. A most extraordinary sensation was produced, and when the resolution was submitted there was one loud-toned overwhelming "No" opposed to the solitary voice of the giver.

Since then, till now, the question has not been seriously raised. The "instantaneous process," which Mr. Scott reckoned the least possible of "ifs," was actually nursed to life by a Congressional appropriation, and now "disseminates the laws." The "seven large boxes" which contained the archives are increased by many thousand tons, and the personnel has become a real army. The President's wife is not now lost on the high-road from Baltimore, nor is it indispensable to live in Georgetown, nor yet do members generally have to lodge in pairs, or frequently decline election on account of the destructive climate. And though the Western traveler does not seek the Kiskiminetas, or frequent the Youghiogheny, he comes from California in less time than it took the member from Connecticut to come in 1791. All of the old objections are removed but one. And as to that, vast as the growth of population in the West has been, there still is force in the old apothegm that "as the West is to the East in point of territory, so is the East to the West in point of population."

Still, Washington is a sparse built and indifferent city. The "good people of this District" have not been "permitted to continue their improvements here without the dread of being sacrificed." Even after 1846 the proverbial timidity of capital required something more than a cessation of debate. The returns of the investments were not flattering, so far, and it may be doubted whether the city would have sold for the amount expended on it; certainly single houses could be bought for less than cost.

WASHINGTON, FROM THE DOME OF THE CAPITOL.

The account between the city and the Government stood somewhat in this wise: The Government received from sales of lots, to 1834, some $750,000, besides $200,000 worth of lots which it had given away, or still held in possession. Against this, Government at different times had granted to the city, in all, $430,000 in lieu of local taxes, none of which it pays, and which would have amounted to several times as much. If the public were not pleased with the city, the city, in its turn, had little reason to be grateful to the public. The account of the past was not encouraging. For the first forty years of its life the growth of the city is reckoned at 550 per annum, a rate of increase almost unworthy the capital of a single American State.

During the ten years following 1840 a general renewal of the public buildings was projected and begun upon a scale which shut out from the minds of most men the idea they would ever be abandoned. The Post-office, the Treasury, the Patent-office, and, above all, the Capitol, were made to loom up as the fit abode and representatives of an enduring government. The result told at once upon the city. Slavery had brought the surrounding country to comparative decay, and repressed at once commerce and manufactures. Yet the annual increase trebled, and after 1850 was increased to 2000. Permanent and costly buildings were the evidence of faith and of activity, until, in 1860, Washington had over 60,000 people. The war did more for it than simply double these; it has brought in freedom and the universal Yankee. The place did not fall off, as was expected, after the cessation of hostilities and the removal of the troops. The workman's house replaced the soldier's tent. Street railroads now afford convenience, as the parks and public buildings educate the taste and offer recreation. There is commerce, and incipient manufactures. The finest school-house in the country indicates the change; the cemetery at Arlington denotes a portion of the cost. The investments in property in Washington have grown beyond a hundred millions, as against the eighty millions which the public has at stake. These it is proposed to throw into the sea. If the public good requires it, it will be rightly done. But if the motive be a different one, it will be felt by the people, as was said in the Senate, that the man who could propose this change from personal considerations deserves the execration of the country. National considerations alone should decide the site of the National Capital.

Washington in Jefferson's Time (1906)

Thomas Jefferson, by Gilbert Stuart.
The property of T. Jefferson Coolidge.

WASHINGTON IN JEFFERSON'S TIME

FROM THE DIARIES AND FAMILY LETTERS OF MRS. SAMUEL HARRISON SMITH (MARGARET BAYARD)

Edited by Gaillard Hunt from the collection of her grandson, J. Henley Smith

PREFATORY NOTE

DURING the first forty years of its existence the city of Washington had a society more definite and real than it has come to have in later days. The permanent residents, although appurtenant to the changing official element, nevertheless furnished the framework which the larger and more important social life used to build upon, and the result was a structure of society tolerably compact and pleasing and certainly interesting. It was emphatically official, but it did not include the lower-class officials, who found their recreation for the most part at the street resorts, and its tone was dignified and wholesome. At any rate, it was genuine and national, even if it was crude, and the day of the all-powerful rich man and his dominance in social life had not yet arrived.

Samuel Harrison Smith, of Philadelphia, a writer and editor in Philadelphia, came to the city in the year 1800, soon after the Government had moved there. He was the son of Jonathan Bayard Smith, a member of the Continental Congress, signer of the Articles of Confederation and colonel of a Pennsylvania regiment during the Revolution; and although he was only twenty-eight years old, he established the first national newspaper printed in America, which he called *The National Intelligencer*. Just before his paper was started he returned to Philadelphia, and on September 29, 1800, married his second cousin, Margaret Bayard, and their wedding journey was from Philadelphia to Washington, where they lived the rest of their lives; and for forty years their house was the resort of the most interesting characters in national public life. The first number of *The National Intelli-*

gencer appeared October 31, 1800, and after conducting it successfully for a number of years Mr. Smith sold it to Joseph Gales, Jr., who afterward associated with himself as editor William W. Seaton. In 1813 President Madison appointed him the first Commissioner of the Revenue of the Treasury Department and on September 30, 1814, Secretary of the Treasury *ad interim*. From 1809 to 1819 he was president of the Bank of Washington, and later president of the Washington branch Bank of the United States until the office was abolished ten years before his death. Undoubtedly, the success of his career was partly due to the assistance given him by his talented wife.

Margaret Bayard was born February 29, 1778, in Philadelphia, the daughter of Col. John Bayard, a famous Revolutionary officer, Speaker of the Pennsylvania Assembly and member of the Continental Congress. Colonel Bayard's nephew and adopted son was James A. Bayard, a distinguished diplomat and Senator from Delaware, and James A. Bayard's son, bearing the same name, was also a Senator from Delaware, as was his grandson, the late Thomas Francis Bayard. Margaret Bayard was twenty-two years old when she married, and it was inevitable that one who wrote so readily should eventually print her pieces, and in due course she fell in with Godey, Mrs. Sarah Josepha Hale, Anthony Bleecker, J. Herrick, and Miss Catherine Maria Sedgwick, and from 1823 up to a few years before her death she was an occasional contributor to the literature of the day. For *Godey's Lady's Book* she wrote "Domestic Sketches," an account of presidential inaugurations, and a serial moral story, printed in March, April, and May, 1837, entitled "Who is Happy?" She also wrote some Spanish tales, "Constantine" and several other Roman stories, "Lucy," "The Sister," and "Estelle Aubert," a translation from the French which Mrs. Hale printed in 1834. In 1835 she printed in *The National Intelligencer* a letter in verse anonymously to Harriet Martineau, and probably contributed to this paper on other occasions which can not be identified. In 1837 she wrote for *The Southern Literary Messenger* and Peter Parley's (Goodrich's) annual "The Token," but anonymously. She contributed to Herrick and Longacre's *National Portrait Gallery*, doubtless the article on Mrs. Madison and probably one or two others. Her contributions were generally moral essays or stories, pitched high as the taste of the day required. The most ambitious product of her pen was a large novel in two volumes, entitled "A Winter in Washington, or Memoirs of The Seymour Family," published in 1824 (New York, E. Bliss and E. White) anonymously. Her authorship was, however, not concealed, and was generally known at the time, and the book, after being a decided success, has since become exceedingly rare. The characters were taken from real life, and it has historical value because of a number of anecdotes, chiefly of Thomas Jefferson, scattered through its pages. Another volume published by her was a little story of two hundred and fifty pages printed in 1828 and sold at a fair held for the benefit of the Washington Orphan Asylum, bearing the title "What is Gentility?" Undoubtedly, Mrs. Smith's most interesting and valuable writings were those which she never intended for publication and which have hitherto never seen the light, being her private letters in which she opens an intimate view of the famous political characters in Washington, whose acquaintance and friendship she enjoyed. These letters present a picture highly entertaining and valuable, and so do some of the reminiscences which she wrote in her note-books.

She was the intimate friend of Jefferson, who was her life's hero, and his family, and one of his most characteristic letters, that in which he discloses his views on religion, was addressed to her; of the Madisons, the Clays, the Calhouns; of William Wirt, the accomplished Attorney-General for twelve years; and of William H. Crawford, whose partisan in his candidacy for the presidency she became, besides many others. She entertained Harriet Martineau when she came to Washington on her famous tour, held long conversations with the socialist Owen of Lanark, and had as one of her intimate friends Madame de Neuville, the wife of Hyde de Neuville, the most popular of the early ministers of France to the United States. She was a remarkably truthful letter writer, and never embellished her correspondence with apocryphal gossip. She judged her fellow-man charitably and believed in her country absolutely, and did not herself participate in any of the party rancor which raged around her. She was, herself, a Republican, to which party her husband adhered, but she came of a Federalist family and looked not unkindly upon her husband's opponents. She died January 7, 1844, and her husband November 1, 1845.

In the valuable manuscript collection in my possession are several thousand of my grandmother's letters and of letters to her from nearly all the prominent characters of her day. They were kept by her son, Jonathan Bayard Harrison Smith, my father, under lock and key during his life and have only been seen since coming under my control after my mother's death. From this mass of material Mr. Hunt has selected only those letters which give an intimate view of the social life of Washington nearly a hundred years ago. Most of the letters are addressed to Mrs. Smith's sisters—Jane, herself a woman of literary accomplishments, the wife of Chief-Justice Andrew Kirkpatrick, of New Jersey, and Anna, who married Mr. Samuel Boyd, of New York; and her husband's sisters, Susan Bayard Smith and Mary Ann Smith; and her son, when he was a student at Princeton. "Sidney," the country-place from which she often wrote, was a farm of two hundred acres, a portion of which the Catholic University now occupies; but the original house is still standing.

J. Henley Smith.

REMINISCENCES*

"And is this," said I, after my first interview with Mr. Jefferson, "the violent democrat, the vulgar demagogue, the bold atheist & profligate man I have so often heard denounced by the federalists? Can this man so meek & mild, yet dignified in his manners, with a voice so soft & low, with a countenance so benignant & intelligent, can he be that daring leader of a faction, that disturber of the peace, that leader of all rank & order?" Mr. Smith, indeed, (himself a democrat) had given me a very different description of this celebrated individual; but his favourable opinion I attributed in a great measure to his political feelings, which led him zealously to support & exalt the party to which he belonged, especially its popular & almost idolized leader. Thus the virulence of party-spirit was somewhat neutralized, nay, I even entertained towards him the most kindly dispositions, knowing him to be not only politically but personally friendly to my husband; yet I believed that he was an ambitious & violent demagogue coarse & vulgar in his manners, awkward & rude in his appearance, for such had the public journals & private conversations of the federal party represented him to be.*

In December, 1800, a few days after Congress had for the first time met in our new Metropolis, I was one morning sitting alone in the parlour, when the servant opened the door & showed in a gentleman who wished to see my husband. The usual frankness & care with which I met strangers, were somewhat checked by the dignified & reserved air of the present visitor; but the chilled feeling was only momentary, for after taking the chair I offered him in a free & easy manner, & carelessly throwing his arm on the table near which he sat, he turned towards me a countenance beaming with an expression of benevolence & with a manner and voice almost femininely soft & gentle, entered into conversation on the commonplace topics of the day, from which, before I was conscious of it, he had drawn me into observations of a more personal & interesting nature, I know not how it was, but there was something in his manner, his countenance & voice that at once unlocked my heart, & in answer to his casual enquiries concerning our situation in our *new home*, as he called it, I found myself frankly telling him what I liked or disliked in our present circumstances & abode. I knew not who he was, but the interest with which he listened to my artless details, induced the idea he was some intimate acquaintance or friend of Mr. Smith's & put me perfectly at my ease; in truth so kind & conciliating were his looks & manners that I forgot he was not a friend of my own, until on the opening of the door, Mr. Smith entered & introduced the stranger to me as *Mr. Jefferson.*

I felt my cheeks burn & my heart throb, & not a word more could I speak while he remained. Nay, such was my embarrassment I could scarcely listen to the conversation carried on between him & my husband. For several years he had been to me an object of peculiar interest. In fact my destiny, for on his success in the pend-

* From Mrs. Smith's note-book. It was written in 1837, but relates to her first arrival in Washington.

* Col. John Bayard, Mrs. Smith's father, was a Federalist.

ing presidential election, or rather the success of the democratic party, (their interests were identical) my condition in life, my union with the man I loved, depended. In addition to this personal interest, I had long participated in my husband's political sentiments & anxieties, & looked upon Mr. Jefferson as the corner stone on which the edifice of republican liberty was to rest, looked upon him as the champion of human rights, the reformer of abuses, the head of the republican party, which must rise or fall with him, & on the triumph of the republican party I devoutly believed the security & welfare of my country depended. Notwithstanding those exalted views of Mr. Jefferson as a political character, & ardently eager as I was for his success, I retained my previously conceived ideas of the coarseness & vulgarity of his appearance & manners & was therefore equally awed & surprised, on discovering the stranger whose deportment was so dignified & gentlemanly, whose language was so refined, whose voice was so gentle, whose countenance was so benignant, to be no other than Thomas Jefferson. How instantaneously were all these preconceived prejudices dissipated, & in proportion to their strength, was the reaction that took place in my opinions & sentiments. I felt that I had been the victim of prejudice, that I had been unjust. The revolution of feeling was complete & from that moment my heart warmed to him with the most affectionate interest & I implicitly believed all that his friends & my husband believed & which the after experience of many years confirmed. Yes, not only was he a great, but a truly good man!

The occasion of his present visit, was to make arrangements with Mr. Smith for the publication of his *Manuel* for *Congress*. Now called *Jefferson's manual*. The original was in his own neat, plain, but elegant hand writing. The manuscript was as legible as printing & its unadorned simplicity was emblematical of his character. It is still preserved by Mr. Smith & valued as a precious relique.

After the affair of business was settled, the conversation became general & Mr. Jefferson several times addressed himself to me; but although his manner was unchanged, my feelings were, & I could not recover sufficient ease to join in the conversation. He shook hands cordially with us both when he departed, & in a manner which said as plain as words could do, "I am your friend."

During part of the time that Mr. Jefferson was President of the Philosophical Society (in Philadelphia) Mr. Smith was its secretary. A prize offered by the society for the best system of national education, was gained by Mr. Smith. The merit of this essay, first attracted the notice of Mr. J. to its author; the personal acquaintance which then took place, led to a friendly intercourse which influenced the future destiny of my husband, as it was by Mr. Jefferson's advice, that he removed to Washington & established the *National Intelligencer*. Esteem for the talents & character of the editor first won Mr. Jefferson's regard, a regard which lasted to the end of his life & was a thousand times evinced by acts of personal kindness & confidence.

At this time Mr. Jefferson was vice-President & in nomination for the Presidency. Our infant city afforded scant accommodations for the members of Congress. There were few good boarding-houses, but Mr. Jefferson was fortunate enough to obtain one of the best. Thomas Law one of the wealthiest citizens & largest proprietors of city property, had just finished for his own use a commodious & handsome house on Capitol hill; this, on discovering the insufficiency of accommodation, he gave up to Conrad for a boarding house, & removed to a very inconvenient dwelling on Greenleaf's point, almost two miles distant from the Capitol.* And here while I think of it, though somewhat out of place, I will mention an incident that occurred which might have changed the whole aspect of the political world & have disappointed the long & deep laid plans of politicians, so much do great events depend on trivial accidents. This out-of-the-way-house to which Mr. Law removed, was separated from the most inhabited part of the city by old fields & waste grounds broken up by deep gulleys or ravines over which there was occasionally a passable road. The election of President by Congress was then pending, one vote

* Thomas Law, a brother of Lord Ellenborough, came to Washington in 1795 with the idea of making an enormous fortune by speculating in real estate. In 1796 he married Eliza Parke Custis, a descendant of Lord Baltimore and granddaughter of Mrs. Washington. They lived unhappily, separated in 1804 and were divorced a few years later. There were rumors that she loved the world and its admiration too much; but Mr. Law was himself an oddity. One of the stories about him is that going to the post-office for his letters one day he could not remember his name till an acquaintance addressed him.

given or withheld would decide the question between Mr. Jefferson & Mr. Burr. Mr. Bayard from Delaware held that vote. He with other influential & leading members went to a ball given by Mr. Law. The night was dark & rainy, & on their attempt to return home, the coachman lost his way, & until day break was driving about this waste & broken ground & if not overturned into the deep gullies was momentarily in danger of being so, an accident which would most probably have cost some of the gentlemen their lives, & as it so happened that the company in the coach consisted of Mr. Bayard & three other members of Congress who had a leading & decisive influence in this difficult crisis of public affairs, the loss of either, might have turned the scales, then so nicely poised. Had it been so, & Mr. Burr been elected to the Presidency, what an awful conflict, what civil commotions would have ensued.

Mr. Jefferson.
Silhouette from life.

Conrad's boarding house was on the south side of Capitol hill & commanded an extensive & beautiful view. It was on the top of the hill, the precipitous sides of which were covered with grass, shrubs & trees in their wild uncultivated state. Between the foot of the hill & the broad Potomac extended a wide plain, through which the Tiber wound its way. The romantic beauty of this little stream was not then deformed by wharves or other works of art. Its banks were shaded with tall & umbrageous forest trees of every variety, among which the superb Tulep-Poplar rose conspicuous; The magnolia, the azalia, the hawthorn, the wild-rose & many other indigenous shrubs grew beneath their shade, while violets, anemonies & a thousand other sweet wood-flowers found shelter among their roots, from the winter's frost & greeted with the earliest bloom the return of spring. The wild grape-vine climbing from tree to tree hung in unpruned luxuriance among the branches of the trees & formed a fragrant & verdant canopy over the greensward, impervious to the noon-day sun. Beautiful banks of Tiber! delightful rambles! happy hours! How like a dream do ye now appear. Those trees, those shrubs, those flowers are gone. Man & his works have displaced the charms of nature. The poet, the botanist, the sportsman & the lover who once haunted those paths must seek far hence the shades in which they delight. Not only the banks of the Tiber, but those of the Potomack & Anacosta, were at this period adorned with native trees & shrubs & were distinguished by as romantic scenery as any

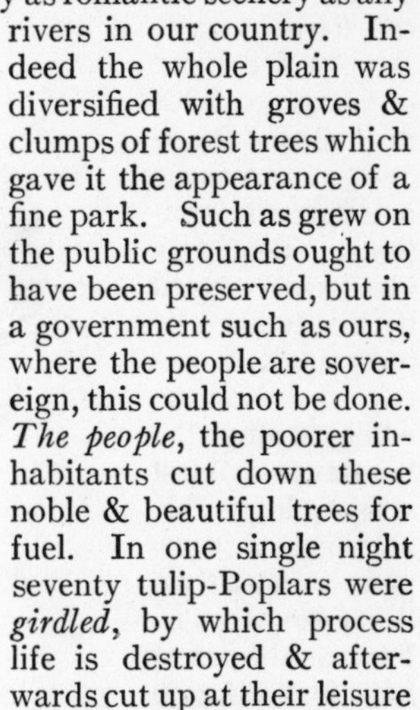

rivers in our country. Indeed the whole plain was diversified with groves & clumps of forest trees which gave it the appearance of a fine park. Such as grew on the public grounds ought to have been preserved, but in a government such as ours, where the people are sovereign, this could not be done. *The people*, the poorer inhabitants cut down these noble & beautiful trees for fuel. In one single night seventy tulip-Poplars were *girdled*, by which process life is destroyed & afterwards cut up at their leisure by the people. Nothing afflicted Mr. Jefferson like this wanton destruction of the fine trees scattered over the city-grounds. I remember on one occasion (it was after he was President) his exclaiming "How I wish that I possessed the power of a despot." The company at table stared at a declaration so opposed to his disposition & principles. "Yes," continued he, in reply to their inquiring looks, "I wish I was a despot that I might save the noble, the beautiful trees that are daily falling sacrifices to the cupidity of their owners, or the necessity of the poor."

"And have you not authority to save those on the public grounds?" asked one of the company. "No," answered Mr. J., "only an armed guard could save them. The unnecessary felling of a tree, perhaps the growth of centuries seems to me a crime little short of murder, it pains me to an unspeakable degree." *

It was partly from this love of nature, that he selected Conrad's boarding house, being there able to enjoy the beautiful & extensive

*This anecdote is given in "A Winter in Washington," Vol. II, p. 40.

prospect described above. Here he had a separate drawing-room for the reception of his visitors; in all other respects he lived on a perfect equality with his fellow boarders, and eat at a common table. Even here, so far from taking precedence of the other members of Congress, he always placed himself at the lowest end of the table. Mrs. Brown, the wife of the senator from Kentucky, suggested that a seat should be offered him at the upper end, near the fire, if not on account of his rank as vice-President, at least as the oldest man in company. But the idea was rejected by his democratic friends, & he occupied during the whole winter the lowest & coldest seat at a long table at which a company of more than thirty sat down. Even on the day of his inauguration when he entered the dining hall no other seat was offered him by the gentlemen. Mrs. Brown from an impulse which she said she could not resist, offered him her seat, but he smilingly declined it, & took his usual place at the bottom of the table. She said she felt indignant & for a moment almost hated the levelling principle of democracy, though her husband was a zealous democrat. Certainly this was carrying equality rather too far; there is no incompatibility between politeness & republicanism; grace cannot weaken & rudeness cannot strengthen a good cause, but democracy is more jealous of power & privilege than even despotism.

Mrs. Madison. *Mr. Madison.*

Silhouettes from life.

REMINISCENCE*

Mr. Jefferson's Election

FEBRUARY, 1801.

It was a day, "big with our country's fate"—a fate not suspended on the triumph or defeat of two contending armies, drawn forth in battle array—but on two contending political Parties, who after years of conflict, were now brought to issue. The power, which had been originally vested in the Federal party, had been gradually diminished by the force of public opinion, & transferred to the Democratic Party. For a while equality of power was maintained—but the equipoise did not last long,—a great & preponderating majority in the Presidential election, decided the relative strength of parties, the Democrats prevailed & brought into office, on the full-tide of popularity, the man who had been long recognized as the head of their Party.

According to the constitutional form, two men were to be run, the one for President, the other for vice President, & he who had the greatest number of votes was to be President. Such was the form of the law of election, but in the execution of that law, the people knowingly designated the vice-President, & voted for him concurrently with the President, this produced an unlooked for result & a constitutional difficulty. In the minds or inclinations of the people, there had been no misapprehensions no dubiousness of choice. They as manifestly gave their votes for Mr. Jefferson as President & Mr. Burr as vice-President, as if each vote had been accompanied with such a designation. With this understanding the votes for one were as unanimous as the votes for the other, & the result, of course, an equality. In this unlooked for emergency what was to be done? The constitution decided. The choice of President was to be made by Congress.

There was not a shadow of doubt or uncertainty as to the object of the people's choice. It had been proclaimed too widely & too loudly for any individual to remain ignorant of the fact.

But this accidental & uncalculated result, gave the Federal party a chance of preventing the election of a man they politically abhorred—a man whose weight of influence had turned the scale in favour of the oppos-

* From the note book.

ing Party. No means were left unattempted (perhaps I ought to say no *honest* means) to effect this measure.

It was an aweful crisis. The People who with such an overwhelming majority had declared their will would never peaceably have allowed the man of their choice to be set aside, & the individual they had chosen as vice-President, to be put in his place. A civil war must have taken place, to be terminated in all human probability by a rupture of the Union. Such consequences were at least calculated on, & excited a deep & inflamatory interest. Crowds of anxious spirits from the adjacent county & cities thronged to the seat of government & hung like a thunder cloud over the Capitol, their indignation ready to burst on any individual who might be designated as President in opposition to the people's known choice. The citizens of Baltimore who from their proximity, were the first apprised of this daring design, were with difficulty restrained from rushing on with an armed force, to prevent, —or if they could not prevent, to avenge this violation of the People's will & in their own vehement language, to hurl the usurper from his seat. Mr. Jefferson, then President of the Senate, sitting in the midst of these *conspirators*, as they were then called, unavoidably hearing their loudly whispered designs, witnessing their gloomy & restless machinations, aware of the dreadful consequences, which must follow their meditated designs, preserved through this trying period the most unclouded serenity the most perfect equanimity. A spectator who watched his countenance, would never have surmised, that he had any personal interest in the impending event. Calm & self possessed, he retained his seat in the midst of the angry & stormy, though half smothered passions that were struggling around him, & by this dignified tranquility repressed any open violence,—tho' insufficient to prevent whispered menaces & insults, to these however he turned a deaf ear, & resolutely maintained a placidity which baffled the designs of his enemies.

The crisis was at hand. The two bodies of Congress met, the Senators as witnesses the Representatives as electors. The question on which hung peace or war, nay, the Union of the States was to be decided. What an awful responsibility was attached to every vote given on that occasion. The sitting was held with closed doors. It lasted the whole day, the whole night. Not an individual left that solemn assembly, the necessary refreshment they required was taken in rooms adjoining the Hall. They were not like the Roman conclave legally & forcibly confined, the restriction was self-imposed from the deep-felt necessity of avoiding any extrinsic or external influence. Beds, as well as food were sent, for the accommodation of those whom age or debility disabled from enduring such a long protracted sitting—the ballotting took place every hour—in the interval men ate, drank, slept or pondered over the result of the last ballot, compared ideas & persuasions to change votes, or gloomily anticipated the consequences, let the result be what it would.

With what an intense interest did every individual watch each successive examination of the Ballot-box, how breathlessly did they listen to the counting of the votes! Every hour a messenger brought to the Editor of the *N. I.** the result of the Ballot. That night I never lay down or closed my eyes. As the hour drew near its close, my heart would almost audibly beat & I was seized with a tremour that almost disabled me from opening the door for the expected messenger.

What then must have been the feelings of that Heroic woman, who had assented to her almost dying husband being carried in this cold inclement season, the distance of nearly two miles, from his lodgings to the capitol?

In a room adjacent to the Hall of R, he lay on a bed beside which she knelt supporting his head on her arm, while with her hand she guided his, in writing the name of the man of his choice. At the return of each hour the invalid was roused from his disturbed slumber, much to the injury of his health, to perform this important duty. What anxiety must this fond wife have endured, what a dread responsibility did she take on herself, knowing as she did & having been appealed to by his physicians, to resist his wish to go, that her husband's life was risked, by his removal from his chamber & the following scene.† But it was for her country! And the American equalled in courage & patriotism the Roman matron.

For more than thirty hours the struggle was maintained, but finding the republican

* *National Intelligencer.*

† Joseph Hopper Nicholson of Maryland was the member He was carried to the House through a snow-storm.

phalanx impenetrable, not to be shaken in their purpose, every effort proving unavailing, the Senator from Delaware [James A. Bayard]* the withdrawal of whose vote would determine the issue, took his part, gave up his party, for his country, & threw into the box a blank ballot, thus leaving to the republicans a majority. Mr. Jefferson was declared duly elected. The assembled crowds, without the Capitol, rent the air with their acclamations & gratulations, & the Conspirators as they were called, hurried to their lodgings under strong apprehensions of suffering from the just indignation of their fellow citizens.

The dark & threatening cloud which had hung over the political horrison, rolled harmlessly away, & the sunshine of prosperity & gladness broke forth & ever since, with the exception of a few passing clouds has continued to shine on our happy country.

Miss Susan B. Smith

Saturday, March, 1809.

I have just returned from the solemn & affecting scenes of this day,—to many they were scenes of greatness, gaiety & exultation. To me they were melancholy. My heart is oppressed, my dearest Susan with a weight of sadness, & my eyes are so blinded with tears that I can scarcely trace these lines. It is some pleasure to me to write to you who participate in my sentiments of affectionate veneration for this best of men. For the last time I have seen him in his own house. He is happy, he has enjoyed all his country can bestow of greatness & honor, he could enjoy no more were he to remain in office his whole life time. He only lays down an irksome burden, but carries with him an increase of popularity, of esteem & love. He goes to be *happy* without ceasing to be *great*. I ought to rejoice, too, but when I think of what *we* are to *lose*, I forget what *he* is to *gain*. To-day after the inauguration, we all went to Mrs. Madison's. The street was full of carriages & people, & we had to wait near half an hour, before we could get in,—the house was completely filled, parlours, entry, drawing room & bed room. Near the door of the drawing room Mr. & Mrs. Madison stood to receive their company. She looked extremely beautiful, was drest in a plain cambrick dress with a very long train, plain round the neck without any handkerchief, & beautiful bonnet of purple velvet, & white satin with white plumes. She was all dignity, grace & affability. Mr. Madison shook my hand with all the cordiality of old acquaintance; but it was when I saw our dear & venerable Mr. Jefferson that my heart beat. When he saw me, he advanced from the crowd, took my hand affectionately & held it five or six minutes; one of the first things he said was "Remember the promise you have made me, to come to see us next summer, do not forget it," said he, pressing my hand, "for we shall certainly expect you." I assured him I would not, & told him I could now wish him joy with much more sincerity than this day 8 years ago. "You have now resigned a heavy burden," said I. "Yes indeed" he replied "& am much happier at this moment than my friend." The crowd was immense both at the Capitol & here, thousands & thousands of people thronged the avenue. The Capitol presented a gay scene. Every inch of space was crowded & there being as many ladies as gentlemen, all in full dress, it gave it rather a gay than a solemn appearance,—there was an attempt made to appropriate particular seats for the ladies of public characters, but it was found impossible to carry it into effect, for the sovereign people would not resign their privileges & the high & low were promiscuously blended on the floor & in the galleries.

Mr. Madison was extremely pale & trembled excessively when he first began to speak, but soon gained confidence & spoke audibly. From the Capitol we went to Mrs. M's, & from there to Mr. Jefferson's. I there again conversed a few minutes; Mr. Smith told him the ladies *would* follow him, "That is right," said he, "since I am too old to follow them. I remember in France when his friends were taking leave of Dr. Franklin, the ladies smothered him with embraces & on his introducing me to them as his successor, I told him I wished he would transfer these privileges to me, but he answered 'You are too young a man.'" Did not this imply, Susan, that now this objection was removed? I had a great inclination to tell him so.

Sunday morning. Well, my dear Susan, the chapter draws to a close. Last night concluded the important day, on which our

* Mrs. Smith's first cousin and adopted brother.

country received a new magistrate. To a philosopher, who while he contemplated the scene, revolved past ages in his mind, it must have been a pleasing sight. A citizen, chosen from among his equals, & quietly & unanimously elevated to a power, which in other countries & in all ages of the world has cost so much blood to attain! Would the size of a letter allow of it, I would allow my pen to follow the current of thought, but to a reflecting mind, which can withdraw itself from the interests & desires of life, which can ascend for a little while to another life, & look down upon this, the differences of rank, grandeur, power, are inequalities of condition, as imperceptible as those the traveller discerns in the valley, when he looks down upon it from the summit of the Alps. The tallest tree of the valley, does not then appear higher than the little shrubs it shelters. The storms roll harmless beneath his feet, clouds which darken those below, obstruct not his view of the sun, & while the inhabitants of the valley are distressed & terrified by the strife of the elements, he enjoys perpetual sunshine.

Thus have I endeavored to raise my own mind, & to contemplate the scenes that are acted before me. Sometimes I can gain this abstraction, but oftener, all the weaknesses, the vanities, the hopes & fears of this vain show, level me with the lowest of earthly minds.

Last evening, I endeavored calmly to look on, & amidst the noise, bustle & crowd,* to spend an hour or two in sober reflection, but my eye was always fixed on our venerable friend, when he approached my ear listened to catch every word & when he spoke to me my heart beat with pleasure. Personal attachment produces this emotion, & I did not blame it. But I have not this regard for Mr. Madison, & I was displeased at feeling no emotion when he came up & conversed with me. He made some of his old kind of mischievous allusions, & I told him I found him still unchanged.† I tried in vain to feel merely as a spectator, the little vanities of my nature often conquered my better reason. The room was so terribly crowded that we had to stand on the benches; from this situation we had a view of the moving mass, for it was nothing else. It was scarcely possible to elbow your way from one side to another, & poor Mrs. Madison was almost pressed to death, for every one crowded round her, those behind pressing on those before, & peeping over their shoulders to have a peep of her, & those who were so fortunate as to get near enough to speak to her were happy indeed. As the upper sashes of the windows could not let down, the glass was broken, to ventilate the room, the air of which had become oppressive, but here I begin again at the end of the story. Well, to make up for it I will begin at the beginning. When we went there were not above 50 persons in the room, we were led to benches at the upper fire place. Not long afterwards, the musick struck up Jefferson's March, & he & Mr. Coles entered. He spoke to all whom he knew, & was quite the plain, unassuming citizen. Madison's March was then played & Mrs. Madison led in by one of the managers & Mrs. Cutts & Mr. Madison, she was led to the part of the room where we happened to be, so that I accidentally was placed next her. She looked a queen. She had on a pale buff colored velvet, made plain, with a very long train, but not the least trimming, & beautiful pearl necklace, earrings & bracelets. Her head dress was a turban of the same coloured velvet & white satin (from Paris) with two superb plumes, the bird of paradise feathers. It would be *absolutely impossible* for any one to behave with more perfect propriety than she did. Unassuming dignity, sweetness, grace. It seems to me that such manners would disarm envy itself, & conciliate even enemies. The managers presented her with the first number,—"But what shall I do with it?" said she, "I do not dance." "Give it to your neighbor," said Capt. Tingey. "Oh no," said she, "that would look like partiality." "Then I will" said the Capt. & he presented it to Mrs. Cutts. I really admired this in Mrs. M. Ah, why does she not in all things act with the same propriety? She would be too much beloved if she added all the virtues to all the graces. She was led to supper by the French Minister,* Mrs. Cutts by the English Minister,† she sat at the centre of the table, which was a crescent, the French & English min-

* This was the first Inauguration Ball. See for an account of it the *Century* for March, 1905.

† In public life and as a writer James Madison was the most solemn of men. In private life he was an incessant humorist, and at home at Montpelier used to set his table guests daily into roars of laughter over his stories and whimsical way of telling them.

* General Turreau de Garambonville.

† David M. Erskine.

Monticello—South front.

Monticello—North front.

isters on each hand, Mrs. Cutts the next on the right hand, Mrs. Smith* the next on the left & Mr. Madison on the other side of the table opposite Mrs. M. I chose a place where I could see Mrs. M. to advantage. She really in manners & appearance, answered all my ideas of royalty. She was so equally gracious to both French & English, & so affable to all. I suspect Mrs. Smith could not like the superiority of Mrs. Cutts, & if I am not mistaken, Mrs. Madison's ——† causes her some heart burnings. Mr. Jefferson did not stay above two hours; he seemed in high spirits & his countenance beamed with a benevolent joy. I do believe father never loved son more than he loves Mr. Madison, & I believe too that every demonstration of respect to Mr. M. gave Mr. J. more pleasure than if paid to himself. Oh he is a good man! And the day will come when all party spirit shall expire, that every citizen of the United States will join in saying "He is a good man." Mr. Madison, on the contrary, seemed spiritless & exhausted.

* Wife of Robert Smith, then Secretary of the Navy, but soon to be Secretary of State.
† The blank is in the orginal.

Samuel Harrison Smith, founder of *The National Intelligencer*.
After the portrait by Charles Bird King.

While he was standing by me I said, "I wish with all my heart I had a little bit of seat to offer you." "I wish so too," said he, with a most woe begone face, & looking as if he could scarcely stand,—the managers came up to ask him to stay to supper, he assented, & turning to me, "but I would much rather be in bed" said he. Immediately after supper Mr. & Mrs. M. withdrew, the rest of the company danced until 12, the moment the clock struck that hour, the musick stopped, & we all came home tired & sick. "And such," said I, as I threw myself on the bed, "such are the gaiety & pleasures of the world! Oh give me the solitude of our cottage, where after a day well spent, I lay down so tranquil & cheerful." Never do I recollect one night, retiring with such a vacuum, such a dissatisfied craving, such a restlessness of spirit, such undefined, vague desires, as I now do. No, the world is not the abode of happiness, for while we have the weakness of humanity about us, vanity, pride, ambition, in some form or other will invade & disturb the breast of the humblest individual. But when far away from such excitements, all within is peace in the performance of known duties; in the enjoyment of intellectual & social pleasures, the best part of our nature is satisfied, the ambition of having the first blown rose, or the sweetest strawberry, lead only to pleasing anxiety & activity, the object of our ambition being attainable, we are not tormented by unsatisfied desires. After enjoying all the pomp & grandeur of the greatest empire in the world, after conquering nations, & the most splendid triumphs, Diocletian, this proud master of the world,

Mrs. Samuel Harrison Smith (Margaret Bayard).

After the portrait by Charles Bird King, in the possession of her grandson, J. Henley Smith, Washington.

voluntarily forsook these delusive pleasures, & often said while tilling his own garden, I take more pleasure in cultivating my garden with my own hands, & in eating the cabbages I have planted & rear'd than in all, that Rome could ever give me. Like him, our good & great Jefferson will taste the sweets of seclusion. But far happier is our president than the Roman Emperor. His retirement is a home endeared by the truest friendship; the most ardent & devoted affection, where his children, his grandchildren & great grandchildren, will lavish on him all the peculiar joys of the heart. How I have rambled in this long letter, but I am sure all these details will be pleasing to you, so I make no apology. To you they will not appear extravagant, to Maria B. perhaps they will.

And now for a little of humbler themes. We propose this week removing to the country, I never felt more impatient to go, as I propose a number of little improvements,—such as having a little poultry yard enclosed with boards, where I intend raising a great many chickens. The well-diggers are to go out very soon, & we shall try to get to water. Mr. Madison last night enquired among other things about this matter. "Truth is at the bottom of a well, is the old saying, & I expect when you get to the bottom of yours, you will discover most important truths. But I hope you will at least find *water*," continued he, smiling. Indeed I hope we will, & I am sure you join in this wish, knowing how much we suffer from the want of it. . . .

MONTICELLO, August 1st, 1809.*

In a visit Mr. J. made our little cottage last autumn, we were speaking of all the various charms of nature, storms of winter, "But," said he, "you can here form no idea of a snow storm. No, to see it in all its grandeur you should stand at my back door; there we see its progress—rising over the distant Allegany, come sweeping & roaring on, mountain after mountain, till it reaches us, and then when its blast is felt, to turn to our fire side, & while we hear it pelting against the window to enjoy the cheering blaze, & the comforts of a beloved family." Well, I have seen those distant mountains over which the winter storm has swept, now rearing their blue & misty heads to the clouds, & forming a sublime & beautiful horrison round one of the finest & most extended scenes the eye ever rested on, —I have seen that beloved family, whose virtues and affections are the best reward & the best treasure of their parent & their country's parent,—I have seen, I have listened to, one of the greatest & best of men. He has passed through the tempestuous sea of political life, has been enveloped in clouds of calumny, the storms of faction, assailed by foreign & domestic foes, & often threatened with a wreck, of happiness & fame. But these things are now all passed away, & like the mountain on which he stands, fogs & mists & storms, gather & rage below, while he enjoys unclouded sunshine. How simple & majestic is his character, my affection for him is weighed with much veneration, that, meek, humble, gentle & kind, as he is in his manners, I cannot converse with him, with ease. My mind is busied in thinking of what he is, rather than listening to what he says. After a very delightful journey of three days, we reached Monticello on the morning of the fourth. When I crossed the Ravanna, a wild & romantic little river, which flows at the foot of the mountain, my heart beat,—I thought I had entered, as it were, the threshold of his dwelling, & I looked around everywhere expecting to meet with some trace of his superintending care. In this I was disappointed, for no vestige of the labour of man appeared; nature seemed to hold an undisturbed dominion. We began to ascend this mountain, still as we rose I cast my eyes around, but could discern nothing but untamed woodland, after a mile's winding upwards, we saw a field of corn, but the road was still wild and uncultivated. I every moment expected to reach the summit, & felt as if it was an endless road; my impatience lengthened it, for it is not two miles from the outer gate on the river to the house. At last we reached the summit, & I shall never forget the emotion the first view of this sublime scenery excited. Below me extended for above 60 miles round, a country covered with woods, plantations & houses; beyond, arose the blue mountains, in all their grandeur. Monticello rising 500 feet above the river, of a conical form & standing by itself, commands on all sides an unobstructed & I suppose one of the most extensive views any spot the globe affords. The sides of the mountain covered with wood, with scarcely a speck of cultivation, present a fine contrast to its summit, crowned with a noble pile of buildings surrounded by an immense lawn, & shaded here & there with some fine trees. Before we reached the house, we met Mr. J. on horseback, he had just returned from his morning ride, & when, on approaching, he recognized us, he received us

Colonel John Bayard, father of Margaret Bayard.

A famous Revolutionary officer. Speaker of the Pennsylvania Assembly, and Member of the Continental Congress.

* From Mrs. Smith's note-book.

Monticello—Entrance hall.

Monticello—Salon.

with one of those benignant smiles, & cordial tones of voice that convey an undoubted welcome to the heart. He dismounted & assisted me from the carriage, led us to the hall thro' a noble portico, where he again bade us welcome. I was so struck with the appearance of this Hall, that I lingered to look around, but he led me forward, smiling as he said, "You shall look bye & bye, but you must now rest." Leading me to a sopha in a drawing room as singular & beautiful as the Hall, he rang & sent word to Mrs. Randolph that we were there, & then ordered some refreshments. "We have quite a sick family," said he; "My daughter has been confined to the sick bed of her little son; my grand-daughter has lost her's & still keeps to her room & several of the younger children are indisposed. For a fortnight Mr. and Mrs. Randolph have sat up every night, until they are almost worn out." This information clouded my satisfaction & cast a gloom over our visit, but Mrs. R. soon entered, & with a smiling face, most affectionately welcomed us. Her kind & cheerful manners soon dispersed my gloom & after a little chat, I begged her not to let me detain her from her nursery, but to allow me to follow her to it; she assented & I sat with her until dinner time. Anne,* (Mrs. Bankhead) who had been confined 3 weeks before & had lost her child looked delicate & interesting; Ellen, my old favorite, I found improved as well as grown. At five o'clock the bell summoned us to dinner. Mr. Randolph, Mr. Bankhead, & Jefferson R. were there. They are 12 in family, & as Mr. J. sat in the midst of his children & grand-children, I looked on him with emotions of tenderness & respect. The table was plainly, but genteely & plentifully spread, & his immense & costly variety of French & Italian wines, gave place to Madeira & a sweet ladies' wine. We sat till near sun down at the table, where the desert was succeeded by agreeable & instructive conversation in which every one seemed to wish & expect Mr. J. to take the chief part. As it is his custom after breakfast to withdraw to his own apartments & pursuits & not to join the family again until dinner, he prolongs that meal, or rather the time after that meal, & seems to relish his wine the better for being accompanied with conversation, & during the 4 days I spent there these were the most social hours. When we rose from the table, a walk was proposed & he accompanied us. He took us first to the garden he has commenced since his retirement. It is on the south side of the mountain & commands a most noble view. Little is as yet done. A terrace of 70 or 80 feet long & about 40 wide is already made & in cultivation. A broad grass walk leads along the water edge; the inner part is laid off in beds for vegetables. This terrace is to be extended in length & another to be made below it. The view it commands, is at present its greatest beauty. We afterwards walked round the first circuit. There are 4 roads about 15 or 20 feet wide, cut round the mountain from 100 to 200 feet apart. These circuits are connected by a great many roads & paths & when completed will afford a beautiful shady ride or walk of seven miles. The first circuit is not quite a mile round, as it is very near the top. It is in general shady, with openings through the trees for distant views. We passed the outhouses for the slaves & workmen. They are all much better than I have seen on any other plantation, but to an eye unaccustomed to such sights, they appear poor & their cabins form a most unpleasant contrast with the palace that rises so near them. Mr. J. has carpenters, cabinet-makers, painters, & blacksmiths & several other trades all within himself, & finds these slaves excellent workmen. As we walked, he explained his future designs. "My long absence from this place, has left a wilderness around me." "But you have returned," said I, "& the wilderness shall blossom like the rose & you, I hope, will long sit beneath your own vine & your own fig-tree." It was near dark when we reached the house; he led us into a little tea room which opened on the terrace & as Mrs. R. was still in her nursery he sat with us & conversed till tea time. We never drank tea until near nine, afterwards there was fruit, which he seldom staid to partake of, as he always retired immediately after tea. I never sat above an hour afterwards, as I supposed Mrs. R. must wish to be in her nursery. I rose the morning after my arrival very early & went out on the terrace to contemplate scenery, which to me was so novel. The space between Monticello & the Allegany, from sixty to eighty miles, was covered with a thick fog, which had the appearance of the ocean & was unbroken except when wood covered hills rose above the plain & looked like islands. As the sun rose, the fog was broken & exhibited the most various & fantastic forms, lakes, rivers, bays, & as it ascended, it hung in white fleecy clouds on the sides of the mountains; an hour afterwards you would scarcely believe it was the same scene you looked on. In spite of the cold air from the mountains, I staid here until the first breakfast bell rang. Our breakfast table was as large as our dinner table; instead of a cloth, a folded napkin lay under each plate; we had tea, coffee, excellent muffins, hot wheat & corn bread, cold ham & butter. It was not exactly the Virginian breakfast I expected. Here indeed was the mode of living in general that of a Virginian planter. At breakfast the family all assembled, all Mrs. R.'s children eat at the family table, but are in such excellent order, that you would not know, if you did not see them, that a child was present. After breakfast, I soon learned that it was the habit of the family each separately to pursue their occupations. Mr. J. went to

* Jefferson's oldest grandchild.

his apartments, the door of which is never opened but by himself & his retirement seems so sacred that I told him it was his sanctum sanctorum. Mr. Randolph rides over to his farm & seldom returns until night; Mr. Bankhead who is reading law to his study; a small building at the end of the east terrace, opposite to Mr. Randolph's which terminates the west terrace; these buildings are called pavilions. Jefferson R. went to survey a tract of woodland, afterwards make his report to his grand father. Mrs. Randolph withdrew to her nursery & excepting the hours housekeeping requires she devotes the rest to her children, whom she instructs. As for them, they seem never to leave her for an instant, but are always beside her or on her lap.

James A. Bayard—Senator from Delaware.
From an engraving of the original painting by Wertmuller.

Visitors generally retire to their own rooms, or walk about the place; those who are fond of reading can never be at a loss, those who are not will some times feel wearied in the long interval between breakfast & dinner. The dinner bell rings twice, the first collects the family in time to enter the room by the time the second announces dinner to be on table, which while I was there was between 4 & 5 oclock. In summer the interval between rising from table & tea (9 oclock) may be agreeably passed in walking. But to return to my journal. After breakfast on Sunday morning, I asked Ellen to go with me on the top of the house; Mr. J. heard me & went along with us & pointed out those spots in the landscape most remarkable. The morning was show'ry, the clouds had a fine effect, throwing large masses of shade on the mountain sides, which finely contrasted with the sunshine of other spots. He afterwards took us to the drawing room, 26 or 7 feet diameter, in the dome. It is a noble & beautiful apartment, with 8 circular windows & a sky-light. It was not furnished & being in the attic story is not used, which I thought a great pity, as it might be made the most beautiful room in the house. The attic chambers are comfortable & neatly finished but no elegance. When we descended to the hall, he asked us to pass into the Library, or as I called it his sanctum sanctorum, where any other feet than his own seldom intrude. This suit of apartments opens from the Hall to the south. It consists of 3 rooms for the library, one for his cabinet, one for his chamber, & a green house divided from the other by glass compartments & doors; so that the view of the plants it contains, is unobstructed. He has not yet made his collection, having but just finished the room, which opens on one of the terraces. He showed us everything he thought would please or interest us. His most valuable & curious books—those which contained fine prints etc.—among these I thought the most curious were the original letters of Cortez to the King of Spain, a vol of fine views of ancient villas round Rome, with maps of the grounds, & minute descriptions of the buildings & grounds, an old poem written by Pierce Plowman & printed 250 years ago; he read near a page, which was almost as unintelligible as if it was Hebrew; & some Greek romances. He took pains to find one that was translated into French, as most of them were translated in Latin & Italian. More than two hours passed most charmingly away. The library consists of books in all languages, & contains about twenty thousand vols, but so disposed that they do not give the idea of a great library. I own I was much disappointed in its appearance, & I do not think with its numerous divisions and arches it is as impressive as one large room would have been. His cabinet & chamber contained every convenience & comfort, but were plain. His bed is built in the wall which divides his chamber & cabinet. He opened a little closet which contains all his garden seeds. They are all in little phials, labeled & hung on little hooks. Seeds such as peas, beans, etc. were in tin cannisters, but everything labeled & in the neatest order. He bade us take whatever books we wished, which we did, & then retired to our own room. Here we amused ourselves until dinner time excepting an hour I sat with Mrs. R. by her sick baby, but as she was reading I did not sit long. After dinner Ellen & Mr. Bankhead accompanied

Aaron Burr.
From a portrait by John Vanderlyn, in the possession of Pierrepont Edwards, Elizabeth, N. J.

us in a long ramble in the mountain walks. At dark when we returned, the tea room was still vacant; I called Virginia & Mary (the age of my Julia & Susan) amused myself with them until their grand papa entered, with whom I had a long & interesting conversation; in which he described with enthusiasm his retirement from public life & the pleasures he found in domestic.

Wednesday morning. Mrs. Randolph was not able to come down to breakfast, & I felt too sad to join in the conversation. I looked on every object around me, all was examined with that attention a last look inspires; the breakfast ended, our carriage was at the door, & I rose to bid farewell to this interesting family. Mrs. R. came down to spend the last minutes with us. As I stood for a moment in the Hall, Mr. J. approached & in the most cordial manner urged me to make another visit the ensuing summer I told him with a voice almost choked with tears, "that I had no hope of such a pleasure—this," said I, raising my eyes to him, "is the last time I fear in this world at least, that I shall ever again see you—But there is another world." I felt so affected by the idea of this last sight of this good & great man, that I turned away & hastily repeating my farewell to the family, gave him my hand, he pressed it affectionately as he put me in the carriage saying, "God bless you, dear madam, God bless you." "And God bless you," said I, from the very bottom of my heart.

Mr. Smith got in, the door shut & we drove from the habitation of philosophy & virtue. How rapidly did we seem to descend that mountain which had seemed so tedious in its ascent, and the quick pulsations I then felt were now changed to a heavy oppression.

Yes, he is truly a philosopher, & truly a good man, and eminently a great one. Then there is a tranquility about him, which an inward peace could alone bestow. As a ship long tossed by the storms of the ocean, casts anchor & lies at rest in a peaceful harbour, he is retired from an active & restless scene to this tranquil spot. Voluntarily & gladly has he resigned honors which he never sought, & unwillingly accepted. His actions, not his words, preach the emptiness & dissatisfaction attendant on a great office. His tall & slender figure is not impaired by age, tho' bent by care & labour. His white locks announce an age his activity, strength, health, enthusiasm, ardour & gaiety contradict. His face owes all its charm to its expression & intelligence; his features are not good & his complexion bad, but his countenance is so full of soul & beams with much benignity, that when the eye rests on his face, it is too busy in perusing its expression, to think of its features or complexion. His low & mild voice, harmonizes with his countenance rather than his figure. But his manners,—how gentle, how humble, how kind. His meanest slave must feel as if it were a father instead of a master who addressed him, when he speaks. To a disposition ardent, affectionate & communicative, he joins manners timid, even to bashfulness & reserved even to coldness. If his life had not proved to the contrary I should have pronounced him rather a man of imagination & taste, than a man of judgement, a literary rather than a scientific man, & least of all a politician, a character for which nature never seemed to have intended him, & for which the natural turn of mind, & his disposition, taste, & feeling equally unfit him. I should have been sure that this was the case, even had he not told me so. In an interesting conversation I had one evening—speaking of his past public & present domestic life—"The whole of my life," said he, "has been a war with my natural taste, feelings & wishes. Domestic life & literary pursuits, were my first & my latest inclinations, circumstances & not my desires lead me to the path I have trod. And like a bow tho long bent, which when unstrung flies back to its natural state, I resume with delight the character & pursuits for which nature designed me.

"The circumstances of our country," continued he, "at my entrance into life, were such that every honest man felt himself compelled to take a part, & to act up to the best of his abilities."

August 4th, MONTPELIER Wendnesd even.

The sadness which all day hung on my spirits was instantly dispelled by the cheering smile of Mrs. Madison & the friendly greeting of our good President. It was near five oclock when we arrived, we were met at the door by Mr. M. who led us into the dining room where some gentlemen were still smoking segars & drinking wine. Mrs. M. enter'd the moment afterwards, &

after embracing me, took my hand, saying with a smile, "I will take you out of this smoke to a pleasanter room." She took me thro' the tea room to her chamber which opens from it. Everything bespoke comfort, I was going to take my seat on the sopha, but she said I must lay down by her on her bed, & rest myself, she loosened my riding habit, took off my bonnet, & we threw ourselves on her bed. Wine, ice, punch & delightful pine-apples were immediately brought. No restraint, no ceremony. Hospitality is the presiding genius of this house, & Mrs. M. is kindness personified. She enquired why I had not brought the little girls; I told her the fear of incomoding my friends. "Oh," said she laughing, "I should not have known they were here, among all the rest, for at this moment we have only three & twenty in the house." "Three & twenty," exclaimed I! "Why where do you store them?" "Oh we have house room in plenty." This I could easily believe, for the house seemed immense. It is a large two story house of 80 or 90 feet in length, and above 40 deep. Mrs. Cutts soon came in with her sweet children, and afterwards Mr. Madison, Cutts, & Mr. Smith. The door opening into the tea room being open, they without ceremony joined their wives. They only peeked in on us; we then shut the door & after adjusting our dress, went out on the Piazza—(it is 60 feet long). Here we walked & talked until called to tea, or rather supper, for tho' tea hour, it was supper fare. The long dining table was spread, & besides tea & coffee, we had a variety of warm cakes, bread, cold meats & pastry. At table I was introduced to Mr. William Madison,* brother to the President, & his wife, & three or four other ladies & gentlemen all near relatives, all plain country people, but frank, kind, warm-hearted Virginians. At this house I realized being in Virginia, Mr. Madison, plain, friendly, communicative, & unceremonious as any Virginia Planter could be—Mrs. Madison, uniting to all the elegance & polish of fashion, the unadulterated simplicity, frankness, warmth, & friendliness of her native character & native state. Their mode of living, too, if it had more elegance than is found among the planters, was characterized by that abundance, that hospitality, & that freedom, we are taught to look for on a Virginian plantation. We did not sit long at this meal—the evening was warm & we were glad to leave the table. The gentlemen went to the piazza, the ladies, who all had children, to their chambers, & I sat with Mrs. M. till bed time talking of Washington. When the servant appeared with candles to show me my room, she insisted on going up stairs with me, assisted me to undress & chatted till I got into bed. How unassuming, how kind is this woman. How can any human being be her enemy. Truly, in her there is to be found no gall, but the pure milk of human kindness. If I may say so, the maid was like the mistress; she was very attentive all the time I was there, seeming as if she could not do enough, & was very talkative. As her mistress left the room, "You have a good mistress Nany," said I, "Yes," answered the affectionate creature with warmth, "the best I believe in the world,—I am sure I would not change her for any mistress in the whole country." The next morning Nany called me to a late breakfast, brought me ice & water, (this is universal here, even in taverns) & assisted me to dress. We sat down between 15 & 20 persons to breakfast—& to a most excellent Virginian breakfast—tea, coffee, hot wheat bread, light cakes, a pone, or corn loaf—cold ham, nice hashes, chickens, etc.

* Of Woodbury Forest, about six miles from Montpelier.

Washington Society
(1893)

WASHINGTON SOCIETY.

BY HENRY LOOMIS NELSON.

I.—OFFICIAL.

WHAT is known as "society" is such a fugitive thing in a true republic that it is next to impossible to locate it, to fix it in a certain quarter, so that it may be said, "Here are the happy beings who reign in the world of pleasure and politeness." There are many different points of view from which the gilded joys are looked at, and many diverse ears that listen to the music of the social spheres. When one undertakes to analyze the ephemera, an initial difficulty is the catching of a specimen: their lives are short, and when they finally quit the world they leave behind them little more than a smudge. And this is truer of the individuals of the social insectivora in the United States than of countries where there are kings and princes, and sometimes even emperors and empresses, around whom circle a definitely appointed and selected host of beings who are part and parcel of the royal or imperial state of things.

It is true, to some extent, as has been smartly said over and over again, that a country's civilization may be learned from the manner in which the people amuse themselves. We understand what manner of folk they are who take a rude delight in the outpouring of blood—whether it be human or taurine blood—and we also realize that one of the evidences of high civilization, and consequently one of the certain signs that civilization has a good deal left to accomplish for the race, is the production of a certain human species with no desire for intellectual or moral advancement, without any purpose whatever except for the joyful expenditure of inherited resources, physical and otherwise. When a human plant begins to revel in the mere pleasure of existence, it is greatly in danger, unless grafting intervenes, of being supplanted by a humbler specimen sprung from newer roots.

It is not possible to weigh the virtues of England or of the United States by the doings and the undoings of their most fashionable people. In this country every one is in society somewhere, although it often surprises a resident of New York, for example, to hear of an unknown fellow citizen or citizeness riding on the top wave of social glory in Washington, or Cleveland, or Bridgeport, or Omaha. And the like is true of strangers venturing into New York from other towns of the country. A man or woman who fails for any reason, usually most illogical, or even absurd, to be familiarly received by the best people of his or her own city or town—best by character or

THE JAM AT THE SENATOR'S.

wealth or intellect, whichever may be the local test of excellence—is very likely to pass on merit in distant places. There is a city in the country whose people are reputed to be of a peculiarly haughty turn of mind, who sustain their reputation for exclusiveness by declining to know irresponsible unfortunates born within their own borders, but on the wrong side of a particular street. Yet

THE LACK OF YOUNG MEN.

they often greet and entertain with a broad and generous hospitality strangers from other parts of the country who at home dwell on the cold side of the street. And at such times, and on such occasions, the humblest of us all is led to realize that in a republic every man has a chance to somewhere make his way to social grandeur as well as to political power.

There is no broader republicanism or democracy than is to be found in the official society of Washington, as undoubtedly there is no deeper-dyed or more abject and revolting snobbery. There are people in this small capital of ours who will tell the on-looker at the tumultuous rush that fills the few weeks before and immediately after Lent with rustlings and hurryings, with the noise of carriage wheels and the excited exclamations and laughter of young women, that all this that is on the surface is very far from being the true society of Washington, that there is an inner and intimate set with which one must become familiar before one can be said to know the society life of the capital and its exquisite and peculiar charm.

These people are basking in their errors. They are pleased to think that they are sitting at the warm heart of the nation, and that their goings and comings, their dinings and gossipings, make up the ebb and flow of all that is first quality in the national circulation. It is strange that clever people who are alert for amusement and recreation should neglect so obvious an object of interest as that society of the republic which wears the official stamp. The society of the capital that is immediately before our eyes is a moving and breathing picture of the life of the country. It is essentially republican. The men and women who compose it come from all ends of the land. Its chief interest lies in the fact that it is not like the society that is to be found at courts or in the charmed circles of those who hedge in kings. Here we have the people doing as best they may what is done by the select of Europe. They may do it crudely, inelegantly, even boisterously, but will any one who has participated in their pleasures say that they do not do it generously, and with a certain nobility of kindliness, that, unfortunately for them, is a stranger to many who look at them through cynical lorgnettes?

From the President's dwelling down, the houses of the official people who care to perform the social function are open to the public. It is absurd, of course, to speak of the social intercourse carried on on such a basis as involving in any but the slightest degree the element of selection or of exclusiveness. There was a time not many

AT THE JAPANESE LEGATION.

years ago when a few persons were invited to the official receptions at the White House, and placed behind a barrier of receiving women and sofas. It was pleasant for those who were thus chosen, and they were people who helped to make Washington unique and peculiar; but the great Washington world, the really interesting and characteristic specimens of humanity, the representatives of the progressive citizenship of the country, tramped on before that President as their like had tramped on before other Presidents, and as they would continue to tramp on before Presidents yet to come, into the great East Room, out into the halls, timidly through the Conservatory—for simple-minded men and women who do not understand all the complications of social relations have not yet learned the delight of remote corners, and are strongly inclined to doubt the propriety of getting beyond the call of the host or hostess, no matter how large the party may be.

At the President's house on a reception night, or at the house of a cabinet officer on a Wednesday afternoon, or of a Senator on a Thursday afternoon, or at any place to which people are asked for their public position, there will be found men and women representing every stage of prosperity in the Union, and every honest calling that leads to prosperity. And that is precisely what is to be found in the public places of the republic—in the House of Representatives, in the Senate, in the cabinet, on the Supreme Bench, and in the White House itself. It is a strange and interesting accumulation of human beings, most of them too timid to be as interesting as they might be. Even when the President issues cards, the people who get together make up a curious conglomerate.

The new Congressman takes his wife to the President's, expecting to find the entertainment not very different, although perhaps on a somewhat grander scale, from that to which he is accustomed in the judge's house at the county-seat during court week. So he goes, perhaps, in his frock-coat, feeling an American prejudice against evening dress, and a white or lilac tie, while his rather fearful helpmate has put on her best black silk, modest or prudish, as you will, with its high neck and its long sleeves. The new Congressman experiences no trepidation in addressing the President. They are both politicians, and the new Congressman may even believe for a moment that some day he may stand at the head of the line of well-dressed women, whose necks and arms now shine in his startled eyes. He does not doubt that the President is aware of the unique vicissitudes of the recent campaign in his district. There are a hundred subjects that the two have in common, but he is disappointed as he is about to utter his first smart phrase of conversation to feel that the President's hand is gently impelling him forward, and that there is a soft pressure of the crowd behind him in the same direction. It is his first introduction to the reticences and restraints of high life, an introduction which is emphasized and made more impressive by the disinclination of the receiving women to shake hands, or to indicate their recognition of the new member by anything warmer or more emphatic than a courtesy, which, however, is quite enough for the timorous wife at his side, who, much more than her husband, shrinks before the grand dames of the White House and cabinet, some of whom were born to polite society, while some have acquired a large amount of social assurance during their husbands' struggles up the ladder of fame.

Other persons besides Congressmen are here, some of them equally uncomfortable, many of them, however, enjoying themselves to the utmost. There is a panorama of all that is prominent in official and political life. There are officers of the army and navy who have been on staff duty at the capital, and are now undergoing, with pleasure or fortitude, as the case may be, the pronounced admiration of young women. There are older officers, who have been more recently on the plains, and who come to the function with their wives and daughters and sisters with a delight or reverence due, to their honest thinking, to the highest and most resplendent social ceremony in this country—the drawing-room not only of the head of the nation, but of the commander-in-chief of the two military services. The army and navy folk of the staff are usually of that inner circle whose peculiar traits and customs are not now under consideration; but the army people who have spent years on the plains know nothing better, or higher, or wiser, or generally more praiseworthy, than their own people. Therefore they will

RECEPTION AT A CABINET MINISTER'S.

be found together, although the excited women, who have for years endured with a noble patience the monotony of life at army posts, are rejoiced beyond words if they may only grasp the hand and hear the voice of some paragon of Congressional wisdom who has been good to their husbands or to the service.

There will be diplomats in dazzling uniforms; Chinese mandarins in silk attire; Japanese officials, the men in the black evening dress of convention, and the

GOING TO THE BALL.

women in the proper costume of Europe and America.

Nearly every one of those who make up this interesting human collection finds somewhere in the moving throng a friend or comrade who will save him from that terrible isolation of an evening party which most persons have felt, and which is often as depressing as the solitude of a great city. There is little need to be alone, and the object of a wondering gaze that freezes the warm blood, in a crush at a Washington reception. As the new Congressman stalks on, followed by the trotting footsteps of his timid wife, his eyes will be gladdened by the sight of a colleague who is apparently as much a stranger as he to the gay scene. And he too may have a wife, a trifle over-resolute, perhaps, a little better assured of the dignity of the place into which her husband's constituents have elevated them. It may be that the two law-makers have only known each other's nod. Perhaps they are of opposing parties, or from different sections of the country. Much that would deter a friendly offering of the hand on other occasions now suggests, even impels it. Who that has not experienced it can tell of the avid pleasure with which an unknown human being, borne helplessly along by the moving tide of a crowded evening party, seizes upon the rescuing hand of a chance acquaintance? The traditional straw of the drowning man, the echoing voices of approaching rescuers, the far-off signal of recognition to shipwrecked sailors—all these are kindred joys to that gratification felt by a stranded soul in a social desert when a face that is known smiles upon its gloom.

Many groups of husbands and wives cling together in the crowded rooms. They fear to give up their grasp on each other. They fear to be cast loose among people to whom they dare not speak, some of whom stare at them wonderingly, and wound them with cruel eyes. So the groups gathered here and there enjoy themselves about as they do at church sociables and ice-cream and strawberry festivals in their home villages. The men clasp their hands behind their backs, rise and fall on their toes, knit their brows, purse their lips, test each other's opinions, try little orations on one another, quote an old saw or two, exhibit themselves to their best advantage, each one inwardly hoping that the others will expect something good from him when he rises for the first time to address the House, and will thus guarantee an audience, a feature of Congressional oratorical performances which, as even new members have learned, is very likely to be lacking.

Meanwhile the women are getting deep into each other's confidences, and they know all about what John says and what James thinks, and what are their peculiar ailments—whatever, in a word, have been the domestic, culinary, social, or medical experiences of the various feminine components of the group. The men touch upon the Constitution, while the women recount the virtues of the leading sarsaparillas or the smartnesses of their children. The men argue a little and the women discuss; but under such circumstances the woman's argument is usually "I think so too," although a moment before she may have stated a proposition entirely at variance with her present imagined thought. Such is the deadening influence of newly made acquaintanceship on the logical powers of femininity.

When some one suggests that the President has prepared a feast, each man takes in his own wife, and there are heard the jests so often repeated—sly jests about "feeling a goneness," about John's appetite for cake, followed by serious assurances on the part of the good wife, lest the jest be taken literally, that John, after all, is not a "good feeder." There is that hilarity in the supper-room which shows that new acquaintanceship is getting on famously, and that there is a loosening of restraint upon the tongues that thus far have been uttering studied phrases.

As likely as not, the dining-room will be pervaded by that kindly matronly person so common among the well-to-do of the country, and, for that matter, of all countries, whose generous nature takes in all the world that she considers good, and who will joke with the great as familiarly as with the little. There will be not only the country lawyer and his wife, but the country merchant, and occasionally a clergyman who has preached himself into politics. There will be the shrewd rural banker, and the quiet speculator from the city.

There will be the vulgar rich man, who for years has been able to buy whatever he desired, and expects to be able to go on buying—friends, social position, and political honors. He will overwhelm the country members with invitations to his "residence." When they go there he will give them cider and mud-turtle, but he will see to it that the sly old lobbyist yonder and the experienced Senator who is a power in the party are served with French champagne and veritable terrapin. He will throw open his doors to all Washington. He will send his cards of invitation to all the newspaper correspondents, whether he knows them or not, and who, if he does not know them, will properly feel insulted, and will decline to honor his entertainment with their presence. And when his party is done with—he will call it a "blow-out"—he will have made a mistake. If he has lavished his champagne and cider, his terrapin and mud-turtle, for political ends, he might have done better by giving a dinner to the politicians at a famous restaurant. The "boys" would have been more comfortable in their own society than they were in the crush of strange men and stranger women. If he has thus sought to force an entry into the inner circles of society, he will be laughed at for his pains. Whatever may have been his object, he has made a mistake, and no one knows it better than the shrewd old trader in legislative desires and frequenter of all the social efforts where the food and drink are likely to be abundant, and who doubtless suggested the giving of the entertainment. It is this same old fox, bred and developed by the ostentatious and vulgar adventurers who are sure to turn up at frequent intervals in Washington, who used to sit at hospitable tables with one bottle of champagne at his elbow and two bottles under his chair. He took the two bottles home to his comfortable lodgings, and kept himself so well supplied that he had always a predatory bottle in good condition for any friend who might happen in with a business proposition worth the sacrifice.

There are occasionally to be seen at these miscellaneous gatherings sharp-eyed and painted women whose business is so well known that they are avoided not only by the honest but by every one of experience and ordinary shrewdness. Congress may be beset by women lobbyists, but it is far from being victimized by them. It is only rarely that one of the tribe finds an escort, and then the quarry is invariably a young member, pert, vain, easily flattered, and, as he parades official drawing-rooms with his vivacious companion, he sadly mistakes the meaning of the glances that he encounters. He will learn fast enough, and next year he will be seen in better company, if he is not altogether bad.

Grave old public functionaries are not wont to lend their presence to the great crushes. When they go, they go perfunctorily, and grumble about the burden imposed upon them as audibly as is consistent with their political and other relations. They wander about discontentedly, bored by the accustomed show. They have outgrown the callow days of their statesmanship; their wives have developed out of high necks and long sleeves, and have become either active or quiescent figures in the social world. Neither the man nor the woman wants ice-cream or strawberries any more. The one drinks tea at five o'clock, nibbles at an eight-o'clock dinner, and endures an evening party, while the other prefers the club and a game of whist, or to sit in slippered converse over a glass of punch with some old crony with whom he has weathered a score or more of political storms.

The healthful American social life is in the ascendency. Among the Congressmen and other public men, and among the guests, there are types as varying as the varying features of the country. The representatives of the somewhat stiff refinement of rural New England are in the throng—the successful lawyer from the mountain or the valley, with his sensible wife, prim and precise in their jointly shared notions of duty, lovers of quiet evenings with current literature, bookish, perhaps, and persistent in maintaining the habits and customs of their native land, strict in their fidelity to the Friday evening prayer-meeting, strong in their devotion to pulpit oratory, quick of wit, intellectually sympathetic, and with a native elasticity that enables them to speedily take on social polish. In the groups which form themselves in the great social sea there are few so interesting as those that are redolent of the eager intellectual life of New England; and of rural New England best of all, for Boston does not count in this heterogeneous aggregate, whose interest depends largely upon the absence of deep sophistication. The Boston merchant who goes to Washington is not very different from the New York or Philadelphia merchant, except perhaps that he has retained a little more sweet homeliness, which increases his genuineness. As to the cultured Bostonian, the pushing samples of the best they have in what was once at least the Athens of America, he is at the heart of things. If social pleasures and dissipations attract him from his dignified labors, he does not habitually seek those that are to be found in the official homes, or, at least, at the official functions. If he goes at all to these, it is to lend his countenance to his party chief, or to satisfy his general longing to sacrifice himself for duty's sake.

As a social animal, the man of tradition, wealth, and education, who has seriously taken up politics as a profession, belongs to the innermost and uppermost of the Brahmins, a few of whom, however, are always present at the large social functions of the capital, where they constitute what may be called a withdrawing class. They and theirs are the correctly garbed and mannered ornaments of such occasions. Like the others of fewer pretensions, they find their amusement in their own set, and their social superiority is recognized by their fellow-beings with a certain fine American lack of envy, hatred, or malice. The quiet, dignified, austere young men who move through the general mass with an ostentatious air of not recognizing that there is any mass do not disturb the placidity of those who are having a good time after their own fashion; but they lend a feature to the occasion, and serve as witnesses that America, like countries that are not republican, or that have not been republican more than a century, possesses a class socially differentiated from the interesting people who are responsible for its real daily life and real character and progressiveness.

Not many years ago—seven from this time of writing—the official parlor of Washington saw, for the first time in many years, the old Southern families creep out again into the warm social sunshine. There is a certain kinship between the New-Englander and the Southerner from one of the older States, and when the Democratic party returned to the White House it was not long in being re-established. Often among the groups of jesting, argumentative, simple-minded statesmen you shall find a courtly Southerner paying fine compliments in his grandiloquent speech to a bright-eyed New England woman used to straightforward words, or to the masculine reserve which believes, whether or not the belief be confessed, in the Puritan subordination of women; and yet there is no New England woman whose femininity does not rise with the shy alertness of a trout after a fly, through superimposed years of hard and restrainful custom, to the shining allurement of flattery. And at the same time—for in society that is purely American the wife is never far from the husband—you shall hear a low sweet woman's voice, mellowed by the Southern accent, arguing learnedly a constitutional point with a New England man whose political opinions are sadly awry; for it has been for ages now the creed of Southern women that to be truly a helpmate to their husbands is to be intellectually helpful and sympathetic. When New England women, before the war, were knitting and putting up famous preserves, and generally looking after the physical welfare of their men folk, the women of the South were reading the works of Edmund Burke and kindred literature to their fathers, sweethearts, and husbands.

And everywhere is the American girl—the pride of prosperous households from the Atlantic to the Pacific; the girl of the period from New York or Philadelphia; the exquisitely tinted Puritan of New England; the Vassar or Wellesley college graduate—determined upon compelling young cavalry officers to bestow upon her their valuable opinions as to Browning's place in literature, or the future of the American woman, or the relative merits of women's colleges and men's universities. There are other girls frankly ignorant, impatient of anything that sounds literary or scientific, but who wear the diamonds bestowed upon them by parental affection with a proud consciousness that there is money in the parental bank to buy many more of them. There are simple rural maidens who are redolent of the soil from which they come. All of them are subjected to a certain forcing process in this atmosphere. All of them will feel the ecstasy that fills each true woman's heart when she imagines that she has been a participant in the highest and brightest of social glories; and the echoes of their delight reverberate from one end of the land to the other, for in nearly every town and hamlet there is some exuberant young being who has shared in the festivities of Washington, who has seen her like from all quarters of the Union gathered together under the roofs of great men—of the President, of cabinet officers, of law-makers, of foreign ministers. She has met young men of different mould from those who make evening calls on her in her own retired village, or small city, or back street. She has felt that there are powers within her which she never recognized before, and which may be wasted in the dull and spiritless place in which she dwells, and where men and women are engrossed by the sordid and confining cares of business and housekeeping, creating and developing the life of which she has been part. She has associated with all that is great in the national life. She has talked familiarly with strange people from the Orient. She has ventured on a little French with an attaché of the legation of the young republic, or perhaps even with the minister himself. She has seen a real Hungarian hussar, and, what is more, she has danced with him. Moreover, she has seen the kind of men she knows at home, the leading lawyers, the principal merchants, the respectable, self-respecting Americans, standing on an even footing with all that controls and directs the country. This fact may not be very impressive to her simplicity, but she feels that she has been among the best there is in all humanity, and that if the men whom she controls can hold their own in these surroundings, why should not she stand on equal terms with Presidents and ministers and Senators and judges, and even with their wives and daughters?

Washington official society offers a great revelation of American character. These people who make the living panorama of a drawing-room are the products of our institutions. In the countries of kings and emperors they could not have come to this. Some of them may be vulgar, many of them may be crude, most of them may be uninteresting to those whose pleasure lies in the alertness and skill of intellectual fence. The latest works of fiction may be unfamiliar to them, they may not know the names of the leading French authors or painters, they may not have heard that Russia has a literature, they may think the equestrian effigy of Jackson more splendid than the graceful figure of Chief Justice Marshall, but they have self-respect and kind considerateness for others, and they recognize the proprieties of speech and manners. They feel their own powers, and have realized their value. They are clean-minded, and they have won their leadership by their own efforts, for this is the congregation of the leaders of the republic—the men and women who inhabit the homes of the country, in city and hamlet, on prairie and mountain, and by sea-shore. They are the source of its power and the products of its culture. From out their sturdy stock come the brilliant double blossoms of that which deems itself the highest civilization. Most of these blossoms die with their generation, but the invigorating soil grows better and better plants as the years go on.

WASHINGTON SOCIETY.

BY HENRY LOOMIS NELSON.

II.—INTIMATE.

THERE are entertainment, instruction, and inspiration in the heterogeneous display of the leaders of the republic and their wives and daughters; and there is no other country where all this is so amply true of the people whose business is "getting on," who have not yet reached the resting-point where they may practise the art of living gracefully. One of the meanest of human vices is shrinking, and in this country there is no valid excuse for it. If an American man or woman fails to stand up at least self-respectfully before the highest of men or the haughtiest of social queens, it is because of the depressing recognition of defeat in the struggle of life. There is little of interest in those who do not live up to their sovereignty--in the women, for example, who stand against the walls at an afternoon reception at which the public is supposed to be welcome. If one is curious about them, they may be found at their desks the next morning, or at their boarding-house tables in the evening descanting on the social glories they have shared by going unbidden and unknown where any one can go, and by extorting, to the utter misery and often unseemly wrath of tired and overburdened women, return cards from the families of cabinet officers and Senators. Poor women! How much insolence they are willing to endure for a pasteboard evidence of familiarity with greatness, the worthlessness of which is recognized by every other seeker after like testimonials!

It would not do to say that the throngs that may be seen in Washington drawing-rooms every afternoon and every evening are not refined. The most refined and delicate morality in the world is that of the American woman—of the woman who has never departed from American traditions, and who has not permitted French innuendo to stimulate her Anglo-Saxon nature. The woman who has made the home, and has not only kept her hearth clean, but has maintained her faith in her husband as in her church, may be untrained in the finer arts of life, may be ignorant of etiquette, of letters, of arts, of all that is deemed essential to the appropriate furnishing of a polite mind, but there is a sweet purity in her heart which forbids us to say that she is unrefined, and which compels us to acknowledge that her spotlessness is more beautiful than the polish of many a woman who considers herself vastly her superior.

We will not say, then, that this living picture of the admirable and prosperous products of the republic is unrefined. It may be crude, angular, sharp of voice, tuneless, cold, uninteresting perhaps, except to one who is studying institutions. The men and women of the world often find it insipid, and if Washington offered nothing more in the way of social attractions than is to be had at the official crushes of the season, it would not be the popular winter resort of wealth and fashion that it is.

It is not always possible to say why fashion or society seeks this place or that and transforms it into a resort. The leader of a set or a social trust, or something of that nature, may determine the momentous matter. But we are not now inquiring why is Newport, or Mount Desert, or Lenox, or Tuxedo. They are, and that is the end of it. But why is Washington popular with those to whom its superficial outward social life must be most aggressively offensive?—with those who have no interest in the problems of that part of humanity which dwells in the outer darkness beyond the pale?

Every town and city that is worthy of any consideration has its intimate life, which is of the very best. Even in New York, where the fashionable mob is so large and glittering as to obscure and nearly blot out what is modest and seemly, there is an inmost core which the gossip of the newspapers does not penetrate. The men and women of Washington who are beings apart in the crowded assemblages of the White House and its kindred dwelling-places, and who look on their fellow-beings with whom they are officially thrown into social contact as strange personalities of comparatively small importance in the universal scheme,

BELLES OF WASHINGTON.

—these are the people who make the inmost life of the capital. They are of the world of American society, and like their kind elsewhere. If a man of the set is in public life, either it is by accident, or he is a social acquisition for purposes of stimulating entertainment.

There was an old Washington, and there is a new. The day has gone by when life was dominated by the first Southern families, whose pride and affections were shared between their genealogical importance and their old madeira. The time has gone by, too, when the circle of the Supreme Court was the innermost of the seven social circles, and when the ponderous anecdotes of the bar, interlarded with law-Latin, furnished Attic salt for heavy feasts. If a judge and his family are now in the innermost circle, it is for other acquirements than those that have made him eminent in his profession. There is no basic reason why society should eagerly accept a great lawyer whose life has been spent in the narrow drudgeries of his office, and whose wife has developed amid the narrow social surroundings of a country town. There have been vulgar and offensive men and women in the Supreme Court circle; and while all who are of the best and brightest at the capital pay due deference to rank and position, the principal reason for their solidarity is entertainment—not necessarily elevating or instructive or sternly moral, but entertainment that is not awkward or shabby.

Not many years ago, according to the veracious wit of a clever woman, Washington relapsed into a village when Congress adjourned, and there are those who have lingered on in the growing city who will tell you that all this is changed, and that the Washington you knew once has departed forever, has been swallowed up by the inrushing tide of new people, who have discovered there attractions that are not to be met with elsewhere. In a large and general way the people who say this are superficial, and they are mistaken, although in the matter of detail they may be perfectly right. It is very easy, at

THE NEW PET.

least not at all difficult, to mistake a change of customs for a change of people—a development of methods for a revolution.

Washington remains essentially what it was. There are more people there, and some of them belong to strange species, but the interest remains the same, the interest of a capital to people of leisure who are blessed with intellects that need something that will add spice and agreeable flavor to their ceremonial functions. The city has spread out wonderfully towards the hills of the northwest, where Mr. Cleveland set his home amid the oaks, on a slope from which the monuments of the city can be seen over the tops of trees. Wealth has made the city one of its pleasant abodes. Society has increased, and the innermost circle is harder to find, and harder, perhaps, to enter, but it is much the same as it was ten or fifteen years ago, although its manner of enjoyment is different. In a word, there are so many eyes upon it, most of them strange, many of them unkindly critical, that its men and women have to be conventional.

Not that Washington was ever a city where perversity and froward disposition prevailed. The benighted person who deems it a city of scandals is likely to mistake the atmosphere of a hotel dining-room for that of a dinner-giving home. There are stories, and there have been whispers, and uncomfortable beings have drawn long faces. Possibly, nay, probably, men and women have often, even in Washington, begun, and perhaps finished, that time-worn burlesque which opens with an argumentative dialogue—usually carried on between two persons who cannot tell whether Plato was a Greek, a Jew, or an Egyptian—a discussion as to whether platonic friendship between a man and a woman is possible. To an old man of the world it may seem hard to believe that this stale device is still in use, but such a one must remember that it was old and stale when he first used it, and the elder men of his time doubtless laughed at him for supposing that fish could still be caught with that bait. And yet it is as true of men and women as it is of anglers and trout, to each generation the old tricks are new, and life must be lived over again each time a human being is brought into the world.

When Washington was in the comfortable habit of relapsing into a village, the manners and customs of the place were most worthy of the commendation and enjoyment of a man or woman of sympathetic nature and abundant leisure. When the jasmine and the forsythia began to burst into blossom, or later, if Congress insisted on legislating into the heats of summer, there was a delightful freedom about life that does not exist now, owing to the metropolitan character which the capital has seen fit to assume. A man might then profitably waste a whole afternoon on a bench in Lafayette Square, listening to the music of the birds and of a feminine voice, and lazily discussing love or art, or other people, or any subject that is dear to a woman's inmost thoughts. It was not improper then to sit on the stoop through the warm evenings, and to continue there the flirtations of the season that was passed, innocuous from their very frankness. There was an open-air life, an unconcealed state of affairs, an indifference to suspicions, that argued both of innocence and intimacy; but as Washington grew and other people went to it to share its attractions, it became improper—that is, unsafe—to walk home from the theatre under the stars and moon, or to linger in the shadows of the doorway, or to do a thousand and one things that one's friends might safely talk about, but that would become flaming swords, injurious to reputation, if they should be gossiped over by impartial strangers coming from the colder commercial metropolises.

There are no simple picnics now to which the privileged once rode by twos

RECEPTION OF THE BARBARIANS.

or threes or fours, held at the hospitable country house of some Washingtonian with rural tastes. Some one as clever almost as the clever woman, but suffering under the misfortune of being a man, has said that there was a time in Washington's social history when a woman might give a ball if she had a case of apollinaris. That simple time has departed. The woman of Washington who undertakes a ball in this day of the city's history faces all the expense and a good many more of the difficulties that confront her sister of New York or Philadelphia or Boston.

It was a great event in the old day when the State Department found itself charged with the duty of entertaining some duly accredited foreign embassy, pagan or Christian, dusky or otherwise. Then what has been dubbed in the navy the "royal yacht," meaning thereby a small, untrustworthy vessel supposed to be useful in time of war as a despatch-boat, was utilized for festal purposes, and the embassy and the guests of the Secretary of State were carried down the Potomac to visit the tomb of Washington. There were lunch and music and talk, bright sunshine and much gayety. If the ambassadors were interesting, they became acquainted with what of Washington the Secretary of State or his family thought to be good enough for themselves; but if they were peculiarly and irreparably pagan, they enjoyed the view of the river and its shores in the society of their accompanying missionaries. Perhaps these pleasant excursions continue to be a feature of Washington society, but if they do, an invitation must be far more rare than it used to be, for necessarily there are many more people in the capital whom the Secretary's family are obliged to consider good enough, while the accommodations of the boat remain limited.

In the old day—the men and women who made part of its panorama call it that, especially if they have moved away and are not of the Washington of the present—in the old day there used to be moonlight excursions down the river to a once ambitious "terminal point"—to use a seductive railroad phrase—and society lunched and gossiped and flirted at so much a head in behalf of the Garfield Memorial Hospital, or of some other equally worthy object of charity.

During the winter the cabinet officers and their families used to hold what were known as "card receptions." They were comfortably crowded, and were pleasant. Other and unofficial families followed the example, and one might go almost any evening of the week, including Sunday, to some particular house, and meet the same people that one met the evening before, and that one would meet the evening following. These were assemblages of friends, with an infusion of whatever distinguished visitors might happen to be in the city. Naturally there was a tinge, sometimes amounting to a taint, of officialism in the gatherings; for the cabinet families cannot neglect the law-makers who provide the means for carrying on their departments. Congress and its wife was asked in due rotation, but the people who were really wanted were invited to the season's series, and there was hardly a single evening in the week when one who was admitted might not meet most of the others at a designated place.

There was no ostentation in these evening parties. There was sometimes a rude intrusion. Occasionally a hostess who, in common with her other receiving friends, had endured the insolence of an unasked intruder—man or woman—felt compelled to take strong measures. The capital of the nation is infested with a human insect that devotes its energies to boring into places where it is not wanted. Possibly its kindred exist elsewhere; but there has been so much freedom of access to the houses of men whose careers depend upon popularity, and so much dread among those in high places of unwittingly trampling upon influential feelings, that the breed is especially encouraged there. Then, again, there are two notable features which mark the society of the capital—the presence of officials and statesmen who are known far and wide, and the absence of men who are distinguished in the sciences and the arts.

The old day was not the day of champagne and terrapin, but of simple tea, and simple tea's ordinary table companions. To think what havoc may be wrought by a single enterprising millionaire! He came, and the tea table vanished. The man with the case of apollinaris hides his diminished head. The cabinet officer who is not very rich, to whom his salary is important enough to make an appre-

AT THE COUNTRY CLUB.

ciable part of the year's income, slinks away among the people who do not entertain—first, because they cannot, and second, because they are not entertained. The day came when the fine old-fashioned family mansions, long considered of most ample proportions, were found to be too small. Ballrooms were added to them, the antique domestic quiet thrummed with sounds of strange instruments, and the domestic gray was touched here and there with gilt. Champagne and terrapin succeeded tea and crackers, while dancing took the place of conversation. The out-of-door life of communities that harbor millionaires was made part of a pageantry to which the capital had thus far been a stranger. Country clubs and hounds, aniseseed bags and beagles, paper hunts and *al fresco* breakfasts—all these made the poor old picnic and its simple luncheons seek the deep shadows of a remote and somewhat impecunious past. Lingering and luxurious dinners made the "card receptions" impracticable. In a word, the Washington society which is not official, which is part of that which fills the ballrooms and dining-rooms of the great commercial cities, which is presented to the Queen and rides on the coaches from Paris to Versailles, which hunts at the Country Club and Cedarhurst, and occasionally in Genesee, and in Kent, which knows what the set of the Prince—the only Prince—does at midnight, which gambles at Monaco, and yachts, and keeps stables, and bets, which makes of pleasure a vocation, and the care of its rents, and often of its mind, an avocation—that society does in Washington as nearly as it can what it does in New York, or Boston, or Philadelphia, or at the various summer places to which it makes its way when the proper time comes. It is becoming a narrower and narrower circle, although, fortunately, no man within it has yet arisen who can draw the line about it sharply, and who can number and name the people who properly belong to it. And doubtless this can never be done in Washington, for reasons that shall be shown further on. But still the narrowing must go on, and the people of the innermost set, who are on the most intimate terms with one another, must continue to grow more and more exclusive, and, for the preservation of their own comfort and pleasures, to increase the circumspection with which they admit to their tables the new-comers who are making their way to the capital.

In essence and in spirit Washington does not change. In outward form and manner transformation is overtaking it, as it overtakes all villages that have the enterprise or that are under the necessity of becoming cities. The singular charm of the place has been always the presence and touch of statecraft. In the earlier time, when the pace was slow, moderate cleverness had a better chance than it has to-day; and when everybody was satisfied with apollinaris and sandwiches, there may have been a trifle more demand upon the intellect, as there was certainly less upon the resources of gastronomy. Wealth certainly has its advantages—sometimes to its possessor alone, but not always—in a contest for social supremacy. There are people to whose entertainments men and women are now flocking whose doors would turn on their hinges most infrequently if it were not for their lavished wealth. They mark the new intrusion. They are of those who not long ago began to seek the capital for a new sensation, and they are responsible for the mighty change which seems so radical to those who are affected by it. The time has come when the moderate people, moderate in means and in wit, must dwell together in Washington, as they do in other cities and villages of the country. The splendors of society are for the richest and cleverest, with an infusion of respectable people who have social traditions and faculties. For in this land of equal rights these things signify what noble birth means in less favored nations. The man or woman whose father and remoter ancestors were distinguished statesmen may count for nothing if the fortunate descendant has not a certain adaptability which is much more likely to be the acquisition of the child of a hard and graceless city trader. There is a certain polite mob in a dinner and ball giving society which is as essential to the *mise en scène* as the supers on the stage. Every one knows the well-bred, agreeable human background. It is in Washington what it is elsewhere. There are the dancing men, some of them clerks of the departments, preferably of the State Department, of course, while many of them were of the army and navy until cruel Secretaries, who, it is boldly charged, wanted to do all the dancing themselves, ordered most of the youngsters off to sea or to distant and dreary posts on the frontier. Excepting the military and diplomatic youth—the lay figures, the necessary filling, as it were—the crowd huddled in the back of the picture, that serves to mark more definitely the distinction of the figures in the foreground, is as familiar and as commonplace as the mass of any society in the world.

It is a subtle change that has come over Washington. The gates are closed to many to whom they once opened gladly. The joys of remoteness, of seclusion, are now unknown to those who once helped to make them. Poverty has done this for many—poverty that a few short years ago was "moderate means," but which is unable to pay its way to the present standard. Once there was a Senator who announced that, having become the leading constitutional lawyer of the Senate, he intended to become a leader in society, and in those days he had opportunities to make his way into the presence of gentility, and to tread on the prejudices of good-breeding with the heavy foot of the clown. He could not do it very well now. He could not do it at all on his mere position. He could only gain his peep into the charmed circle if his political influence should become of importance to a social leader. Rank does not count unless it is accompanied by social attributes, or unless its power or influence is worth conciliating. A seat in the cabinet no longer necessarily elevates the holder's family to social heights. It may be—nay, it has been—that the daughters of a cabinet officer have been known only in official circles, and in what may be termed the suburbs of the real citadel. Even a Chief Justice and his *ménage* may go unsought, although it is not to be imagined that his social progress would be barred if he should do any seeking.

Yet, notwithstanding the change, the reason why people enjoy Washington remains the same. The clever people who make life at the capital enjoyable are those who are engaged in the work of statecraft. Once they used to make their own pleasures. They used to command and direct. That part of society which had accomplished nothing beyond the accumulation of a pile of gold and the polishing of itself to some semblance of worthiness used to sit at the feasts of statesmen with humble gratitude, and to drink the tea of statesmen's wives with becoming reverence for those who dwelt continuously under the roofs that sheltered greatness. Now, in a great measure, statesmen sit at the feasts of wealth, if they have wit and conversation and manners, and are capable of affording amusement to those who give the feast, who drive the coach, who own the hounds, who have the magic power to furnish inspiration to wit, to surround its possessor with the stimulation of beauty, and to satisfy all his sensuous nature with the delights that wealth can conjure with.

It is not true that fewer people are enjoying the richness of the inmost life of the capital. Nor is it true that the delights are either less or different. There are more people at the very core because Washington is larger, and the gain is greatest in the leisure classes. There are some people who were, and who are not, and they regard the changed aspect of affairs with a jaundiced eye; but there is much the same kind of intercourse now at the long and luxurious dinners as there was a dozen years ago at the less ostentatious and perhaps more democratic assemblages. If there is any important departure, it is in the increase in number of eager women who are in touch with public men for the first time, and who find their natural capacities enormously gratified and stimulated by the insight they obtain of the intrigues by which men rise to power, the very men with whom they dine and talk, and on whom they use their exquisite arts of coquetry. It is one of the most beautiful experiences in their lives, this introduction to the finer arts of politics, of the larger game that is played for great stakes on the national field. A true woman never fails to find infinite pleasure in watching the rise of a politician in whom she has a personal or a friendly interest, and the downfall of his enemy; while, as for the statesman, is it necessary to say that hours of labor are assuaged by the subtle flattery of this feminine adulation?

The women of Washington have a rational interest in the subjects that are of the utmost importance to the national life, taking sides and entertaining hopes with the men in whose careers they have most interest. The people who were at the capital on the evening when the news came of Mr. Blaine's nomination had an

GENIUS IN SOCIETY.

take more than an affected interest in what appeals so little to the mind as the doings of the men about town; and, in their season, even hunting, dogs, horses, and the vast variety of out-of-door sports must pall upon clever women. They fancy a little art, a little literature, and a little charity in their turn, and therefore in the commercial cities artists and literary men furnish a mild form of the entertainment that in Washington is supplied by the statesmen, the difference being that artists and literary men in the great cities are subject to a somewhat infrequent demand, and stand no chance whatever against the millionaire, while the statesman is always and everywhere the superior. They do not talk current literature in Washington society, at least not in that kind which is now under consideration, nor do they talk much of the arts or philosophy or science of the times. Occasionally some one goes to the capital at a time when a literary sensation is the victim of gossip, and society catches up with the literature of the day while its maid is brushing its hair in the morning.

The great affairs of nations, and the distinguished men of this and other countries, are the reigning food for thought and sentiment in Washington drawing-rooms and at Washington dinner tables. The talk of society is the better because the proportion of clever men is very

exceptionally good opportunity to know how intense is feminine enthusiasm for a political champion, and can therefore readily understand why it is that a poor unfortunate male being who is cursed with principles may find himself left out of many pleasant houses if he has the folly to permit his principles to make him an obstacle to the progress of the favorite.

Are not women thus the world over? In New York they like to know about men's clubs. They organize parties for the purpose of seeing what men see behind the scenes. But they cannot all

much greater than it is in other cities; and it is another wonderful tribute to the adaptability of the American people that the wit and conversation of society are so quickly taken up by many men who enter national public life well on towards the middle period, coming out of provincial towns and small cities, emerging from the shadows of rural law offices, and from homes of the chromo period. It is not alone distinction and ability that society demands, but agreeable and entertaining distinction and ability. Society only tolerates men and women who are witless and dumb if they have traditions.

The inmost and best life of Washington rests upon the same basis as the official society, but there must be a spot in the garden reserved for the rarest plants. To the average man and woman the game of politics is the most entrancing that is played, and on the large board of the nation it is full of a noble interest. The chit-chat of art and letters does not figure largely in the social talk of the capital, but there must be a fine flavor of the best that has been written in the talk of cultivated people who are not artisans of the craft, and you may find that in Washington, as it has been always found in the society of capitals.

The tourist and the unfortunate often find Washington society crude and vulgar, and the majority knows no more of what makes up the inner life of the capital than the majority is likely to know of the inner and best life of other places. To those who see life and judge Washington from a herdic, or in the vestibule of the hotels, or from the stairway of the White House on a crowded night, or from the newspapers that lash its most patent vices, may be repeated what a clever woman once said to one of their kind:

"I think that perhaps you would like Washington better if you knew it."

Washington in 1859
(1859)

HARPER'S NEW MONTHLY MAGAZINE.

No. CXV.—DECEMBER, 1859.—Vol. XX.

VIEW FROM THE UPPER TERRACE, CAPITOL GROUNDS.

WASHINGTON IN 1859.

BY referring to the number of *Harper's Magazine* published in December, 1852, our readers will find an accurate portrayal of the Federal Capital as it then appeared. We know of no fact which can supply so much reason for the patriotic pride of every citizen as the immense changes which, even in the short period that has since elapsed, our political metropolis has undergone. Seven years of American progress might furnish material for an epic. We count our cycles not by centuries but by months. It is a wonderful thing, and instructive, to be permitted to witness the process of that new creation which records the work of its days in the completion of stately marble palaces and lofty domes; it is also a very inspiring thing to feel that every grand building, every noble avenue, and the constantly repeated demands for a broader area of beauty, are but faint symbols of the working of that mighty providential fiat which, from the chaos of a continent overbrooded by the still darkness of barbarism, has in two short centuries called forth villages, towns, cities, states—a whole nation—full of restless enterprise, and led continually forward by the prompting of some yet unrecognized purpose. During the last five years Washington has made amazing strides toward permanent grandeur; and already the "City of Magnificent Distances" has become more remarkable for its magnificence than for its distances. No longer are our legislators compelled to wade through a morass in order to pass from the Capitol to the White House, and the sportsman must find his quarry in regions more remote than the Centre Market, although malice asserts that some incipient Nimrods still find that the surest place to obtain their game.

Before entering upon a description of the beautiful public buildings which have recently lent such a marked improvement to the capital, perhaps it may be well to rescue from dusty archives, and to place on record where they will be forever accessible to the people, some of the facts which attended the selection of Washington for the seat of the Federal Government.

During the Revolution the Continental Congress sat for the most part at Philadelphia, although it was compelled by the movements of the British army to vacate that city, and to pass through a migratory career at Baltimore, Lancaster, York, Princeton, Annapolis, Trenton, and New York. The Federal Government, under the present Constitution, was inaugurated at New York in 1789. At the first session, which commenced immediately, petitions came in from various town and state governments in regard to the permanent location of the seat of Government. The Eastern States and New York were opposed to the premature agitation of the question when there were other measures which their representatives considered of greater national importance demanding immediate attention. Among these important matters was the proposition to assume the debts of the States by the Federal Government—a measure in which the New England States were doubly interested: first, because, as they alleged, they had made the greatest pecuniary sacrifices in support of the war; and, secondly, because their citizens were in possession of an undue share of state securities. They were also averse to the removal of the capital to any point south of New York; and the latter State, as a matter of course, concurred with them in this policy. Pennsylvania was divided between Philadelphia and a point on the Susquehanna called Wright's Ferry, not far from Havre de Grace. New Jersey was for Philadelphia; Delaware would perhaps have preferred a point lower down the river; Maryland was divided in its preferences between Baltimore and some point on the Potomac. The Southern States, including Virginia, North Carolina, South Carolina, and Georgia, were unanimous for the Potomac.

In the first session the House passed a resolution for the permanent establishment of the seat of Government at Wright's Ferry, on the Susquehanna, as soon as suitable buildings could be erected; and in the mean time the Government was to remain at New York. This resolution was matured into a bill and was sent to the Senate, where it was amended by the substitution of Germantown for Wright's Ferry. Going back to the House, this important amendment was agreed to. But an amendment being added, that the laws of Pennsylvania were to remain in force until repealed by Congress, by preventing the immediate consummation of the plan, spoiled Germantown of its destiny. The Senate, availing itself of this trifling amendment, postponed the whole subject until the next session of Congress.

In the mean time, before the meeting of the next Congress, the Legislature of Virginia adopted a resolution offering ten miles square of its territory on the Potomac to the Federal Government for the location of the capital. It also offered one hundred and twenty thousand dollars for the erection of public buildings on condition that the offer of territory, or a portion of it, should be accepted. At the suggestion of the Virginia authorities, Maryland made a similar offer of territory with seventy-two thousand dollars. The Southern people were deeply aroused and agitated about the subject; and Mr. Madison said that Virginia would not have ratified the Constitution except with the understanding that the seat of Government was to be located south of Pennsylvania.

A compromise was at length agreed upon. The capital was to be permanently located at some point on the Potomac "between the East Branch and some point on the Conecogeague;" and until suitable buildings could be erected, the Government was to reside at Philadelphia. By an amendment, the ten miles square might extend below the mouth of the East Branch, so as to include Alexandria on the Virginia side of the main Western Branch, but the public buildings were to be on the Maryland side. The unpronounceable Conecogeague, which is "named in the bill," was forgotten in the execution of its provisions, and is practically as far from the seat of government as the jilted Germantown; and, we believe, it has never ceased to murmur its discordant complaints to the hills and gorges of Washington County, Maryland, beyond the Blue Ridge.

Immediately after the settlement of this question the Funding Act, with an amendment providing for the assumption of the State debts to the amount of twenty-one millions, was taken up in the House and passed, "two members representing Potomac districts" changing their votes and coming to its support. "Others," says Judge Marshall, "would have done likewise if necessary to carry the bill." He subjoins, by way of apology, that the gentlemen who changed their votes were understood to have been all the while favorable to the policy of assumption; but if the capital was to be located north of Maryland, they were opposed to any measure calculated to strengthen the Federal Government.

Mr. Jefferson, whose writings were not published until long after Judge Marshall wrote, gives a full explanation of the transaction in his "Anas," substantially agreeing with the above, except as to the feelings which governed the "Potomac members" in changing their votes.

He states that never, in his day, was the Union so near its dissolution as at the date of the above transactions. The most serious grounds of sectional discord were the questions of assuming the State debts and the location of the capital. The North laid great stress upon the former, the South upon the latter. The President and Cabinet were at their wit's ends for some plan of adjustment. He (Mr. Jefferson), then Secretary of State, met Mr. Hamilton, the Secretary of the Treasury, opposite the President's mansion. The latter, with an air of grave solicitude, took Mr. J.'s arm, and walked him back and forth for half an hour in earnest conversation upon the perplexing state of affairs. Hamilton thought that an accommodation or compromise might be effected by connecting the two vexed questions with each other. Jefferson, who had just returned home after a long residence in Europe, was wholly unacquainted with the financial affairs of the country, and complains that General Hamilton tricked him into the support of his plans. At any rate he invited General Hamilton to dine with him the next day, and promised to have other parties present who could join in the friendly conference. He only listened, or exhorted to moderation. Hamilton thought if the South would concede the assumption of the State debts, the North would consent to the location of the capital on the banks of the Potomac. "So," says Mr. Jefferson, "two of the Potomac members (White and Lee; but White with a revulsion of stomach almost convulsive) agreed to change their votes, and Hamilton undertook to carry the other point."

Hildreth connects the name of Robert Morris with that of Hamilton in the negotiation of this compromise, and concedes to the former the merit of its suggestion. We may observe, in passing, that, according to Mr. Jefferson's own statement of the case, it is difficult to understand how he was cheated by Hamilton into the office of "candle-holder" to his plans of stock-jobbing. The matters seem to have been arranged in the most business-like manner, with no other disagreeable incident than the "convulsive revulsion of stomach" of one of the "Potomac members;" whose travail, considering that he was giving birth to a great capital, will excite but little wonder.

Washington is situated at the head of tide-water and of navigation—or, more accurately, these points are included within the District of Columbia, but extend a short distance above the city. The ebb of the tide is arrested at the Little Falls, about three miles above the corporate limits, and navigation ceases at Georgetown, which is separated from Washington by Rock Creek, the streets of the two places being connected by the bridges which cross the stream. On the east the city is bounded by the East Branch, a small tributary from the northeast, which, penetrated by the tides, was formerly navigable for sloops as far as Bladensburg, six miles from the Capitol. Seventy-five years ago this town shipped tobacco to London; but for many years past all navigation, except by canal boats, propelled by poles, has ceased, in consequence of the filling of the channel with the accumulated washings of the neighboring fields. The town, however, notwithstanding its traditional glories as a sea-port engaged in the foreign trade, probably never had more population than at the present moment—viz., about five hundred.

Georgetown was, and still is, a place of much higher pretensions. Like Bladensburg, its commercial glories have departed. It no longer boasts of its commerce with London and Liverpool; although the harbor is good, and it still carries on a languid West India and coasting trade in coal and flour; with return cargoes of groceries, furniture, etc. The population increases slowly, and is now two or three times greater than when the town had a brisk and prosperous foreign trade. As a suburb of Washington it is destined to become famed for its princely private residences, the abodes of foreign ministers and wealthy citizens.

Alexandria, town and county, which were included within the original limits of the District, were, in 1846, retroceded to Virginia. It is difficult to understand why they were made a part of it, in the first instance, coupled with the condition that no public buildings were to be erected on that side of the river. Since its re-annexation to Virginia its prospects have greatly improved. The State has granted charters to railroads terminating at this point, which were refused so long as it remained a foreign territory; and these works have been prosecuted with vigor. The improvement in trade has been marked; and the town has now a population of about fifteen thousand. It has a high and healthy location, with a fine grain-growing region back of it, which is rapidly improving under the spur of railroad facilities as well as of Northern immigration.

The situation of Washington itself is one of great beauty. From the top of the Capitol, or of the unfinished Washington Monument, the city is seen to be situated in an amphitheatre surrounded by graceful hills on the east, north, and west; while on the south the broad and beautiful Potomac opens out a magnificent vista, where placid waters mirror the hills and tree-tops of Virginia and Maryland for many miles. The view down the river, of a fine summer morning or afternoon, from any elevated point in Washington or Georgetown, is one of surpassing loveliness.

But the most essential advantage of position possessed by Washington is the salubrity of its climate. No city in America of equal age and population, perhaps, has suffered so little from pestilence. The cholera, that terrible plague, which has repeatedly scourged other cities, North as well as South, has paid only one visit to the National Capital; yellow fever, we believe, has never made its appearance. Small-pox has never produced a panic; and notwithstanding the many swamps, marshes, and standing pools by which the sparsely-peopled city is surrounded,

WASHINGTON, FROM THE DOME OF THE CAPITOL.

the whole family of febrile diseases barely gives wholesome exercise to the physicians.

It was argued by those who favored the location of the capital on the Potomac that it was important for the Legislature and Government to be beyond the control of large commercial cities. It was insisted that at Philadelphia or New York the ruling powers would be liable to intimidation by mobs, and to be biased in their acts by the proximity of wealthy merchants and bankers. How keen must have been the strife for the settlement of this question we may learn from the contemporary newspapers and correspondence, as well as from the various magnificent plans for laying out the city and for building the public edifices; showing that the prize must have been regarded by all interested in the location as of incalculable pecuniary value. It may serve to allay any alarm that may have been created in rural districts by the large sums recently expended on the improvement of the capital to remind the reader that, even to this hour, great as have been the expenditures of the last five or six years, many of the plans submitted by General Washington have not yet been attempted; although perhaps the size of the buildings, which the unparalleled and unexpected growth of the country has forced the nation to construct for the public service, far exceeds the wildest speculations of the projectors of the city.

Our engraving is a faithful representation of the new Capitol. The corner-stone of the old Capitol was laid on the 18th of September, 1793, by George Washington, in the presence of a large concourse of citizens, public officers, the Masonic fraternity, and many military companies. The building was designed by Dr. William Thornton, who, although not a professional architect, was well versed in architectural matters. His plan had been submitted to the President the previous year, and was approved, but referred to Mr. S. Hallet, who, after some slight changes in the design, commenced the construction of the edifice. He was soon removed, and his place supplied by Mr. Hadfield; who, in turn, was superseded by Mr. James Hobson, the architect by whom the President's mansion had been erected. Under Mr. Hobson's direction the north end of the building was completed. Again the designs were modified, but this time to a much greater extent, by Mr. Latrobe, who, in 1803, was appointed by President Jefferson architect of the Capitol.

In 1811 the south wing was completed; but the breaking out of hostilities between England and the United States caused a suspension of the work. It was in this unfinished condition when those ever-to-be-deplored acts of spoliage took place which were more disgraceful to the British arms than injurious to this country.

When peace was restored, Mr. Latrobe having resigned his position, President Monroe appointed Mr. Bulfinch to fill the vacancy, and under his faithful oversight the work was at last completed in 1825. The length of the old Capitol, which now forms the centre of the new edifice, is 352 feet 4 inches; in width, the wings are each 121 feet; and the centre, including the portico and steps, is 290 feet deep. The west front has a receding loggia 100 feet in length, and containing ten columns. This recessed portico is approached through the library, and affords a magnificent view of the city and its environs; southward, the vision is carried to Alexandria, Fort Washington, old Arlington (the seat of the late Mr. Custis), and along miles of the beautiful sloping banks of the Potomac. In the city, right under the spectator's gaze, are the Smithsonian Institution, the Washington Monument, the Patent-Office, the Observatory, the Treasury Department, and various beautiful edifices, while in Pennsylvania Avenue, from the Capitol to the White House, he sees the panorama of life reduced to a mimic scale. The rotunda is 96 feet in diameter, and was surmounted by a dome, shown in the engraving of the Capitol, in *Harper's Monthly* for December, 1852, but now demolished to make way for the noble construction which is to replace it. The new dome will rise 241 feet above the building, which is itself 69 feet in height, making 310 feet above the level of the ground, to which must be added the terracing, which increases the height above the ordinary level 86 feet, making a total elevation of 396 feet, being 4 feet less than the height of St. Paul's Cathedral in London, and 36 feet less than St. Peter's at Rome.

The original building was constructed of a very poor yellow sandstone, obtained in the neighborhood, and it was found necessary to paint it, both to preserve it and, if possible, to beautify it. The extensions are of white marble, which is procured from the State of Connecticut, and it is a matter of great importance that as soon as possible the sandstone in the old walls may be replaced by the same stone that the new portion of the building is constructed of, and that here and at the Patent-Office the really grand design may not be marred by a want of uniformity in the materials. The extensions are connected with the old building by very fine corridors, each 44 feet in length, and 26 feet wide, with outside colonnades, consisting of four columns, making a total width of 56 feet. The new wings, which constitute the extension, are each 324 feet in length from east to west, and 152 feet wide from north to south, making the total length of the new building, comprising the old edifice, the corridors, and the width of the extension, 745 feet 8 inches. The corner stone of the south wing was laid with very imposing ceremonies by President Fillmore, on the 4th of July, 1851, and the occasion was made memorable by the delivery of an eloquent oration by Daniel Webster.

The whole building has a rustic basement, supporting an ordonnance of Corinthian pilasters. A noble portico, 160 feet in length, supported by a double row of columns, each 30 feet high, adorns the centre on the east front, and furnishes a fitting Forum for the inauguration of the Presidents

THE CAPITOL.

PEDIMENT OF THE NORTH WING.

of the Republic. This is really the main entrance to the Capitol, although from its relation toward the city it is generally supposed by strangers to form the rear of the building. A grand flight of steps leads us up to the porch, which contains two singularly inappropriate representations of Peace and War (by Persico); War being represented by an individual in ancient armor who, despite his Roman garb, seems to have violated the military law by falling asleep at his post; while Peace, though clad like a lady, has a more masculine and forbidding countenance than we usually assign to the gentle goddess. The Discovery of America is fitly symbolized by the figure of Columbus with a miniature globe in his hand, while an Indian maiden crouches at his feet; the latter work is by the same artist, and does more justice to his fame. On the other side, the early struggles of our Pioneers are symbolized by a group representing the rescue of a mother and an infant from the scalping-knife of an Indian; executed by Greenough. Overhead is a pediment 80 feet in length, ornamented with a group of statuary, representing Liberty, attended by Hope and Justice, while in the beautiful garden which lies before the portico is Greenough's colossal statue of Washington.

On the eastern or main side of the new wings are porticoes in the centre of the façade, supported by twenty-two Corinthian columns; the pediment of the north wing (which contains the Senate chamber) is one of the triumphs of American art; it contains twelve exquisite figures, designed by the lamented Crawford, and executed in American marble by Italian artists resident in Washington. In the centre of this beautiful work of art is the genius of America, behind whom the rising sun typifies youth and prosperity, and on either side are figures emblematic of the mechanic, the pioneer, the soldier, youth, education, commerce, the hunter, the Indian chief and his family (whose posture near a grave, with the abandoned tomahawk by his side, sadly pictures the passing away of the aborigines).

On the western front of both wings are porticoes, 105 feet in width, with Corinthian columns. On the south side of the south wing, and also on the north side of the north wing, there are porticoes 121 feet in width, and having ten Corinthian columns. The exterior of the edifice is one of the finest achievements of architectural science in modern times. Without the pretension of the British Houses of Parliament, it stands grand, solitary, overlooking the city, while on the highest point, a landmark visible far down the river, is to be, unmoved by storm and sunshine, the last and best work of Crawford, the colossal figure of "America," crowned with stars, bearing the arms of the warrior and the wreath of victory, and forming a fitting apex for the majestic fabric!

The present inclosure around the Capitol contains only thirty-five acres, a space quite too contracted to permit the construction of the ornamental grounds necessary to do justice to a building which itself covers 62,000 square feet. The necessity for purchasing several squares of land adjoining the present grounds is so manifest, and has been so frequently admitted by the successive administrations, that persons owning the property necessary for the enlargement have from year to year delayed the erection of buildings, so that at this time the houses immediately surrounding the Capitol are of the commonest sort, with a few exceptions. During the thirty-fifth Congress an attempt was made to bring the negotiations to a close, but although well advanced when the adjournment occurred, the all-absorbing Kansas discussion occupied so much time that this important matter was again deferred. It is to be hoped that the new Congress about to assemble may determine to purchase the required land; for as the matter lies, it commits a double injustice. The demand for land for the erection of first-class dwellings has been forced to seek the west end of the city, from the prospect that Congress will condemn the larger part of "Capitol Hill;" while, on the other hand, the value of the property is annually increasing, and public policy would seem to dictate an early purchase, because the public necessity should be supplied with the least expense.

The interior decorations would require more space for their description than we can afford in a single article; the corridors and committee rooms are richly ornamented, the visitor walks upon the finest encaustic tiles, carved marble columns are on either side of him, and beautifully frescoed and gilded ceilings are over his head. The Representatives' Hall, in the south wing, is 139 feet long, and 93 feet wide, and although at first regarded as too ornate, in a few years, when time shall have toned the colors, it will be found as nearly faultless in its ornamentation as can be expected from so vast an undertaking. The criticisms upon its acoustic properties we believe to be exceedingly unjust; standing in the clerk's desk we have found no difficulty in being distinctly heard, with a very moderate exercise of our vocal powers, in any part of the vast chamber. The true reason of the imaginary acoustic defects will be found, we fancy, in the absurd arrangement for giving each member a desk. On the opening of the next Congress a very salutary and long-desired reform is to be inaugurated by the removal of all reading and writing facilities from the floor of the House. Formerly, instead of watching the debates, each member was engaged in franking, writing, or reading his correspondence. The business of the country will be expedited, and the comfort of the members vastly enhanced, by the adoption of the English system. Moreover, being brought into near contact, less space will be required; and having no unnecessary noises to distract

"AMERICA," THE APEX OF THE DOME.

their attention, members will find the new hall a very easy place to speak and hear in. A new plan of lighting the hall from above has been introduced, and is found to work admirably, except that the heat generated by the burning gas is sometimes very oppressive. The arrangements for heating and ventilating are excellent, and reflect great credit upon the architects. The new Senate Chamber is even richer in its appearance than the Hall of Representatives. It was occupied last winter, and gave entire satisfaction; the Senators, however, vacated their cheerful hall in the old building with great reluctance, and still regret the loss of their old-fashioned fire-places and the pleasant outlook from the windows. The approaches to these two halls are worthy of the great nation whose strength the Capitol so well symbolizes. The display of marbles, all from American quarries, could hardly be surpassed by any of the older countries. But, delightful as we find the theme, we must leave the description of the interior, with a single word of thanks to the architect, Mr. Walter, and the superintendent, Captain Meigs, for the excellent service they have done the State.

The Congressional Library, which was destroyed in 1851, has been replaced by a perfectly fire-proof building of great beauty, in which a superb collection of books is already classified and arranged. Immediately after the destruction of the former Library, Congress made an appropriation of $75,000 for the purchase of books; the judicious expenditure of this sum, and the annual appropriation of $7500, places at the disposal of Congress a very large and excellent library, to which access is, by courtesy, granted to literary men and others. The necessity for such an arrangement was foreseen by Mr. Jefferson, who succeeded in obtaining about 2500 volumes, which were all consumed in the British raid upon Washington in 1814. Under the management of the very efficient Joint Committee of Congress the present Library bids fair to become all that could be desired in a national collection of books.

In the article to which we have twice referred the hope is expressed that in five or six years what is known as the Mall would be improved so as to furnish a park worthy of the capital of the great republic; but, alas! even while the anticipation was being penned the master-spirit of that noble enterprise was passing through a painful exit from the beautiful, which always surrounded him below, to the beautiful above. In the melancholy death of Downing, America lost a man who had the wide vision to perceive, and the genius to execute, a work such as would have done honor to the nation. Since his decease but little has been done toward beautifying the space between the Capitol and the Potomac which is set apart for the people's park. It is only justice, however, to except the Congressional green-house, which has been vigorously and untiringly advocated and fostered by the Hon. James A. Pearce, Senator from Maryland, whose refined taste and true gentlemanly instincts make him the unwavering friend of all that appertains to literature, art, or beauty. Under his judicious management the Congressional green-house, instead of being a mere flower-shop, has become, in floriculture, a central influence felt to the remotest verge of the country, wherever people love flowers, and wish to increase the number or virtue of these gentle ministers of the good and loving in nature.

Midway of the Mall stands the Smithsonian Institution, which has undergone little change, except that the various objects of curiosity, including articles brought home by the Japan and other exploring expeditions, have been removed from the Patent-Office, and placed here. In front of the building is the monument erected to the memory of the lamented Downing.

Just beyond the Smithsonian Institution, going toward the President's mansion, is the unfinished shaft which was originally intended to be a monument to Washington; but the spacious gallery which was to furnish us an American Walhalla exists only on paper, and the shaft seems to grow no higher. However, as the direction of this commendable enterprise has been recently returned to its original managers, we hope for more active measures. It would be a relief to those who have seen this unfortunate affair day after day, for seven years, to witness some energy expended upon it, even if it were only to pull down what has been erected.

In point of magnitude the extension of the Treasury Department, so as to form a suitable building for the Department of State, is, perhaps, the greatest undertaking at present in progress. The following engraving shows the south and west fronts of the new edifice. The work has been going on about three years, and is rapidly approaching completion. The original building is 342 feet long, fronting on Fifteenth Street, immediately east of the President's mansion. It presented an unbroken colonnade, the ends having been purposely left unfinished with the expectation that the present extension would ultimately be built. It produced a very unsatisfactory impression on the mind of the spectator, the imposing nature of the attempt not being fulfilled in the execution. The style of architecture is that known as Grecian Ionic—a perilous selection, for the attempts made in this country and in Europe to apply the Grecian style of architecture, either to public or private edifices of the present day, have generally been failures, so far as harmony, appropriateness, simplicity, and gracefulness are involved. Neither the taste nor the invention of the architects have usually been able to retain the spirit of the original when applied to buildings constructed for modern use.

Perhaps in no case is this more strikingly exemplified than in the old part of the Treasury building, as it stood when the extension commenced. The east front was a portico or colonnade, consisting of a long, uninterrupted line of Grecian Ionic columns, adopted for this work from the most elaborately ornamented examples of that order, but deprived of their entases, and mostly denuded of their proper ornamentation; both of which are essential to give to the columns their true dignity, grace, and character. Those columns are placed upon a perfectly plain base or podium, forming the basement story of the building, to light the rooms in which its face is pierced between the columns with plain rectangular openings for windows. This podium has neither base, die, nor cornice, but rises smooth from the foundation, and is terminated at the top by the square arris or edge of the portico floors; nor have the windows in it any casings whatever. To add to its uncouthness, when an entrance to the building through the colonnade was required, it was found necessary to bring forward the podium some seven feet, as a screen to the stairs and platform required for the use of the public; thus making an unfortunate adjunct to the architecture of its façade. The wall under the portico (in Grecian architecture known as the wall of the cell) has a series of antæ, or pilasters, which correspond with, and are immediately in rear of, the columns. These antæ should have had a close correspondence, in style and character, with the columns; but by depriving their capitals, in a great measure, of their ornamentation, they detract from the beauty and harmony of other parts, to which they ought to add relief and support. In each of the spaces between the antæ are three openings, one above the other, for windows and doors, the upper tier being but one half the size of the two below. The three openings for doors are characterized by a very meagre architecture, not at all in keeping with the style of the building.

The entablature of the columns exhibits the fewest faults of any part of the arrangement, and the balustrade is tasteful and appropriate. The ordonnance of the rear of the old building consists of a Grecian Ionic anta or pilaster of the same intercolumnation, derived from the same example of the order as the east front. But the capitals, though composed of the same moulding, lack the necessary embellishment to give them distinctive character, and to harmonize them with other architectural parts of the building. The design for the extension, as prepared by T. U. Walter, Esq., upon the plan suggested by the Hon. R. M. T. Hunter, Senator from Virginia, and approved by committees of both branches of Congress, gave the general outline, in most respects corresponding with the old part; but the details varied so much that it was not possible to harmonize them, or intelligently carry them out. This led to the decision not to confine the details of the extension strictly to the details of the old building, but to make them such as would give the best effect to the style of architecture. It then became a question how far deviations could safely be made from the original work without departing from the principles of good taste. By reference to various buildings, ancient and modern, it was found that

SOUTH AND WEST FRONTS OF THE TREASURY EXTENSION.

great latitude has always been used in architectural details. And if authority is wanted, sufficient is found in the single example of the Erectheum (the temple of Minerva Polias, and the Pandrosium being but parts of it), to warrant far greater deviations than it has been found necessary to make in this case. The general design of the exterior was to flank the eastern front of the old building by pavilion terminations of the south and north wings, projecting some seven feet in front of the face of its columns. By this means it was to a great extent isolated from the extension, and all necessity for following its details avoided. Thus being left at liberty to make any judicious changes, the first point was to arrange the basement story so that it would not be liable to the objections of dampness, want of light and ventilation, incident to the old part. To effect this the floor was lowered two feet, which the gradual slope of the ground renders appropriate, and thereby the story is increased to 13 feet in height, and the windows, instead of being square and unsightly holes, are enlarged to proportions suggestive of comfort and elegance. Beneath this basement there is a cellar 12 feet in height. By this arrangement there is an extra wall of hammered gneiss extending from one foot above the cellar bottom to the grade of the surrounding ground. The walls of the extension, from the bottom of the cellar to the top of the building, viz.: cellar, basement, second and third stories, with the attic above, are of hammered granite. For the cellar wall the coarse granite, or gneiss, from the quarry at Port Deposit, Maryland, was originally selected, on account of its strong and durable character; but, after innumerable delays, it was found that sufficient quantities from that quarry could not be delivered with a rapidity consistent with economy in the prosecution of the work. Attempts were then made to obtain it from other points in the vicinity, and also from Richmond, Virginia, but without success; and the superintendents were compelled to procure much of the large stone for this purpose from the same quarries from which the material for the superstructure is delivered. The entire granite for the superstructure, and most of that for the foundations, is obtained from a quarry at Dix Island, near Rockland, off the coast of Maine. This is a barren island of granite, cresting out of the ocean, about five miles from the main land. The large blocks of granite taken from that quarry have a beauty, compactness, and uniformity nowhere else equaled in the world. So steep and sheer are the sides of the island that vessels drawing thirty feet of water come in direct contact with it, and the large masses of rock are quarried out and swung aboard without intermediate hauling. Vessels of peculiar construction and of great strength are made for the special purpose of shipping the immense pilasters, columns, and other large stones to Washington. The absence of all necessity for land-carriage renders this stone cheaper than that from Quincy and other places, much nearer the seat of Government than Dix Island.

The walls of the Treasury Extension above the cellar, are: a basement story forming a stylobate, and, resting on it, an ordonnance of antæ of the Grecian Ionic order, 45 feet in height. The stylobate is intended to be decidedly of a Grecian character, its base, die, and cornice, are beautiful in themselves, but as here brought together they have an effect peculiarly appropriate and pleasing. The window openings in the die are managed so as to give them all the character needed, without loading them with ornament; and the whole arrangement of sills and piers, and the continued cornice, which serves as a window cap, is entirely novel. The antæ, and the filling of the spaces between them, are so arranged as to accomplish the very difficult combination of the adaptation of Grecian architecture to modern uses, without spoiling its inherent beauties. The style of architecture is more fully preserved, and its design carried out by the use of single blocks for the columns and antæ. These enormous masses are raised by means of machinery, designed by the superintending architect of this work, and used in raising the pillars of the Boston Custom-house, which was also built under his superintendency. The arrangement of the interior of the new building varies essentially from that of the old, and from public offices generally, in being divided into larger and more commodious rooms. Instead of the narrow, cell-like apartments, with one or at most two windows, into which the public departments in Washington are subdivided, the Treasury Extension will present the health-promoting novelty of spacious and airy saloons, capable of accommodating the clerical force of a bureau. The superintending architect has made a laudable and successful attempt to nationalize the interior embellishments, without in any degree impairing the general architectural effect. Indeed, in many cases, the elegance and symmetry of the details are improved by his national adaptations; for instance, the moulding, known as the "egg and dart," is substituted by an acorn and Indian's arrowhead; and while the transformation is too slight to alter the general effect, the symbols to the close observer are more satisfactory because more significant. This attempt to characterize by some well-known American emblem the leading points of the ornamentation, has also been successfully applied to

AMERICAN CAPITAL IN THE INTERIOR OF TREASURY DEPARTMENT.

THE GENERAL POST-OFFICE, NORTH AND EAST FRONTS.

the elaborate capitals of the interior columns. In these, while the general character of Grecian architecture is followed, in the composition the national eagle is made to perch proudly under each of the graceful volutes, surrounded by other characteristic emblems, adroitly blended, so as to produce an effect similar to other composite capitals adapted to this style.

In this way, through the whole interior, the common error has been avoided of adopting for the ornamentation the stereotyped scroll work, which, though graceful in itself, has no special significance, and has, besides, been degraded by its uniform application to the decoration of eating saloons and barbers' shops. In its place elegant designs of fruits, flowers, and other products of the American soil have been substituted. These details were designed by A. B. Young, Esq., the supervising architect. The old unfinished edifice was 342 feet in length, from north to south, the building as enlarged is 465 feet long, exclusive of the porticoes, by 266 in width; when completed it will present four fronts upon as many streets; and the long rectangular space between these four fronts is subdivided by a centre building, extending from east to west, into two courts, each about 130 feet square. These large interior courts, which are essential to the occupants of the range of interior apartments for purposes of light and air, will be adorned by grass, flowers, and the play of fountains of pure water.

The material of the old building is a very inferior, as well as unsightly sandstone, similar to that of which the old portions of the Capitol and Patent-Office and the President's House are constructed. Paint and putty, or mortar, have been resorted to for the double purpose of preventing disintegration, and of disguising the deformities of the walls; and in all the cases, except that of the Treasury, with decided success. Numerous, or, more properly, innumerable holes, from the size of a pea to that of an apple, have been plugged, and the sickly yellow of the stone in the other buildings has been covered by pure white. But less taste has been displayed on the Treasury. The columns and the pilasters are a pale or whitish yellow, and the walls between the pilasters are a dark yellow, or brown color. The gray granite basement has also been desecrated with paint, whether for the sake of uniformity or variety it is difficult to say—the result a very pale blue, being near enough to that of the colonnade above to leave the matter in doubt.

The General Post-Office has been enlarged by extending the building around the entire square, leaving a court-yard in the centre of 95 feet by 194 feet for light and air. The architectural style is palatial, and the order a modified Corinthian. The columns of the new portico each consist of a single block of Italian marble very beautifully chiseled, the capitals are of the same material, the design and the execution of these columns affording the most cheering evidence of the advance of American Art. On the Seventh Street front there is an open vestibule, the ceiling of which is composed of richly ornamented marbles, supported by four marble columns in the Doric order; the walls, niches, and floors, are also of marble, all being finely polished except the floor, which is richly tesselated in white and black. This is the grand entrance for the General Post-Office department, and harmonizes with the entrance to the Patent-Office which is on the next block north in the same street. The entrance for the mail wagons on Eighth Street consists of a grand archway, the spandrils of which are ornamented with sculpture representing Steam on one side, and on the other Electricity, while a mask representing Fidelity forms the key-stone. The F Street front is arranged for the accommodation of the City Post-Office; it has a deeply-recessed portico in the centre, consisting of eight columns grouped in pairs, and flanked by coupled pilasters, supporting an entablature which girts the entire work. The portico is supported by an arcade, which furnishes the most ample convenience for the delivery of letters to the public. Mr. T. U. Walter, the architect of the Capitol, who designed this extension of the Post-Office, has given the best evidence of his ability to discharge fitly his important obligations to the people, in the excellent arrangements he has here devised to combine simplicity, convenience, and beauty. We doubt if there is a building in the world more chaste and architecturally perfect than the General Post-Office as now completed. Without the imposing grandeur of its neighbor the Patent-Office, it is so symmetrical, and the details so faithfully executed, that it carries us back to the palmy days of Italian Art.

The immense building which is devoted to the Department of the Interior, including the Bureau of Patents, Indian Affairs, and General Land Office, has been enlarged, and its capacity more than doubled, the extension being demanded by the incredible amount of business transacted in the Department. We have not at hand the statistics of the patents issued in America since the establishment of the Government; but we venture to say that, startling as is the following statement, which we extract from a work published under the authority of the British Government, of the increase of the mechanical development in that country, the same period in American history would exhibit a more remarkable evidence of the wonderful impetus which the last century has given to material progress. In Great Britain,

From 1610 to 1700	there were patented		267	inventions.
" 1700 to 1800	"	"	2,067	"
" 1800 to 1851	"	"	11,000	"
" 1851 to 1855 (only four years)			10,000	"

Admitting only a similar increase in the patent business of our country, bearing in mind the constant and rapid opening of the Western wilderness to civilization, and the majestic Patent-Office, as now completed, will not seem unduly magnificent. It stands indeed as a very hopeful and significant sign of the growth, en-

THE PATENT-OFFICE.

terprise, and keen intellect of the nation. On a clear moonlight night there is nothing more beautiful than this immense edifice of pure marble, glistening with the moonbeams, and almost speaking to the beholder of the vastness of his country's power and the worth of its Union. The order of architecture in which this grand edifice is built is Grecian Doric; there are porticoes on the south, east, and west sides—the south portico being copied from the Pantheon. The total height is 74 feet 11 inches; it is 275 wide by 406 feet 6 inches long. In the third story are saloons for the exhibition and preservation of models, although until recently the space was occupied by an immense collection of curiosities which is now more properly deposited in the Smithsonian Institution..

We have been thus particular in describing these new buildings, because the architecture and taste of the nation ought to be represented by its public edifices. If it is true that the architecture of a people records their mental and moral condition, then certainly the contrast between the new and the old public buildings in Washington must be gratifying to every patriot. And we say this, not only as regards the greater size, but the marked regard for truthfulness in the designs, and the employment of material. We regret that at the Capitol, Treasury, and Patent-Office, the granite and marble should still be obliged to endure the company of the wretched sandstone used in the older portions of those buildings, and we are not without hope that the day is not far distant when this decaying stuff will be removed to make room for stone that needs neither paint nor putty to make it endurable. Unfortunately the General Post-Office, though built of marble, exhibits two very distinct kinds in the old and in the new portions of the edifice.

There is one other public work, which has just been completed, to which we beg briefly to call the reader's attention. The idea of supplying the City of Washington with water by an aqueduct extending to the Great Falls of the Potomac, is an enterprise which dates back to the beginning of the Federal Capital. It was a part of the original plan, approved and submitted to Congress by President Washington, and was then considered necessary as a safe-guard against fires, as well as for the purposes of health, convenience, and ornament. In that plan large and beautiful parks were to be laid off around the public buildings, to be ornamented with trees and shrubbery, and to be refreshed with fountains. It was probably Mr. Jefferson who proposed the Great Falls as the most proper source of the supply. His residence in France had given him large and liberal ideas as to the scale upon which such works should be planned, and satisfied him, economist and strict constructionist as he was, that any thing small or contracted in the display of national taste would be ten-fold worse than actual barbarism. Those who object to the expenditure of public money upon works of art and ornament about the national capital do so generally for want of reflection. They ask, "Why should the citizens of Washington be favored above those of all other cities in the Union? Why should the Government build streets, and parks, and aqueducts for Washington, and give not a cent for such purposes to Philadelphia, New York, New Orleans, or St. Louis?" The answer is easy. Nothing is given for the people of Washington. They may reap incidental advantages greater than the citizens of other places, because they have chosen Washington for their abode; but all such expenditures are made in order to render the seat of Government worthy of the nation.

Washington was founded in the wilderness. The President and Cabinet and members of Congress found it difficult to traverse the "magnificent distances," either in carriages or on foot, for many years after the Government resided here. The population was small and poor, and utterly incapable of paving any one of the immense streets, which the accommodation of the public officers demanded. What was to be done? Whose duty was it to provide for the public accommodation? Was it not, and is it not, as clearly the duty of the Federal Government to incur these expenses as to build a Capitol? To this day there is but one street in Washington paved by the Government for more than a few squares. Pennsylvania Avenue, from the Capitol to Georgetown, a distance of about two miles and a half, is the exception. The other paving, save that around the public buildings, has been done by the citizens, and that without the privilege of taxing public property.

It is due to the national dignity that Washington should be, if not a great city, a great centre of whatever is noble and beautiful in architecture and the fine arts. The President could live in a log cabin, and Congress might meet under a tent, in good weather, or perhaps your rigid economist would grant a large square brick building, such as is used for cotton factories. But the public intelligence and taste demand that the halls of legislation and the departments of Government shall be noble in construction and of the best materials; combining the greatest degree of comfort with the highest style of beauty. Any thing short of this would be derogatory to the national character, and for that reason we might almost say unconstitutional! Hence the Capitol, the President's House, and the Departments must be marble palaces, adorned with statuary and painting, and surrounded by parks, and trees, and flowers, and fountains. There should be libraries, and picture-galleries, and museums, and whatever illustrates civilization in its highest walks. This is what people expect to find when they visit Washington, and they never fail to complain when they are in any respect disappointed.

The aqueduct now being constructed was projected during the latter part of Mr. Fillmore's administration. The President, in a letter dated September 13, 1852, committed to the Engineer Department the duty of making a survey and estimates of the best manner of introducing into Washington and Georgetown "an unfailing and abundant supply of good and wholesome water." Captain Frederick A. Smith, of the corps, was assigned by Colonel Totten, its chief, to the performance of this duty, from which he was removed within a few weeks thereafter by sudden death. He was succeeded on the 3d November of the same year by the present Superintendent of the work, Captain, then Lieutenant, Montgomery C. Meigs, of the same corps. The Report of this officer, dated February 12, 1853, presents an elaborate statement of the advantages of three available sources of supply: Rock Creek, a small tributary of the Potomac, which divides Washington from Georgetown; the Little Falls of the Potomac, at a distance of four miles above the city; and the Great Falls, sixteen miles above. The latter was adopted. To bring the water from this place it was necessary to construct a conduit fourteen miles in length. But the elevation is such as to render pumping unnecessary. The height of the water above the dam which turns it into the aqueduct is 150 feet above high tide at the city wharves; and the inclination of the conduit is only about nine inches to the mile; so that the head of water in the distributing reservoir is nearly 140 feet above tide-water, and 14 feet above the upper floors of the Capitol. The dam across the Potomac is 2100 feet in length and 8 feet in height. The water thus diverted from the river passes by a tunnel or culvert under the Chesapeake and Ohio Canal into a receptacle known as the Gate-House. It is excavated out of the solid rock, and will be surmounted by a structure of beautiful sandstone from the Seneca Quarry, a few miles above. This Gate-House will exclude drift-wood and other foreign substances from the conduit.

The river, from the falls to Georgetown, passes between high ranges of hills, often rugged and precipitous in outline, but always picturesque. "The traveler," says Captain Meigs, "ascending the banks of the Potomac from Georgetown to the Great Falls, would conclude that a more unpromising region for the construction of an aqueduct could not be found. Supported by high walls against the face of jagged and vertical precipices, in continual danger of being undermined by the foaming torrent which boils below, the Canal (the Chesapeake and Ohio) is a monument of the energy and daring of our engineers. The route appears to be occupied, and no mode of bringing in the water, except by iron pipes secured to the rocks, or laid in the bed of the canal, seems practicable. Such were my own impressions; and though I knew that in this age, with money, any achievement of engineering was possible, I thought the survey would be needed only to demonstrate by figures and measures the extravagance of such a work. But," he continues, "when the levels were applied to the ground, I found, to my surprise and gratification, that the rocky precipices and difficult passages were nearly all below the line which, allowing a uniform grade, would naturally be selected for our conduit; and that, instead of demonstrating the extravagance of the proposal, it became my duty to devise a work presenting no considerable difficulties, and affording no opportunities for the exhibition of any triumphs of science or skill."

The obstacles encountered in the construction of the aqueduct may have been less serious than an engineer would have anticipated upon a casual inspection of the ground; but they can not fail to astonish the unscientific spectator; and it is not impossible that Captain Meigs's decided preference for the Great Falls as a source of supply may have caused him, in his report of surveys, from which we quote, to underrate obstacles of which he had in the first instance formed an exaggerated estimate. The original plan was to make the conduit, which was to be tubular in form, seven feet in diameter; but at the same time one of nine feet in diameter was suggested as preferable, and was adopted. The difference of only two feet in the width of the conduit makes the immense difference of nearly two to one in its capacity. One of seven feet will discharge but thirty-six millions of gallons in twenty-four hours, while a nine-foot conduit will supply above sixty-seven and a half millions. The larger dimensions adopted of course adds something to the expense of the work, but not in any proportion to the additional supply of water. There are in all eleven tunnels, some of them several hundred feet in length, and six bridges. The largest of the bridges is one of the most stupendous achievements of the kind in this country. It spans a small tributary of the Potomac. called the Cabin John Creek, by a single arch 220 feet in span, and 100 feet high. The receiving reservoir is formed by throwing a dam across a small stream known as the Powder-Mill, or Little Falls Branch. The dam is of pounded earth and floods above fifty acres, making a reservoir of irregular shape, containing, at a level of 140 feet above high tide, 82,521,500 gallons. The water leaves it at a distance of 3000 feet from the point where it enters, and, in slowly passing across this pool, which deepens to 30 or 40 feet near the exit, it will deposit most of its sediment. The Powder-Mill itself supplies two to three millions of gallons of pure water daily to the reservoir. The estimated cost of the Washington Aqueduct is $2,500,000, and the daily supply 67,596,400 gallons; the Croton Aqueduct cost $10,375,000, and furnishes New York with a minimum supply of 27,000,000; Philadelphia is provided with a daily supply of 15,000,000; and Boston with 10,176,570 gallons. These comparisons give the best illustration of the magnitude of the work undertaken and nearly brought to a successful completion at Washington.

In the midst of all the magnificence of the public buildings, it is a little surprising that, with a population of sixty-five or seventy thousand, there should not be a single church whose architecture justifies ever so brief a notice; without exception, the church edifices present an appearance that would be considered a disgrace to a Western city of twenty thousand inhabitants.

Among the ancients the capital city, or seat of empire, was the State. The denizens of the country, even in the republics, had no political rights except such as the city to which they owed allegiance chose to concede to them. We read of the republic of Athens, not of Attica, of Sparta, not of Laconia, of Carthage, of Rome, and so on, not of the subject provinces. The Roman empire, in the first centuries of the Christian era, embraced nearly the whole of the then civilized world, with a large portion of that which was recognized as barbarous, and all the immense countries from the Pillars of Hercules, or Straits of Gibraltar, on the west, and the frontiers of Caledonia on the north, to the confines of Persia, acknowledged the sway, and bore the name of the imperial city of Rome. Under the more ancient despotisms we discover the same pre-eminence of the cities over the country, in the histories of Babylon, Nineveh, Tyre, and the Egyptian capitals. In the modern nations of Europe, which have risen upon the ruins of the Roman empire, new elements of power have come into play—new elements of race, of language, of religion, and of political principles—society, in fact, resting upon a stronger foundation of ideas. The most powerful and extensive of modern empires is not the "London empire," but the British; the power and importance of a whole people are thus recognized in the style of the empire, and London, though perhaps more wealthy and populous than Rome in her palmiest days, has less political power than any half-dozen representative boroughs. The city has not made the kingdom, but has grown up with it, and been fostered by its trade. It has been the seat of government immemorially, though not uninterruptedly, simply as a matter of public convenience, and by the choice of the rulers of England. The same may be said of Paris; the proverbial saying that "Paris is France," is a scarcely warrantable exaggeration. Whatever liberties are enjoyed in France, are enjoyed equally by the whole population without regard to locality. The representation is apportioned with reference to population, and we believe that Paris, like London, is not particularly favored in this respect. The American capital, although voted into being by a free people, occupies the anomalous position of being the only one in history which is denied the privileges that are accorded to the meanest hamlet in the remotest department of the empire. For even our Territories may each send a delegate to the National Legislature; and being incipient States, sovereignties in embryo, may look forward to the time when they are to participate in all the privileges of the proudest of the Old Thirteen. Not so the capital. She may rival Rome in populousness, wealth, and magnificence; her citizens may live under the shadow of marble palaces, or promenade on avenues paved with mosaic work, or stroll through gardens shaded with evergreens and exotics, perfumed with flowers, and cooled with fountains and sparkling waterfalls—but *they can not vote!* They can have no Senators, no Representatives—no voice in the election of President. This anomalous condition of the national capital, so different from the capitals of the ancient republics, illustrates the complete revolution which has taken place in the affairs of mankind and the policy of nations in the course of two thousand years.

We have endeavored to confine our article to a review of existing things, and yet, in examining it, we perceive that we have slightly drawn upon our anticipations; but we are comforted with the reflection that America is entitled to a large use of the future tense. Foreign criticism properly wonders at our constant employment of the phrases, "going to be" and "going to do," but it is also true that abroad—except in Russia—they can only use the past tense; for their noblest monuments and most beautiful surroundings are only the heir-looms and old clothes of departed generations. Their noblest mission is preservation, ours is creation. For a long period Washington expectancy was a laughing-stock for every wandering Englishman, who chose to dish up our national peculiarities in a hash of guide-books, private journals, Munchausen stories collected in cars and stage-coaches, and confused recollections of three months devoted to diligent examination into the properties of sherry-cobblers, large oysters, and Catawba wine. And yet, at this hour, London is paying a fearful penalty for its neglect of that planning for the future which foreigners thought so ridiculous in the wide avenues and green spaces of Washington. Spacious pleasure-grounds are the best friends of law and order; it is well for the people to play, and the instinct of childhood points to the open air as the best place for recreation. A grass-plot has a magical virtue for "clearing the breast of perilous stuff." During the fierce heat of summer, it is pleasant to see the large concourse of people which pours into the Capitol grounds, or those around the President's mansion, sitting under the shade of the trees, while the Marine Band furnishes the choicest music; and it requires no poetic enthusiasm to picture the coming day when the Mall, stretching from the Capitol to the margin of the noble Potomac, shall be one continuous shade, covered with glorious foliage, and vocal with the rippling of fountains and the song of birds. Then hard-handed toil and weary brains shall find in every sight and sound of beauty not only rest, but hope—hope for the perpetuity of that strong *Union* which, having created this costly capital, may find it a centre of attraction sufficiently strong to marshal around it the orderly States, and to control even the wildest comets that seek to fly off into new orbits. Then the seat of Government, adorned as becomes the representative city of America—not claiming to be the fountain of power—shall be a beautiful lake, formed by the rills that flow into it from north and south, from east and west, and shall forever mirror, on its placid bosom, the great forms of the mountains from whose sides it is fed.

The New Washington (1884)

THE CENTURY MAGAZINE.

MARCH, 1884.

THE NEW WASHINGTON.

WITHIN the past ten years Washington has ceased to be a village. Whether it has yet become a city depends on "the point of view." It has no elevated railroads, no palace hotels, no mammoth elevators, no great commercial establishments; it has no opera and but indifferent theaters, and for a park it borrows the grounds of the old soldiers of the army. In short, it has none of those evidences of commercial prosperity which are proudly shown to the traveler in every thriving town, all the way from New York to San Francisco. On the other hand, it has large public buildings and monuments and numerous statues; it has a mild climate, clean, well-paved streets, and no "local politics"; its chief inhabitants are those persons who guide the action and control the interests of fifty millions of people — so far as they are guided or controlled at all in a nation which so largely governs itself. Washington is thus a place quite out of the ordinary run; whether city or no, it is certainly unlike other cities. Its origin and inception were novel and unusual in character. Other cities have originated in the necessities of trade, and have grown in proportion as that trade increased. Washington, on the contrary, was made to order on a map; and so far from extending its limits as its population increased, its population has not yet grown up to the limits which were originally laid out. It found its origin in the rivalry existing among the various States after the Revolution, all being jealous of the increased importance which would result to any one of them from having the federal city established within its limits. This feeling was increased by the mortifying spectacle which occurred at Philadelphia, in 1783, when Congress was insulted in its own halls and driven across the river by a handful of mutineers from the army,— the State and local authorities being either powerless or unwilling to protect them from injury. Many of the members of that Congress were delegates to the Constitutional Convention four years later, and the recollection of this indignity was so fresh in their minds that they determined that Congress should itself make the laws for the place where it met. The result was the well-known clause in Section 8 of Article I. of the Constitution, which conferred on Congress the power "to exercise exclusive legislation in all cases whatsoever" over such district as might be ceded by the States and accepted by Congress as the seat of government. The selection of such a district was one of the very first questions which arose in Congress. As soon as laws had been passed organizing the various departments of the government and putting the new machinery in motion, the question of the location of the government came up, and it gave rise to long and acrimonious debate. Not only was it claimed by the large cities, like New York and Philadelphia, but each of the middle States, from New York to Virginia, inclusive, was ready with a piece of territory on which to found an entirely new city. It was finally settled by a curious compromise — the first recorded instance of "log-rolling" — in this manner. Hamilton was then (1790) engaged in his projects for funding the debt, all of which had passed except the final one assuming the debts of the States. This was a popular measure in the North, but somewhat unpopular among the Virginians. He needed some votes from the South in order to carry the measure through. Jefferson had then but lately returned from France, and, as he claimed, was not very familiar with the funding projects, which he subsequently opposed so violently. He was, however, greatly interested in locating the new capital in the vicinity of Virginia. Hamilton was a foreigner by birth, accidentally settled in New York by reason of his marriage, but quite devoid of any feeling of local or State pride. He cared nothing for the location of the capital, but was anxious concerning his financial projects, which he considered of vital importance. It was therefore arranged — at a dinner-party — between himself and Jefferson, that the latter should persuade the Virginia delegation to vote for assumption, while Hamilton was to induce the New York delegation to yield their preferences concerning the capital. The two measures were thus carried, one on the 16th of July and the other on the 4th of August, 1790. The former prescribed that the permanent seat of government should be in the district ceded by Maryland and Virginia on the banks of the Potomac, and that the Government should be moved there in the year 1800. President Washington had remained neutral during the discussion, but he was much pleased at the selection made; and he gave his personal attention to the matter with unflagging interest throughout his administration, and, indeed, to the day of his death. Commissioners were at once appointed to acquire the land, which was obtained on the most liberal terms, the owners giving to the United States the fee of all ground necessary for streets and public buildings, and one-half of all the building lots in addition; with the understanding that these lots were to be sold and the money applied to opening and improving the streets and erecting the public buildings. With these commissioners there was associated, for the purpose of making plans and surveys, a certain French engineer named L'Enfant, who had served under Washington's notice during the Revolution. His plans were as comprehensive and far-reaching in their way as was the Constitution itself. He planned for centuries, and for a population of half a million of people.

THE STATE, WAR, AND NAVY DEPARTMENTS.

The plan was simple in its general outline, though its details were very elaborate. Three principal points were selected for the legislative, executive, and judicial buildings respectively; from two of these points avenues radiated like the spokes of a wheel, affording short lines of communication to all parts of the city and forming numberless little parks at their intersections; a rectilinear system of streets was added, running north and south and east and west, the first being designated by numerals and the second by the letters of the alphabet. The avenues were named after the States of the Union, with much care and discrimination in guarding their respective susceptibilities by giving to those which were intended to be most important the names of the principal States. Everything was on a scale of large proportions, the avenues being grand boulevards of one hundred and fifty to one hundred and sixty feet in width, and even unimportant streets being ninety or one hundred feet wide.

STATUE OF GENERAL GEORGE H. THOMAS, BY. J. Q. A. WARD.

The proportion of streets and open squares, which in most cities is about one-fourth, was thus laid out in this capital city at more than one-half of the whole surface. It was to be the capital of a mighty nation, and no one was to be pinched for space in it.

The plan was thus drawn on paper, and nothing remained but to fill up the uninhabited fields through which the imaginary streets ran. This was not so easy. The Government came there in 1800, and great expectations were formed, but they were not realized. For more than half a century the place remained a straggling Southern village, giving rise to much ridicule as a "city of magnificent distances." The diaries and chronicles of the first third of the century give curious accounts of the uncomfortable and dreary life in such an uninviting place; it was particularly amusing to the members of the diplomatic corps, and the contrast to London and Paris and Vienna must certainly have been very great. It was originally intended that the city should grow to the eastward on the broad, high plateau beyond the Capitol, and that the President's house and other executive buildings should form a sort of suburb like Versailles. But the lots on Capitol Hill were all bought up by speculators, and held at such high prices that people were forced to turn in the other direction, and the city thus took a course which it has never been possible to reverse. Its growth, however, was extremely slow. The commercial advantages which were expected to result from the navigation on the Potomac and the transportation routes to the westward proved to be delusive. Commerce went to other cities. It was a city of office-holders simply, and at first these were not numerous. Gaunt rows of "six buildings" and "seven buildings" were erected here and there, principally as boarding-houses to accommodate the members of Congress and those who had business with them during the winter. But no one came there who did not have urgent business, nor did any one stay longer than was necessary. Its character changed but little down to the period of the war, and at that time—sixty years after it had been founded, and when the country had grown to contain thirty-two millions of people—it had attained a population of only sixty thousand inhabitants, who were scattered over a territory of several miles; its streets were so filthy and ill-kept that they were a by-word of contempt; none of its citizens were rich, and there were no handsome dwellings or other indications of private wealth; it had the usual government of a mayor and council, which had neither the means nor the disposition to beautify the

THE TREASURY DEPARTMENT—FIFTEENTH STREET FRONT.

THE U. S. POST-OFFICE DEPARTMENT.

city; the General Government had neglected its godchild, and while it spent lavishly for its own public buildings, it paid little or nothing to improve the general appearance of the city.

With the resumption of prosperity in the period following the war, the place first began to change; the business of the Government had greatly multiplied, and the number of its public servants had correspondingly increased; the population of the city had nearly doubled between 1860 and 1870, and among the new-comers were many energetic Northern men. It began to be realized that it was a disgrace to have such a city for a capital, and that the General Government and the citizens must all unite in efforts to improve it. The result was the formation, in 1871, of a territorial government, with a Governor and Legislature and a Board of Public Works. The master-spirit of this government was Alexander Shepherd, a native of the city, who, though still young, had raised himself by his energy and talents from the apprenticeship of a manual trade to a position of means and importance in the community. The results of his government are too recent and too well known to call for fresh comment. Vast plans were again matured, founded, as in the past century, not on the actual necessities of the moment, but on the requirements of a generation hence. Costly improvements were undertaken and prosecuted far beyond the limits of habitation. Miles upon miles of expensive pavements and other works were laid across swamps and streams, and through waste places where nothing but frame shanties and government stables of the war period had as yet penetrated. In less than three years Shepherd plunged the city into a debt which, for the numbers and wealth of the population, has no rival in all the world. No

THE OLD CARROLL MANSION ON CAPITOL HILL.

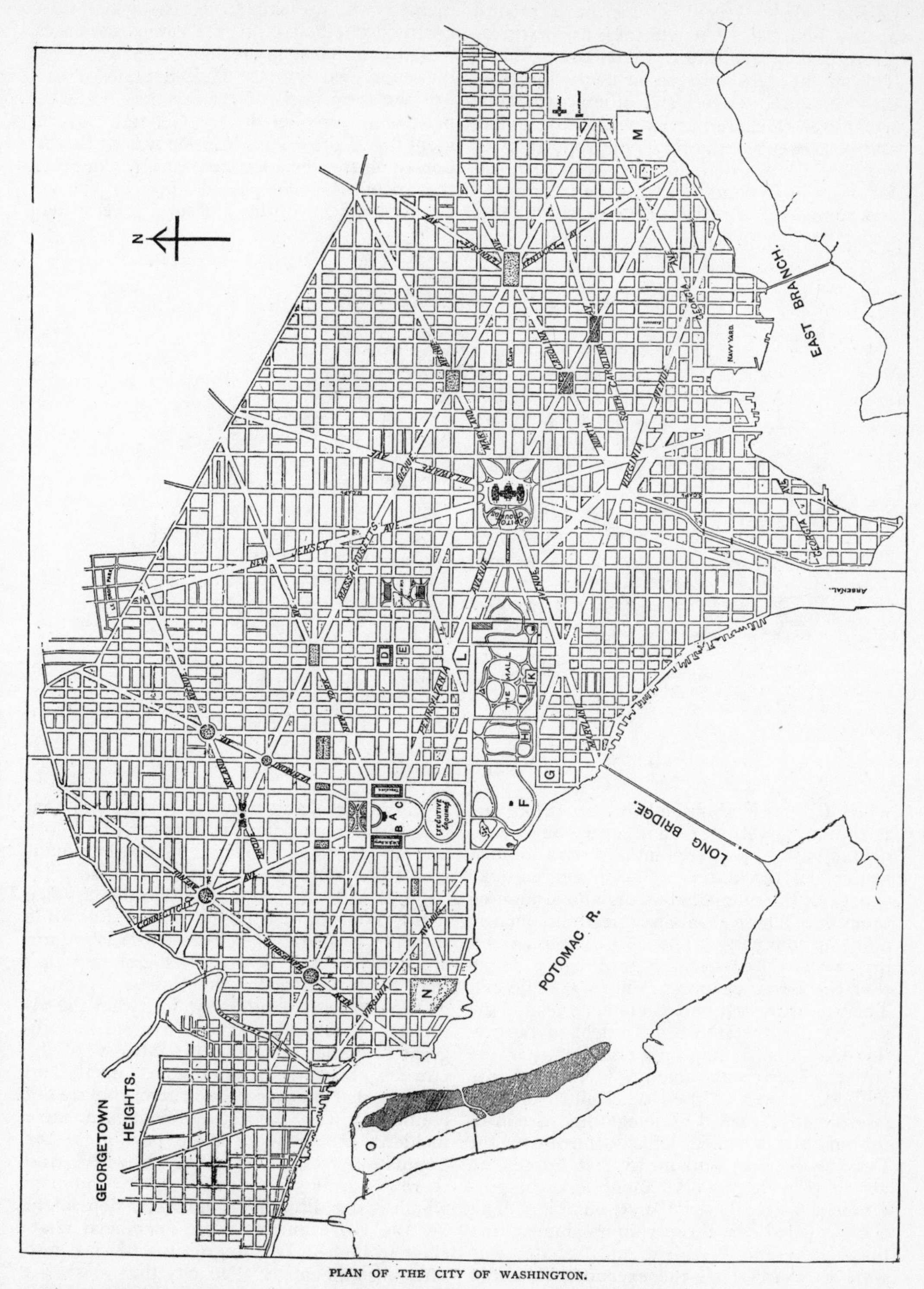

PLAN OF THE CITY OF WASHINGTON.

A. Executive Mansion. B. State, War, and Navy Department Building. C. Treasury. D. Patent Office. E. Post-office Department. F. Washington Monument. G. Bureau of Engraving and Printing. H. Department of Agriculture. I. Smithsonian Institution. K. National Museum. L. Market. M. Congressional Cemetery. N. Washington Observatory. O. Analostan Island.

personal dishonesty has ever been proved against him, but the recklessness and extravagance in the expenditures were extraordinary. The streets were torn up in every direction on a "comprehensive plan" of improvements, which was estimated at six millions of dollars and cost twenty; the rights of property-owners were disregarded, and they were assessed for "improvements" when their property was ruined. The result was a crash in 1874, when Congress abolished at one stroke the territorial government and everything connected with it, and appointed three Commissioners, in the nature of receivers, to take charge of the municipal affairs and straighten them out. These Commissioners remained in office for four years. The work of reconstructing the city had been so thoroughly begun that there was no option but to complete it. This was cautiously and carefully done, and the net result was stated to be a debt of twenty-three millions, resting on a community whose entire property was valued at less than eighty millions. Congress then determined to exercise directly, instead of delegating, its constitutional power of legislative control over the Federal district; and in 1878 it framed an act to provide "a permanent form of government for the District of Columbia." This act provided for three Commissioners, appointed by the President and Senate, who were to exercise all the executive functions necessary for the city, and who were to appoint and remove, and be responsible for, their own subordinates. The legislative power remained wholly with Congress, which also assumed one-half of all the annual expenses, including interest on the debt. The taxes were to be covered into the United States Treasury and form one-half the revenue, the other half being provided by the General Government; and the entire revenue was to be disbursed on specific appropriations by Congress, the accounts being passed upon by the accounting officers of the Treasury. This system

"ABOVE THE GRADE."

is still in force, and after nearly six years' trial it is, in the main, quite satisfactory to all concerned. It would appear at first to be fundamentally opposed to the spirit of American institutions, for the people have no direct voice in the choice of their public officers. But while this is true as far as the citizens of Washington are concerned, it is to be remembered that the Federal city is the creature and protégé of the Federal Government, and that the interests of that Government are overwhelmingly great in comparison with the interests of the citizens. It is the seat of government, and the fact that persons reside there who are not connected with the Government is a mere incident. As a fact, a large portion of the population retain a residence elsewhere, and there is only an inconsiderable minority which is not directly or indirectly dependent on the Government. Were its official character to be lost, Washington would sink into utter insignificance. The city thus exists for the people of the whole country, and the people govern it through their elected representatives in Congress.

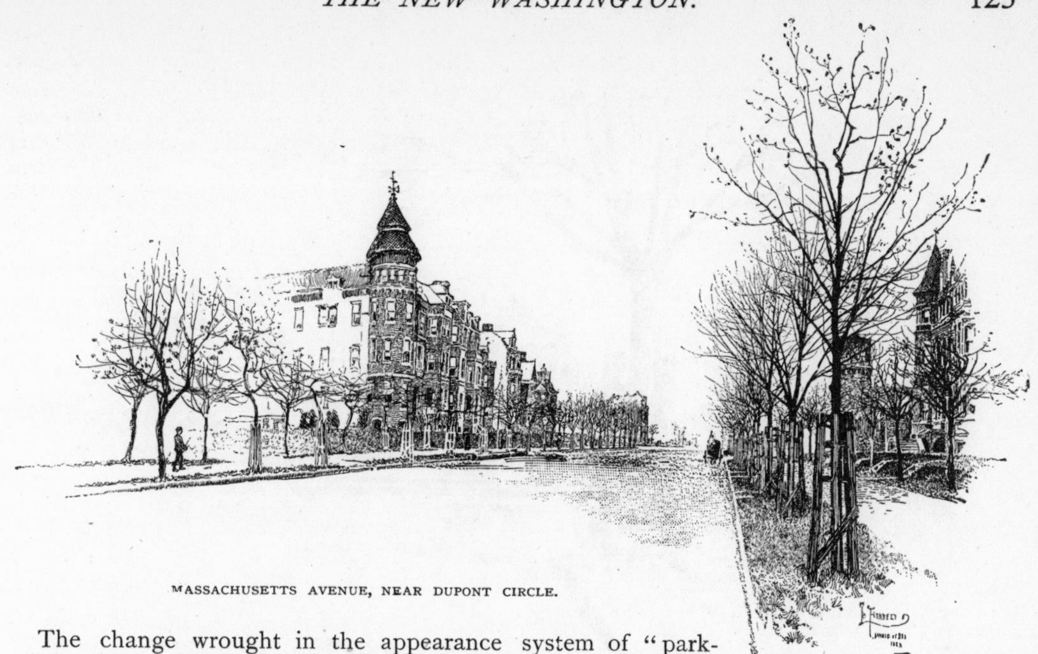

MASSACHUSETTS AVENUE, NEAR DUPONT CIRCLE.

The change wrought in the appearance of the city by the Shepherd government and its successors was fundamental and revolutionary. It might have been done more cheaply, but it was better to have it done extravagantly than not at all. Possibly, it never could have been done at all but by some man of Shepherd's intolerant energy, which sacrificed individual rights for the future benefit of the whole community. Had it been attempted prudently and cautiously, these individual rights would have defeated the whole scheme, for the community was not wealthy enough to compensate the injury done to them.

Fortunately, during all the years that the place had remained a wretched village, its grandiose plan had never been intrenched upon in any way; and when the work of development was taken in hand in earnest, it was at once manifest what immense possibilities the plan contained. The great boulevards, or avenues, were three times as wide as was necessary for purposes of communication; it was determined to use a portion of them only for a roadway, another portion for foot-walks, and to devote fully half of the street to lawns in front of the houses. The idea was not novel, for it had been carried out to a limited extent in many cities of Europe and America, where, on a few streets, the houses are built well back from the front line of the lot; but, as a general rule, city real estate is too valuable to allow such a luxury. In Washington, however, the streets were wide enough to permit this without sacrificing any private property, and the system of "parking" thus became the rule, and not the exception. At the same time, the city was torn up from one end to the other, and regraded, filling up here and cutting down there, without regard to the existing positions of houses. Many were banked up to their windows, others were left high in the air; but the general result was a system of streets with such gradual slopes that there is hardly a place where an ordinary carriage cannot proceed at a trot.

The roadways being narrowed and the streets graded, the next step was the planting of trees, forming miles on miles of shade. This was systematically done, the trees being carefully selected by experts, certain varieties for certain streets, planted with great care, and protected by boxing. They have been wonderfully successful, fully ninety-five per cent. having thriven. The quick-growing maples and poplars were principally used, but there are large numbers of elms, lindens, box elders, and buttonwoods, besides other varieties, amounting to more than twenty. One feature of the tree-planting project was a continuous drive of several miles under lindens; a part of this extends for over three miles on Massachusetts Avenue, where there are four rows of the lindens, two on each side of the road-way, already of sufficient size to unite with their summer foliage in an arch over the sidewalk. In this matter of trees, Washington is unrivaled among all the cities of the world. Other cities have trees in their parks and here and there on

THOMAS CIRCLE.

a few streets, but nowhere else has it been attempted to plant trees systematically and thoroughly on every street, except those devoted exclusively to business purposes. Nowhere else are there one hundred and twenty miles of shaded streets. The effect of this planting is not yet fully developed, the elms and other slow-growing varieties being still quite small; but the quick-growing maples and poplars are now seven and eight inches in diameter and forty feet high. The view in the spring and early summer of the streets thus shaded, and flanked by lines of lawn or terrace or flower-garden, is novel and beautiful. Its beauty is increased by the flowers and vegetation of great numbers of little triangular spaces, which have been formed by the intersection of the avenues with the streets, and which have all been tastefully laid out, according to their size, either as simple lawns or flower-beds, or as parks, with walks, fountains, etc.

As the trees were the most successful and the most inexpensive of all the works of the Shepherd government, so were the pavements the most costly and the most unsuccessful. They were principally of wood, and they went to pieces very quickly, leaving the streets for some time almost impassable. Year by year the wood has been replaced with asphalt, which now covers a length of fifty miles, and is a great luxury for all who use the streets, whether with cushioned carriage or heavy express wagon. By far the greater part of the streets used for residences are covered with these asphalt pavements, which are somewhat similar to those in Paris, but cover an extent three times as great.

It was but a short time after the city had been thus remodeled, when the natural result came in a new class of houses. And here again the French engineer's plan was found to be full of possibilities which hitherto had not been thought of. In a city laid out like New York and most other cities, in monotonous parallelograms, all the lots are of the same pattern. What can an architect do with the unvarying 25 x 100 feet? He may double it, and make it 50 x 100, and he may expend vast sums upon it, but it is still the same. The streets of Washington, however, with its various intersecting avenues, afforded building lots of every conceivable variety of shape; and the architects were not slow to cover them with every conceivable variety of houses,—square houses and round houses, houses with no two walls parallel, with fantastic roofs and towers and buttresses and bay windows and nameless projections. Some of them were good and some bad, but hardly any two were alike. Even after making all deductions for the mistakes and failures, the result of this variety is certainly pleasing. The two miles of Fifth Avenue in New York between Washington

Square and the Central Park present an imposing manifestation of wealth ; one may visit many cities without finding its equal. But in the whole length — excepting a few recent structures — there is not a house which has any individuality. So similar are they that they might all have been made on a machine, and one cannot but be oppressed by the interminable monotony of the long vista of brown-stone walls on either side, with gray-stone flags underfoot, and very little sky overhead, and no trace of vegetation of any kind. In Washington there is no such wealth — and no such monotony. As the eye wanders along the street, it constantly finds some new shape, some odd design, some strange combination in color. Many of these alleged "Queen Anne" houses, with their rooms cut up into all sorts of angles, are reputed to be most uncomfortable places to live in ; but they serve an admirable purpose in street decoration. With streets, however, laid out for more than double the actual population, one has a wide range in which to choose a lot. This option has been freely availed of, and there are, consequently, three vacant lots to one which is built upon. The new buildings have clustered about the Scott Square and Dupont Circle, and the other little squares and circles, forming small settlements, separated from each other by long distances of vacant fields, unbroken except by the asphalt roads and the lines of trees. This scattering of the new building forces has given a very incongruous and ludicrous appearance to some of the most handsome avenues. Everywhere there are superb residences looking out upon fields of red clay and weeds, and flanked on either side by such shanties as perch on the rocks in the upper part of New York. This incongruity reaches its height on the principal street of the town, Pennsylvania Avenue, which is of unrivaled width, beautifully paved both for vehicles and pedestrians, flanked at either end by the magnificent Capitol and Treasury buildings, and possessed of every requisite for a famous boulevard — except buildings. There are, perhaps, a dozen large structures in its length of more than a mile, which tower high in the air, and are suited to the character of the thoroughfare. All the rest are dilapidated and wretched little houses of ancient date, which look singularly out of sympathy with their surroundings.

PENNSYLVANIA AVENUE.

This is naturally to be expected in a place which was first planned, and subsequently improved, out of all proportion to the requirements of the moment. It grows in spots, which, like the settlements in the Far West, form each a little center of development, radiating and extending toward its neighbor, until finally they will all join and form a civilized whole. When this process is completed in Washington, it will be, among cities, the wonder of the world.

Such is the outward appearance of the Federal city. What sort of people live in it ? It has no commerce, no great merchants, no powerful corporations, none of the classes

LONG BRIDGE.

persons of leisure and moderate means. Its mild climate, its quiet streets, free from the hurried bustle and noise of a commercial center, and the character of its society, prove more and more attractive to certain classes. The merchant who has acquired a fortune in the fierce struggles of trade goes there to build himself a house and quietly enjoy with his family the results of his labors in a place where there is no business talk. The retired army or navy officer finds nowhere

which form the controlling elements in other cities. Its one hundred and eighty thousand inhabitants are, roughly speaking, the families of office-holders, or of persons who supply office-holders with food, clothing, shelter, and the other necessaries of life. It is hard to realize to what extent the Federal business has grown. The official register contains the names of nearly fifteen thousand persons, beginning with President and ending with "cuspadorians," who serve the United States in the city of Washington. Perhaps one-half of these are clerks and writers, busy in settling accounts and claims; nearly one-fourth are employed in mammoth establishments like the Printing Office and Bureau of Engraving and Printing. Others are engaged in the various scientific departments under Government control. Finally, a number, small in amount but large in importance, comprise the prominent men in public life—the Senators and Representatives in Congress, the great lawyers on the Supreme Bench, the members of the Cabinet and chief bureau officers, the most prominent officers of the army and navy, the representatives of foreign governments. These form the ruling element in what is called "society" in its restricted sense. But they do not form the whole of it. Every year Washington becomes more and more a winter residence for

else so many friends or so much consideration,—in fact nowhere else can he live on his pay with any comfort. The man of science goes there because he can find nowhere else so many men engaged in his own specialty, no matter whether it be in the domain of physical or biological investigation, and nowhere else can he prosecute his studies to such advantage. The man of letters finds there more than one distinguished author, and a library which has no equal on this continent. Other cities have probably more scientific and literary men, but they are relatively insignificant among the vast numbers engaged in commercial pursuits. They form their little societies apart, and are almost unnoticed in the great current of affairs; but in Washington they form an important part of the whole. Finally, during the winter all the world and his wife goes there for a visit—some for sight-seeing, to see what Congress and public men are like; some because it is the fashion to go to Washington in winter as to Newport in summer; some because they have cases to argue in the Supreme Court; some because they have their little measures to look after in Congress. The society is thus ever changing and kaleidoscopic; it is perforce completely revolutionized every four years, and partly so every second year, while every winter brings its fresh supply of mere temporary residents. The "old-resident" element which, in the days of Southern supremacy before the war, ruled Washington society, is becoming every year more and more in a minority, buried out of sight in the avalanche of Northern wealth and numbers. It is this thoroughly cosmopolitan character which gives to Washington society its characteristic feature. It is the common meeting-ground of people of different tastes and different habits, representing communities and ideas as wide apart as the poles, but truly representing them, and all men of mark in their own localities, even though their importance dwindles when exposed to a national glare.

OUTSIDE THE MARKET.

Not the least interesting among the features of Washington is the opportunity which it affords to study the results of emancipation. These results can there be seen at their best, as in South Carolina and Mississippi they appear at their worst. The war brought into Washington a large influx of negroes, principally refugees, who came tramping over the Long Bridge after each successive battle, hoping to find the promised land after they had crossed the Potomac. Their numbers are given in the last census at sixty thousand, or one-third of the whole population. They are as a rule industrious, sober, and orderly; and, although they figure in the police court more numerously than the whites in proportion to their numbers, yet the offenses are nearly all trivial, most of them being petty larceny and sneak-thieving. Crimes of any magnitude are extremely rare among them, and they are not inferior to the whites in morality or in freedom from the lower vices. They know their legal rights, and are quick to enforce them if imposed upon, but if treated fairly they seldom give trouble. They find employment as laborers in the various public and private works, as household servants (for which they are admirably adapted), as hucksters and purveyors for the markets. Others have improved their condition, and have learned trades as masons, carpenters, blacksmiths, etc. Many are sufficiently educated to carry on a small business or become messengers and clerks in the departments, and a few have held offices of importance, and have discharged the duties of them in such a manner as to gain the respect and esteem of all with whom they are brought in contact. Unlike the plantation negroes of the South, they are provident and economical, accumulate their savings, purchase comfortable homes for themselves, build expensive churches, and conduct a great number of coöperative and benevolent societies with marked success. Even the poorer laborers are not without food and lodging, for which they are ready to work hard and long, and professional beggary is almost unknown among them. Good schools are provided for their children and filled with thousands of pupils. Those who have the means attach great importance to their dress, and although fond of gaudy colors, they are usually neat in their appearance.

Altogether, the negroes, as seen in Washington, form a very useful and unobjectionable portion of the community, incomparably superior in every respect to the low foreign element which forms the dregs of Atlantic cities. When one sees the intelligence and prosperity of those who have been educated, and the industry and good order which characterize the uneducated laboring class, it instills new hope for the future of their race. The dark past of the ante-bellum period, when slaves were herded in pens on the grounds now used as a botanical garden at the foot of the Capitol, and when the voice of the auctioneer, as he sold them, could almost be heard in the halls of Congress — these days seem to be separated from the bright present by centuries rather than years.

The society of Washington has of late years been the subject of much discussion and not a few novels. It was cleverly satirized three years since by the author of "Democracy." His book was hardly noticed in his own country, save by a few who imagined that they identified the originals of the types so baldly presented, and were amused to see the faults of their acquaintances thus made sport of. But in due time the book traveled to England, and was there gravely considered as an analytical thesis upon the results of a century of self-government. The "Quarterly Review" moralized at great length upon the remarkable spectacle thus presented of a mighty people rushing to self-destruction for lack of a ruling class. People at home then began to inquire for a book which excited such profound interest abroad, and the demand was met by a cheap edition, which all the world has now read.

The society represented in this book centers around a widow of an "assured position in society," who, having traveled everywhere and exhausted everything, comes to Washington in search of a new sensation; to whom court is paid by two men intended to form an antithesis — one a Senator from the West, distinguished as a leader in his party and a Presidential candidate, and the other a Southern gentleman ruined in fortune by the war and now practicing his profession as a lawyer. Incidentally, there is a President who is a mere puppet in the hands of the Senator, a cynical diplomat, a historian who clamors for a foreign mission, a young miss of startling freedom of manner, and a host of constituents who throng the gaunt lodgings of the Senator, spitting tobacco juice on his floor and pressing their "claims" for office. The slender thread of the story hangs upon the rivalry of the two suitors for the heroine's affections, and the climax is reached after the Southern gentleman is disposed of by sending him off to Mexico as counsel for some sort of claims commission, and the Senator is about to win his suit — when the heroine discovers that he had formerly sold his vote in Congress on a bill for a steamboat subsidy. He tries to explain this, while admitting the fact, by saying that he used the money solely for political purposes in the crisis of an election on the result of which he believed the safety of the country to depend. But she scorns his sophistries and flies a place where no one is free from corruption.

The story is full of hits which, though local in their character, are cleverly made, and it is altogether an amusing little satire; yet no one but a ponderous reviewer would ever find in it any adequate justification for its comprehensive title of "Democracy."

It cannot be denied that certain measures in Congress have been tainted with corruption; the Crédit Mobilier and other investigations have distinctly proved it. But neither can any one deny that cupidity is the ruling vice in the nature of most men the world over; nor that in a place where the public business of fifty millions of people is planned, enacted, and conducted, there should be manifold opportunities for dishonesty of every shade, from open bribery to the most remote indirect benefit. But in spite of cupidity, human nature is not wholly bad; and in spite of its temptations, Washington society is not wholly, nor even principally or mainly, corrupt. There are professional lobbyists who go there in numbers every winter; their doings and their methods, with their restaurant dinners, their hotel life, their intrigues, and their secret conferences, can be traced by the aid of a detective reporter; and the spectacle is by turns exciting and repulsive, instructive and indecent. But the lobbyist and his companions are no more to be found in good society than the social outcast among decent people. The most that is known about the lobby and corrupt bills is derived from the principal newspapers, and one may live in Washington for years and never meet a live lobbyist. It is highly probable that the amount of legislative dishonesty is at least not greater in Washington than in London or Paris. The difference lies in the amount of publicity given to it in America, and to the public craving for that sort of news which stimulates the supply of it, to an extent far exceeding what is warranted by mere truth.

Nevertheless, the lobby and corruption are legitimate subjects for satire. But the satire must not be accepted as a well-proportioned picture. If one should write a book and call it "Commerce," in which the principal character should be a notorious stock-jobber who amassed a great fortune by assiduously circulating lies which affected the value of the property he bought and sold, and in which the other characters should be a chief municipal officer and a judge who were mere hirelings of the stock operator, a minister of the Gospel who was a gross libertine, a merchant who made false returns of his income and false invoices of his goods, and a host of idle young men who scorned the trades in which their fathers gained the fortunes they were spending, and whose principal occupation was to assemble every night in a club to talk scandal and play cards — who would accept it as a faithful picture of New York society? and what would be thought of the foreign philosopher who should gravely discourse upon it as showing the inevitable results of engaging in commercial enterprises?

The prominent men of society in Washington are the prominent men of the country at large, and their morals and their character, their honesty and dishonesty, are a faithful reflection of the tone of public sentiment in regard to morality throughout the country. Those who believe that the people in general are corrupt will believe the same of their representatives; and those who believe that the prevailing sentiment in America and elsewhere throughout the world is in favor of honesty will find the same sentiment in public men.

ENTRANCE TO NAVY YARD.

Leaving aside the question of political morality, few people who have passed a winter in Washington will deny the charm of its society. Acknowledging all its faults, its crudeness — narrowness, perhaps — and its lack of form, it must yet be acknowledged that it differs from all other American society in the fact that it is not founded on wealth. It is the only society which is really republican, though it has little resemblance to the "republican court" of the first administration,— the only one in America which has a well-defined basis. And that basis is public station, temporarily conferred, whether directly or indirectly, by the expressed wishes of fellow-men. The holding of such public station necessarily implies intelligence, and thus it is intelligence, as distinguished from lineage or wealth, which is the fundamental basis in Washington society. Such a society does not feel obliged to adopt certain customs because it is reported at second hand that they are good form in London. Its opinions are robustly independent, its information is extensive, and its subjects of conversation are many and varied.

It is not to be imagined that such a society is well defined, or that its rules are clearly established—though it is true that the "Etiquette of Social Life in Washington" has been most elaborately formulated in a little pamphlet, of which a fresh edition is perennially produced, and which is said to sell in great numbers. It is, undoubtedly, open to the criticism of being raw, to the same extent—but no more—that society in London is subservient and snobbish, and in New York illiterate and commercial. Nothing can be more ridiculous than the public levees of the President, where the doors are thrown open that every person in the street may enter them in a crush, and stand in a slowly moving procession for two hours, in order that during half a minute of that time the President may be seen and his arm may be wrenched. But this is not peculiar to Washington alone. Such "public receptions" are inflicted upon presidents in all cities which they visit. Hardly less incongruous are the Wednesday afternoon receptions of the wives of Cabinet officers, when their doors are also thrown open and hundreds of strangers tramp through their parlors "to pay their respects." The wives of Judges and Senators and Representatives have to endure the same thing on other afternoons of the week. It has come

STREET SCENE NEAR NAVY YARD.

ST. JOHN'S CHURCH.

to be considered as part of the price of public station. But, no matter what office a man may hold, no one may come to his dinner table without an invitation. And it is in dinners that Washington society excels. Diplomats and travelers from every part of the world; men distinguished in political life, on the bench, and in war; men of science and men of letters; women of intelligence and culture, with the native grace and beauty for which American women are justly celebrated — there is no such wealth of choice in any other American city, and there are no other dinner-parties so entertaining as those of Washington.

Of great balls there are not many. Few people have the means, and still fewer have the disposition, to incur the expense and domestic nuisance of a ball at home. But those who think that society exists only for dancing have ample opportunities for their amusement in the constant number of balls given by the different german clubs in public halls.

Of evening parties, where there is occasionally dancing, but which can hardly be dignified as balls, there is an incessant round night by night, from Christmas to Ash Wednesday. There are perhaps two score of houses where people are at home one or two evenings in every month. As the society is still so small that there is but one set in it, one meets everybody, *i. e.*, some four or five hundred persons, at these different houses. It would be absurd to say that these affairs are the equals in brilliancy of the salons of the famous French women of the last century, but they are of that type, and will gradually approach that ideal. A considerable minority — often a majority — of the company is composed of distinguished men and brilliant women; and it is the constant reunion of such people at dinners and small evening parties which makes up the most agreeable part of Washington society.

What, then, to sum up, are the attractions of Washington? It has a climate which is mild in winter and unrivaled in spring and autumn. It is a cleanly and convenient place to live in. It has many things to interest the curious. At the Capitol one may see in the Senate the most orderly and dignified legislative body in the world; in the House one may watch a debate of such turmoil and confusion that it seems an unintelligible Babel; in the Supreme Court one may hear the most profound legal argument, and study the proceedings of a court which has no equal in the extent of its jurisdiction and powers. Going up the avenue, there will be seen at the White House a building rich with memories of everything that is prominent in American history for the past seventy years, and in it the curious spectacle of a man performing the chief executive business of the nation in a small office where there is less ceremony than is usual with the president of a bank. On either side of this building is a vast aggregation of granite containing each many hundreds of rooms filled with busy

THE TREASURY DEPARTMENT.

clerks. In the one which is devoted to the State, War, and Navy Departments, there can be seen the original draft of the Declaration of Independence, much correspondence of Washington and others during the Revolution, and the original draft of every law which has been passed and every treaty which has been made since the foundation of the Government. On the walls of one of the rooms are the photographs of the successive Secretaries of State, and their faces are worthy of study. Beginning with Jefferson, Randolph, Pickering, and Marshall, the collection goes on with Madison, Monroe, Adams, Clay, Webster, Calhoun, Everett, Marcy, and Cass, and ends with Seward, Fish, Evarts, and Blaine. Few offices can show such a famous list of occupants.

GENERAL LEE'S HOUSE, ARLINGTON.

Crossing over to the other great pile of granite, one comes into an atmosphere of money and the evidences of wealth which probably no other building contains. Here are between two and three thousand people, men and women, busy with figuring and settling accounts. In the vaults there are a hundred and fifty millions of hard cash; this is not shown to visitors, but must be accepted on the faith of the monthly Treasury statement. But in the safes of the National Bank division there are over three hundred millions of dollars in bonds, deposited there to cover the circulation of the banks. They are piled up in brown paper parcels, and visitors who are properly accredited sometimes amuse themselves by holding five millions or more in one hand. Going down a quarter of a mile to a new brick building on the banks of the Potomac, under the shadow of the now nearly completed Washington monument, one may see this paper money and bonds and stamps in every stage of its manufacture — the making of the paper, the mixing of the inks, the engraving of the plates, the printing, numbering, cutting, and counting. It is like any other four-story factory, yet even to the most philosophical mind there is a certain interest in the wholesale manufacture of money — or its representative.

Just across the street from this building, in the midst of a park most elaborately laid out, is the Department of Agriculture, where the theoretical farmer can learn all the processes of the latest experiments in agriculture, from the culture of expensive tea to the improvement of the common potato. In the continuation of the same park are seen two large buildings, side by side: one a graceful Gothic structure of dark sandstone, and the other a modern heap of red, blue, and yellow bricks. One is the Smithsonian Institution and the other the National Museum. The latter building covers five acres under one roof, and is the best stocked museum in this country, though it is yet far behind its foreign rivals.

And so the sightseer can go on, inspecting Washington's old clothes and camp chest, surrounded by countless models of machines at the Patent Office; penetrating the mysteries of weather predictions at the Signal Office; looking at pictures in the Corcoran Gallery; examining skeletons at the Army Medical

SOLDIERS' GRAVES, ARLINGTON.

Museum; driving out northward to the Soldiers' Home to get a bird's-eye view of the city from the hills which form its northern boundary; and finally, riding across the Potomac to Arlington to see the beautiful home which Lee left after so long and painful a struggle between his duty to his country and to his State, where now his majestic oaks look down on long lines of white headstones, covering those who laid down their lives in the great war with no reward save that

> "On Fame's eternal camping-ground
> Their snowy tents are spread,
> And Glory guards with solemn round
> The bivouac of the dead."

To such sightseeing there is no limit, so long as curiosity and physical strength remain unabated. But after all it is the people which form the chief attraction of any place. And Washington is the place of all others to study America and the Americans. It has no local types of its own; it is simply cosmopolitan and representative of every type, from Michigan to Texas, and from Maine to California. Here these types meet every year in closer fellowship, every year broadened by mutual intercourse and a better knowledge of each other's characteristics, and ever more and more mindful of the great destiny which binds them all together into one mighty whole. Here one may gain faith to believe — what is usually disputed — that America has an individuality of its own, not Anglo-Saxon, but distinctly American, as different from that of England as France from Italy; to perceive the slow but incessant process by which this individuality is losing its angularities and its dissimilarities and becoming shapely and homogeneous; to realize that the New World, having risen to might and power, is ceasing to consider

> "This Western giant coarse,
> Scorning refinements which he lacks himself,"

as its highest type, and is gradually evolving a society of its own, not founded on caste or wealth, yet not lacking in grace or refinement. It is different from other society, and is well worth study.

The White House
(1884)

THE CENTURY MAGAZINE.

APRIL, 1884.

THE WHITE HOUSE.

THERE is a deal of architecture in Washington — Doric, Ionic, Corinthian, Composite, Elizabethan, Gothic, Norman, African too,— an amazing jumble of styles borrowed from all nations and all ages; but among it all there is no building quite as satisfying to my eye as the White House, with a reservation to the prejudice of the northern portico, which was added when the structure was repaired after the British invasion of 1814; but happily the portico is half hidden by the foliage of noble trees.

There is no sham or pretense about the house; none of the straining after striking effects, which is the fault of so many of our modern constructions; no effort to look like a temple, or a cathedral, or a castle. It tries to be a spacious and dignified dwelling and nothing more, and in this it is entirely successful. The public-office feature, which has converted many of its rooms into tramping and lounging places for office-seekers and political plotters, was no part of the original plan, but has come from the modern system, introduced in a small way by President Jackson, and since grown to monstrous dimensions, under which nine-tenths of a President's working hours are devoted to hearing and considering the applications of place-hunters. The mansion would now be adequate to all the domestic and social uses of a republican chief magistrate, if other quarters were found for the business of the Executive office.

When James Hoban, the Irish architect, who had established himself in Charleston, and was building substantial houses on the Battery for South Carolina planters and tradesmen of that town, received notice that his plan for the President's house had been adopted, he hastened to Washington to claim the prize of five hundred dollars, and to take charge of the erection of the building. Hoban had not seen much of the world, and had modeled his plan pretty closely upon one of the best houses he knew — that of the Duke of Leinster, in Dublin. The Duke's house was in imitation of one of those spacious and stately villas which the Italians learned to build when the rest of Europe was living in uncouth piles of brick or gloomy fortified castles. Indeed, the world has not improved much to this day on the Italian house of the middle ages, save in inventions for water-pipes, warming, and lighting. Thick walls secured warmth in winter and coolness in summer; the windows were made to admit plenty of air and sunlight, the wide doors for ingress and egress, without jostling, of people walking by twos or threes; the stairs were easy to climb, the rooms high, well-proportioned, and of a size fitted for their several uses. Thus was the White House built. The corner-stone was laid in 1792, in a bare field sloping to the Potomac, the Masons conducting the ceremonial and George Washington gracing the occasion. At first it was proposed to call it the Palace, but against this suggestion a lively protest was made by people who feared the young Republic would be governed by an aristocracy aping the ways of courts and kings; so it was determined by Congress that the building should be officially named the "Executive Mansion"—mansion being then a term of common use for the better-class dwellings of the gentry in Virginia and Maryland. It would be hard to say when the name White House was first applied to it, but it did not, probably, gain currency until the edifice was rebuilt after the British soldiers had partly destroyed it, and was painted white to hide the black traces of smoke and flame upon the freestone walls.

President John Adams, Washington's immediate successor, was the first occupant of the Mansion; and everybody has read, in Mrs. Adams's letters, how she used the unfinished East Room for drying clothes, and of the literal "house-warming" she made to take the dampness out of the walls, with no end of trouble to obtain fire-wood enough for the purpose. This East Room, by the way, was intended for a banqueting hall; and here we have a souvenir of the aristocratic notions of the Virginians and South Carolinians of that day. Hoban must have been encouraged in his idea that a President of the United States would occasionally give a mighty feast, like those given by kings and princes and powerful noblemen in the Old World. Probably neither he nor Washington, whom he must have consulted, imagined that the room would be needed, and besides be much too small, for the miscellaneous crowd which, in another generation, would overflow the Mansion at public receptions.

When the British army, under General Ross and Admiral Cockburn, came marching across the country from the Patuxent River, in August, 1814, scattering like sheep the militia drawn up at Bladensburg, and taking possession of the raw, rambling, uncouth village of Washington, the White House was still unfinished—an unsightly pile standing in the midst of ill-kept grounds, surrounded by a cheap paling fence. After the soldiers had burned the Capitol, and just as they were about to countermarch to their ships, having pillaged the house quite at their leisure for twenty-four hours, they brought fire from a beer shop and set it ablaze, and then trudged off quite merrily in the light of the conflagration till caught in the historic thunderstorm of that summer night, which so pelted and battered them that they thought it was the wrath of Heaven upon their vandalism. There is only one memento of the fire in the House to-day—the picture of Washington which hangs in the East Room—once called a Gilbert Stuart, but now known to be the work of an English artist of no fame, who copied faithfully Stuart's style. The fraud was not discovered until some time after the original had been shipped to England—too late to recover it. Every visitor is told that Mrs. Madison cut this painting out of its frame with a pair of shears, to save it from the enemy when she fled from the town; but in her own letter describing the hasty flight, she says that Mr. Custis, the nephew of Mrs. Washington, hastened over from Arlington to rescue the precious portrait, and that a servant cut the outer frame with an axe, so that the canvas could be removed, stretched on the inner frame. The story of the shears is a pretty one, but, like so many other entertaining historical anecdotes, is a fiction.

There is probably no building in the world where, in less than a century, more of history has centered than in this shining, white mansion, screened by trees on the city side, and looking out from its southern windows

REAR VIEW OF THE WHITE HOUSE, FROM NEAR THE GREENHOUSE—TREASURY BUILDING IN THE DISTANCE

THE WHITE HOUSE, FROM THE FRONT.

across the placid Potomac to the red Virginian hills. Twenty-one Presidents have lived in it, and two have died in it. One went from its Red Room with a group of friends, at the close of the four years' civil war, to be struck down by an assassin's bullet in a theater, and to be carried unconscious to a death-bed in a strange house. One, in full mid-current of life, sturdy of brain and body, and glowing with patriotic purposes, was shot in a railway station and carried up the vine-bordered steps shown in the picture, to languish through weeks of pain, struggling manfully with death, all the world looking on with a universal sympathy never before shown to mortal man, to be borne, as a last hope, to the sea-side, and there to die.

There have been marriages and merry-makings too, jovial feasts, and ceremonial banquets; grave councils of state that shaped the destiny of the nation; secret intrigues and midnight conclaves that made or unmade political parties; war councils that flashed forth orders, on telegraphic wires, which moved great armies and set lines of battle in deadly front. The history of the White House is a governmental and political history of the United States from 1800 to this day; it is also a history of the domestic lives, the ambitions, and the personal traits of twenty-one Presidents, their families, and their near friends and advisers. I shall attempt no part of it here, and shall only remark, in passing to a survey of the building itself, that it has left few traces behind in the way of memories or traditions in the Mansion. The history must be sought out piecemeal in libraries. One cannot even learn which was the room where Harrison died, after his brief four weeks of power, or where bluff, honest Zachary Taylor, the "Rough and Ready" of the Mexican war, breathed his last. The few traditions that cling to the house are incongruous mosaics of tragedy and gayety. "Here," says an attendant, pointing to a particular place on the carpet in the East Room, "is where Lincoln lay in his coffin; and here"—moving a few steps away—"is where Nellie Grant stood when she was married to the young Englishman, Sartoris." Your attention is called to the smoked-blue color of the furniture in the Blue Room, and you are informed that at such a place the President usually stands at receptions, and in the next breath are told that "this is the window where they brought poor Garfield in after he was shot, taking him up the back-stairs because of the crowd in front."

It seems as if the memory of the two martyred Presidents were alone destined to haunt the White House, all others fading away with the lapse of time. Indeed, if one wants to find some trace of the angular and resolute personality of Jackson, or of the polite and graceful Van Buren, or of that hardy soldier Zachary Taylor, or even of occupants as late as the courtly Buchanan, he will be disappointed; and a still more recent President, Grant, finds his permanent fame dependent far more upon his career as a general than on that as chief magistrate, and has left in the building he occupied for eight years few memories that are still fresh. The White House is, in fact, an official hotel. The guests come and go, and when they leave they take with them, along with their trunks, whatever of personality they diffused through its stately apartments while they remained. Some have lived in the house in the spirit of a freehold owner, sure of undisturbed possession; some, like short-term tenants, never feeling quite at home. Of the latter were the family of President Johnson, one of whose daughters said: "We are plain people from the mountains of Tennessee, called here for a time by a great national calamity. We hope too much will not be expected of us." Whether proud or modest in their temper or belongings, however, the Presidents, when once they have surrendered the reins of power, soon drop back into the dim and ghostly procession of their predecessors. One of the saddest spectacles connected with official life in Washington, and one to which no pen has done adequate justice, is the hasty packing of the effects of an outgoing President just before the fateful fourth of March which ends his power. After noon of that day the family has no more right there than the passing stranger on the street; and while the cannon are firing salvos of welcome to the new President, and the long procession is moving up Pennsylvania Avenue to the Capitol front, where he is to be inaugurated, the White House family are gathering their personal effects together and taking last looks at the rooms where they have been honored and courted and flattered for years, the delightful sense of greatness and power they have enjoyed so long now cut short in a single day.

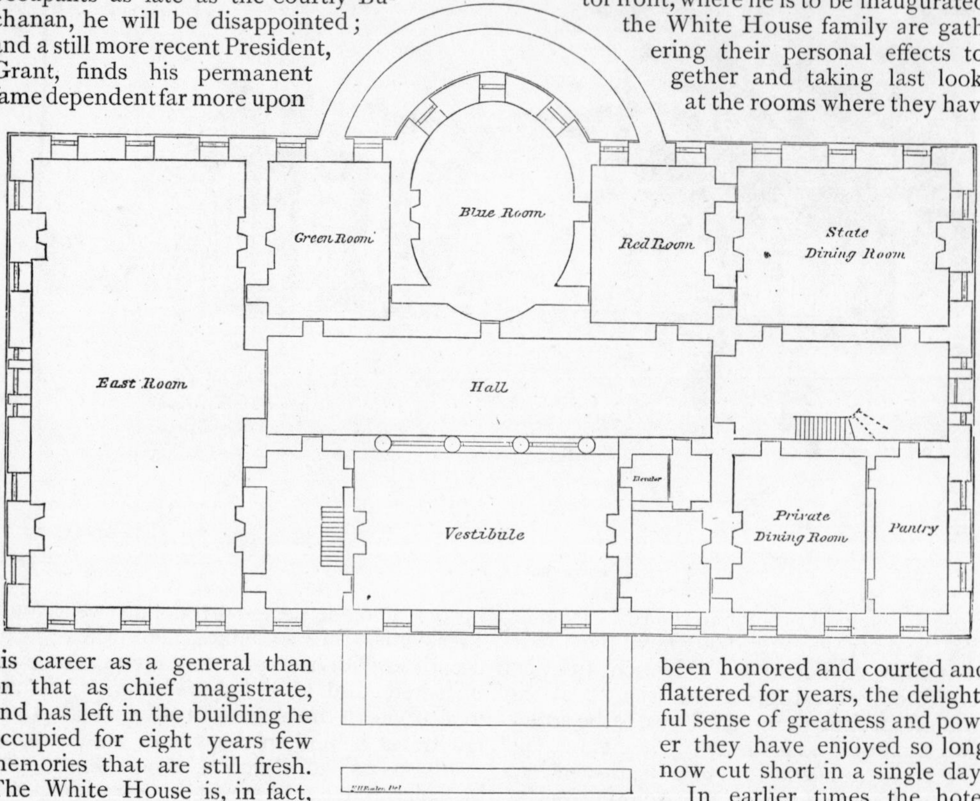

GROUND PLAN OF THE WHITE HOUSE.

In earlier times the hotel character of the Mansion was well reflected in the stiff, formal, half-furnished appearance of the rooms. It was thought enough to have thick carpets on the floors, and strong furniture and a few decorative pieces, too heavy to be carried off by servants during the quadrennial migration; but of late Mr. Louis C. Tiffany's decorative association has metamorphosed the place, and made the smaller rooms look like the abode of people of luxurious tastes. Perhaps the most successful of all this new work is in the long corridor, which leads from the East Room to the Conservatory, and from which open the Red, Green, and Blue Rooms. The light coming through the partition of wrinkled stained-glass mosaic makes a marvelously rich and gorgeous effect, falling upon the gilded niches where stand dwarf palmetto trees, the silvery net-work of the ceiling, and the sumptuous furniture. Indeed, the

THE WAITING-ROOM.

only dark tints in the apartment are found in the portraits, which become the more conspicuous by reason of their contrast with their brilliant setting. Only one of these need arrest our attention now — the full-length portrait of Garfield, by Andrews. The artist, seeking to give the face the dignified statesman-like expression which is supposed to be essential in Presidential portraits, has almost lost sight of the genial, buoyant, warm-hearted character which lay at the bottom of the man's nature. No one looking at the picture of Lincoln in the Red Room would gather from the face the hearty love of jest and anecdote, the tender pity for suffering and distress, and the warm fraternal sympathy, which lit up the homely features with the interior beauty of a kindly soul; and I fear coming generations of visitors who pass through this grand corridor will see nothing in the stern, sad face of Garfield to remind them that here was a man who loved to play croquet and romp with his boys upon his lawn at Mentor, who read Tennyson and Longfellow at fifty with as much enthusiastic pleasure as at twenty, who walked at evening with his arm around the neck of a friend in affectionate conversation, and whose sweet, sunny, loving nature not even twenty years of political strife could warp.

The Red Room, used as a reception parlor by the ladies of the President's household, already had a home-like look, from the presence of a piano, a handsome embroidered fire-screen (a present from the Austrian commissioners at the Centennial Exhibition), and some small adornments; and in the recent general renovation of the Mansion, it has been given an imposing carved-wood mantel of thirteenth century style, set off with tiling of tortoise-shell glass. Some beautiful work has been done, besides, in the ceiling and in the walls, and the whole effect of carpet, furniture, and wall-tints is exceedingly rich and warm. Opening from this room is the State Dining-room, only used when large companies are entertained at dinner — a rather chilling apartment, in spite of the glowing yellows Mr. Tiffany has given to the walls. In early times this room was called the "company dining-room," to distinguish it from the family dining-room across the hall. The long table seats thirty-eight persons. In the middle sits the President, and opposite him the mistress of the Mansion. No order of precedence is observed in going in to dinner, or in seating the guests. Something of this sort was attempted in early times, but abandoned as not practicable, and perhaps also as not sensible, in a country with democratic institutions. These state dinners are rather dull affairs. The cold-water régime lasted four years, and has left behind an interesting souvenir in the fine portrait of Mrs. Hayes, by Huntington, which stands in the Green Room, and was presented to the Government by the Women's National Temperance Association, the money ($3,500) being raised by a general subscription. With the exception of a small picture of Mrs. Tyler, which hangs in the corridor on the second floor, this is the only portrait of a President's wife to be found in the Mansion.

If a description of upholstery were of any interest, we might linger in the Green and Blue rooms to speak of the manner in which their historic hues have been preserved in the invasion of the modern zeal for decoration. The East Room has not been much changed since President Grant's time, when the ceiling was broken into three panels by heavy beams supported by columns, and the profuse gilding was done. The ebony and old-gold furniture and the "greenery yallery" carpet are new. Gilding and color have been lavished of late all over the White House. Even the heavy iron railings in front of the house are tipped with gold, and the bomb-shells, supported on iron tripods, glisten like the balls of a pawnbroker's shop. In one of these bombs, during the war-time, a pair of birds built a nest, and gave John James Piatt a theme for his well-known poem.

The upper floor of the Mansion is approached by two stair-ways, one leading from the grand corridor, used only by the family and their guests, and the other coming down from the office part of the building to the small hall between the vestibule and the East Room, forming a general passage-way for all people having business with the President or his secretaries. A broad hall runs from end to end of the second story, terminating in semicircular windows; but the fine effect of the ample length and width of this corridor is spoiled by two low cross partitions: one long ago put in as a necessity to keep the throng of Congressmen and place-hunters from blundering into the family rooms, the other a cheap affair, looking as if it came second-hand from some junk-shop, erected lately to gain an additional office-room. It was no part of the plan of the White House, as we have said, that it should be a public office; but with the growth of the country and of the political patronage system, the proper use of the building as a dwelling for the chief magistrate has been more and more subordinated to its official use as a bureau of appointments and a rendezvous for the scheming politicians of the two Houses of Congress, who claim the Government offices in their States as their personal property, to

THE WHITE HOUSE BY NIGHT.

IN THE RED ROOM.

be parceled out by the President in accordance with their wishes. It will doubtless surprise many people to learn that hospitality, save in the restricted sense of giving dinners, is almost an impossibility to the President of the United States, for the reason that he has no beds for guests. There are only seven sleeping rooms in the Mansion, besides those of the servants on the basement floor. If a President has a moderately numerous household, as General Grant, Mr. Hayes, and Mr. Garfield had, he can hardly spare for guests more than the big state bedroom. A President may wish to invite an ambassador and his family, or a party of distinguished travelers from abroad, to spend a few days at the White House, but he cannot do so without finding lodgings elsewhere for members of his own household. It has been said over and over again, in the press, that Congress should either provide offices for the President, or should build for him a new dwelling, and devote the Mansion exclusively to business purposes; but Congress is in no hurry to do either.

The present office system in the White House is an affair of quite recent growth. Before President Johnson's time, no records or files were kept, and there were no clerks. President Lincoln had two secretaries, Mr. Nicolay and Colonel Hay; but the law recognized only one, the other being an army officer detailed for special service, —any extra clerical work being done by clerks detailed from one of the departments. Now there are four rooms occupied by the private secretary and his staff of clerks. Big ledgers of applications for office are posted up daily, numerous pigeon-holes are filled with letters and petitions, the newspapers are read and scrap-books made, one room is devoted to telegraph and telephone service; in short, here are all the paraphernalia of a busy public office. One of the files of letters would furnish curious reading to students of human nature. It is called the eccentric file, and contains the epistles of advice, warning, and "gush" mailed to the President by cranks, fanatics, absurd egotists, and would-be philanthropists; and how numerous these peculiar people are, only those in high station know. A President gets two or three hundred letters a day, and probably not one-fourth of them are upon any subject that can properly be brought directly to his personal notice.

One might well suppose that in the White House, where the clerks and servants come into close relations with the President, there would be numerous changes with each new administration; indeed, there would be more excuse for rotation in office here than in any other branch of the Government, for a President might naturally prefer to have old friends in whom he had learned to confide in care of his house and correspondence; but the wise rule of service during good behavior obtains here to a greater extent than in any one of the departments, except perhaps the Department of State. One of the servants dates back to Fillmore's administration, and has seen thir-

A CORNER OF THE STATE DINING-ROOM.

ty years of service; one of the clerks and one of the door-keepers were appointed by Lincoln; others came in under Grant. The private secretary is, of course, always the personal friend and confidant of the President, and goes out with his chief; but the rest of the staff remains, as a rule, and constitutes an efficient working force, familiar with the precedents, customs, and etiquette of the Presidential office, and very valuable on this account to a man entering upon its trying duties.

IN THE CONSERVATORY.

Visitors who have business with the President wait in the antechamber, or walk impatiently back and forth in the hall. The President receives in the Cabinet Room—not the historic room where Lincoln signed the Proclamation of Emancipation. Mr. Johnson converted that into the private secretary's room, and took the former anteroom for the Cabinet meetings. At the door stands a quiet, sagacious, gray-haired man, who has an instinct for distinguishing people of consequence from the general multitude. Senators, judges, governors, and other men of note find their cards taken directly to the President; persons of small account are referred to a polite man of color, who is the warden of the private secretary's door. Their business must be explained to the secretary, and few of them ever get any nearer to the seat of power. The hours for callers are from ten to one, save on the days of regular Cabinet meetings. In the afternoon the President sees visitors by special appointment, and most of his evenings are filled in the same way,—the business in ninety-nine cases out of a hundred concerning the disposition of offices. The late President Garfield once said that he was obliged to see an average of about thirty persons for every office to be filled. If the question was one of removal, the number was much greater, including the friends of the incumbent as well as the candidates for the place. There is an amusing story, not a new one by any means, of the method Mr. Lincoln adopted to settle a contest over a postmastership which had greatly annoyed him. There were two candidates in the field, and petition after petition had poured in upon the weary President, and delegation after delegation had rushed to the White House to argue the claims of the rival aspirants. Finally, after he had been bored for half an hour by a fresh delegation, Mr. Lincoln said to his secretary, "This matter has got to end somehow. Bring

THE LIBRARY.

a pair of scales." The scales were brought. "Now put in all the petitions and letters in favor of one man, and see how much they weigh, and then weigh the other candidate's papers." It was found that one bundle was three-quarters of a pound heavier than the other. "Make out the appointment at once for the man who has the heaviest papers," ordered the President, and it was done.

There is no necessity for a President giving up nine-tenths of his working hours to the consideration of claims to office, thus unfitting himself for the study of public questions, and depriving himself of time which should be given to social intercourse with men of ideas and high public station. The Constitution says he shall make appointments, but it also says he shall be commander-in-chief of the army. He is no more required to examine petitions and hear applications concerning all the post-offices, consulates, and collectorships, than he is to buckle on a saber, mount a horse, and maneuver the troops. All the details of

THE WHITE HOUSE, FROM NEAR THE TREASURY.

Social life at the White House varies with different adminstrations. A tendency toward making it less public and more discriminating is noticeable of late years. President Johnson gave a public reception once a week during the winter season, and even in the stress and agony of the war-time President Lincoln shook hands with a mob of two or three thousand people surging through the Mansion as often as once a fortnight. Now, one or two public receptions during a session of Congress are thought a sufficient concession to the democratic principle. A New-Year's Day reception is demanded by the unbroken custom of three-quarters of a century. First, the members of the diplomatic corps present themselves in all the splendors of court dress—the only occasion when they can display the uniforms, cocked hats, gold lace, and decorations of that costume, without being mistaken for people on their way to a masquerade ball; then come the Senators and Congressmen, officers of the army and navy, and last, the public in general and in mass, going in at the door and out of a window on a temporary bridge. Once or twice each season, a reception to Senators and Representatives in Congress and their families is given. For these occasions cards are usually sent out. Not long ago this custom was disregarded, and in place of cards an announcement of the event was published in one of the newspapers. The witty wife of an Eastern member of Congress, who attended the reception, said, when presented to the host, "Mr. President, you advertised for me, and I am here."

THE PORTICO.

appointment business should be left to the members of the Cabinet, whose recommendations should be final, except in relation to a few of the most important offices, such as foreign missions, high posts in the military and naval service, and perhaps a few of the great collecting agencies in the chief cities which supply the Treasury with the greater part of its funds. Some day there will come to the White House a man of strong will and of a lofty patriotic purpose, with no relish for wielding personal power in the distribution or refusal of official favors; and he, revolutionizing the customs of the Executive office, which are stronger than law, will resolutely shut his door upon all place-hunters and their advocates in Congress, and be the President of the people and not the President of the office-seekers and office-holders.

Formerly it was thought the duty of the President to invite each Senator and member of Congress to dinner once a year; but as the two Houses have grown in their membership,

WEST WINDOW. (NEW DESIGN.)

this burdensome custom has fallen into disuse. President Johnson was the last to adhere to it. If a President's dinner invitations include, in a single season, the Senators, the Justices of the Supreme Court, the members of the Cabinet, the foreign ministers, and a sprinkling of influential members of the lower House and distinguished officers of the army and navy, he is now thought to have done his duty in this direction with sufficient liberality. Much the best of White House sociability is found at informal dinners and lunches, at which only a few guests are present with the President's family, and at evenings "at home," for which no cards are sent out. Then there is conversation and music, and one may meet a score of famous men with their wives and daughters. Some Presidents are remembered for the number of their state dinners, others for their receptions, and others for the cordial social tone they gave to the life of the Mansion by small entertainments, by being accessible to all the world, and by making people feel at home. Each Presidential household has modified in some degree the customs of the place to suit its own tastes and habits. Perhaps the most important innovation on long-established precedent was made by General Grant, who broke through the traditional etiquette which forbade a President to make visits. Formerly a President saw the inside of no house but his own, and was in some sort a prisoner during his term of office. He could drive out or go to the theater, but he could not make a social call, or attend a reception at a friend's house. Now he goes to weddings and parties, makes calls, and dines out, as freely as any other citizen. Indeed, the tendency of White House customs is toward less formality, and more ease and freedom of social intercourse, rather than in the other direction; and this is remarkable at its coachman and footmen in powdered wigs and its white horses with blackened hoofs, would make a sensation on Pennsylvania Avenue in these modern times. It is safe to say that no chief magistrate nowadays, entertaining any hope of reëlection, would venture to make a display in servants, equipage, or mode of living. The ado made over Martin Van Buren's gold spoons in the political campaign of 1840 has not been forgotten.

CORNER OF THE EAST ROOM.

a time when our new moneyed aristocracy is aping the manners of courts and surrounding itself with liveried flunkies. No servant at the White House wears a livery, unless the coachman's coat can be called such. It is often easier to get an interview with the President of the United States than with the editor of a metropolitan daily newspaper, or the president of a great railroad company. The ways of the Executive Mansion are much simpler now than in the days of the first Presidents. Washington's gilded coach, with The country is wiser than it was then, and makes no outcry about the sumptuous decorations or elegant table furniture in the White House; but if the servants who attend the front door should appear one day in livery, the innovation would be condemned. Presidents no longer smoke corn-cob pipes as Andrew Jackson did, or take whisky at dinner, or put their feet on the table while talking with visitors — a rudeness I have myself seen within the last twenty years; but they are expected to be quiet, unpretentious

THE CABINET ROOM.

gentlemen in their manners and surroundings, and nothing more nor less. Wielding more real power to-day than any sovereign in Europe, save the Czar and the Sultan, they must avoid all the pomp and ceremony of courts, and meet people face to face with a shake of the hand and a "How d'ye do?" like plain citizens. No coats of arms adorn their coach panels, and no soldiers clear the way or ride at their heels. In the war period, when Lincoln rode out to his summer residence on the hills near the city, he was attended by a cavalry detachment; but this was necessary for his protection in a time of raids, surprises, and murderous plots. Since the war, no President has had a body-guard. Even the two cavalrymen who used to wait at the White House portal, to ride with messages to the Capitol or the departments, have disappeared since the telephone came into use.

Looking at the portraits of the "Ladies of the White House" in a volume recently published, and reading the meager annals of their lives, one cannot resist the conclusion that Presidents' wives, with few exceptions, have been simple matrons who on their elevation to the first social station in the country have performed their duties creditably, with that ready adaptation to new conditions which is so marked a peculiarity of American women. In recent times there has been a mistress of the Mansion who taught her boys Latin and Greek and read the best of current literature, and another who is remembered for her kindly and cordial ways and earnest interest in charities and reforms. One has left a tradition of elegant manners; one never appeared in public, but lived in seclusion, devoted to domestic duties, and making with her own hands butter from the milk of a favorite cow.

Coming back now from the social life of the White House to the house itself, let us note that the family sitting-room and parlor is the oval library above the Blue Room — a spacious and comfortable apartment; that the second room beyond is the bedroom occupied by Lincoln and Grant, and the one made historic by Garfield's long suffering; that President Arthur occupies as a bedroom a chamber across the hall looking toward Pennsylvania Avenue, and has fitted up for a private office one of the adjoining chambers, where he works late at night; and that the broad corridor between the two lines of sleeping-rooms is used as picture gallery, promenade, and smoking-room. The Executive Mansion, in these modern days of wealth, luxury, and display, appears a small and modest dwelling for the chief magistrate of fifty millions of people.

E. V. Smalley.

Our Fellow-Citizen of the White House (1897)

THE CENTURY MAGAZINE

MARCH, 1897.

OUR FELLOW-CITIZEN OF THE WHITE HOUSE.

THE OFFICIAL CARES OF A PRESIDENT OF THE UNITED STATES.

A PRESIDENT who should not carry into the White House a relish for drudgery, business habits of the nicest discrimination, and a constitution of iron, would be President only in name, even as regards his more important duties. His signature on the papers which he is told will not otherwise be legal might be as good as the custodian of his bank account would require, but within the meaning of the law it would be as often as not a moral forgery. Yet no complaint should be offered on this account. Presidents are made for better or for worse. Such as they are in natural faculties and strength, so they must serve—some of them leaning on official advisers and bureaucratic clerks in every step they take; and some of them putting the stamp of their own individuality on the papers and acts which make up an administration.

When a President-elect, facing the Chief Justice, has repeated the Constitutional oath, « I do solemnly swear that I will faithfully execute the office of President of the United States, and will, to the best of my ability, preserve, protect, and defend the Constitution of the United States,» he has indentured himself for four years of the heaviest servitude that ever fell to the lot of any mortal. By comparison the « hired man » talked about in the last canvass would lead a pampered existence, and a constitutional monarch is a man of leisure. A President equal to his oath is both king and premier; he reigns and he rules; he is bowed down by the crown of authority and is encompassed by the mantle of care.

A paragraph in the first article of the Constitution, and the section in the second article following the oath, define the meaning of a promise to « execute the office of President.» As commander-in-chief of the army and navy he is accountable to the people for the personnel and efficiency of both services; he is the supervisor of the acts of the members of

DRAWN BY JAY HAMBIDGE.

THE WHITE HOUSE AT NIGHT, FROM THE EAST CARRIAGE ENTRANCE.

the cabinet, who are the heads of the executive departments; with him rests the power to grant reprieves and pardons; on him devolves the responsibility of our relations with all other nations; with few exceptions among the higher officers, and not including the minor clerks, who are responsible to the heads of departments, he must select men to fill all vacancies in the vast army of public officials, from a judge of the Supreme Court to a third-rate postmaster. Furthermore, after the selections have been made he must undergo the clerical drudgery of signing every nomination and commission; and finally, it is his duty to sit in judgment on all legislation, to impart information to the houses of Congress on the state of the Union, and to suggest measures necessary to the furtherance of the domestic and foreign policy of his administration. Even in Lincoln's time, with a powerful majority behind him, the legislative feature of the President's rule was a galling care; and it is only four years since a retiring President compared that particular task confronting his successor to the driving of «a team of wild horses.» Such are the President's obligations to the government as defined in the fundamental law; yet they do not include a great many collateral cares. When the Constitution, which Mr. Gladstone has called «the most wonderful work ever struck off at a given time by the brain and purpose of man,» was framed in 1787, the population of the United States was three and a quarter millions, or only half as numerous as that of the State of New York at the present time. If it may be said that under the original instrument a President is still able to shepherd seventy million souls, it is also undeniable that a large distribution of his cares to responsible officers is inevitable and near at hand.

After a fellow-citizen has been, as it were, condemned to the herculean task, he looks about him for a man whose tact will serve for a private secretary, and whose capacity will master the crowd of the anteroom and the rushing stream of executive business. As a rule, the stress of the canvass has brought the right man to the right hand of the President-elect. This was true of Lincoln's secretary, Mr. Nicolay, who also conformed to a view which frequently commends a trained journalist to that office. General Horace Porter accompanied his war chief to the executive mansion as «military secretary,» though General Grant once said jocosely, «I suppose in a railway company he would be called Assistant President»; Mr. Phillips had been private secretary to General Arthur as collector of the port of New York; while Daniel S. Lamont is an example of a jour-

PHOTOGRAPH BY GEORGE C. COX.

PRIVATE SECRETARY THURBER AT HIS DESK.

nalist who has stood on every rung of the ladder of executive advisement. As chief clerk in the office of Secretary of State under John Bigelow during the administrations of Governors Tilden and Robinson, and as secretary of the Democratic State Committee of New York, he revealed tact and energy which marked him as the fittest man for private secretary to Governor Cleveland; and when the latter broke the spell which for a generation had barred Democratic candidates from the White House, his secretary accepted the same office with the higher responsibility. On the return of Mr. Cleveland to the White House in 1893, Mr. Lamont again became an official adviser as Secretary of War, the only other man who has passed from the laborious anteroom to executive functions being Lincoln's assistant private secretary, Colonel John Hay, who, after long diplomatic service abroad, was Assistant Secretary of State under President Hayes. In view of the unusualness of Mr. Lamont's promotion from the inner circle of executive experience, it is worthy of note that army officers give him credit for being the only civilian secretary in their generation who has mastered the complex details of that department, instead of being largely a signature clerk to the heads of the different bureaus.

For his new private secretary President Cleveland went to his own profession, choosing Mr. Henry T. Thurber, a law partner of his former Postmaster-General, Don M. Dickinson of Michigan, who has filled this difficult position with most essential cheerfulness and courtesy. When it became known that Mr. Lamont would not return to his former position, it is said that a journalistic caller undertook to do Mr. Cleveland a service by way of suggestion.

«We are hoping,» said the journalist, «that

DRAWN BY JAY HAMBIDGE.

HALL BETWEEN THE PRESIDENT'S OFFICES ON A BUSY DAY.

you will appoint a man who will be good to us newspaper men.»

«I had a notion,» replied the President-elect, «of appointing a man who would be good to me.»

Cabinet-making is a more difficult matter. A private secretary, it is safe to assume, will adapt himself to the views and methods of his chief; but the official advisers of the cabinet, according to their political stature and idiosyncrasy, are liable to have policies of their own, or even ambitions, which will not exactly dovetail one with another around the council-table. Mr. Lincoln, with a wisdom suited to a peculiar emergency, gathered about him his political rivals, who were to some extent rivals among themselves; but in discomforting one another they very largely spared him, and their abilities were so extraordinary that the work he had in hand prospered in spite of family jars. The one who persisted in presidential aspirations, Mr. Chase, finally left the cabinet, and suffered the usual failure of aspirants for the chieftaincy by way of the cabinet door. Mr. Blaine's success in securing the nomination was no exception to the rule, for he left the cabinet a few months after the tragic succession of President Arthur, and by securing the nomination in 1884 effected the latter's humiliation. A different outcome to the indomitable secretary's candidacy of 1892 was partly due, no doubt, to his position in the cabinet and to President Harrison's determination that his official family should be loyal to him or wage open warfare on the outside. Blaine's resignation came late, but none the less it placed him in the position of a secessionist whose following was in a minority.

By contrast, President Cleveland's two cabinets have proved not only free from these ambitions, but also remarkably harmonious and single in purpose. Evidently they were chosen for work. Each of his cabinets has shown the coöperation of strong individualities with complete subordination to the official head. It is safe to say that more industrious cabinets, reflecting the disposition of the President, were never gathered around the council-table.

Even when political reasons do not shape the choice of a cabinet officer, a deference to the geography of the nation is always discernible. Aspirants are expected to be as mum and as coy as a maiden pining for a young man, and as a matter of fact they are not as persistent as those who aspire to the other offices; for tradition enforces upon a cabinet officer the attitude of conferring a favor; still a President is not wholly deprived of suggestions from the friends of willing statesmen; nor are the go-betweens always on the side of the wooer; and it will be remembered that the celebrated conferences at Mentor were attended by circumstances suggestive of the negotiations of a matrimonial agency.

Still, the official family of a President-elect is seldom known with accuracy before the inaugural day. A variety of tactful reasons prescribe this, and determine also the purely formal intercourse between the outgoing and incoming Presidents. For one thing, it is felt that a dignified aloofness on the part of a successful adversary is only a proper deference to the zeal of his supporters in belittling the expiring administration; and where the latter belongs to the same political party reasons of a more personal nature are apt to prevail. But this attitude seldom interferes with an exchange of pleasant courtesies; for instance, in 1885 President Arthur invited Mr. Cleveland to dine with him the night before the inauguration, but in this case Mr. Cleveland had made arrangements which compelled him to decline. In 1889 General and Mrs. Harrison dined with the President and Mrs. Cleveland, alone, on the eve of the transfer of power; and when Mr. and Mrs. Cleveland returned to Washington to resume their life in the White House, the same courtesy was extended to them, and with the same privacy.

On March 3, 1889, at an hour privately arranged by the secretaries, and according to the established usage, General Harrison and his private secretary, Mr. Halford, drove to the White House, and were received by President Cleveland and Mr. Lamont in the Blue Room, reserved for diplomatic and official courtesies. While the chief magistrates conferred for a moment, the secretaries exchanged greetings at one side, and the interview was soon over. About an hour later Mr. Cleveland and his secretary returned the call at the hotel. Four years later these civilities were repeated exactly, with the exception that the order was reversed, and Mr. Cleveland was accompanied by Mr. Thurber, this being the only instance in our history where a retiring President has succeeded his successor.

With the shifting of such gigantic cares there is a peculiar poverty of helpful suggestion; affairs of state are avoided with graceful dexterity. In receiving Mr. Cleveland, President Arthur alluded jocosely to the daily ordeal in store for his successor, and said: «You will suffer most from two classes of visitors: the man who desires to pay his respects, and the man who wants to catch a four-o'clock train.» Mr. Arthur had the reputation of holding a firm check on fellow-citizens with such aspirations, believing as he did that the personal comfort of a President had something to do with the dignity of the office.

When a ruler of the old royal order is installed with ostentatious joy, his predecessor is comfortably dead. But a President, who wields more power than most monarchs, is forced by custom to grace his successor's triumph; unless, like John Adams, he chooses to be frank with whatever feelings of disgust he may have for the new situation, and bolts the ordeal. On the way from the White House to the Capitol he occupies the right-hand seat of honor, but when the procession is ready to return he takes the seat of retired greatness on the left, and breathes more freely. Soon after reaching the White House the ex-President bows himself out into private life.

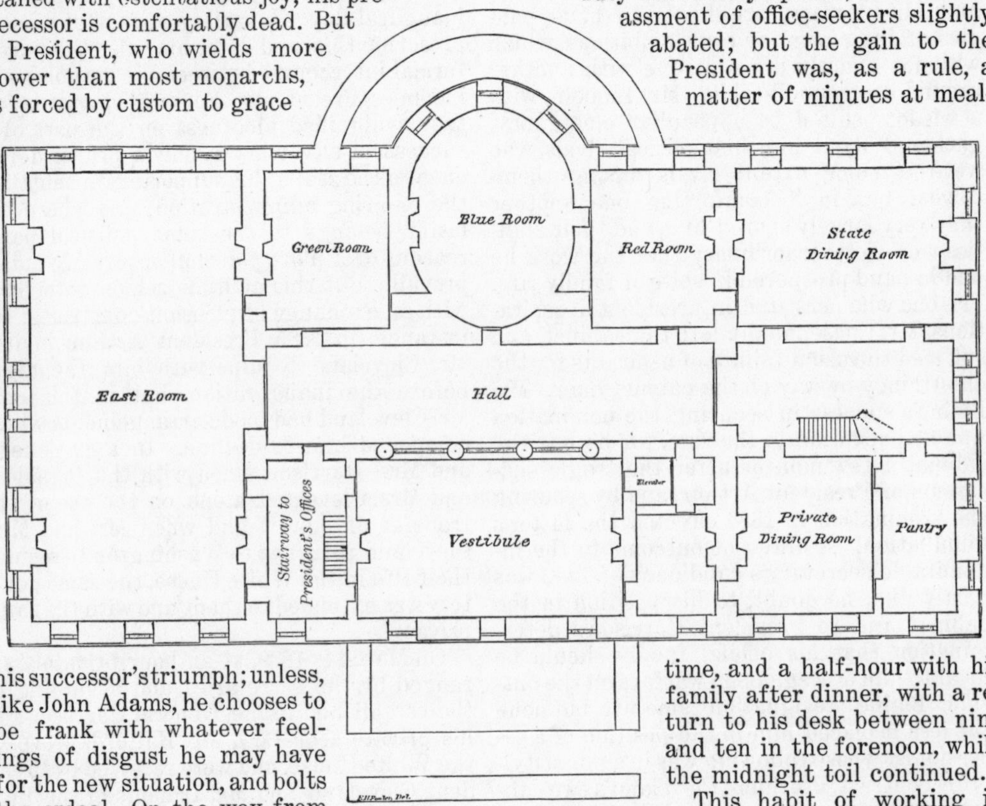

After the fatigue of reviewing the vast procession that followed him «home,» and of leading the promenade at the inauguration ball, the President is left alone in his glory, the first manifestation of which is a stack of boxes reaching half-way to the ceiling, filled with applications for office. Now he is President indeed. Those preliminary boxes, nearly every caller, letters by the thousand, and large willow trunks full of papers delivered with regularity from the departments, remind him that the United States expect every President to do his duty by the party which elected him. With a large experience of this sort of thing, extending over a longer series of years than ever before fell to the lot of an American executive, Mr. Cleveland began his second term with months of labor, broken each day in the small hours of the morning. By this effort the path of executive duty was merely opened, and the harassment of office-seekers slightly abated; but the gain to the President was, as a rule, a matter of minutes at meal-time, and a half-hour with his family after dinner, with a return to his desk between nine and ten in the forenoon, while the midnight toil continued.

GROUND PLAN OF THE WHITE HOUSE.

This habit of working in the quiet of midnight is the secret of Mr. Cleveland's ability to understand for himself the nature of every paper which receives his signature. It is a habit which he acquired in Buffalo, where his living-rooms were over his law offices, his tendency to a sedentary life heightening the attractions of midnight oil for reading and work that required quiet. First as sheriff, and then as mayor, these hours were devoted to the studious part of the public business; when he reached the gubernatorial mansion the habit had become a second nature; and on taking the reins of national government it alone enabled him to discharge his duty in the light in which he sees it—as a personal and literal responsibility. Accordingly, President Cleveland has been so little seen in Washington outside the White House for recreation or amusement, that in the minds of many credulous people his personality is shrouded in mystery. The mystery has attached even to the occasional outings for a little rest at shooting, the secrecy attending them being made necessary by the fact that little privacy is accorded him except by a dash through the pickets of the press for a government steamer and a disappearance into unsuspected waters; for if his coming were heralded, the object of the outing would be partly defeated by the well-meant attentions of the citizens of the neighborhood. In vacation time he enjoys the reputation of a devoted fisherman, whereas the daily package from the White House entails as much business, even at that season, as a man of ordinary strength would care to do in the active season. Providence and government never rest from their labors.

Within the White House there is no mystery except as to the copiousness of the work that is done. There is even little ceremony which would not be observed in an ordinary business house. The average citizen strolls up the imposing oval walk to the magnificent portico with the ease with which he would approach his own front door. His general view was indicated in the conversation of two young men approaching to examine the home surroundings of «our President.»

«It 's fine,» said one.

«*We* pay for all this,» said the other; «every time we smoke a cigar we help to keep it going.»

The only restriction on these gentle masters is that the cigar may not be smoked within the doors; and in fact there are but few freemen who do not leave their internal-revenue tobacco at the gates.

No soldier walks his beat before the portal, as before all executive offices and palaces in other lands. Several years ago, a Spanish gentleman who was being conducted over the lower floor in the hour when visitors were shown the state apartments, inquired in the dining-room after the immediate whereabouts of the President, the fact of his being in the room where that great personage actually dined implying to his mind executive absence. When told that at that moment the President was in the room overhead, he exclaimed with surprise, «But where are the soldiers?» When told that there never were any about the White House in the capacity of guards, his ideas of propriety underwent a shock.

There have been no soldiers as guardians under the shadow of the great Ionic columns since the war; and even then, on one fierce winter night, the boy in blue who was on guard was not allowed to maintain professional decorum. Mr. Lincoln emerged from the front door, his lank figure bent over as he drew tightly about his shoulders the shawl which he employed for such protection; for he was on his way to the War Department, at the west corner of the grounds, where in times of battle he was wont to get the midnight despatches from the field. As the blast struck him he thought of the numbness of the pacing sentry, and turning to him, said: «Young man, you 've got a cold job to-night; step inside, and stand guard there.»

«My orders keep me out here,» the soldier replied.

«Yes,» said the President, in his argumentative tone; «but your duty can be performed just as well inside as out here, and you 'll oblige me by going in.»

«I have been stationed outside,» the soldier answered, and resumed his beat.

«Hold on there!» said Mr. Lincoln, as he turned back again; «it occurs to me that I am commander-in-chief of the army, and I *order* you to go inside.»

At ten o'clock a hardly discernible sign against the glass of the barrier announces to the citizen who has arrived under the grand portal that the executive mansion is «open» to visitors; at two o'clock the sign is changed to «closed.» The doorkeepers swing the doors open to everybody. Within the large vestibule nothing is seen which indicates the arrangement and purposes of the different parts of the mansion. It was not always so, for originally the now concealed corridor, or middle hall, with the staircase on the right was a part of the entrance-hall; now the spaces between the middle columns are closed with colored-glass partitions, and the vestibule is simply a large square room pleasant to get out of. No way appears to open to the state apartments in the center, or to the west wing, which is devoted to the private apartments; yet glass doors are there, though as imperceptible to the stranger as a swinging panel. To the left there is a door which is always open. It admits to a small hall across which a similar door is the side entrance to the great East Room. About this splendid room, comprising the whole east end of the mansion, the visitor may wander at will before the portraits, or enjoy from the windows the beauty of the Treasury building to the east or the impressive landscape to the south, including the towering shaft of the Washington monument, and, beyond, the ever-charming Potomac spreading with enlarging curves toward Mount Vernon; and in the private garden under

DRAWN BY JAY HAMBIDGE. FROM A PHOTOGRAPH BY GEORGE C. COX.

ASSISTANT SECRETARY PRUDEN ARRANGING THE SEATING FOR A STATE DINNER.

the windows he may chance to see a merry band of little ones, two of them the President's older daughters, with a few playmates belonging to a kindergarten class.

From the small hall between the vestibule and the East Room a stairway ascends toward the medial line of the building to a wide middle hall, on each side of which are the offices of the President. The arrangement is simple, and in the floor-plan covers the space occupied below by the East Room and the Green Room, the latter being the counterpart of the small hall with the public stairway, just mentioned. At the head of these stairs, over the Green Room, is the Cabinet Room, which is the first apartment on the south side of the hall; a jog of two steps, at the private door into the President's room, marking the raised ceiling of the East Room below. The President reaches his office through the Cabinet Room, entering the latter from the library, which corresponds on the second floor with the Blue Room of the State apartments. President Arthur, indeed, used the library as his office, and the cabinet chamber for an anteroom, while his private secretary was domiciled in the traditional office of the President. During his first term Mr. Cleveland preserved the same arrangement; but General Harrison went back to the office hallowed by Lincoln's occupancy, and Mr. Cleveland, on his return, found the arrangement so satisfactory that he continued it.

Beyond the President's large square office is the corner room where Private Secretary Thurber is always either wrestling with the details of executive business or standing with his shoulder braced against the crowd struggling to see the President. It is a narrow apartment, and might be called appropriately the «Hall of the Disappointed,» the suggestion being emphasized by portraits of the greatest of presidential aspirants, Clay and Webster, to which Mr. Thurber has added, as his private property, an engraving of the closest contestant for the office, Governor Tilden.

On the north side of the hall there are two rooms which correspond to those on the south side just described, the small one being occupied by Mr. O. L. Pruden, the assistant secretary since General Grant's time, and the custodian of the office books as well as of the traditions which govern the public social routine of the executive mansion; in his room sits the telegraph clerk at his instrument, and by the window is a telephone, which saves a great amount of messenger service between the President and the departments. Occasionally a congressman, with less ceremony than discretion, attempts to get an appointment with the ear of the President over the telephone, and there is record of a stage earthquake produced in the private secretary's room by a furious congressman who found the telephone ineffective, and his Olympian style even less so.

The large room on the north side, corresponding to the President's office south of the hall, provides for the mail clerk and his assistants, and the stenographer and letter secretary; it is also a store-room for official papers and the office books, a new set of which is made ready by each private secretary for his successor.

In the hallway there are always several attendants, among them the colored messenger who was recommended to President Lincoln by Secretary Stanton.

On this historic floor the weary Lincoln buoyed desponding patriots with hearty hope and merry joke; here have been discussed and formulated the policies which have saved and maintained the republic; here the strong men of the country have chafed at the barriers to the source of appointments; and here the queue of office-seekers, stretching from the private secretary's door, has drawn its weary length, most of them departing with a hollow straw of hope, and some of them, after many calls, taking the stairs with the lingering step of despair.

More accommodation for the President is a necessity; but the White House, from the point of view of beauty and tradition, is one of the relics of our past which belong unimpaired to posterity. The perfect inadequacy of the executive offices to the present demands is apparent at a glance; nor is the lack of room less obvious at the social functions which custom as well as reasons of state impose upon the President.

At every large public reception in the White House the guests are taken in with a limited amount of style; but their departure is virtually over a stile, since the halls could not be cleared if the guests were not passed out by steps to a window-sill from which a bridge spans the basement area. These receptions and dinners occur much in the order of the winter fêtes of 1895–96, which were ushered in with the President's usual drag-net levee on New Year's day, beginning at an early hour with the cabinet, the Supreme Court, the diplomatic corps, the army and navy, Congress, heads of departments, etc., according to cast-iron rules of precedence, and finishing with the unofficial citizen.

As it happened in 1896, the cabinet dinner occurred the day after New Year's; and on January 9 the diplomatic reception, from 9 to 11 P. M., which is looked upon as the brilliant function of the year. About three thousand invitations are issued, which go to every person of some degree of responsibility in the government services and in the departments, and to the social friends of «The President and Mrs. Cleveland,» as the invitation reads. This is the reception for which every new aspirant to social position hungers and thirsts, since it is felt to be so inclusive as to leave the stamp of negative gravity on anybody of social pretensions who has been overlooked. But the number of invitations indicates sufficiently the perfunctory character of the entertainment. The members of the cabinet and their wives assemble in the private apartments on the second floor. At nine o'clock, when the Marine Band begins to play, they march down the west staircase, the President and his wife at the head of the procession. Passing from the corridor into the Blue Room, the President and his wife take position near the door leading from the Red Room, with the ladies of the cabinet at their right, the cabinet members themselves passing into the background. Meantime the diplomatic corps have assembled in the Red Room. As they are received by the President and his wife, they pass behind the line and join the cabinet. Then the members of the Supreme Court and other dignitaries are received, and afterward the invited guests in general pass in a steady stream from the anteroom by the group of honor, through the Green Room into the East Room, and crowd the halls and corridors, emerging, often with a considerable sense of relief, through the aforesaid window.

DRAWN BY JAY HAMBIDGE.

A DISAPPOINTED OFFICE-SEEKER.

On January 16, 1896, the diplomatic dinner

was given; January 18 Mrs. Cleveland gave a large private reception; January 23 occurred the reception to Congress and the Judiciary; January 30 the Supreme Court were dined; February 1 was the date of Mrs. Cleveland's public reception, from 3 to 5 P. M.; February 6 the usual evening reception was held in honor of the officers of the army and navy and marine corps; and on February 13, from 9 to 11 P. M., the so-called «public reception» crowded the White House and marked the close of the official social season.

Thereafter Mrs. Cleveland continued to receive friends and special visitors on Mondays at 5 P. M., her day «at home,» which is made also the occasion for getting acquainted with the wives of diplomats recently accredited to Washington. According to etiquette, the ambassador or minister sends a formal note inquiring when his wife may pay her respects to the wife of the President; and the private secretary replies, in the third person, that Mrs. Cleveland will be happy to receive the lady at a given time.

For the official family dinner, so to speak, to which the members and ladies of the cabinet are invited, the state dining-room is still adequate. The ordinary table will seat thirty-six persons, and if widened at the ends with curved indented sides, fifty may be accommodated, though there will be no room between chairs for political or other animosities. As there are always officials who are wifeless or daughterless or for a time deprived of family companionship, a hostess of Mrs. Cleveland's tact and generosity will ask the necessary number of matrons and young ladies of her social acquaintance to complete the requisite couples and honor the serious gentlemen of state with their conversation. Yet this resource sometimes fails to balance the company, owing to eleventh-hour accidents.

At the Supreme Court dinner on January 30 thirty guests appeared, but the even number does not necessarily indicate that the grave and reverend signiors were all provided with partners; nor does it follow that the dignity of the Supreme Bench does not conceal a humor equal to every prandial situation. As a matter of fact, the judges always have partners, because, under the rules of precedence, they are first considered; and if a man goes in alone, it will be the Attorney-General or one of the chairmen of the Committees on the Judiciary.

An incident of one of President Arthur's dinners to the Supreme Court will illustrate some of the perplexities of such a ceremonious occasion. The Attorney-General, then Mr. Brewster, was a gentleman of decided character and brilliancy, who in society looked upon converse with the ladies as quite indispensable to his happiness and dignity. On finding that the envelop bearing his name in the gentlemen's dressing-room inclosed a table-card which merely denoted his chair at the board, his sense of a profound emergency was aroused, and instead of joining the other guests he made straight for the dining-room, where his suspicion was confirmed by the plate-cards, which showed that he was to be sandwiched between two other lone adjuncts to judicial greatness. Then he spoke in accents, not of anger, but of calm commiseration, that some one should have made so unheard-of a mistake. It was courteously explained that, owing to the limited number of ladies, some of the gentlemen must necessarily go in alone. But this did not impress him as applying logically to himself. And when it became apparent that he was not carrying the situation by storm, he proceeded to try a state of siege by dropping into a chair by the door, and near the foot of the President's stairway. His plaintive reproach, «They have even taken my wife away from me!» reached the ears of the Chief Magistrate, who, alarmed by the controversy below, had come out into the upper hall.

President Arthur summoned the assistant secretary, and on learning that the trouble had been caused at the last moment through a redistribution of the guests by the private secretary, the President exclaimed, «This is an outrage on Attorney-General Brewster, and he would be justified in leaving the house.»

But how could the fault be remedied? Only by a dash on the dressing-room, in the hope that some congressman who had been accorded a partner had not yet arrived! Fortunately, one card remained which allotted to General Logan the wife of a distinguished congressman.

«It won't do,» sighed the President. «General Logan is one of the most sensitive men in the world.»

But the strategy had to be tried; and so it happened that the card bearing the lady's name was handed to the gallant Attorney-General, who, wholly appeased, joined the company in the drawing-room and proceeded to claim his partner with the courtly elegance which always distinguished him; while General Logan, unaware of the deed, marshaled the odd guests, and helped to relieve with his jollity the seclusion of his end of the table.

An incident of this kind cannot happen at a diplomatic dinner such as was given on January 16, 1896,—at least not among the foreign guests who have seen their names printed in the « diplomatic list » provided by the Department of State, in which their rank and the date of their presentation are indicated, the two facts which determine the precedence to which, if accurately followed, there can be no demur. At that dinner sixty-six guests were present. For the second time the table was set in the long main hall which separates the Red, Blue, and Green rooms from the vestibule. Though of course not designed for such a function, the decorative effect was fine.

The seating of the guests devolves upon the assistant secretary, who has invented a table-plan which serves for all such occasions. An oblong piece of pasteboard has many slits on the four sides near the edges; into these slits are thrust narrow cards on both sides of each of which has been written the name of a guest. At the diplomatic banquet the seating begins with the President, who sits in the middle of the north side of the table, with Lady Pauncefote on his right, and Mrs. Cleveland, who sits opposite with the British ambassador at her right, since Sir Julian is at present, by priority of reception, at the head of the list of ambassadors. The other ladies and gentlemen are placed, according to precedence, alternately with reference to the President and to Mrs. Cleveland. The problem is so complicated as to be equal in the laying out to a game of solitaire; the four ambassadors are in a class apart from the ministers, and the absence of a chief relegates his representative to a less prominent place. If a mistake has been made with one of the cards, it may be moved, or by turning it over shifted to the other side. When the seating has been both proved and approved, table-cards for the gentlemen are prepared by writing in the center the name of the lady to be escorted, and checking off with a pencil the chair numbers printed on the edges of the small diagram of the table which is given to each guest; also, the name of each guest is written on a plate-card bearing a gilt eagle with stars, which is the crest of the United States and is used on the stationery connected with state ceremonies. Here and there a social difficulty appears, as when the Chinese minister and his wife, out of supporting distance of each other, convey by smiles and signs the good humor they feel, and the quips and oddities they would be glad to exchange.

It was at the entertainment to the diplomatic corps that Mrs. Hayes inaugurated her anti-wine policy. The Presidential dinner to the Grand Duke Alexis had impressed her unpleasantly; so it was decided to blend the diplomatic reception with the diplomatic dinner, and to serve a collation lavish in elegance and quality, and abounding in every kind of liquid refreshment that was free from alcohol. As a consequence the party broke up with amazing punctuality, some of the diplomats reconvening at the State Department opposite, where the waggish Secretary of State had made provision against a chilly condition of our foreign relations.

The weekly routine of executive business is at its highest pitch during the two winter months of social activity. Congress is then in session, the diplomats are pressing whatever business they may have with the government, and the capital is full of visitors, promoters, and the higher order of birds of prey. A reading of the « Executive Mansion Rules » which adorn Mr. Thurber's mantel will give the impression, of themselves, that the President leads a methodical and social existence not unmixed with the joyful consciousness of bestowing the gifts of a great father on seventy millions of grateful children; but the facts do not give credit to this view.

What could be more indicative of leisure than the first rule, which says that « the cabinet will meet on Tuesdays and Fridays at 11 o'clock A.M. »? As the eight gentlemen of the cabinet, each of whom has too much business on his mind for one man, have the entrée at any hour of any day or night, and actually avail themselves of it according to the gravity of their business, the two formal meetings of the cabinet each week are given up mainly to the discussion of questions of domestic policy and foreign relations. And as the cabinet hour approaches, as likely as not the chair by the President's desk will be occupied by some caller who is too important a personage for abrupt dismissal, and who may not dislike the sensation of seeing the cabinet officers, one by one, popping like impatient apparitions up the steps of the cabinet doorway, and receding with an air of « O Lord, how long! » Separate interviews with the members of the cabinet occur almost every day, and the difficult work, such as consultations over the papers involved in a fight for a post-office, usually takes place at night, when the President and the Postmaster-General will be closeted for hours, with the cabinet table loaded with applications and flanked by willow trunks filled with relays of papers. This is labor, and not to be compared with the deliberations of the full cabinet, which may involve a burden of care, but are often relieved by amusing incidents.

«Mondays will be *reserved* by the President for the transaction of public business requir-

DRAWN BY JAY HAMBIDGE.

THE PRIVATE SECRETARY'S DOORKEEPER.

ing his *uninterrupted* attention,» is the second rule; but the raid on the private secretary's office continues just the same, and persons will call who, in exceptional cases, do get into the big room if the President happens to be alone with his never-ended task.

The third paragraph lays down this rule: «The President will receive Senators and Representatives in Congress from ten to twelve o'clock on other days, except cabinet days, when he will receive them from ten to eleven o'clock.» And what a variety of human nature and irrelevancy that rule covers! As fast as they can be passed in and listened to, the merry round of importunity goes on. A local sarcasm, that a new congressman, impressed by the importance of his surroundings, spends his first day at the Capitol wondering how he ever got there, and the second day wondering still more how his colleagues ever got there, is true enough as a key to the *raison d'être* of the «errand-boy» business of a congressman. With the eyes of his constituents upon him, the average congressman accepts as a blessing the chance of having «leave to print,» and of using the inalienable privilege of running errands to the departments and telling the President about the worthy men in his district who want, actually need, and in fact ought to have, berths in the ship of state. As the last or sixth paragraph of the rules is a gentle admonition to congressmen, it should be given here. It reads: «The President intends to devote the hours designated for the reception of Senators and Representatives *exclusively* to that purpose, and he requests their coöperation in avoiding encroachments upon the time set apart for their benefit.» And yet the impressive act of leading magnates of the cross-roads into the presence of their President goes merrily on.

Much gentleness is couched in the fourth rule: «Persons not Senators or Representatives *having business* with the President will be received from twelve to one o'clock every day except Mondays and cabinet days.» But in the working of the rule there is plenty of room for more oil, and for less sand, which the private secretary is constantly sprinkling on the cogs. It is his duty to learn if the line of callers really «*have business*» with the President, and in nine cases out of ten he discovers that they would like to have, but that a prior condition to that state is a siege of some one of the departments. He briefly interests himself in the case, points out the road to be followed, and tells them to come back when their ambition has been actually furthered as far as the President's threshold. These quixotic enterprises are frequently pitiful, and sometimes amusing; it follows, also, that oftentimes they are successful. Many a President who has dropped his fist on his desk with the vocal declaration that «if that man calls again I won't give him the place,» has been thwarted by the hypnotic influence of magnetic «cheek.»

But the majority of these visitors «having business» with the President wish merely to pay their respects. They are moved by a conscientious desire to do their duty as citizens who placed him in power. Some of them know the number of their vote in the small majority which secured him the electors of their State. «It 's blanked strange I can't see *my* President,» roars some disgusted politician from the back districts, after several offered reasons for doing so have been parried. A few of this type yield grace-

DRAWN BY JAY HAMBIDGE.

IN THE PRIVATE SECRETARY'S ROOM—WAITING TO SEE THE PRESIDENT.

fully, and retire with the remark, «Tell the President I called; I want him to know that I have n't forgotten him.» Then there are delegations with «organized» claims on the President's courtesy, and estimable people who bear the same surname of whom he never heard; for at this hour «relatives» are visited upon a President back to the fourth and fifth generation. Most appealing of all are the people, some of them influential in the professions, who are in Washington on their wedding trip, and would like to grasp the President's hand—it would so please the bride to observe that the President remembered her husband. Then there are the large class who accept the ear of the private secretary as a substitute, and fill it with advice on the weightiest measures of state, including suggestions for the annual message, particularly when they are told that the bar is up because it is November, when the President has to devote much time to the constitutional duty of «informing» Congress. This work President Cleveland always does with his own hand, sometimes making several drafts. He also writes his own Thanksgiving proclamation, which most Presidents have had drafted by the Secretary of State. «Tell the President to use these suggestions freely,» said one adviser on the message, adding, «*I* can't help it if people detect the ear-marks.»

A great many visitors who ascend to the offices to pay their respects are referred to the fifth rule, which says: «Those having no business, but who desire merely to pay their respects, will be received by the President in the East Room at 1 o'clock P. M. on Mondays, Wednesdays, and Saturdays.» No part of his social duties, it is said, gives President Cleveland more pleasure than this public levee, which brings him in contact with visitors to Washington from all parts of the country and from abroad. A line forms about the East Room, the President emerges from the double doors of the main hall, and without ceremony extends his hand to the head of the line, which is soon moving so rapidly as to disconcert those who have primed themselves for a chat. Often the smile on the President's face will represent more than his kindliness of feeling, for the effort of the visitor to be impressive (as in the case of the young lady who, in her self-consciousness, waltzed by) is often amusing. Recently an old lady in the line with something to say was struck dumb by the suddenness of her arrival before the President; but after she had been propelled past she recovered herself, and, turning, condensed the expression of her solicitude over a delicate international complication by shouting back, «How 's Cubay?»

In the message season there is a marked increase in the President's mail, and, indeed, every important public question calls out hundreds of letters of advice from watchful patriots. Upward of a thousand letters a day arrive in the busy season, and two hundred or more are received in the dullest times. During the first year of Mr. Cleveland's second administration the letters averaged over fifteen hundred a day. Eighty per cent. of them are referred by the clerks to the different cabinet officers, a type-written blank of acknowledgment being sent, for instance, to the applicant for office who has forwarded letters of recommendation. Polite type-written expressions of the President's inability to meet all the demands made upon his charity are mailed to the incredible number who feel that the President's salary is too large for the needs of his family. These appeals have often aggregated twenty thousand dollars in a day. Exaggerated rumors of what the President has done for some namesake always bring out letters reminding him that other namesakes, just as worthy and probably in greater need, have been overlooked; and there is a popular impression that triplets are rewarded by the government. The «baby compliment,» so to speak, and the attendant correspondence, with which every President is honored, amount almost to a special department of the public business, and more than ever when there is a baby in the White House. This is carried on by persons who are actuated by one of the finest human sentiments, but who overlook the fact that the sentiment is too general to be safely indulged in toward a public officer who is constantly in the thoughts of seventy millions of people. Nor does the President escape being taken for a very capable errand-boy. It occurs to a great many veterans that if he would drop in on the pension officer and mention their claims, it would cost him little trouble and do them a great service. The friends of a public clerk who is in difficulty appeal without compunction for the President's personal interest in the case; and a public officer in another town once asked him to run into a bank in Washington just to say that it would be safe to renew a loan, since the President was aware that the officer's official sureties were good. Not a little humor percolates through the mass, as when an office-seeker wrote: «If,

DRAWN BY JAY HAMBIDGE.

MIDNIGHT SESSION OF PRESIDENT CLEVELAND AND POSTMASTER-GENERAL WILSON WITH THE APPLICATIONS AND RECOMMENDATIONS OF WOULD-BE POSTMASTERS.

after the poor and dependent relatives of Senator —— are satisfied, there is anything remaining to the quota of our State, I would like to be considered.» Occasionally letters are received from England and Ireland inquiring as to the whereabouts of persons who emigrated to this country years before. As a matter of necessity, the President sees only a small part of the letters addressed to him; but every letter of special interest and importance reaches the private secretary, and through him receives the President's attention. The merely complimentary letters are politely acknowledged, while, with the aid of Mr. Thurber and his own pen, the President each day accomplishes a large correspondence.

The executive record-books of each administration are also an index of the vast business which burdens the life of a President. One book is a register of all appointments made by the President; and as in making the appointments for the different departments Mr. Cleveland is not in the habit of depending on the briefs of the recommendations submitted in behalf of applicants, the task of selecting from among many the man best fitted for public service at home or abroad may be imagined. Another book contains a record of recess appointments which must be renewed when the Senate reconvenes.

One book is devoted to laws approved or vetoed, and this discloses another field of labor which President Cleveland has broadened by applying for reports and opinions of the different departments as to the expediency of legislation submitted to him for approval, and when the time for his final action arrives by requiring that the reports of congressional committees on the bill shall be included with the papers for his private study. A book is set apart for the entry of congressional resolutions of inquiry, another for executive orders and proclamations, and still another for copies of the President's indorsements on the business of the several departments requiring his decision. A stick of fallen timber on a public acre or on an Indian reservation cannot be sold for the benefit of the treasury or for the relief of the wards of the nation without the President's approval of the contract. It is not long since it fell to the President to discover that the terms of such a contract implied a misapprehension of the law—a case of minor importance, perhaps, but indicative of the slips that may be made, despite the efforts of able and faithful officers, if a President discharges his duty without legal experience and in a perfunctory spirit.

A most impressive chapter of the record-book last mentioned is that relating to pardons. Prior to President Cleveland's first term it was the custom of Presidents to follow the recommendations of the Attorney-General, through whom applications for pardons and reprieves must come. In Lincoln's time a large part of the pardon business pertained to the army engaged in war, and the whole world knows how he gave it his personal attention, and how his great heart was wrung by the conflicts of mercy and duty. In President Arthur's time the pardon papers seldom, if ever, reached his table. The record of 295 cases from March 4, 1881, to March 4, 1885 (which includes a few months of President Garfield's service), does not show a single case considered by the President and «denied.» According to usage, the clerks noted that the Attorney-General recommended the pardon, and affixed the executive order, «Let a pardon issue.»

But when President Cleveland came into the White House he soon let it be known that he would assume a personal responsibility for pardons. To him «the quality of mercy» enjoined by the Constitution was one of the most sacred trusts reposed in a President; and besides, as a governor who had dealt with pardons, he felt qualified to say to his advisers: «Some of you may know more than I do about certain lines of the public business; but if there is one thing I do understand, it is pardons.»

Consequently the papers in every pardon case were sent to his desk, were exhaustively considered, the petition was granted in whole or in part, or denied, and his reasons were indorsed in his own hand on the folder.

The amount of labor which this revolution in method added to the burden of the President may be inferred from the fact that President Harrison, who followed the new custom, considered during his term 779 pardon cases (not including reprieves), 527 of which were granted in whole or in part, and 252 denied. His indorsements, sometimes extended, are often brief and pointed. On one case President Harrison wrote: «I will not act in these cases without the facts»; and a few days later, on another case: «Pardon denied. I request that the Attorney-General will in all cases hereafter insist that some statement of the facts, as developed upon the trial, shall be submitted by the judge or district attor-

DRAWN BY JAY HAMBIDGE.

IN LINE AT THE PRESIDENT'S LEVEE.—I.

ney.» Again he wrote: «I will not examine a petition for pardon while the petitioner is a fugitive from the process of the court.» These are indicative of the kind of papers which under the old usage slipped through in the name of «justice tempered with mercy.»

As time goes on, offenses against the federal laws naturally increase, and the pardon cases wax more numerous. From March 4, 1893, to November 13, 1896 (a period of one hundred and ninety weeks, or four months less than his full second term), President Cleveland has considered 907 pardon cases (or an average of nearly five a week), 506 of which have been granted in whole or in part, and 401 denied; and it should be said that many cases of pardon, with all presidents, are merely slight commutations for the sake of relieving from political disability convicts who have behaved well in prison.

DRAWN BY JAY HAMBIDGE. IN LINE AT THE PRESIDENT'S LEVEE.—II.

President Cleveland has said that «Sundays are a good time to consider pardons.» The hours, amounting to many days, spent on them, and the general character of such cases, may be indicated by a few extracts from the public record-book. It may there be easily discovered that the President has a severe front for crimes against the mails, the pension laws, and public decency. In an Idaho case of violation of the registration laws he wrote:

> The pardon of this convict is recommended by the judge who sentenced him and the district attorney who tried him. This being an offense against suffrage, and committed in a locality where public interests require a firm execution of the laws passed to protect the ballot, I cannot bring myself to do more than to commute the sentence as above stated.

In a noted case of embezzling he added to his other reasons:

> I confess that, in addition to other considerations, I cannot miss the fact that the granting of a pardon in this case will bring comfort to a wife and daughter whose love and devotion have never flagged, and whose affection for a husband and father remains unshaken.

To an appeal relating to aiding and abetting the abstraction of funds from a national bank, he replied:

> Denied. My sympathy is very much awakened for the family of this convict, but my ideas of public duty will not permit me to grant the pardon asked.

But reconsidering two years later, he wrote:

> Granted. This convict is one of five persons convicted of conspiring together to criminally obtain the funds of a national bank. All the rest have been pardoned from time to time, except one, whose sentence was so commuted that it has expired. This prisoner's term of imprisonment began about six months before any of the others, and he has now been confined almost three years and six months. The social position of these convicts and the circumstances surrounding these cases, have led to earnest efforts for their relief. If there was any difference in the degree of their criminality, this one was certainly not more guilty than the others, and considerable evidence has been presented to me, which was not adduced on the trial, tending to show that the condition of the convict's mind was such at the time the offense was committed as to render it doubtful if he should be held to the strictest accountability. In view of all the circumstances of his case, I have, upon a reëxamination, concluded that he should not remain imprisoned after his co-conspirators are discharged. I am also fully satisfied that the ends of justice have been answered by the punishment he has already suffered.

In the case of a Tennessee «moonshiner» he said:

> Denied. Those who shoot at revenue officers when in the discharge of duty should be constantly taught that such offenses are serious. I do not agree with the district attorney that if those who are shot at are willing that the offender should be pardoned, their inclination should regulate the conduct of those charged with executing and upholding the law.

Two counterfeiters of Illinois, a man and wife, petitioned; and the President wrote this decision:

> On the facts presented in this case, I am not clear that these convicts should be pardoned on the merits; but aside from any other consideration, I have determined to pardon the wife and mother on account of the child born to her in prison, and now less than three months old.

A Virginia case of selling liquor without a license called forth a laconic inquiry:

> If the petitioner in this case went to jail, pursuant to his sentence, his term has already expired. If he did not go to jail, he seems to be doing pretty well without a pardon. Where has he been since sentence?

Another change in the business life of the White House concerns its relations to the public press. President Cleveland has not felt able to reciprocate the intimate attitude of the «new journalism,» which in its first overtures outraged the rights of privacy in a manner never before heard of, and probably never since equaled. This was followed up with betrayals of official confidences of various kinds, and finally with efforts to force the administration into cordial intimacy by the method of concerted abuse until it should cry: «Enough! Take all we know, whether public interests will suffer by publication or not, and treat us with ordinary decency.» Even this method failed. During his present term news of finished business has been given by Mr. Thurber to the two press associations, and intimations of probable events have been withheld from everybody. Little effort has been made to draw out public opinion in advance of official action by guarded revelations to journalists of ability and respectability: not because correspondents of that character no longer abound in Washington, but because such aims would be checkmated by the acts of newspapers which appear to take pride in the frustration of official purposes, and prefer sensationalism, to a judicious treatment of views and facts. The method of frustration is simple and effective. When a crisis arises a guess is made at every imaginable contingency, and all the probable moves in the case are elaborated. Some one of the guesses will be sure to impinge on the facts. By the use of such phrases as «it is intimated at the White House» (which may mean no more than that one lobe of the correspondent's brain has made inquiry of another lobe, and obtained an answer suited to the purpose), the desired amount of deception is injected into the «news.» Journalism of the old order finds it difficult to compete with such «enterprise.» And so long as it pays, men who have the guise and education of gentlemen will no doubt be ordered to do disreputable things. The latter, as a rule, do the work grudgingly, and no one pities them more than the large body of able correspondents who indirectly are the chief sufferers from the new enormity.

DRAWN BY JAY HAMBIDGE.

VISITORS IN THE GREEN ROOM.

While the public life of the White House is constantly open to the public view, President Cleveland has succeeded in preserving the sanctity of its home life in spite of efforts to invade it which until recently grew in recklessness in proportion as they proved to be futile. To the President, who spends twelve to fourteen hours a day in the east wing of the executive mansion, harassed by all sorts of importunities, and often worried by the duty of deciding questions involving the happiness of thousands, or even the welfare of the nation, the overshadowing importance of the home life in the west wing may be dimly imagined by the private citizen who looks to his fireside for surcease of the ordinary cares of life. And there has been vastly more of the domestic character associated with the idea of an American home in the White House, under the gracious sway of Mrs. Cleveland, than would naturally be ascribed to an official residence. The laugh-

SCENE OUTSIDE THE WHITE HOUSE DURING A DIPLOMATIC RECEPTION.

ter of romping children has rippled as merrily in the halls of the executive mansion as in any private home; and never has public sentiment been more unanimous than in regarding President Cleveland's domestic good fortune as also a public good fortune.

When cares of state have been most perplexing, President Cleveland has been known to say, in answer to inquiries concerning the welfare of his family: «There everything is well. If things should go wrong at that end of the house, I should feel like quitting the place for good.»

President Cleveland has not followed the custom of going to Congress at least once a year. His messages to the legislative branch are delivered in person by Mr. Pruden, the assistant secretary, all executive papers for the departments being transmitted by the regular White House messenger, who may be seen in the mansion burdened with a heavy budget, or on horseback without, waiting for an urgent missive. Presidents have usually occupied the President's room at the Capitol on the last evening of a session; but except in emergencies President Cleveland has declined to betake himself to the Capitol, because he believes that his duty to legislation cannot be properly fulfilled under such conditions of haste and personal pressure.

A President is the chief officer among 174,596 persons connected with what is called the executive civil service. This does not include the legislative and judicial branches, that bring the total up to 200,000. Nearly half of the executive service (80,407) are now classified under the merit system, outside of which there still remain 66,725 fourth-class postmasters, and 4815 Presidential places subject to the Senate's confirmation. It has been the privilege of President Cleveland to contribute more than his predecessors to the lightening of the President's burdens by reinforcing the merit classes through executive action. He is understood to be well pleased with the working of the system, though persuaded, by a tendency among the protected employees to combine for doubtful purposes, that some amendment of the law may be necessary. But that is one of the unsettled questions which on the 4th of March, with a meaning grasp that only an incoming Magistrate may understand, President Cleveland will hand over, with the good-will of the office, to President McKinley.

C. C. Buel.

Inauguration Scenes and Incidents (1897)

INAUGURATION SCENES AND INCIDENTS.

FROM the first the American people elected to make of the inauguration of a President a great national festival. They did this spontaneously, and in quiet disregard of all efforts to prevent them. Washington desired to be installed as first President without pomp or parade, as was natural in a man who looked upon his consent to serve as the greatest sacrifice he had ever been called upon to make, and who entered upon his task with a most unfeigned reluctance, and with a real diffidence, for which he did not expect to receive credit from the world.[1] Yet his journey from Mount Vernon to New York, which he wished to make as private as possible, was converted by the people, overflowing with veneration and gratitude, into an unbroken triumphal progress, which culminated in a series of public demonstrations and ceremonies that surpassed anything of the kind yet seen in the young republic. Each succeeding inauguration of a new President has been celebrated in much the same way, with a steadily increasing multitude of spectators, and a swelling measure of pomp and pageantry. In outward appearance there has been much similarity in these recurring quadrennial demonstrations; but each has had a distinct individuality shaped by the personality of its central figure and by the forces which prevailed in the election.

So long as Washington was on the scene he dominated it completely. He came much nearer to having his own way at his second inauguration, in Philadelphia, than he had been able to at his first, in New York, chiefly through the desire of his political rivals to prevent a fresh demonstration of the popular adoration for him. Jefferson's immortal devotion to republican simplicity had its origin in this desire; for he favored the abolition of all public exercises at the second inauguration, and wished to have the oath of office administered to Washington privately at his house, a certificate of it to be deposited in the State Department. Hamilton took the same view, but other members of the cabinet favored exercises in the open Senate-chamber, and their opinion prevailed. There was as large an attendance as the hall would hold, but no parade or other popular demonstration. The people went on worshiping their hero with undiminished fervor, however. They celebrated his birthday with such honors, and in so general a way, that his rivals were more distressed than ever, and began to see in this infatuation a menace to the republic, a threat of monarchy.

The chief sufferer from this condition of affairs was John Adams when the time came to inaugurate him as Washington's successor. He is the only President we have had, with the possible exception of Mr. Van Buren, who can be said to have played a secondary part at his own inauguration. The people had no eyes for him; they saw only the stately figure of Washington passing forever from the scene. The ceremonies were held in Independence Hall, Philadelphia, in the House of Representatives. Washington drove to the hall in his coach and four, and was lustily cheered both outside and inside the building. He passed quickly to his seat, as if eager to stop the applause. Adams entered a few minutes later, dressed in a light drab suit, and passed slowly down the aisle, bowing in response to the respectful applause which greeted him. He took the oath, and then delivered his inaugural address. He described the scene subsequently as a solemn one indeed, made more affecting by the presence of Washington, whose countenance was as serene and unclouded as the day. There was a flood of tears, which he sought in various ways to explain, though no explanation was necessary. There was, he said, more weeping than there had ever been at the representation of a tragedy; but whether it was from grief or joy, whether from the loss of their beloved President or from the accession of an unbeloved one, or some other cause, he could not say. He suspected that the novelty of the sun setting full-orbed, and another rising, though less splendid, may have had something to do with it. For several days after the exercises he was still bewailing the tendency to weep. Everybody was annoying him by talking of tears and streaming eyes, but nobody told him why; and he was forced to believe that it was all for the loss of their beloved. Two or three had ventured to whis-

[1] Letters to Benjamin Lincoln and Samuel Hanson.

per in his ear that his address had made a favorable impression, but no other evidence of interest in him had reached him. One thing he knew, and that was that he was a being of too much sensibility to act any part well in such an exhibition.[1]

If the tears at the inaugural exercises made Mr. Adams unhappy, what followed must have added greatly to his sufferings. When, at the close, Washington moved toward the door, there was a precipitate rush from the gallery and corridors for the street, and he found a great throng awaiting him as he emerged from the door. They cheered him, and he waved his hat to them, his countenance radiant with benignity, his gray hair streaming in the wind. He walked to his house, followed by the crowd, and on reaching it turned about for a final greeting. His countenance assumed a grave and almost melancholy expression, his eyes were bathed in tears, and only by gestures could he indicate his thanks and convey his farewell blessing.[2]

No inauguration myth has been more tenacious of life than that which pictured Jefferson, attired as a plain citizen, riding on horseback to the Capitol, hitching his horse to the palings, and walking unattended into the Senate-chamber to take the oath as President. To have done this would have been in accordance with his previous utterances, for he had strongly condemned as savoring of monarchy all public ceremony at the swearing in of a President. When the time for his own inauguration arrived, however, the case seems to have looked different to him. Whether it was because he was to be the first President inaugurated at the new Capitol, or because of an unwillingness to disappoint the large numbers of his friends and partizans who had assembled to honor him, is not clear; but the fact is that he did permit a considerable display at the ceremonies. He was met at the door of his boarding-house, which was only a stone's throw from the Capitol, by a militia artillery company and a procession of citizens, and, escorted by these, he went on foot to the Capitol. The horseback story, or «fake,» as it would be denominated in modern journalism, was the invention of an Englishman named John Davis, who put it in a book of American travels which he published in London two years later. In order to give it an air of truthfulness, Davis declared that he was present at the inauguration, which was not true. A veracious account of the ceremonies was sent to England by Edward Thornton, who was then in charge of the British legation at Washington; and in this Jefferson was described as having walked to the Capitol. These facts, together with a great mass of interesting matter about Jefferson's inauguration, are set forth in detail by Henry Adams in his «History of the United States,» and leave no doubt that the Davis version was a pure fabrication.

On reaching the Senate-chamber, in which he was to be inaugurated, Jefferson became a member of one of the most striking groups ever gathered in a public place. On one side of him stood John Marshall as chief justice to administer the oath, and on the other Aaron Burr, who was to be sworn in as Vice-President. As described by his contemporaries, Jefferson was very tall (six feet two and a half inches in height), with a loose, shackling air about his slender figure, a very red freckled face, and neglected gray hair. He was clad in a blue coat, a thick, gray-colored, hairy waistcoat with a red under-waistcoat lapped over it, green velveteen breeches with pearl buttons, yarn stockings, and slippers down at the heels—his appearance being very much that of a raw-boned farmer. Marshall, as described by Joseph Story in 1808, was tall and slender, not graceful and imposing, but erect and steady, with black hair, small and twinkling eyes, and rather low forehead, plain and dignified in manners, and very simple and neat in dress. Burr was rather small in stature, but dignified and easy in manners, and dressed with aristocratic care. The three men were alike in one respect: they distrusted and disliked one another thoroughly. Jefferson both feared and hated Marshall, saying of him that he had a mind of that gloomy malignity which would never let him forego the opportunity of satiating it on a victim. Marshall said of Jefferson, shortly before the inauguration, that by weakening the office of President he would increase his personal power, and that his letters had shown that his morals could not be pure. Both Jefferson and Marshall looked upon Burr as a political and social adventurer who was living up to his own creed, «Great souls care little for small morals.» The outgoing President, Mr. Adams, was not present at the exercises; but he undoubtedly took a grim pleasure in the presence of Marshall, whom he had made chief justice, greatly to the wrath of Jefferson, only a few weeks before. After the ceremonies the new

[1] Letters of John Adams to his wife.

[2] Personal recollections of Wm. A. Duer, once president of Columbia College.

President proceeded to the Executive mansion, or «the Palace,» as it was then styled, in the same manner as he had gone to the Capitol.

Washington set the example, which has been followed at frequent intervals by new Presidents even to our day, of wearing at the first inauguration ceremonies clothing of American manufacture. He was dressed in a suit of dark cloth made at Hartford. I have been able to find no mention of the nationality of the «light drab suit» which John Adams wore. Jefferson was inaugurated in his «every-day clothes,» which may or may not have been exclusively American; but before the end of his service as President he appeared at his New-Year reception dressed in an entire suit of homespun. Madison carried the matter a step further; for, as he passed down the aisle of the House of Representatives to be inaugurated, he was spoken of as a «walking argument in favor of the encouragement of native wool.» His coat had been made on the farm of Colonel Humphreys, and his waistcoat and small-clothes on that of Chancellor Livingston, all from the wool of merino sheep raised in the country. John Quincy Adams says in his Diary that the house was very much crowded, and that its appearance was magnificent, but that Mr. Madison read his address in a tone so low that it could not be heard. Contemporary descriptions of Madison picture him as a small, modest, and jovial man. Washington Irving spoke of him in 1812, at the time of his second election to the Presidency, as «a withered little apple-john,» and an English observer as «a little man with small features, rather wizened, but occasionally lit up with a good-natured smile.» He was habitually neat and genteel in his appearance, says another writer, dressed like a «well-bred and tasty old-school gentleman.» American wool seems, therefore, to have made its first appearance as a «walking argument» under favorable conditions.

Monroe's inauguration, in 1817, was remarkable chiefly for being the first one held out of doors since the seat of government had been moved to Washington. There had been out-of-door exercises when Washington was installed in New York, but all his successors till Monroe had been inaugurated within doors. It is said by some authorities that the proposal to change to the open air in 1817 was the outcome of a long and bitter wrangle between the two Houses as to the division of seats in the House at the ceremonies. Agreement being apparently impossible, some one suggested that by going out of doors room enough could be found for everybody, and the idea was acted upon joyfully. An elevated platform was erected for the occasion under the unfinished portico of the Capitol, and from this Monroe delivered his inaugural address to the largest assemblage that had yet been gathered there. The day was balmy and beautiful. There were no outdoor exercises at Monroe's second inauguration, the weather being stormy, rain and snow falling throughout the day. The attendance on this occasion did not exceed two thousand persons. John Quincy Adams was also inaugurated indoors four years later, and it was not till the advent of General Jackson, in 1829, that the outdoor exercises became the established custom.

Jackson's entry upon the Presidency has been likened repeatedly to the descent of the barbarians upon Rome. It was accompanied with a huge multitude of people from all parts of the land, and by an amount of uproar altogether unprecedented. Webster wrote from the capital, several days before the inauguration, that the city was full of speculations and speculators, there being a great multitude, too many to be fed without a miracle, and all hungry for office. «I never saw such a crowd before,» he added. «Persons have come five hundred miles to see General Jackson, and they really seem to think that the country is rescued from some dreadful danger.» They surged through the streets shouting, «Hurrah for Jackson!» They swarmed about Gadsby's tavern, where the general lodged, in such masses as completely to hem it in and make access to his presence nearly impossible. When inauguration day arrived, fully ten thousand people gathered about the eastern portico of the Capitol, which was to be used for the first time for these ceremonies, and a ship's cable had to be stretched across the long flight of steps, about a third of the way from the top, to keep the portico clear. It was with great difficulty that the procession which escorted the general was able to reach the Capitol. He went first to the Senate, as usual, where the chief justice and other dignitaries joined him to proceed to the outdoor platform.

An eye-witness, who took a somewhat jocose view of the day's events, wrote that the most remarkable feature about Jackson as he marched down the aisle of the Senate with a quick, large step, as though he proposed to storm the Capitol, was his double pair of spectacles. He habitually wore two pairs, one for reading and the other for seeing at a distance, the pair not in use being placed across the top of his head. On this occasion, says the eye-witness, the pair on his head reflected the light; and some of the rural admirers of the old hero were firmly persuaded that they were two plates of metal let into his head to close up holes made by British bullets. When he appeared on the portico, we are told that the shout which arose rent the air and seemed to shake the very ground. The ceremony ended, the general mounted his horse to proceed to the White House, and the whole crowd followed him. «The President,» says a contemporary writer, «was literally pursued by a motley concourse of people, riding, running helter-skelter, striving who should first gain admittance into the executive mansion, where it was understood that refreshments were to be distributed.» An abundance of refreshments had been provided, including many barrels of orange punch. As the waiters opened the doors to bring out the punch in pails, the crowd rushed upon them, upsetting the pails, and breaking the glasses. Inside the house the crush was so great that distribution of refreshments was impossible, and tubs of orange punch were set out in the grounds to entice people from the rooms. Jackson himself was so pressed against the wall of the reception-room that he was in danger of injury, and was protected by a number of men linking arms and forming a barrier against the crowd. Men with boots heavy with mud stood on the satin-covered chairs and sofas in their eagerness to get a view of the hero. Judge Story wrote that the crowd contained all sorts of people, from the highest and most polished down to the most vulgar and gross in the nation. «I never saw such a mixture,» he added. «The reign of King Mob seemed triumphant. I was glad to escape from the scene as soon as possible.»

The outgoing President, Mr. Adams, was not present. He and his father have been the only outgoing Presidents, alive at the time of the inauguration of their successors, who did not attend the ceremonies. The reason why the younger Adams did not was stated tersely in «Niles's Register» of March 27, 1829: «It is proper to mention, for the preservation of facts, that General Jackson did not call upon President Adams, and that Mr. Adams gave not his attendance at the installation of President Jackson.» This conduct must have been a cause of grief to the editor of the «National Intelligencer,» for four years earlier he had written, when describing the scene which followed the inauguration of Adams: «General Jackson, we were pleased to observe, was among the earliest of those who took the hand of the President; and their looks and deportment toward each other were a rebuke to the littleness of party spirit, which can see no merit in a rival and feel no joy in the honor of a competitor.» General Jackson was very conspicuous at the inauguration of his successor, Mr. Van Buren. The two rode side by side from the White House to the Capitol, and back again after the ceremonies, in a carriage made of wood from the frigate *Constitution*, presented by the Democrats of New York. But the general was at all moments the central figure; the crowd along the route and at the Capitol paid only slight attention to the new President.

Of the inauguration of General William Henry Harrison in 1841, John Quincy Adams says in his Diary that it was celebrated with demonstrations of popular feeling unexampled since that of Washington in 1789. It had more of a left-over campaign flavor than any other inauguration either before or since. The great «Tippecanoe» canvass, with its log cabins and hard cider, its enormous processions, its boundless enthusiasm and incessant uproar, got under such headway that it could not be stopped with election day. Enough of it was still in motion in March to make the inauguration of the general a virtual continuation of it, so far as the procession was concerned. The log cabins were brought to the capital for the occasion, and many of the clubs came with their regalia and banners. A magnificent carriage had been constructed by his admirers, and presented to General Harrison, with the expressed wish that he ride in it to the Capitol; but he declined to do so, insisting upon riding a horse instead. The crowd of visitors along the avenue from the White House to the Capitol was the largest yet seen in Washington. The procession created such enthusiasm that the novel expedient was put in operation of having it march and countermarch several times before leaving its hero at the Capitol. For two hours it went to and fro in the avenue before the spectators were supposed to have their fill of it. Mr. Adams, who saw it from his window, under which it passed, describes it in his Diary as a mixed military and civil cavalcade, with platoons of militia companies, Tippecanoe clubs, students of colleges, school-boys, a half-dozen veterans who had fought under the old hero in the War of 1811, sundry awkward and ungainly painted banners and log cabins, and without car-

THE CRUSH AT THE WHITE HOUSE AFTER JACKSON'S INAUGURATION.

DRAWN BY G. WRIGHT.

A SCENE AT WILLIAM HENRY HARRISON'S INAUGURATION.

riages or showy dresses. The *coup d'œil*, he adds, was showy-shabby; and he says of the general: «He was on a mean-looking white horse, in the center of seven others, in a plain frock coat or surtout, undistinguishable from any of those before, behind, or around him.» The day was cold and bleak, with a chilly wind blowing. General Harrison stood for an hour exposed to this while delivering his address, and at its close mounted his horse and returned to the White House with the procession again as an escort.

The inauguration ball dates from the very beginning. There was a ball when Washington was inaugurated in New York, but owing to the pressure of other demands upon his time, it did not take place till the evening of March 7. Washington attended, and performed a minuet with Miss Van Zandt, and danced cotillions with Mrs. Peter Van Brugh Livingston, Mrs. Maxwell, and others. There was no ball at his second inauguration because of its extremely quiet character, and there was none when Mr. Adams came in because of the general grief over Washington's departure. I can find no mention of a ball when Jefferson was inaugurated, but there was one when Madison came in, and since then there has been no break in the custom. There were two when Polk was inaugurated, and two when Taylor succeeded him—an administration and an opposition ball on each occasion, both very well attended. The crush was so great at the Taylor administration ball that many persons narrowly escaped injury, and there were loud complaints because of the inadequate supply of refreshments.

The crowds at Polk's inauguration were said to be the largest yet seen at the Capitol, which was undoubtedly true; for as the country has advanced in size, the number of people going to Washington to witness the advent of every new President has steadily increased. Evidence that the outdoor custom had become firmly established in Polk's time is furnished by the fact that, although rain fell steadily throughout the day, he delivered his address from the portico to a wide, moving sea of umbrellas, with no protection save an umbrella which was held over his head. The crowds amused themselves during the progress of the procession along Pennsylvania Avenue by repeating the favorite cry of the opposition in the preceding campaign, «Who *is* James K. Polk?» Roars of laughter always followed this somewhat worn but always amusing query. An interesting contemporary note of this inauguration is the following: «Professor Morse brought out his magnetic telegraph to the portico platform, close to one side of it, from which point he could hear everything that went on, having under view all the ceremonies performed, transmitting the results to Baltimore as fast as they transpired.»

There was little that varied the now well-established monotony of inauguration ceremonies when Franklin Pierce came in in 1853, and James Buchanan in 1857. Pierce was one of the most buoyantly self-poised men who ever entered upon the Presidency. He made the journey from the White House to the Capitol standing erect in the carriage beside President Fillmore, and bowing constantly to the cheers with which he was greeted. At the Capitol he distinguished himself by being the first President to deliver his address without notes, speaking in a remarkably clear voice, and arousing great enthusiasm by his handsome appearance, dignified bearing, and somewhat unusual oratorical powers.

DRAWN BY IRVING R. WILES.

THE APPROACH TO THE CAPITOL DURING POLK'S INAUGURATION. (BASED ON A CONTEMPORARY PRINT.)

Lincoln's inaugurations have been so fully described in recent years in the columns of THE CENTURY that it is unnecessary to say much about them now. Perhaps the most dramatic phase of the first inauguration, always ex-

DRAWN BY IRVING R. WILES. FROM A CONTEMPORARY PICTURE IN "HARPER'S WEEKLY."

BUCHANAN'S INAUGURATION.

cepting the address itself, was that described in Dr. Holland's «Life of Lincoln,» when the new President stood on the portico to take the oath of office, with President Buchanan, Chief Justice Taney, author of the Dred Scott decision, and Stephen A. Douglas prominent in the group about him, and the latter, his famous rival in debate, holding Mr. Lincoln's hat while he was delivering his inaugural address.

The chief characteristic of later inaugurations has been the steadily rising number of people in attendance. At both inaugurations of General Grant the crowds were enormous; but those which have gathered every four years since have shown no diminution from the standard of bigness then fixed. That standard, which stood at from five to eight thousand in the early years of the century, will have passed one hundred thousand before the century closes. The managers of President McKinley's inauguration predict the finest pageant and the greatest throng ever seen in Washington, and doubtless their prediction will be verified.

Joseph B. Bishop.

The Capitol at Washington (1883)

THE CENTURY MAGAZINE.

APRIL, 1883.

THE CAPITOL AT WASHINGTON.

When in the early days Congress turned its back upon the cities in which it had been hospitably entertained, to adopt Washington's cherished idea of founding a "Federal City" on the bank of the Potomac, no time was lost in inviting proposals for a plan of a "Congress House." The architectural competition thus solicited was a serious disappointment to the young French engineer who had laid out the future city — Major Pierre Charles L'Enfant. He had served gallantly under Baron Von Steuben in the Revolutionary War, — his artistic taste had been recognized by the Society of the Cincinnati when it had adopted his designs for its insignia, — and his architectural ability had been formally approved by Congress, after he had fitted up a building for its accommodation in the city of New York. Commissioned by President Washington as the engineer who was to plot the Federal city, Major L'Enfant had selected the most commanding spot as the site for the legislative halls, which he was the first to designate, on his map, as "the Capitol." From this site, and from that selected for the erection of an executive mansion, a mile and a quarter distant, radiated broad avenues, intersecting at a variety of angles, rectangular streets laid out like those of ancient Babylon and modern Philadelphia.

President Washington approved Major L'Enfant's plan as well adapted for a great city of the future, and was especially pleased at the adoption of his suggestion that the Capitol should be placed at such a distance from the executive offices as to prevent the too frequent visits of congressmen. East of the site of the proposed Capitol was a broad plateau, where it was expected that the finest residences would be erected. The greater portion of this land, therefore, was immediately purchased by the agents of foreign capitalists, who then asked such high prices for building-lots that no one would purchase, and it was for this reason that the new city was begun in the swamps and on the hillocks west of Capitol Hill, and now lies mainly at the back door of the Capitol. Major L'Enfant meanwhile quarreled with the commissioners, and one of the rebukes which they administered to him was their advertisement for designs for the "Congress House," offering a premium of five hundred dollars, or a gold medal, for the best plans offered. Sixteen designs were submitted, and they have all been pronounced by modern architects very bad, — many of them below contempt, and some bordering on the ludicrous. When they were shown to President Washington, he was "more agreeably struck with Judge Turner's plan than with any other," as it embraced a dome, which, in his opinion, "would give a beauty and grandeur to the pile." The President finally gave his formal approval to a plan drawn by Dr. William Thornton, a native of one of the British West India Islands, who had been made the first clerk in charge of patents, and who possessed many accomplishments, among them an acquaintance with architectural drawing. Of his water-color sketch of the proposed edifice, showing a central rotunda, crowned by a dome, Washington wrote that, in it "grandeur, simplicity, and convenience were combined." But Thornton was not a practical architect, and the commissioners were obliged to engage Stephen Hallett, a professional French architect, to reduce Thornton's designs to practical form.

President Washington, aided by his brother Freemasons of Georgetown and Alexandria, laid the corner-stone of the Capitol under what is now the Law Library, on the 18th day of September, 1793. The exterior walls were constructed of yellow sandstone, from a quarry opened for the purpose on a small island at the mouth of Acquia Creek, where it empties into the Potomac River. The brick for the interior work was made and burned in kilns upon the spot, and much of the timber was cut on the neighboring hills. The north or Senate wing was first erected. The architect and the commissioners soon disagreed, and Hallett was superseded by James Hoban, an Irishman, who had come from Charleston to superintend the erection of the President's house. Nor was it long before Hoban was in turn superseded by George Hatfield, an Englishman, who was recommended by Benjamin West as possessing a knowledge of the theory of civil architecture superior to that of any other young man in England.

The Federal Government migrated from Philadelphia to Washington in October, 1800, and it became necessary to crowd both Houses of Congress into the north wing, which was the only finished portion of the building. The Senate Chamber was an imposing and beautiful apartment, modeled after the ancient Greek theaters, with a gallery behind the chair of the presiding officer, supported by caryatides representing the States. North and South Carolina stood as sisters, with interlocked arms, while Massachusetts led, as a child, Maine, then a district dependent on her. When Thomas Jefferson, as Vice-President of the United States, called the Senate to order for the first time in its new chamber, on the 17th of November, 1800, there were only thirty-two senators representing the sixteen States. Now there are seventy-six senators, representing thirty-eight States. As the Senate generally sat with closed doors, all that is known of its deliberations is what has been preserved in the private journals kept by some of the senators. These show that the men who are now alluded to as dignified and patriotic statesmen, who shaped with unswerving purpose and firm hands the new system of national government, were very much like the senators of to-day,—some of them possessing fiery tempers, great personal ambition, sensitiveness to criticism, and obstinate adherence to hastily formed opinions. Speeches were then never written in advance of their delivery, to be read from the manuscript or from printed slips; but it was a common thing for senators to write full reports of what they had said, for publication in the newspapers. The first House of Representatives which met at Washington had Theodore Sedgwick of Massachusetts as its Speaker, and was, as a legislative body, far abler than the Senate.

The grounds around the Capitol were roughly graded, and stables were erected for

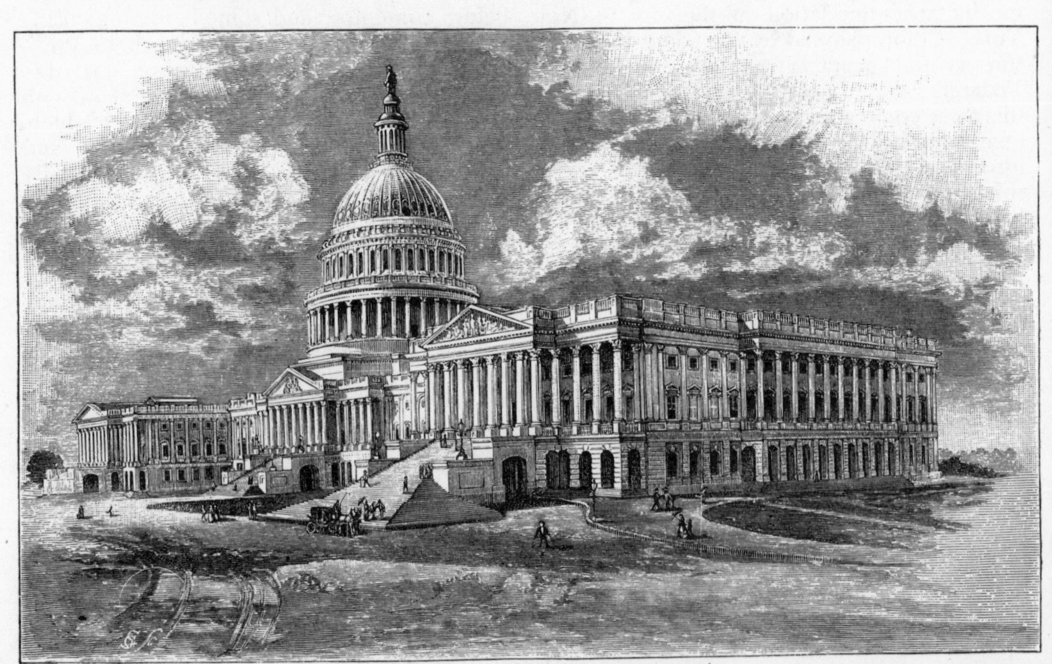

THE CAPITOL AT WASHINGTON (EAST FRONT).

THE CAPITOL, FROM PENNSYLVANIA AVENUE (WEST FRONT).

the accommodation of those congressmen who came from Georgetown to attend the daily essions on horseback, or in the English mail-coach belonging to the Union Tavern there, with seats on the top and behind, which John Randolph christened "The Royal George." Near the Senate wing of the Capitol was a barber's shop, the interior of which was surrounded by glass cases filled with the wigs belonging to those senators and representatives who had not discarded them. They would visit the barber's shop in the morning, be shaved, and have a freshly dressed wig put on, leaving the wigs that they had worn to be combed, oiled, and brushed for the next day.

The House of Representatives, at first located in a room designed for the Secretary of the Senate, removed in 1801 into a low building of elliptical shape, which had been temporarily erected within the foundations of the external walls of the south wing, and which, from its general appearance, was familiarly known as "the oven." Seven years later, the House took possession of the majestic hall designed for it, although the decorations had not been completed. This hall, which is modeled after the theaters of ancient Greece, is now the National Statuary Gallery, containing what a wag told a verdant sightseer were "the United States statutes at large."

The central rotunda (*rotundo* it was always called in the "National Intelligencer") had not then been begun, and the extremities of the Capitol, in which the Houses of Congress were located, were connected by a covered wooden passage-way. President Jefferson appointed Benjamin Henry Latrobe, a well-educated Englishman, architect, under whose direction a great deal of ornamental work was sculptured in freestone by a number of Italians imported from Rome. Jefferson, when President, used personally to supervise the work of these sculptors, in which he took a great interest, especially in the columns supporting the dome of what is now the vestibule to the Law Library. The design for these was composed of a bundle of corn-stalks with

LATROBE'S CORN COLUMN.

the half-husked ears as the capitals—"the corn-cob capitals," as John Randolph called them. The suggestion of this "American order" came from Mr. Latrobe, who also designed some capitals in a measure resembling the Corinthian, but composed of the leaves and blossoms of cotton, and of tobacco, instead of the traditional acanthus.

As there were no stationery shops in the then infant city, the officers of each House of Congress used to make annual purchases in the northern cities of stocks of stationery, penknives, scissors, pocket-books, etc., which were disposed of to Congressmen at cost,—a practice which has been continued to this day. It also appears, by the accounts of the "contingent expenses" of Congress early in the present century, that large quantities of "sirup" were purchased for consumption at the Capitol; and there is a tradition that this "sirup" was French brandy, Holland gin, and Jamaica rum. Each House had among its officials "pen-makers," who became acquainted with the exact kind of pen used by the senator or representative whose goose-quills were intrusted to their care, making or mending pens which had "fine points" or "broad nibs." There was also in an anteroom of each House a "sealer," who stood behind a table on which was a lighted candle, and sealed with red wax packages or letters brought him, using the private seal of the member sending them, or an official seal.

The impeachment of Judge Samuel Chase of Maryland, in 1805, marks an era in the chronicles of the Capitol. The Senate chamber was elaborately fitted up as a high court of impeachment, with the senators sitting as judges on a semicircular platform on either side of the Vice-President presiding,—Aaron Burr. Places were assigned for the members of the House, the Diplomatic Corps, and a few spectators. The trial demonstrated the violence of party feeling, and showed that while Judge Chase was an arrogant and impulsive man, with strong political prejudices, he had not rendered himself liable to dismissal from the bench. It was said of Aaron Burr at this trial, that he "presided with the dig-

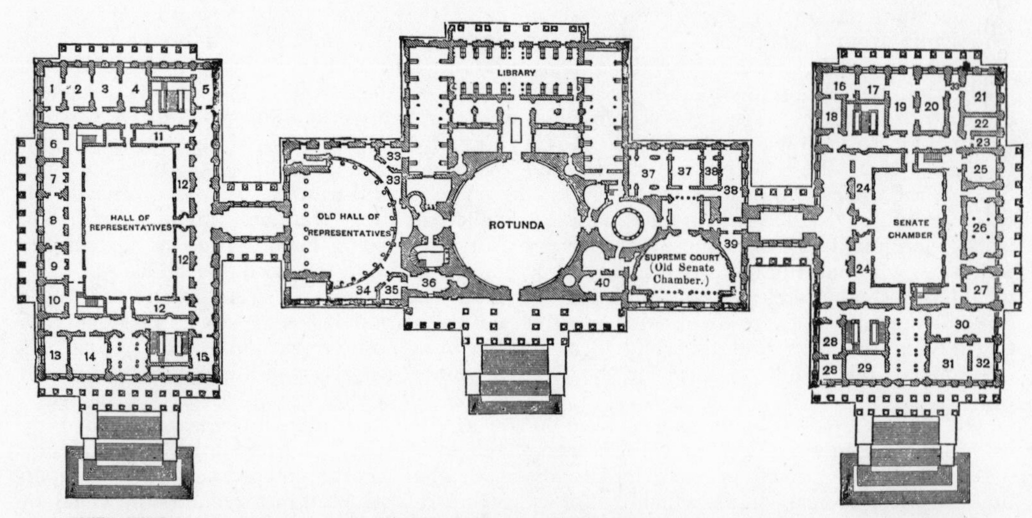

SOUTH WING. GROUND PLAN OF THE CAPITOL. NORTH WING.

1. Office of the Speaker. 2. Office of the Sergeant-at-Arms. 3. Engrossing Clerks of the House. 4. Journal and Printing Clerks. 5. Office of the Clerk. 10. Lobby. 12. Cloak-rooms. 13, 14, 15. Committee-rooms. 16. Office of the Secretary of the Senate. 17. Executive Clerk. 18. Financial Clerk. 19. Chief Clerk. 20. Engrossing and Enrolling Clerks. 21. Committee on Appropriations. 23. Committee on Enrolled Bills. 24. Cloak-rooms. 25. The Room of the President of the United States. 26. The Senators' Withdrawing-room. 27. The Vice-President's Room. 28. Committee on Finance. 29. Official Reporters of Debates. 30. Reception-room. 31. Post-office. 32. Office of the Sergeant-at-Arms. 33. House Document-room. 34. House Stationery-room. 35, 36. House Committee-rooms. 37. Office of the Clerk of the Supreme Court. 38. Robing-room of the Judges. 39. Withdrawing-room of the Supreme Court. 40. Office of the Marshal of the Supreme Court.

IN THE SENATE LIBRARY.

nity and the impartiality of an angel, but with the vigor of a devil." A few years later he was himself on trial for treason, while Senator John Smith, of Ohio, one of those who had sat in judgment in the Chase impeachment trial, only missed by one vote expulsion for his connection with Burr and Blennerhassett.

The "War of 1812," as it was called, gave great importance to Congress, and both Houses often sat with closed doors, discussing plans submitted by the Executive for organizing success. In August, 1814, an invading force ascended Chesapeake Bay, landed without opposition, and marched on Washington. After the main body of the British troops had reached the Capitol, Admiral Cockburn (who commanded jointly with General Ross), ordered a regiment to march into the hall of the House of Representatives, the drums and fifes playing "The British Grenadiers." When the hall was filled with troops, Admiral Cockburn seated himself in the Speaker's chair and said: "Attention! Shall this harbor of Yankee Democracy be burned? All for it will say Aye! Contrary opinion, No!" There was an affirmative shout, and the soldiers soon scattered themselves through the building, firing army rockets through the roof and building fires on the floors with the books, papers, and furniture. Much of the lumber which had been used in the interior construction was pitch-pine, which burned freely, while the columns and ornamental work of sandstone were calcined into dust.

The people in every section of the United States appeared to feel deeply the wanton and barbarous destruction of the Capitol and other public buildings at Washington, and urged their reconstruction in accordance with the original plans. Liberal appropriations for this purpose were voted with great unanimity, and Latrobe, who had gone West, was recalled to superintend the rebuilding of the Capitol. He resigned, however, in 1817, and Charles Bulfinch, of Massachusetts, an educated and accomplished architect, was placed in charge of the work.

The halls of the Senate and of the House of Representatives were immediately rebuilt,

Congress meanwhile occupying a structure erected by the citizens of Washington for their temporary use. The Senate chamber, now the Supreme Court room, was the first portion of the Capitol reconstructed, and it became the scene of the famous oratorical contests that took place between the intellectual giants who occupied its curule chairs, whose memories, like the remains of the mastodon, will long excite the wonder and admiration of posterity. Generally speaking, the proceedings in the Senate were colloquial, resembling the meetings of boards of directors of banks or similar institutions. A resolution would be offered, amended, discussed, and passed, within a quarter of an hour; and the Senate, with an occasional day for set speeches, managed to transact its business between twelve and three o'clock, invariably adjourning over from Thursday until the following Monday. This dispatch of the real business of the session was ended when the proceedings were reported verbatim by stenographers. When every word was recorded, to be printed and distributed over the land at public expense, senators became prolix.

This was the beginning of the period of great constitutional debates, in which the prominent figure was Daniel Webster. When it was known that he was to have the floor in the Senate chamber, it would be crowded by people who often cared but little for the subject under discussion, but wanted to see and to hear Webster. Nor were they ever disappointed, either in the personal appearance of the orator or the intellectual banquet which he provided. His stalwart figure was always arrayed in the old Whig colors of "blue and buff"; his massive head was firmly set on his square shoulders; his swarthy complexion was at times radiant with smiles, displaying his excellent teeth; his black, wily eyes gleamed in cavernous recesses beneath shaggy eyebrows, and his firm jaws showed his mastiff-like grip on whatever question he took hold of. He rarely spoke in the Senate without preparation, and he would never permit the publication of the reports made of his remarks by the stenographers until he had carefully revised them, often rejecting pages and substituting new sentences. His genial and liberal nature made him a great favorite among the senators, who were always ready to enjoy his hospitality, either at Washington or at Marshfield.

Henry Clay, who left a seat in the Senate for one in the House, but after many years' service at the other end of the Capitol returned to the Senate chamber, exercised a powerful control over the politics of the republic. Idolized by the Whig party, his wonderful powers of personal magnetism, and his rich, manly voice would enable him to hold an audience for hours. He made but little preparation, and used but few notes in speaking; but when he wrote out his remarks for the press, his manuscript was remarkably neat, without interlineations or blots. He seldom indulged in classical allusions, and his occasional attempts to make quotations of English poetry were generally failures. On one occasion, he used the well-known phrase from Hamlet, "Let the galled jade wince, our withers are unwrung," but misquoted the last syllable, calling it "un-*strung*." The gentlemen who sat on either side of him noticed the error, and simultaneously whispered "unwrung." This double prompting confused "Young Harry of the West," who straightened himself, and with stronger emphasis repeated "unhung." This raised a general laugh, at the close of which Clay, who had meanwhile ascertained his mistake, shook his head, and said with one of his inimitable smiles: "Ah! murder will out! Unwrung's the word." The fascination which he exercised over all with whom he had personal intercourse,— even his political adversaries,— was remarkable; but he was imperious and domineering, exacting unconditional and unqualified support as the price of his friendship.

John C. Calhoun was among the purest of American statesmen. His political enemies could find no opprobrious epithet for him but "Catiline," and could accuse him of no crime but an inordinate political ambition. As Webster said, when pronouncing his eulogy: "He had no recreations, and he never seemed to feel the necessity for amusements." He never was subjected to that ordeal of newspaper slander through which nearly all of our public men have had to pass, and his only fault was a thirst for political power, to gratify which he would rather "reign in hell than serve in heaven." When he last entered the Senate chamber, during the discussion of the compromise measures of 1850, he looked like a skeleton summoned from the tomb and inspired by indomitable zeal. Unable to speak audibly, he gave the argument which he had prepared to Senator Mason to read, but his eagle eyes followed the utterance of every word, occasionally glancing at Clay and Webster as if to note the effect produced on them. Not many days had elapsed before they were called upon to eulogize him in the Capitol.

Inferior in intellectual ability to Webster, Clay, or Calhoun, Thomas Hart Benton had no superior as a man of iron will and haughty

Danl Webster

PLASTER COPY OF HOUDON'S WASHINGTON.

disposition, during the twenty-nine years and seven months that he served continuously in the United States Senate. Aggressive, bold, and defiant, he would occasionally strike out recklessly at everything and everybody about him, like the huge wild buffaloes of the Missouri prairies, treading his opponents beneath his feet in his angry rush. His greatest display of ungovernable rage in the Senate chamber was when, in an angry debate, he advanced with threatening gestures toward Senator Foote, of Mississippi, who, fearing that he was to be attacked, drew a small pocket-pistol. The sight of this weapon made Benton uncontrollable, and, endeavoring to shake off the grasp of friends who seized him, he shouted: "The cowardly assassin, let him shoot me if he dares. I never carry arms, and he knows it. Let the assassin fire!" After quiet was somewhat restored, Clay suggested that both senators should enter into bonds to keep the peace, upon which Benton rose and exclaimed: "I will rot in jail, sir, before I will do it! No, sir! I will rot in jail first!" and he proceeded to pour forth a torrent of bitter invective on Foote before he could be quieted. Even when he was defeated in seeking a reëlection for the sixth time to the Senate, and was forced to accept a seat in the House of Representatives, Benton failed to display a chastened ambition or a softened heart.

VICE-PRESIDENT DAVID DAVIS.

There were other senators who were dwarfed by the great reputations of the four great leaders, but who were far above the average senator of to-day as orators and useful legislators. Preston of South Carolina, and Pinckney of Maryland, silver-tongued speakers, would hurl their well-rounded sentences upon their audiences, like the discharge of shot from a Gatling gun. Silas Wright, making no pretentions to oratory, dealt with facts as he found them, and made speeches that the farmers and mechanics of the country regarded as judicial decisions. From the South and West came other noted senators, some of them spicing their sentences with the idiosyncrasies of the "stump" oratory of their respective localities,—men whose utterances exercised a potent influence in shaping the destinies of the republic. The senators always spoke extemporaneously until Isaac Hill, of New Hampshire, an editor by profession, set the example of reading long speeches.

The old hall of the House of Representatives, now the National Gallery of Statuary, was rebuilt, after having been destroyed by the British troops, in its original fine proportions, except that the semicircular colonnade was ornamented with columns of breccia, or "pudding-stone," with capitals of white Italian marble, modeled after those in the temple of Jupiter Stator, at Rome. They were once referred to in debate as "colossal Bologna sausages, with the upper ends dipped in table-salt." Noble as are the proportions of this grand old hall, it was found ill-adapted for legislative debate. The representatives could hear the Speaker, but they could not hear each other, and there were perplexing echoes which still remain, and are revealed to visitors by the attendants, who also show curious resemblances to distinguished faces in the cemented pebbles which form the columns.

It was in this old hall that Henry Clay,

JOHN RANDOLPH.

then Speaker of the House, welcomed Lafayette as the nation's guest, and John Quincy Adams pronounced the gallant Frenchman's eulogy. There, the great parliamentary battles were fought over the admission of Missouri, the tariff, the United States Bank, and nullification, with their kindred issues. There, that pernicious doctrine, "To the victors belong the spoils," was infused like a malignant poison into our body politic. There, the old Whig party had its rise and fall, and there the Republican party was launched upon the stormiest of political seas.

The despot of the debates for many years was the eccentric John Randolph, who would ride on horseback from his lodgings in Georgetown to the Capitol, and enter the House, wearing a fur cap with a large visor, a heavy great-coat

EDMUNDS. LAMAR. ANTHONY.

BAYARD. HARRISON. WINDOM.

A GROUP OF SENATORS.

over a suit of Virginia homespun, and white-topped boots with jingling silver spurs. Striding down the main aisle, followed by his brace of pointer-dogs, he would stop before his desk, upon which he would deliberately place his cap, his gloves, and his riding-whip, listening meanwhile to the debate. If he took any interest in it, he would begin to speak at the first opportunity, without any regard to what had previously been said. After he had uttered a few sentences (and had drunk a glass of porter, which an assistant door-keeper had orders to bring whenever he rose to speak), his tall, meager form would writhe with passion; his long, bony index-finger would be pointed at those on whom he poured his wrath; and the expression of his beardless, high-cheeked, and sallow countenance would give additional force to the brilliant and beautiful sentences which he would rapidly utter, full of stinging witticisms and angry sarcasm. So distinct was his enunciation, that his shrill voice could be heard in every part of the hall; his words were select and strictly grammatical, and the arrangement of his remarks was always harmonious and effective.

Randolph, having had a dinner-table difficulty with Willis Alston, of North Carolina, never let pass an opportunity for alluding to him in the most bitter and contemptuous manner. Alston, enraged one day by some language used by Randolph in debate,

A CARD TO A "MEMBER."

A PERSISTENT LOBBYIST.

IN THE CLOAK-ROOM.

Hancock. Sheridan. Sherman.
General Officers of the Army.

Members of the Cabinet.
SKETCH OF THE SCENE IN THE HALL OF REPRESENTATIVES

said, as the representatives were leaving the hall and Randolph was passing him: "The puppy has still some respect shown him." Whether the allusion referred to Randolph or to one of his pointer-dogs, which was following him, was afterward a question, but Randolph immediately began beating Alston over the head with the handle of his heavy riding-whip, inflicting several wounds. The next day the Grand Jury, which was in session, indicted Randolph for a breach of the peace, but the court allowed him to offer the remark about the puppy as evidence in extenuation, and inflicted a fine of twenty dollars.

Among a little corps of Congressional adherents which Randolph ruled with a scepter of iron, was Daniel Sheffey, one of his Virginian colleagues in the House, who had risen by his ability and his industry from a shoe-maker's bench to a seat in Congress. After having obediently followed Randolph's lead for some time, Sheffy ventured, during a debate, to speak and to act for himself in opposition to the "Lord of Roanoke." This Randolph resented, making a personal attack upon the deserting henchman, in which he upbraided him with his low origin, and quoted the Latin proverb: "*Ne sutor ultra crepidam*,"—"The cobbler should stick to his last." Sheffey did not receive his punishment with humility, but retorted pluckily, admitting his humble origin, but asserting that, had Mr. Randolph been in his place, he never would have risen from it, but would have remained a cobbler all his life. Replies and rejoinders were kept up for nearly two days, and the once friendly leader and follower worried each other like angry bull-dogs, until the House dragged them apart.

PART OF BRONZE STAIRCASE BY BAUDIN IN THE SENATE WING.

During the debate on the Missouri question, Mr. Philemon Beecher, a native of Connecticut who had emigrated to Ohio, and had there been elected a representative, became somewhat impatient as his dinner-hour approached, and at last, when Randolph made a somewhat lengthy pause, moved "the

The President. Mr. Blaine.
DURING THE GARFIELD MEMORIAL SERVICES.

previous question." The Speaker said, "The gentleman from Virginia has the floor," and Randolph proceeded, to be again interrupted when he paused again to collect his thoughts, by a demand for "the previous question"; nor was it long before the demand was made for the third time. Randolph could stand it no longer, but said, in a voice as shrill as the cry of a peacock: "Mr. Speaker, in the Netherlands, a man of small capacity, with bits of wood and leather, will in a few moments construct that which, with the pressure of the finger and thumb, will cry 'Cuckoo! cuckoo!' With less ingenuity and with inferior materials, the people of Ohio have made a toy that will, without much pressure, cry, 'Previous question! previous question!'" and, as he spoke, Randolph pointed with his attenuated index-finger at Beecher, who did not attempt a reply.

Years afterward, John Quincy Adams rivaled Randolph as a fomenter of discord, whose delight it was to raise a storm of debate. When "the old man eloquent" would rise to address the House, during one of the cyclones of sectional passion which he had started, his bald head resembled a polished globe of white marble; but, as he proceeded (assailed on all sides, but standing like a sturdy oak in a tempest), it began to assume a scarlet look, and would at last become a bright crimson. Cold-blooded, clear-headed, logical, and merciless,—caring nothing about consistency or inconsistency, except as a weapon to use against others,—no insinuation or sarcasm exasperated him, and attacks on him were like throwing fire-crackers at an iceberg.

It was in the old hall of the House that Caleb Cushing displayed that political sleight-of-hand which enabled him to make the flimsiest supposition appear like a "fixed fact"; and there Robert Toombs, towering above those around him like a Titan, poured forth with rapid utterance his caustic antagonism to the budding doctrines of emancipation. There Corwin convulsed his hearers with his wit and humor, and Edward Everett, fresh

THE MACE.

IN THE ROTUNDA.

from his pulpit, established his reputation as an accomplished orator.

When the old hall was first occupied by the House, many of the representatives came from the backwoods, and were but little acquainted with the courtesies and refinements of civilized life. There was a striking difference between them and the dignified, polite, soldier-statesmen of the Revolutionary epoch, and occasionally, when angry, they would draw in debate the weapons which they invariably carried, while the sergeant-at-arms, bearing aloft his "mace," would hasten to place himself between the excited combatants. Yet this type of an American citizen, which has been portrayed in fiction as "Nimrod Wildfire" and "Roaring Ralph Stackpole," possessed many of those stern Roman virtues that teach the personal sacrifice of the legislator to the rights, the interests, and the welfare of his constituents.

OLD MIRROR IN THE VICE-PRESIDENT'S ROOM.

It was not until 1818 that Congress made the necessary appropriations for building the central rotunda. When its eastern portico was completed, its tympanum was adorned by an allegorical group, sculptured in high relief from designs by John Quincy Adams, when Secretary of State. Beneath this group, on a temporary platform built over the broad stair-way, the oath of office has been administered to each successive President during the past half-century. The impressive scene reminds one who has passed Holy Week in Rome of the assembled populace congregated before St. Peter's on Easter Sunday to receive the blessing of the Pope. The resemblance is heightened by a salute from a light battery stationed near by, which is echoed by the great guns at the Navy Yard, at the Arsenal, and at Fort Washington.

In the central portion of the Capitol, west

of the rotunda, is the Library of Congress. After the destruction of the original library by the British, Congress purchased the collection of books made by Mr. Jefferson, and there are now about six hundred thousand books and pamphlets, many of which are piled up, waiting for shelf-room in the proposed new Library building. For many years, the Library,—with its portico overlooking the city,—its books, and its engravings, was the favorite morning resort of the literary and fashionable society congregated at Washington during the sessions of Congress.

In 1827 Mr. Bulfinch, the architect of the Capitol, reported the edifice completed, and returned to Boston. The stately building, with its low dome and its ranges of columns, was the admiration of architects; and William H. Seward once spoke of it as "perfect in design, perfect in proportion, perfect in all its adaptations." Even Mrs. Trollope, mother of the recently deceased novelist (and the author of a sarcastic book of travels in the United States), was impressed with "the beauty and majesty of the Capitol, standing so finely high and alone,—an object of imposing beauty to the whole country adjacent."

As the nation increased in size and in importance, the Capitol became too circumscribed for the use of Congress, and it was thought by many devoted friends of the Union that the enlargement of the edifice might serve as an additional tie to bind the country together. Several plans were presented, but the first suggestion that north and south wings should be added was made by Jefferson Davis, then a senator from Mississippi, and a member of the committee on public buildings and grounds. Mr. Mills, a Washington architect, adopting this suggestion, submitted to Congress designs for the proposed wings and a new dome. The necessary appropriations for commencing the wings were made, and the corner-stone of one of them was laid with Masonic ceremonies on the 4th of July, 1851, Daniel Webster delivering an appropriate oration. The construction was begun by contract, under the direction of Thomas A. Walter, a Philadelphia architect; but great abuses were discovered, and the inspection of the work was given to Captain M. C. Meigs, of the United States Engineer Corps, an honest and efficient officer, who sacrificed the comfort of the congressmen by so changing the plans as to immure the two Houses in the centers of their respective wings, thus forming two hollow squares, in accordance with military tactics. The wings are built of white marble from the quarries at Lee, Massachusetts, with monolithic columns from Cockeysville, Maryland. The Senate chamber has room on its floor for one hundred and twenty senators, and its galleries will accommodate a thousand spectators. The hall of the House is much larger than the Senate chamber, and will accommodate four hundred representatives on its floor, and two thousand spectators in its galleries.

Each House has its "Diplomatic Gallery," set apart for the diplomatic representatives of foreign powers, who, however, are rarely seen there. Above and back of the chairs of the presiding officers are the "Press Galleries," with adjacent telegraph offices, frequented by some sixty quick-witted and generally well-informed representatives of the leading journals of the country, who, like the Athenians, "spend their time in nothing else but either to tell or to hear some new thing." Through the afternoon and late into the night the telegraph wires leading from the Capitol are busy with the reports of these correspondents, from which millions of citizens derive their daily information concerning legislative action.

The offices and committee-rooms of the Senate and the House, in the new wings, are elegant apartments, handsomely furnished, some of them having ceilings elaborately decorated in fresco. In the Vice-President's room (where Henry Wilson closed his active and useful life), visitors are shown in a closet the modest mirror, used half a century ago, the purchase of which was denounced in debate as a piece of extravagance. The committee-rooms are the hot-beds of legislation, in which the seed sown in the shape of petitions and memorials grows into bills and resolutions.

Descending into the subterranean regions of the Capitol, visitors find themselves in the heating and ventilating departments, where they are shown the intricate machinery, propelled by steam-engines, for removing the foul atmosphere from the legislative halls, and replacing it with pure air, heated in winter and cooled in summer.

During the great and angry discussions of the Kansas-Nebraska questions, the architect of the Capitol gave a supper at a night-session, at which he asked for an appropriation of one hundred thousand dollars for removing the old dome of the Capitol and beginning the construction of one better suited to the proportions of the enlarged edifice. The desired appropriation was made that night, and when Congress re-assembled the following December, the old dome had been removed, and every cent of the appropriation had been expended. There was much grumbling by the economists when another hundred thousand dollars was asked for, for the construction of a new dome; but the money was voted, and the new structure was constructed of large plates of cast iron, bolted together on huge upright iron ribs, like those of a vessel. Its total weight is nine millions of pounds, and it is crowned with a bronze figure of America, by Crawford, which weighs nearly fifteen thousand pounds more, and stands about three hundred feet above the earth. The statue faces the east, turning its back upon the present location of the city, and looking down on the level plain where it was meant to be.

While the new dome was unfinished, the war of Secession broke out, and the Capitol grounds became the rendezvous of numerous regiments of loyal soldiers, who had hastened to the defense of the city. Many of these militiamen were quartered in the Capitol. Every pleasant afternoon they were drilled, and they were often visited by a tall, gaunt, ungainly man, whose high silk hat towered above helmets and pompons, and whose kind words to the soldiers secured their devotion to "Honest Old Abe," as they called him. Twice, during the first years of the war, the Capitol was used as a hospital, and scores of brave fellows died there.

The daily sessions of Congress are much the same. As the hour of noon approaches, the senators begin to congregate in their chamber. Sometimes little groups are formed, which chat merrily until a rap from the presiding officer commands silence. A prayer is then offered by the chaplain, who does not always have many devout hearers, and his "amen" is echoed by an order from the presiding officer that the journal of the last day's proceedings be read. Before he has concluded, nearly every senator is sure to be in his seat. Petitions are presented by senators, received, and referred by the presiding officer to the appropriate committees—usually never to be heard from again. Bills are introduced and ordered to be printed. Executive communications are received and referred to committees, and reports are made by committees on subjects which have been previously intrusted to them, often accompanied by bills which are at once considered and passed, or placed on the calendar, to be taken up in their order. After this routine business, bills on the calendar are successively considered until two o'clock, when the bill which has been made the order of the day is taken up. There is no limit to speaking in the Senate, and entire days are often occupied by a senator in giving his views on some measure which he regards as of importance to his constituents, although he may not have a dozen listeners.

Usually, one of the private secretaries of the President presents himself in the main aisle of the Senate chamber about two o'clock in the afternoon. The assistant door-keeper stands at his right hand, and the presiding officer, availing himself of the first pause in the remarks of the senator having the floor, arrests him by saying: "The Senate will receive a message from the President of the United States!" The assistant door-keeper, making a profound obeisance, announces "A message from the President of the United States," and the secretary then says: "Mr. President, I am instructed by the President of the United States to present a message in writing." He then bows and hands his package of manuscript to the assistant door-keeper, who carries it to the presiding officer, after which the senator whose remarks were interrupted resumes them. Messages brought from the House of Representatives by its clerk are received with similar formalities. Later in the afternoon, a motion is generally made that the Senate proceed to the consideration of executive business. If it is carried, as is generally the case, the presiding officer directs the sergeant-at-arms to "clear the galleries and close the doors!" Then the proceedings of the Senate, relieved from the restraint of spectators and of newspaper correspondents, become somewhat free and easy. Cigars are lighted, comfortable positions are assumed, and often a good deal of humor —with an occasional dash of bad temper —is displayed in the confidential canvass of the history and the qualifications of the presidential nominees. The proceedings of the Senate while in executive session are regarded as confidential; but senators are often willing to tell correspondents what has happened, in order that they and their political friends may be placed advantageously before the country.

The House of Representatives is opened in the same manner as the Senate, except that after prayers the sergeant-at-arms places on a stand, at the Speaker's right hand, the mace which is his emblem of authority. Petitions are presented in the House by placing them, without any announcement, in a box, from which they are distributed by the clerk among the committees. The order of morning business is unintelligible to strangers, and is merely the successive recognition, by the Speaker, of those members who have obtained from him a promise that they can have the floor. In keeping these promises, the Speaker often pays no heed to members in the front seats who are endeavoring to attract his attention by cries of "Mister Speaker!" in every note in the gamut, accompanied by frantic gesticulations, and "recognizes" some quiet person beyond them.

"I have been a member of this House three successive sessions," said an indignant Tennessean who had vainly tried to obtain the floor, "and during that time I have caught the measles, the whooping-cough, and the influenza, but I have never been able to catch the Speaker's eye."

In the debates on appropriation bills, each member has the right to speak for five minutes, and those closing the debate have an hour each, parts of which they often farm out to their friends. When a member takes the floor for a long speech, especially if he reads it, he receives but little attention. A few of his colleagues and friends, tipping their chairs back to an angle which they suppose is comfortable, pretend to listen; but a large majority of the representatives go on reading the newspapers and writing letters, or retire to the cloak-rooms. When a vote is taken by tellers, a member of each party is named by the presiding officer, and the two take positions in front of the Speaker's table facing each other. Here they shake hands, and the voters pass between them—first those voting in the affirmative, and then those voting in the negative. The voters are counted by each teller as they pass, and a report of the result is made by one of the tellers to the presiding officer.

The proceedings of the Senate and of the House are taken down in short-hand by the experienced official reporters, revised in manuscript when those reported so desire, and promptly put in type at the Government Printing Office. Proof-slips are sent out when asked for, and some congressmen change, correct, and polish their sentences until but little of what they originally said remains; while others, notably Senator Edmunds, never look at a proof. The proceedings of each day, no matter how voluminous they may be, appear in the "Congressional Record" of the following morning, when another opportunity is given for correction before the pages are stereotyped for the bound edition. Each congressman receives twenty-four copies of the "Congressional Record." The revised edition is thoroughly indexed, and is bound in volumes at the close of a session.

It is a curious fact that a number of the present senators and representatives were, earlier in life, employés of Congress. Senator Gorman, of Maryland, was a page, and rose by promotion to be postmaster of the Senate. Representatives R. R. Hitt, of Illinois, and Samuel F. Barr, of Pennsylvania, were clerks of senate committees, and Representative N. F. Deering was a clerk in the office of the Secretary of the Senate; while Representatives R. W. Townshend, of Illinois, and George D. Wise, of Virginia, were pages in the House of Representatives. The transfer of these gentlemen from humble positions in the Capitol to seats in Congress illustrates the simplicity of our republican institutions.

Ben: Perley Poore.

The Improvement of Washington City (1902)

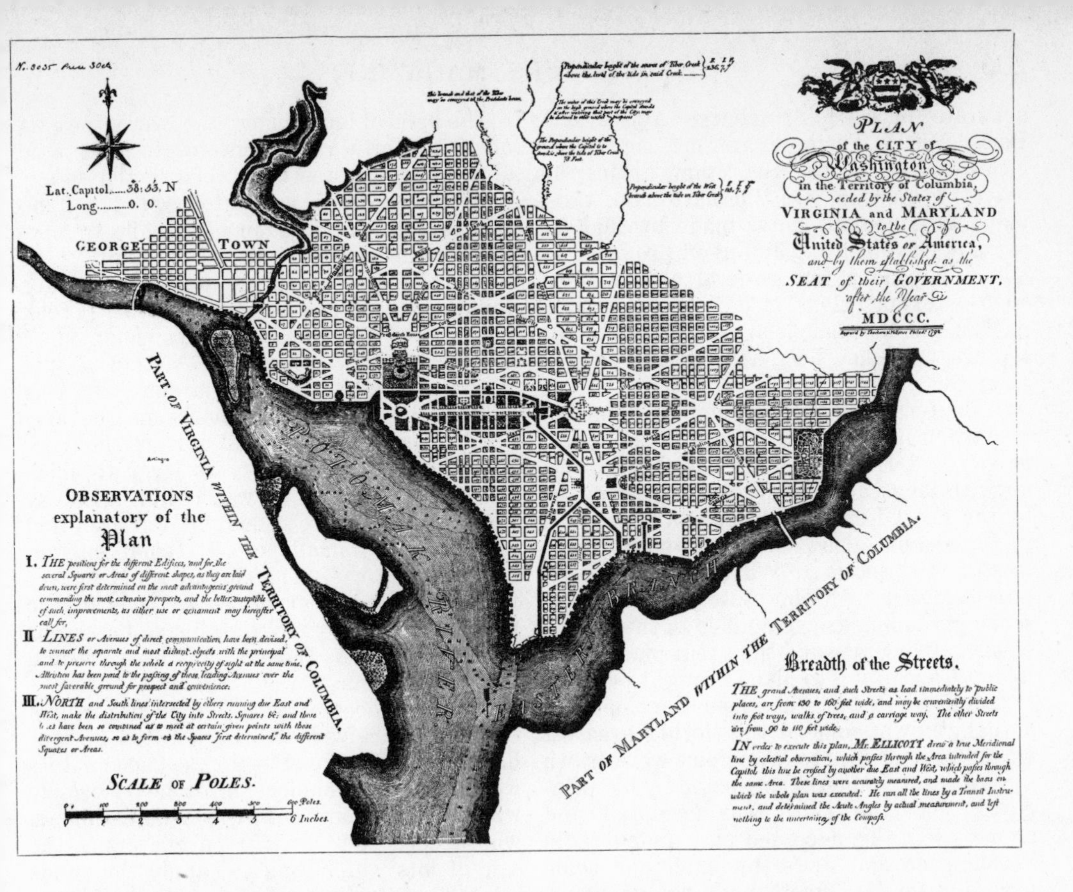

THE IMPROVEMENT OF WASHINGTON CITY.

FIRST PAPER.

BY CHARLES MOORE,

Author of "The Northwest under Three Flags," Clerk of the Senate Committee on the District of Columbia.

WHEN President Washington was charged by Congress with the duty of superintending the creation of a capital city on the banks of the Potomac, he sent Major Andrew Ellicott to mark the metes and bounds of the federal territory, and immediately afterward commissioned Major Peter Charles L'Enfant to make drawings "of the particular grounds most likely to be approved for the site of the federal town and buildings." During the Revolution Count d'Estaing had commended L'Enfant to Washington, and the latter had formed a good opinion of the young French engineer's abilities. When peace had been conquered, L'Enfant settled in New York city, where he was enjoying a lucrative practice when Washington summoned him. Such was his confidence in the President that he immediately gave up his private work, and threw himself heart and soul into the task that, while it won for his name enduring fame, brought to him personally nothing but disgrace, neglect, and poverty prolonged through more than a quarter of a century.

Arriving in Georgetown in the March of 1791, L'Enfant was soon joined by Washington, and the two tramped over hills and through forests to discover the most advantageous sites for the Congress house and the President's palace. These two points having been located, L'Enfant began his congenial task of laying out a city, reporting by mail twice a week to Thomas Jefferson, then Secretary of State. Calling on Jefferson for maps, he received large and accurate ones of Strasburg, Amsterdam, Paris, Milan, Turin, Frankfort, and other cities visited by the Secretary during his travels in Europe. On the margins of these maps were copious notes made by that observant traveler; but Jefferson proffered no advice beyond a few general observations, such as exhortations to adhere to classical models and those modern examples of architecture which had been approved by persons of taste.

A lieutenant in the French provincial service when he came to America at the age of twenty-two, L'Enfant must have been familiar with landscape-architecture as practised by the great Lenôtre, whose work, not only in France, but also in England and in Rome, is still unsurpassed. Washington was not unacquainted with the stately art of landscape-gardening as exemplified in the capital of his native State and the great plantations laid out according to plans brought oversea; and Jefferson's taste had been developed by actual study of some of the world's greatest examples of civic art. Two plans were drawn by L'Enfant, only to be rejected by his principals; but the third was accepted and adopted. In this accepted plan undoubtedly Washington and Jefferson each had some part, and for it Ellicott made valuable suggestions; but the origin and development of the general scheme belong alone to L'Enfant.

The commissioners who had the general oversight of all matters pertaining to the District of Columbia had decided on a system of streets running from north to south and from east to west. Upon this rectilinear arrangement L'Enfant imposed those diagonal avenues, radiating from the Capitol and the White House, which give to Washington its distinguishing feature. He also made disposition of the public buildings so as to secure to each its appropriate landscape setting; and he was most particular to preserve the axial treatment which is the cardinal principle of Lenôtre's work. In a word, he planned the capital city as a work of art, in which each feature should have a distinct relation to every other feature; and thus he gave to the scheme that feeling of unity which to-day excites the interest and admiration of the visitor in Paris.

In L'Enfant's plan the one great park of the city was to be the space connecting the Congress garden with the President's park south of the White House. Here a grand avenue four hundred feet broad and about a mile in length, bordered by gardens flanked with buildings, was to dignify the approach to the halls of legislation; and where the axis of the White House intersected the axis of the Capitol was to be placed the equestrian statue of Washington voted by the Continental Congress in 1783. The twenty-five springs within the limits of the city were to furnish an abundant water-supply for fountains and cascades, and Tiber Creek was to be utilized as a canal to accommodate commerce, save where the waters should flow through the public gardens. In this manner he proposed to overcome the arid conditions which prevail during the long Washington summers, or at least to mitigate them. The canal was built; in its day it served its full commercial purpose, and even now the small portion remaining uncovered is in use. The cascades were never realized; and the most urgent need of the capital city to-day is fountains as numerous and as copious as those which give life and beauty to Rome.

L'Enfant became so absorbed in his plan that he conceived an exaggerated idea of his own importance. Fearing lest speculators would select the choicest sites, he perversely withheld his map from the commissioners, who needed it to satisfy purchasers at the sale of lots which was to supply the funds for the construction of the public buildings. Washington, who had received L'Enfant "not only as a scientific man, but one who added considerable taste to professional knowledge," and who regarded him as, by all odds, the person best qualified for the work in hand, intimated to the commissioners that the feelings of men of genius "are always alive," and that it is policy to humor them, or to put on the appearance of doing so.

Unfortunately, however, it was found impossible to employ Major L'Enfant "about the federal city in that degree of subordination which was lawful and proper," and so Jefferson dismissed him after he had been employed only a single year. The President urged that his compensation be ample—twenty-five hundred or three thousand dollars: but L'Enfant placed the value of his services at fifty thousand dollars, and refused to accept a less sum, nor would he accept an appointment as professor of engineering at West Point; and until the day of his death, in 1825, the tall, erect figure of the courtly Frenchman trod the corridors of the Capitol as he vainly pleaded with Congress for the reward he believed to be his due.

Washington and Jefferson not only adopted L'Enfant's plan, but so long as they were in power they protected it from perversions, just as they also guarded Thornton's plans for the Capitol from threatened changes by builders claiming to be architects; and by the time these two worthies had passed from the scene the main features of the original scheme were fixed beyond possibility of loss, although not beyond neglect and temporary perversion. Lack of money in the federal treasury at first prevented a full realization of those elements which made for beauty, and in later years there was a marked decline in public taste.

The Civil War found and left Washington a straggling Southern town, ill built, unpaved, with cattle and swine roaming the streets at will. During the war the poor and homeless negroes, who naturally drifted to the capital, squatted upon its vacant lands and built a cordon of huts on the range of hills that commands the city on the north.

Then came the Shepherd régime, during which Washington was improved with a ruthless hand. Grades were changed, streets cut down and hastily paved with wood; Congress was outwitted and defied; judges were lured on excursions from the city in order to prevent them from restraining the demolition of unsightly structures; money was poured out like a Potomac flood; taxes were doubled, and an enormous debt was piled up: but, after all has been said, the fact remains that the result was amply worth the cost.

Meantime two great works had been accomplished. The Capitol extension, planned by Walter, had been finished during the war by the completion of the superbly proportioned dome; and in 1884 the half-built Washington monument, which had been an eyesore for a generation, was carried to its present splendid height. Unfortunately, however, the engineers, despairing of building a firm foundation at the intersection of the two axes as planned by L'Enfant, placed the monument off center as regards both the Capitol and the White House. Moreover, the space where was to have been the grand avenue connecting those two monumental buildings had become a common pasture, watered by a canal lined with wood-yards; and, as if with the purpose of destroying forever L'Enfant's conception, in 1870 the citizens invited, and Congress sanctioned, the location of a railroad across the Mall.

It is true that the parks and circles which L'Enfant had reserved for improvement by the States came to be adorned with statues of heroes of the Rebellion, until to-day Washington can boast of more bronze horsemen than any other city on the globe possesses; that, year by year, the small parks have been improved, the streets have been well paved, and many excellent residences have been built; and that large park areas have been either purchased or reclaimed from malarial marshes. The one thing lacking in the development of the capital has been that unity for which L'Enfant strove.

Such was the situation when, at the special session of the Senate, last March, Senator McMillan of Michigan, for some years the chairman of the Senate Committee on the District of Columbia, secured the adoption of a resolution directing that committee to report a plan for the development of the entire park system of the District, and authorizing the employment of experts to prepare such a plan. A conference with the Institute of American Architects resulted in the selection of a commission composed of Daniel H. Burnham of Chicago, Charles F. McKim and Augustus St. Gaudens of New York, and Frederick Law Olmsted, Jr., of Brookline, Massachusetts. It so happened that these men had worked together to produce the results achieved at the Chicago Exposition, and thus they were able to bring to their new task a familiarity with like problems, and, what was more important, the ability to work together in entire accord.

No sooner was the membership of the commission announced than requests for aid and advice came from a number of the officers of the government who had duties to perform in relation to parks and buildings in the District of Columbia; and at the very outset was established a feeling of confidence and coöperation that promises well for the success of the undertaking.

When the commission began to study the problem presented to them, they were satisfied that their first duty was to return to the original plan of L'Enfant, which had found favor with Washington and Jefferson. In order to treat the Mall as a unit, the removal of the railroad-tracks and the station was absolutely essential. Happily, the appeal of the commission found sympathetic response on the part of President Cassatt of the Pennsylvania Railroad. Most fortunately, also, the common ownership of the two railroad lines entering Washington makes possible the creation of a monumental union station, a consummation long hoped for in the District of Columbia. Thus the commission has been able to secure terms on which the removal of the tracks from the Mall may be

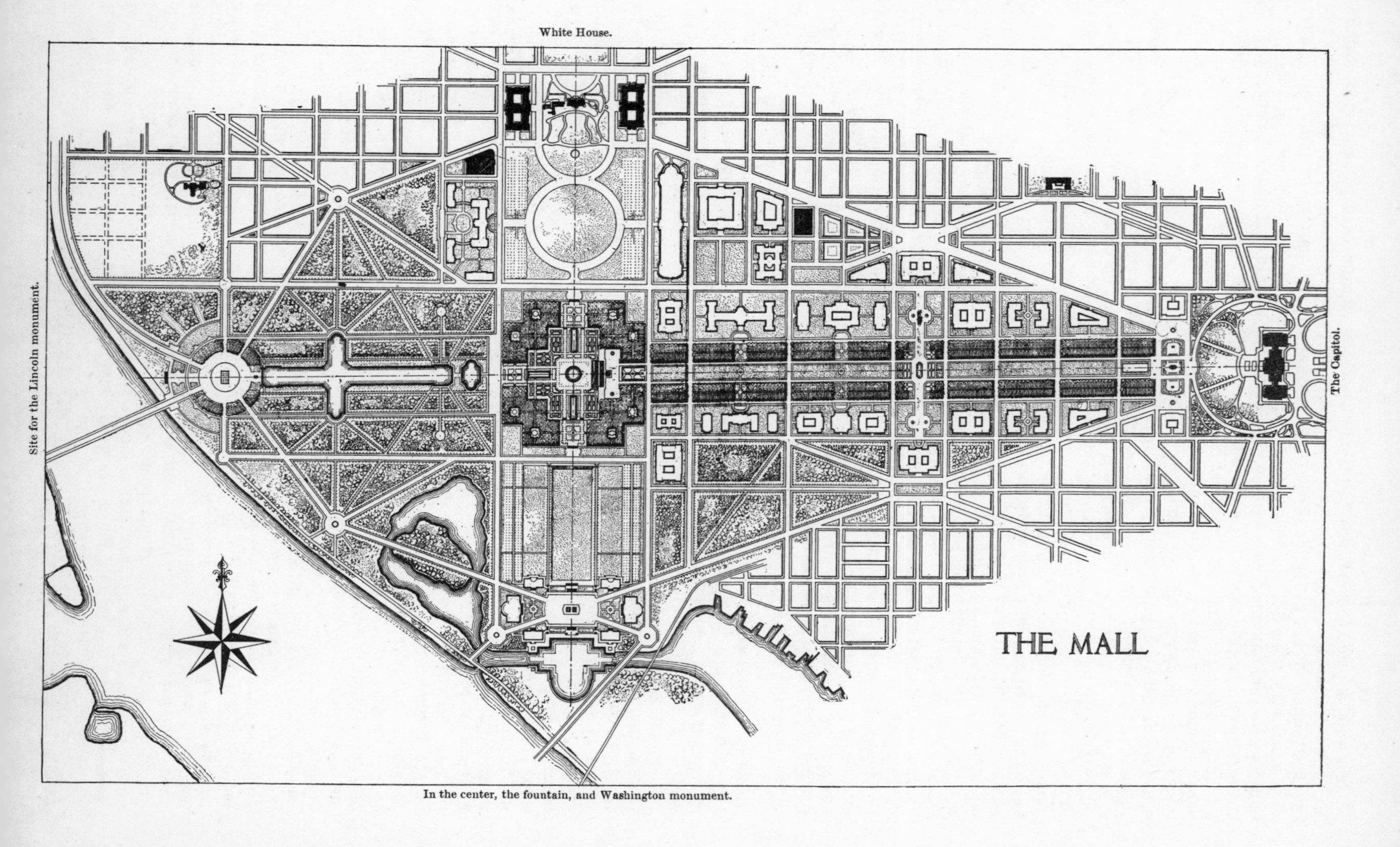

In the center, the fountain, and Washington monument.

BIRD'S-EYE VIEW OF THE MONUMENT AND APPROACHES, LOOKING EAST—THE CAPITOL IN THE BACKGROUND.

brought about by the favorable action of Congress.

The plans now before Congress contemplate not only the improvement of the Mall and the monument grounds, but also driveways, boulevards, and park connections, the reclaiming for park purposes of the Anacostia Flats, the acquisition of additional park areas in those portions of the District now ill provided with breathing-spaces, and the development of areas already possessed and awaiting improvement.

When one recalls the setting of many foreign capitals and their flat topography, one realizes that with so superb a beginning, and with the majestic monument in a vista closed by the Potomac and the Virginia hills, the possibilities for beautiful treatment of Washington are unequaled. The new plans open the way to realize these possibilities.

Let one imagine himself standing on the western terrace of the Capitol on a summer afternoon. At the foot of the extended grounds great fountains toss clouds of refreshing spray into the heated atmosphere. From the foot of the Capitol hill to and up the monument slope, a mile and a half distant, two lines of stately elms march majestically in column of fours, one column on each side of a carpet of greensward three hundred feet wide. Buildings of white marble gleam behind the rows of elms; where the streets cross the Mall great bands of light lie across the stretches of tree-shadow; carriages and riders pass and repass on the roadway half covered by the grateful shade, while pedestrians linger under the wide-spreading trees. Thus, by a simple device of planting, the monument is brought into the vista of the Capitol.

VIEW OF THE TERRACES AND THE MONUMENT FROM THE GARDEN.

Or suppose that the observer stands at the monument, with his gaze still directed to the setting sun. The space about him, as extensive as the piazza facing St. Peter's, is flanked by elms beneath which children play. At his feet broad stairs lead down to a formal garden inclosed by wooded terraces; and from this garden the broad opening leads to a long canal, tree-bordered, as at Versailles. Nearly a mile away, where the axis meets the Potomac, is a great *rond-point* surmounted by a Doric portico commemorating the one man in our national history who is worthy to stand with Washington—Abraham Lincoln.

From this point of divergence a memorial bridge leads straight across the broad Potomac to the terraced slopes of Arlington, surmounted by the temple-like mansion, which, once the home of Robert E. Lee, now stands sentinel among the thousands of graves of Union soldiers. From the same point of departure one road leads up the river to the valley of Rock River, and thence

VIEW OF THE MONUMENT AND GARDEN FROM THE SOUTH TERRACE, LOOKING TOWARD THE WHITE HOUSE.

to the great park which takes its name from that stream; while a second drive extends down the Potomac to the park formed by the engineers in reclaiming those malarial flats whose miasmal emanations, in Garfield's case, are believed to have completed the work of Guiteau's bullet.

From the portico at the rear of the White House the eye looks off over, first, the circular parade-ground, and thence over the garden at the foot of the monument, which is treated as an adjunct to the towering needle, thus establishing the reciprocity between the two structures that now is missed by reason of the construction of the monument off the axis. The space still farther to the south, between the garden and the Potomac, is arranged with basins for swimming and boating, with gymnasiums and ball-fields, with a stadium for games and displays of fireworks, and with all those means of athletic recreation which now are a necessity in civic life. The White House vista may be completed, perhaps, by a colossal figure, emblematic of the republic, standing serenely on the shore of the broad river, or even rising from the smooth surface of the water.

Fronting on the White Lots, as the parade-ground is called, public or semi-public buildings may well be placed—on the east perhaps an armory, to be occupied by the battalion of District militia, and to be used for inaugural balls or other large gatherings; on the west, continuing the line of the Corcoran Art Gallery, the administration building of the contemplated National University. So, too, the spaces fronting on Lafayette Square may come to be occupied by buildings for the Departments of State and of Justice, and by such other monumental structures as the growing needs of the republic may demand. Possibly, too, it will be found advantageous to build for the President an office building, and thus relieve the present overcrowded condition of the White House.

The historic Pennsylvania Avenue, also, will have its south side lined with such structures as a municipal building for the District of Columbia, a modern market in which the space is ample to accommodate the traffic now done on the public streets, and a hall of records for storing in safety government archives. And the Capitol grounds, too, should be faced only by public buildings, of which the number already projected is sufficient to complete the square indicated by the Capitol and the Library of Congress.

The return to the original type of treatment for the development of the Mall was not determined without most careful consideration. During the summer of 1901 the commission studied the great parks of Europe: in the Borghese Gardens, on the broad terraces of the Villa d'Este, amid the still splendid ruins of Hadrian's Villa, on the Grand Canal at Venice, on the magnificent Maria Theresia Platz at Vienna, on the swift Danube curbed between miles of stone quays at Budapest, in the Gardens of the Luxembourg, and amid the splashing fountains of Vaux-le-Vicompte they threshed out many a perplexing problem. Bushy Park and Windsor Great Park, while they emphasized the beauty of long stretches of green, warned the commission against disturbing the central space by a commonplace roadway; and Hatfield House showed conclusively the surpassing beauty of a *tapis vert* bordered by tall trees.

Will these plans, developed after much study by competent men, be carried out? That is for Congress to determine; but there is good reason to believe that the work will begin at once and be prosecuted continuously. The new building for the Department of Agriculture is to form a portion of the Mall improvement; and the supervising architect of the Treasury sought and obtained the aid of the commission in preparing the program, in selecting the architects for the competition, and in making the award. The removal of the railroad-tracks from the Mall will necessitate the improvement of the space vacated, together with the adjoining areas.

The Secretary of War has made the approval of plans for two new bridges across the Potomac contingent on the approval of the commission; and various other projects that have been delayed for the want of agreement as to the sites to be occupied now will have that obstacle removed. Moreover, there has been manifested throughout the country a conviction that the day has come to develop Washington according to a well-considered plan, rather than continue the haphazard building that has gone on since the L'Enfant plan was lost sight of.

The large degree of interest and coöperation the commission have met with since the beginning of their work is decidedly encouraging; and if only the people of the United States will support their representatives in Congress in making the necessary appropriations, the improvement of the national capital along the lines laid down by Washington and Jefferson will be accomplished speedily.

It is not essential to the success of the plans that large appropriations be made immediately. Considerable amounts of money are appropriated annually for carrying on the development of the District of Columbia in order to meet the needs of the increasing population, and from year to year new buildings are being erected by the government. The public offices are now scattered about the city, many of them being located in private buildings, the rentals of which are out of all proportion to the interest paid by the government on its loans.

There is every reason to believe that in the near future a number of the bureaus will be provided with buildings adequate to the demands of the work to be done; and the two houses of Congress are considering the question of erecting office buildings of a monumental character for the use of their members individually. What the new plans do contemplate mainly is that when appropriations are made from time to time, the buildings shall be placed and the parks shall be developed according to a definite system; and if this principle shall be established, the result must follow that the capital of the United States, already beautiful for situation, will stand as one of the most beautiful cities of the world.

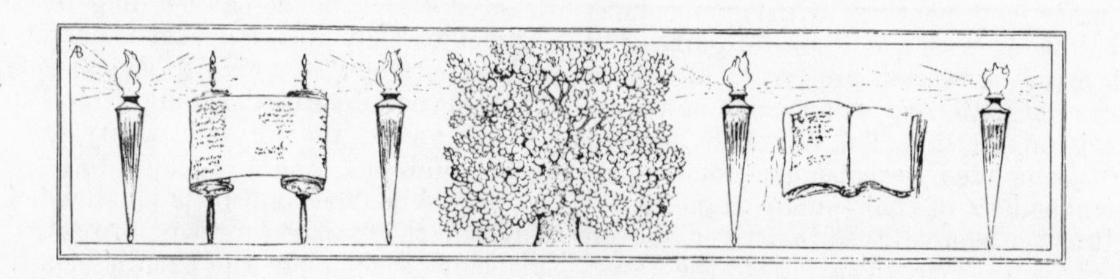

DRAWN BY JULES GUERIN. HALF-TONE PLATE ENGRAVED BY H. DAVIDSON.

VIEW OF THE MONUMENT TERRACE, LOOKING SOUTHWEST.

THE IMPROVEMENT OF WASHINGTON CITY.

SECOND PAPER.

BY CHARLES MOORE,

Clerk of the Senate Committee on the District of Columbia.

ALBERT GALLATIN, writing from Washington in 1801, expressed the optimistic opinion that the portion of the Federal City near the President's house might, in a short time, form a town equal in size and population to Lancaster or Annapolis, a prediction based mainly on the proximity of the locality in question to the well-established tobacco port of Georgetown. Mr. Thomas Twining, an English traveler who visited the site of the capital city in 1795, thought that Georgetown must share the advantages of Washington, but be independent of its failure. If Twining and Gallatin could revisit the national capital and stand on one of the antiquated bridges that span Rock Creek, they would look down into the deep ravine and see nearly the same conditions that met their gaze when first their eyes beheld that thread of water twisting between steep banks overgrown with trees. Officially the name of Georgetown is obsolete; but not until that portion of the Rock Creek Valley which lies between the ancient town and the modern city shall have been developed into a parkway will the line of demarcation be obliterated and Georgetown become in fact, as it is now in theory, a part of Washington.

Certain Georgetown families still keep alive traditions of the days before the seat of government was removed to the banks of the Potomac; and upon proper introduction one may be permitted to gaze on priceless miniatures of the piquant Martha Custis, together with many of the household belongings of the Father of his Country, relics cherished by persons who have the right to refer to those illustrious personages by the titles of intimate relationship. These families have ever held aloof from transitory Washington society as quite beneath consideration on the part of those whose title-deeds run back in direct line to royal grants. On the other hand, in Washington itself, of late years, several social circles

DRAWN BY JULES GUÉRIN. HALF-TONE PLATE ENGRAVED BY R. C. COLLINS.

THE MONUMENT AND THE TERRACE AS SEEN FROM THE WHITE HOUSE.

DRAWN BY JULES GUÉRIN. HALF-TONE PLATE ENGRAVED BY F. H. WELLINGTON.

VIEW OF THE MALL, LOOKING TOWARD THE CAPITOL.

DRAWN BY HENRY McCARTER. HALF-TONE PLATE ENGRAVED BY C. W. CHADWICK.

A SMALL TEMPLE IN THE MONUMENT GARDEN.

have developed quite independently of Presidents, cabinet ministers, and senators. With a few notable exceptions, the great houses of Washington are occupied by those who have no direct connection with the government; and high officials are welcome guests at these houses, not so much because of their position as because they also are in pursuit of social pleasures.

Then, too, Washington has a winter population numbering thousands of persons drawn thither from all parts of the country by the comparative mildness of the climate, and the fact that it is the only city in the country where a man may have an interest in what is going on without being himself actively engaged in any pursuit. The debates in Congress, questions of foreign and domestic policy and the like, furnish subjects for conversation at the round of official receptions which occupy the first four afternoons of each week, and which any respectable person is privileged to attend; so that the sojourner at the capital is sure to make acquaintances at the homes of the representatives of his State, and speedily one's social circle may be enlarged as inclination and length of purse may dictate. Also, there are the retired army and navy officers who regard Washington as the home of their declining years; and the scientific people, a greater body numerically than is to be found in any other city, at least in this country; and the thousands whom public business or pleasure calls to the capital for a few days or weeks at a time. So that Washington has become the representative American city; and any improvements which Congress may undertake in the District of Columbia will be made not alone for the benefit of the comparatively few permanent residents, but for the much greater number of American citizens who have a just pride in seeing that the capital of the United States is made worthy of the advancing power and taste of the people.

Primarily, however, the District of Columbia was created for the seat of government of the United States. The city of Washington, its public buildings, its parks and driveways, its great library, even its municipal government, all are maintained to serve the purposes of the national legislature and of those portions of the executive and judicial branches of the government which must be located at the capital.

Of late a theory has been put forth that the federal government simply finds a local habitation in the city of Washington, District of Columbia, and that there is a reciprocal relation between the government on the one hand and the municipality on the other. This view has support neither in the Constitution nor in history. Indeed, the capital was removed from New York and Philadelphia for the very purpose of giving to Congress exclusive jurisdiction over any territory which might be selected as the seat of government; and neither Washington nor Jefferson, L'Enfant nor Ellicott, ever had even a suspicion that they were not planning a city which in all its features

DRAWN BY JULES GUÉRIN. HALF-TONE PLATE ENGRAVED BY J. W. EVANS.

VIEW FROM THE TERRACE, LOOKING NORTH.

DRAWN BY JULES GUÉRIN. HALF-TONE PLATE ENGRAVED BY H. DAVIDSON.

VIEW OF THE MONUMENT AS SEEN FROM THE MALL.

should be the expression of the stability, the dignity, the taste, and the wealth of the government of the people of the United States. So that while the District of Columbia may offer attractions to private citizens, or opportunities to business and professional men, the District is, first of all, the abiding-place of the highest representatives of the people, and its development should be prosecuted in accordance with this fact.

The work of improvement is by no means a new enterprise. For years Congress has been laying the foundations. Those very necessary measures of civic housekeeping, a perfect sewer system and an adequate supply of pure water, are rapidly nearing completion; and lands have been either purchased or reclaimed for all the larger parks, so that what now remains to be done is to develop areas already possessed, and to make suitable connections among them. The city that L'Enfant planned has outgrown its boundaries, and now the task is to extend to the entire District of Columbia as comprehensive and as well-considered treatment as he gave to the forests and plains with which he was called to deal.

In a former paper the Senate Park Commission's scheme for the treatment of the Mall and the Monument grounds so as to restore the axial relations planned by L'Enfant was outlined. Leading from the Lincoln memorial site, at the western end of the Monument grounds, the improvement plans contemplate a roadway skirting the Potomac and carried on a higher level than the wharves, so that one may look down on the busy and interesting scene of commercial activity. On reaching Rock Creek, the driveway turns up the valley and skirts the stream, while the street-cars and the general traffic continue to be carried on bridges spanning the narrow ravine, and the great thoroughfares of Massachusetts and Connecticut avenues cross the valley on stone viaducts already in process of construction. Two miles of parkway bring one to the Zoölogical Park, a well-developed tract of one hundred and seventy acres, where the Smithsonian Institution aims to preserve specimens of those animals which advancing civilization threatens with destruction. Adjoining the Zoölogical Park is the Rock Creek Park, throughout the length of which a single road winds along one bank of the stream to the boundary of the District. Across the park run a few country roads; and on its wooded knolls stand a few ancient stone houses, among them the Klingle place, one of the owners of which, on his wedding-night, returned to town on an errand, and, within sight of the lights and hearing of the voices of the merrymakers, was drowned in the torrent into which a sudden storm had turned the creek. Tumbling over boulders, darting around corners, spreading itself over shallows, Rock Creek is a picturesque stream; and no matter how thickly populated the District may become, Congress has provided for isolation and quiet within the long, cool valley.

The region between Rock Creek and the northwestern line of the District has so many natural beauties that the Commission found difficulty in restraining their desires to acquire a very considerable portion of it for park purposes. Washington, following the rule with cities, is growing most rapidly toward the northwest; and already the pick and shovel of the real-estate speculator are at work tearing down wooded hills to fill picturesque valleys, after a fashion that called forth the vehement protest of Cicero against those who, in his day, were making monotonous the surroundings of Rome.

A permanent system of highways, approved by Congress, regulates the subdivision of lands in the District, and the engineers have paid more or less attention to topography in their plans for this section; but for the most part the only possible recourse is immediately to acquire those ravines and heights which will afford the most desirable park connections, and leave to government or other public institutions and to seekers for villa sites the preservation of a few from among the multitude of natural beauties.

Already the ample grounds of the long-established Georgetown University command the Potomac and the Virginia hills; and farther to the north gleam the white buildings of the Naval Observatory, standing in a circle encompassed by Massachusetts Avenue. The observatory, one of the most satisfactory of Richard M. Hunt's creations, can be seen for miles across the District, affording a fine example to be followed in future building. The newly established Bureau of Standards (by means of which the United States purposes to create a set of standards that will make the manufacturers of this country independent of Germany and England) has acquired a fine site in the northwest section, where are also located the Episcopal Cathedral Foundation, which includes the Phœbe A. Hearst School for girls; and the American University, for which the Methodists have already gathered several millions of dollars.

Here, too, the District has placed a high-service reservoir on the beautiful and commanding site of Old Fort Reno, one of a chain of fortifications that protected Washington during the Civil War.

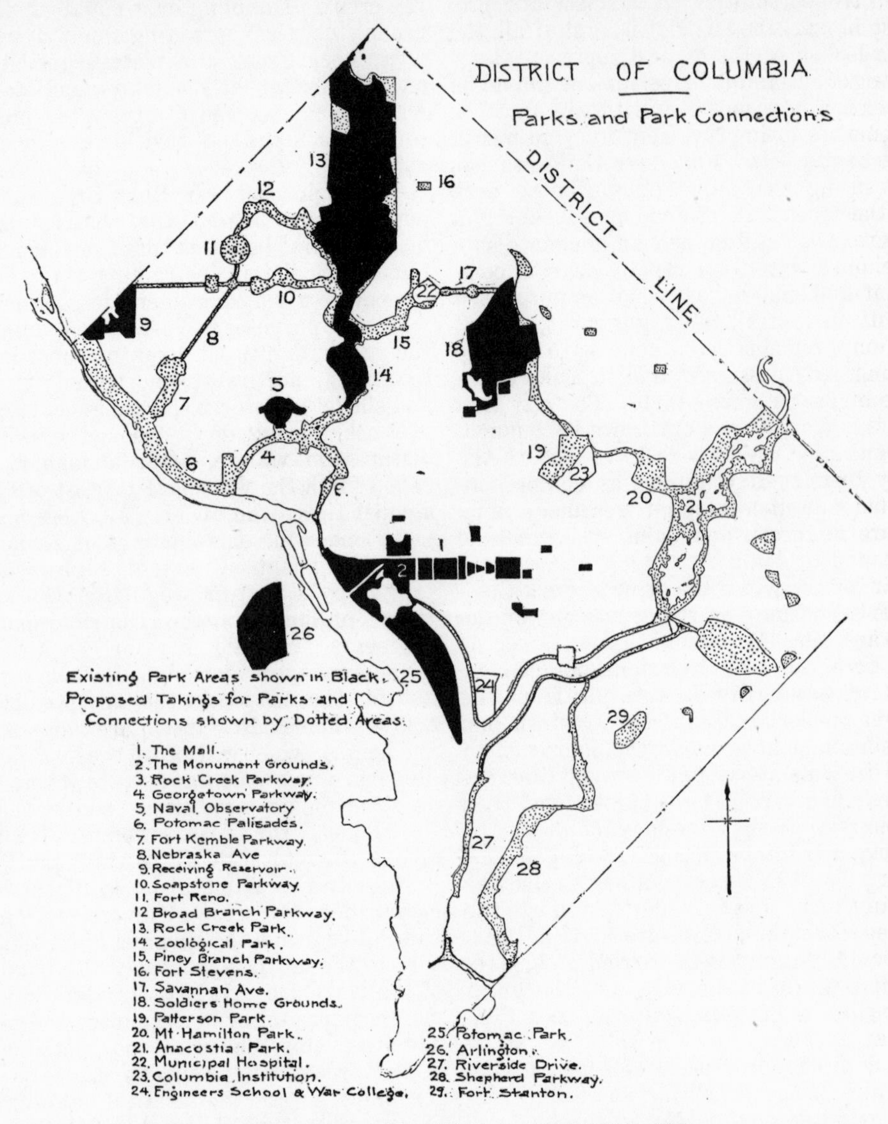

MAP OF THE PARK SYSTEM OF WASHINGTON CITY.

When the highway system was laid out all of these abandoned forts were connected by streets; and the Park Commission advise that the grass-grown earthworks be brought into the park system, because the same reasons that made them available for fortifications now make them desirable for small parks. One of them, Fort Stevens, possesses a unique interest. On July 10, 1864, General Jubal Early, with Ewell's corps of Lee's army, suddenly appeared at Rockville, ten miles from the District of Columbia, and the next morning marched down the Seventh street pike to capture the capital. At Fort Stevens Early was met by the Sixth Corps, which had been detached from Grant's army and sent up the Potomac for the protection of Washington. Surprised and baffled by finding a veteran body of men where he had reasonably hoped to encounter only department clerks and the remnants of regiments left in Washington, Early was himself attacked, and in the hot engagement that followed, one of the coolest and keenest observers who stood on the parapet of Fort Stevens, amid whistling bullets and screeching shells, was Abraham Lincoln. When a surgeon standing by the President's side was wounded by a Minié ball, General Wright ordered Lincoln down. The President reluctantly obeyed the order; but nevertheless he would persist in climbing up again and again to have a look at a real battle.

Along the eastern side of Rock Creek Park extends Sixteenth street, running in a mathematically straight line from the White House to the District boundary. Where the street surmounts the hill, a mile and a half from the President's house, is a superb site for a great memorial arch or column, whence the beholder may command the entire panorama of the city, dominated by the graceful dome of the Capitol and the serene shaft of the Monument, and having for a background the long silver band of the river and the purple hills of Virginia. The beauty of the scene is marred to a degree by the restless roof of the State, War, and Navy Building, and by the impertinent tower of the city post-office, as insistent as a spoiled child, both architectural warnings for future guidance.

Near the northern boundary of the Zoölogical Park, the Piney Branch falls into Rock Creek; and not only is the wild valley of the tiny tributary highly picturesque, but also in its westerly course it cuts across both the great thoroughfares of Sixteenth and Fourteenth streets, and thus it is fitted by nature to form in part the parkway to the Soldiers' Home. Where Piney Branch Valley rises to the level of the plain is a tract of thirty acres recently purchased as the site for a group of municipal hospital buildings; and by a suitable arrangement these proposed structures may be brought into reciprocal relations with the new building to be erected at the Soldiers' Home, so that by widening the connecting avenue a fine parkway may be completed between the parks on the axis of the White House and those on the axis of the Capitol.

The grounds of the Soldiers' Home, now five hundred acres in extent, are highly developed in an informal manner, with borders of forest and great central meadows, through which flows a small stream that forms ponds and miniature cascades. The white stone buildings on higher land at the northern end of the grounds command an extensive view of the city. For years the Soldiers' Home was the only driving-park in the District, as it is now the only one of any considerable extent. The original purchase was made in 1853, with the proceeds of the indemnity that General Scott exacted from Mexico for the benefit of the soldiers of the United States army. During the Civil War Lincoln often used the quarters of one of the officers as a refuge from the cares and worries of the White House, and on hot summer evenings he found strength in the cool of the hills and serenity in the wide prospect. To-day the grounds are the favorite drive alike of Washingtonians and of visitors, while the blue-coated soldier inmates of the home willingly share with the black-gowned students of the neighboring Catholic University of America the enjoyment of well-shaded walks and wide stretches of meadow.

From the Soldiers' Home westward the parkway extends to the high wooded hill adjoining the extensive grounds of the Columbia Institution, a national college for the higher education of the deaf and dumb; thence it continues until it strikes the Anacostia or Eastern Branch of the Potomac, including in its course one or two tree-topped elevations that should be acquired for breathing-spaces, in anticipation of the not distant day when the growth of population will lead to the occupation of the entire District.

There was a time when the town of Bladensburg, at the head of navigation on the Anacostia, disputed with Georgetown and Baltimore for preëminence as a shipping-port of tobacco. In 1755 a portion of Braddock's army was quartered on its people, and from thence marched to death on the banks of the Monongahela. There, too, was the famous dueling-ground which claimed Commodore Decatur among its victims. And in Bladensburg streets was fought a disastrous battle of the War of 1812, after which the British marched unopposed to burn the Capitol and the President's house. For General Ross, who committed the vandalism of destroying the public buildings of a nation, a place in Westminster Abbey was prepared, and his family were permitted to add to their titles that of Ross of Bladensburg.

It is many decades since the meanest wood-scow went up with the tide to the wharves of Bladensburg; and of late years the sewage-polluted flats of the Anacostia have been a menace to the health of the people of Washington, seriously retarding the growth of a large portion of the District. Subjected to the miasmal emanations from these vast stretches of tide-washed mud are more than two thousand insane persons confined at St. Elizabeth's, besides the prisoners in the jail and the work-house, the poor in the almshouse, the sick in the city hospital, hundreds of workers in the great gun-shops at the navy-yard, and the marines in barracks—a striking example of the cruelty of governmental neglect.

The new plans contemplate dredging these flats to create within the area a water park with encircling driveways and wooded islands. Some six hundred acres will thus be changed into a place for boating and swimming in summer and skating in winter; and, as a result, sports now indulged in but sparingly for lack of opportunity will be encouraged. In recent years the object seems to have been to push the river away from the city, and to deny to the people most enjoyable forms of recreation. A change in this particular cannot come too soon; and those who are familiar with the large use that Londoners make of the narrow Thames will appreciate how welcome to the people of Washington must be any line of improvement that shall utilize the lavish pleasure resources of the Potomac.

Where the Anacostia unites with the Potomac are the old arsenal-grounds, long occupied as an artillery post, but recently set apart by the Secretary of War for the higher instruction of the officers of the corps of engineers. Within the next few years it is proposed to rebuild the post and to add a war college, where the officers of the United States army shall receive the highest possible training in all subjects pertaining to their profession. When this work is completed the place will become a great military park, with ample parade-grounds flanked by tasteful quarters for the officers, barracks for the enlisted men of the engineer corps, and halls of instruction, the whole surrounded by a riverside drive connected with the boulevard coming from Anacostia Park.

Directly opposite the arsenal-grounds a long, low island separates the Washington channel of the Potomac from the main or Georgetown channel. The engineers have created this island out of the shoals and bars on the river-bottom, and have planted willows along the water's edge. Although the work of sucking up river-sand to enlarge the reclaimed area is still in progress, all that is necessary to turn the island into a most attractive park is a dike to keep back possible floods, a roadway on the raised land, and informal planting of the rich alluvial lands of the central space. The almost immediate effect of such treatment will be a pleasure-ground that will rival in beauty and availability the famous Margarethen Island at Budapest.

By a recent decision of the Supreme Court the title to the wharf property of Washington has been decided to be in the United States as the riparian owner; and when the courts shall have determined the value of the improvements thereon, the District will enter into possession of the property. This will afford an opportunity to rebuild the wharves as permanent structures of stone, with a terraced roadway carried on masonry arches to form the connecting parkway between the proposed war college and the Monument grounds, thus completing the inner circle of park connections, and forming a continuous drive around the city.

No park system for the District of Columbia would be complete that did not include ample driveways up the Potomac, not only to the District boundary, but even to the Great Falls, sixteen miles above the city, whence comes the water-supply. A well-constructed roadway covers the conduit through which the water for the city flows; and in one place, where a deep ravine is crossed, a stone arch with a span equal to the height of Bunker Hill Monument has been constructed—the longest single span as yet built of masonry. The river for miles is narrowed between high wooded banks, whose sky-lines are as wild as they were when Captain John Smith gazed upon them. To add to the picturesqueness, a half-used canal creeps along the river's edge, its frequent locks, with the whitewashed buildings for the keepers, giving a quaint flavor to the prospect. Down the Potomac, on the Virginia side, it has been proposed to build a roadway to Mount Vernon, and in time doubtless this project also will be carried out. The plans already laid out, however, will provide work enough to employ the attention of Congress for many years to come.

The expense of almost all the improvements mentioned in this paper will be borne by the District of Columbia, and the money will be appropriated according to the Organic Act of 1878 providing a permanent form of government for the District. That is to say, one half of the amounts appropriated by Congress will be paid from the revenues of the District, which are raised by the taxation of the real and personal property (including franchises) within the District, and the other half will be paid from the Treasury of the United States, such division having been found to be the most equitable method of providing for the expenses of the seat of government. Moreover, the projects are so arranged that the appropriations for them can be made from year to year, as the District finances may warrant and as population increases; and the increase in land valuations consequent on the improvements should provide for the additional expense by larger revenues from taxation.

There is no question that the moneys appropriated will be expended honestly and efficiently, because it is beyond question that the government of the District of Columbia is conducted with entire honesty, with a very high degree of intelligence, and without political partizanship. This result is not reached, as most writers on the subject have assumed, because of the denial of suffrage to the citizens of the District, thus making a paradox in a republican government. The true explanation is to be found in the fact that under the express provisions of the Constitution the nation's capital is governed by the citizens of the United States, who choose its aldermen and the members of its legislature when they elect senators and representatives; and that Congress deals with the District of Columbia in an enlightened spirit, and with an understanding that comes of familiarity with large affairs.

Making Laws at Washington (1902)

THE CENTURY MAGAZINE

JUNE, 1902.

MAKING LAWS AT WASHINGTON.

GOVERNMENT BY THE HIERARCHY.

BY HENRY LOOMIS NELSON.

WITH PICTURES BY ARTHUR I. KELLER.

WHEN this article was being written, the old-time caucus seemed to be reviving in the national House of Representatives, but it was probably only a momentary awakening. Meeting after meeting was held by the Republican members for the purpose of reaching a conclusion on the President's proposition to grant tariff concessions to Cuba in order that the chief industry of the island might not meet with disaster. As we learned from the scribes of the press, who hear what is said in the council-chamber though the doors be closed, the speeches for and against relief to Cuba were many, vigorous, and even acrimonious. It sounded like the caucus of an elder day, when party policies were agreed to, and the agreements kept. Then caucus was really king, but years have passed since his rule was broken. Now his subjects seldom come together; even on this momentous occasion many of the leaders do not attend, and the meeting is a mere debating-club, whose decision does not control a single vote in the open House.

The caucus is now held for the information of the three men who rule the House with the power of an ecclesiastical hierarchy. Its orders are obeyed by consent, so that, in a party crisis, it must learn the temper of the House before it dare direct its party following to consider and adopt a given measure. Debate in open session is nearly a thing of the past, and the revival of the caucus is intended rather to furnish a vent for excited feeling, and to measure and sum up the relative strength of different opinions, than to frame a policy upon which the party will unite.

"Who is speaking?" I recently asked a newspaper correspondent as we looked down from the press gallery.

"I don't know," he answered.

"And who is he, and he, and he?" I went on, pointing out one member after another.

TYPES OF CONGRESSMEN.

"I don't know," he said again.

"We used to have to know members; don't you?" I asked in some astonishment.

"Not at all. This gentleman thinks that he is debating, but he is n't. The fate of this bill is known in advance to the three gentlemen who determined that it should be considered. They permit a little talk on it, but they shut off the oratory at the precise minute they have fixed upon, and take the vote. In our day we have to know only those three men and a few chairmen."

Usually the hierarchy knows how the House stands through its feelers, the committee chairmen and a few others. Just now it thinks it well to inform itself through a caucus. When it receives the information sought, it will do as it pleases as to permitting consideration. It will be governed by its view of what is best for the party. The House votes, but it does not deliberate; the hierarchy thinks for it. The mischief is that the power of these rulers is not accompanied by responsibility, and that the country does not always know the reasons for their conclusions.

What is the hierarchy of the federal House of Representatives, and who compose it? It consists, primarily, of the majority members of the Committee on Rules, and is a natural growth from the rules devised by Mr. Thomas Brackett Reed when he was first chosen Speaker. Mr. Reed's new rules were based upon a large and aggressive contempt for parliamentary precedents, and especially for those which were known as the "muniments of the rights of the minority." Among other revolutions, he wrought a change in the method of securing a hearing for bills, and he put an end to obstructive tactics. He invented the system of considering a measure under a rule, made for each occasion, which prescribes the number and kind of amendments that may be offered, the length of time during which debate may run, and the precise moment when the vote is to be taken. As Speaker he had the right to say who should address the House. Irreverent newspapers called him "Czar"; and he certainly had power enough to start an evolutionary movement which resulted in the present system. The majority of the House consented to carry out the orders of its members of the Committee on Rules, and gradually the habit of obedience strengthened. At first the old-fashioned caucus continued its time-honored endeavor to declare, with more or less success, the policy of the majority; but at last this ancient instrument of party management lost its power and fell to its present state. The hierarchy now does what the caucus used to do, and does it more effectively; for it is notorious that three men can reach a conclusion more readily than three hundred.

The revolution was not accomplished without protest, without discussion, without angry outbursts from the minority that was suppressed, and also from members of the majority who felt themselves injured when their pet measures were killed and when their amendments were arbitrarily declined.

"Sir," said a Democratic member from the South to a New England Republican, as the two walked out of the House after some discussion of the new Reed rules, "you 're slaves. I 'm ashamed, sir, to think of such a subservient crowd as free American citizens. Your party, sir, has voluntarily assumed the yoke of a tyrannical czar."

"It is not precisely true that we are subservient, although it may be true that we are gagged," mildly responded the cautious New England Republican.

"Well, sir, if you 're not subservient, and feel that you 're gagged, why don't you rebel? Why don't you rise in your might as freemen and break your shackles?"

"Oh, we can't do that very well."

"Can't!" sneered the Democrat. "Then I say that you 're so like slaves there 's no telling the difference. Why is n't it subserviency, eh?"

"It is n't subserviency at all; it 's loyalty to the party, a desire for party harmony."

"And is Reed the party?"

"That 's what his rules say."

Mr. Reed was a masterful man, and his was the word of the committee of which he was chairman. Mr. Henderson, the present Speaker, is only chairman, and the three Republican members united—the other two being Mr. Dalzell and Mr. Grosvenor—utter the command.

When a momentous question of party policy arises, there is the voluble caucus, or a score or so of other leaders may be invited into conference. These are usually the chairmen of the more important committees, but there are also some who are not chairmen, rising men with influence. The policy being determined on, the majority usually obeys, for obedience, for the moment at least, has become almost second nature, while the rule of the powers is aided by the desire for party unity or harmony, which stands near the head of the list in the catalogue of a politician's virtues. This power of the few is,

HALF-TONE PLATE ENGRAVED BY F. H. WELLINGTON.

THE LOBBY: A MEMBER AND HIS CONSTITUENTS.

however, in process of formation; it is far from being firmly established. The signs of revolt at the present session, and the threats that have been heard of "beating the Ways and Means" on the Cuban question, may be ominous of another change. It is not likely, however, that the House will consent to become inefficient. The power of the hierarchy—though obedience to its decisions is by common consent—rests on the substantial basis of the rules which prescribe the duties of the Speaker and his Committee on Rules. Protest against the outcome of these rules as members may, they really approve of them. At the opening of each session some one pretends to urge an amendment to the end that debate may be more free; but that he is content to be defeated is indicated by the remark of one of these momentary rebels:

"It 's a great deal better as it is, no doubt," he said. "If we were allowed to talk all we wanted to we 'd certainly make fools of ourselves."

OUR ACTUAL GOVERNMENT.

We say that ours is a government by a President and a Congress guided by the judiciary, and the English say that theirs is parliamentary government. We are wholly wrong, and the English are only partly right. Ours is government by Congress, while that of Great Britain is parliamentary government "veiled in monarchical forms, and containing in its organization large survivals of aristocratic privilege." In our republic the executive department is under the control, extended to most minute and insignificant details, of the legislative department; and the judiciary, theoretically the guardians of the folk-made law, are yearly more inclined to accept, as the ultimate command of the republic, the word of their supposed coequals and coördinates, the representatives of the people and the States. In Great Britain the administrators of the law are the servants of the House of Commons, but every-day administration is usually independent of the law-making power, because it follows monarchical tradition, and because Parliament, by self-imposed restraints, has made vexatious interference difficult, whether by itself or by the crown. In our country the President does little that he is not directly commanded to do by the legislative branch of the government; in Great Britain the Parliament frequently leaves to the executive and administrative officers of the empire a wide discretion, without which there can be no real responsibility.

The framers of our government started out deliberately to tie down the executive, and their work was so well performed that the President, in ordinary times, seems like the big elephant in the zoo: he agitates the atmosphere by swaying back and forth and by trumpeting; but when he attempts to take a step forward, he is suddenly reminded of the steel bracelet and chain by which he is bound to a wooden peg. In times of dire necessity, when the nation is in danger or when war is threatened, Congress sometimes abandons its usurpations and even imposes its rightful duties upon the President. It did so in the War of Secession, when it passed over to Mr. Lincoln its own power to suspend the writ of habeas corpus. On the outbreak of the war with Spain it gave fifty million dollars to Mr. McKinley to spend as he would. In emergencies it almost invariably throws all the responsibility upon the President, giving him at the same time, it is fair to say, all the power essential to the accomplishment of his task. Mr. McKinley was really the head of the government, partly because Congress saw the necessity of a strong executive in the crisis through which we were passing, and partly because the President knew its will, its character, its attitude, and its moods. He dealt with it tactfully, and obtained from it nearly all that he desired. He was unable, however, even in the midst of war, to secure at once the consent of Congress to the adoption of modern tactics for the army, and his reciprocity treaties are yet unratified. Still, none of our Presidents ever managed Congress so adroitly as Mr. McKinley did. He often paid extravagantly for the laws he desired, but often, too, he won over an angry lawmaker by mere amiability.

"It 's like going into a beautiful conservatory," said one senator to another, speaking of a visit to the White House from which he had just returned. "You may go there mad clean through; but when you get there the air is soft and kindly, and is rich with perfume. Delicious and tempting fruits delight your eyes. Your visit is happiness itself. But when you get back home you realize that you 've brought away nothing but the memory of the perfumes and of the rich colors of the fruit: you have n't anything in your pocket."

The needs of the hour drove Congress back into its proper sphere,—far within it,—and Mr. McKinley's way did the rest. But when

HALF-TONE PLATE ENGRAVED BY F. H. WELLINGTON.

SCENE IN THE HOUSE OF REPRESENTATIVES: A WITTICISM FROM THE CHAIR.

ordinary times return after a strenuous period, the steel bracelet and the chain are slipped back on the elephant's leg, and he returns to his trumpeting and swaying, cunningly devising means for tempting a stray legislative peanut his way.

The progressists, to borrow a term from our old ally and "sister republic," love to speak and to think of the Constitution as a "living organism," and it is true that they have made our institutions move on, sometimes to their betterment and sometimes to their injury; on the whole, it is probably true that whenever the motion is too rapid the effect is not happy. The law-making branch of the government was not intended to be all that it has become. Notwithstanding the eighteenth-century hatred and distrust of executive power by which the fathers of the republic were actuated, they supposed that the principal business of Congress would be the enactment of laws for the promotion of the general welfare. The legislators were indeed charged to keep a jealous eye on the executive; to repress his inevitable ambition to become an absolute ruler; to keep control of the army and the navy in order that he might not have the opportunity, which it was known that he would desire, to seize upon the government and to set up a throne. The framers of the Constitution, deeply impressed by Roman history and French philosophy, also knowing much of Magna Charta and the Bill and Petition of Rights, were jealous of the executive. The first grant of power to the Senate is that of jurisdiction over impeachments, while the President is the first to be mentioned as a possible accused. Other powers were granted to Congress which have enabled the legislative branch of the government to impair, and in some instances to destroy, the wholesome discretion of the President. Congress gives money for the maintenance of the army, for example, but it directs him to expend it for an army organized and drilled in accordance with its notions of formations and tactics. It permits him to build war-ships on patterns which it chooses. It makes him the paymaster of officers whom he commands, but whose rise in their profession is governed by its hard-and-fast rules of promotion, the commander-in-chief being denied the natural privilege of rewarding his subordinates for exceptional merit or conspicuous gallantry. "If you want

HALF-TONE PLATE ENGRAVED BY J. TINKEY.

A SUBCOMMITTEE MEETING, WHERE THE SERIOUS WORK IS DONE.

this man confirmed," says the Senate, "you must give us the right to name So-and-so; if you want this treaty ratified, you must insert in it these articles of ours." So the

HALF-TONE PLATE ENGRAVED BY R. C. COLLINS.

"'DOUBTLESS ONE OF THE MOST NOTABLE SPEECHES.'"

independence of the President has been diminished, although his influence on the country may still be deep; the system of checks and balances has often brought about the very conditions which it was framed to avoid; and Congress, at present under the domination of the Senate, is the government.

The character of this power, its capacity for the work which it ought to perform and for that which it has absorbed, its methods, its manners, its intelligence, and its virtues and vices, are very well worth a more general investigation than they often receive. Skipping over the past, leaving behind us the First Congress, with its small-clothes and ruffles, its sectional jealousies, its prolonged debates about titles and precedence, its wisdom, for it had much, and its bargains over debts and the site for the national capital, of which there were many; passing by the days of big events and of such giants as those over whose departure Benton grieved, we bestow only a glance upon the "great Senate" of our own generation, the Senate of Thurman, Edmunds, Carpenter, Matthews, and Bayard. It was the Senate into which the prodigal Southern son returned, with an utter incapacity to understand that questions had changed, an absolute refusal to put his mind to the knotty and confusing problems of the new order, but with an oratory which burned, and of which he and his friends were finely proud.

"Indeed, madam, it was; it was a remarkably fine oratorical effort—doubtless one of the most notable speeches that the Senate has listened to since befo' the wah, madam," said a former Confederate soldier, and then senator, to one who stirred his gallant pulses with feminine congratulations on one of his own speeches.

These old-fashioned Southerners are gone now, with their economic incapacities, their florid oratory, their childlike vanities, their gentle dignity and courtesy, and their warm patriotism; for it is true, and worthy of record, that, their struggle over, the best of them transferred to the nation the hot passion of loyalty which had inspired them in the battle for their States. Their successors are not like them, but are no less the products of their time.

TYPES OF THEIR SECTIONS—MEN OF FORCE.

It is with the lawmakers of to-day that we are to deal, and we look over the roll of the two houses to learn something of their fitness for their tasks—the task of making laws, which is theirs of right, and the other task, which is not theirs, that of prescribing, with minute detail, precisely how the President shall expend each dollar they bestow upon him. Most of them are lawyers, and many of them are business men. Lawyers should certainly know the ethics of legislation, the history of parliaments, the meaning of words, and the value of grammatical construction and lucid expression; business men are supposed to know the material needs of the country. On the other hand, none but high-minded lawyers ever get beyond their attorneyships, and none but great merchants can understand that the general welfare is not always expressed on the profit side of their own ledgers. We are not considering exceptional men, nor the average man, but men who are higher than the average and yet far from being the highest; because, under existing conditions, men of the highest character cannot get into politics, save by happy accident, and men of the highest intelligence, barring one here and there, do not want to get in. The mental activities of the period find happier employment in the wide realm of commercial and industrial adventure than they could possibly enjoy in the cramped ring of politics, and, so far as we can now see, this is likely to continue to be true.

On the whole, one sees the country in the senators and representatives. These lawmakers are types of their various sections. The New England member is racy of the soil. The Philadelphian bears the impress of his city. The time was when as much might be said of the New York member, but that is a remote day. The New York city member of the present is too often a person whose kind the stranger would be obliged to search for in parts of the town where he would need a guide. With the exception of these seeming strange folk from the metropolis and of certain far Westerners, the usual senator or representative suggests to one who has traveled through the country the section whence he comes to Washington. As for the far Westerners, though this is especially true of the senators, not including those from California, perhaps, or maybe Oregon, there is about them the air of the tall buildings, of the mining-camps of the Atlantic seaboard, and one is irresistibly inclined to think of their relations to things as proprietary. They have unmistakably the habit of ownership.

Still one would say, glancing down at these lawmakers from the gallery of either house: "Here is the country: that punctilious gentleman who is speaking on the subject of propriety is the same kind of man who displeased the querulous Maclay in the First Congress; he who listens with rumpled hair, endangering the fit of his broadcloth coat by his easy attitudes, is from the Middle West; and he who is so extraordinarily busy with telegraph- and cable-blanks is nominally from the Rocky Mountain region, although his name is on the glass door of a New York office, and his most occupied chair within the room behind that door." One will note the Southerner from the city, and will distinguish him from the gentleman from the Southwest to whom walking is only another means of expressing a preference for sitting down, but whose intelligence is alert enough, once he is aroused.

Having noted these distinctions by a glance, one will discover, on better acquaintance, that these legislators are, without question, almost without exception, from among the superior people of their States and neighborhoods; that they are men of probity and intelligence in their private affairs,—trusted counselors, loyal friends,—and if some of them have not always been good citizens, their offenses have been committed in obedience to the exigencies of party politics. Most of them are patriotic; at least, they have a pride in the achievements of the country, in its progress, in the place which it holds among nations, but especially in its wealth, in its mechanical ingenuity, its industrial enterprise, in its "resources" and its "output." There is no more apathetic body in the world than Congress when a question of political science is under consideration, but there is no more alert body when the question touches the pockets of the constituencies, or the wealth-producing powers of the country.

The oleomargarin bill was under consideration. It was the bill which the House of Representatives debated at the present session for several days immediately before passing by unanimous consent, and without any debate whatever, the bill abolishing seventy-five million dollars of our annual revenue. It proposed to tax oleomargarin in order to destroy the industry; in the language of the House, it was "a bill for the cow." A prominent member had spoken long and well, and on a high plane, against such vicious class legislation. He was opposed to the employment of the taxing power for any such purpose.

When he finished, the man whose seat was next to his rose to reply. He eulogized his neighbor's high-mindedness, but added that, in searching for the author of certain other bills of like viciousness, he had been disappointed in finding that this patriotic gentleman was the sponsor for every one of them. He had introduced, among other measures, a bill to punish people for selling any but pure wool unless the baser quality was clearly marked "Mixed wool." So drastic were the provisions of this bill that, under them, the tailor who made clothes from "mixed wool" was liable to imprisonment if he did not mark them as the law prescribed.

"Do you think that 's fair treatment?" asked the high-minded assailed, as the other took his seat.

"Why not?"

"You know well enough why I had to introduce that 'pure-wool' bill," said the victim of the disclosure. "Besides," he added, "your constituents wanted that bill passed. I 've got hundreds of letters from them."

"Who wrote them?" asked the oleomargarin member.

"Sheep-raisers," responded the wool statesman.

"Bah! I have n't got a sheep in my district. The fact is, Charles, that all the cows are in my district and all the sheep in yours."

It is in the nature of the human mind that constant dwelling upon material grandeurs induces a belief in the primacy of wealth, and in the righteousness of means by which wealth is gained. It was very recently that a statesman exclaimed, in hot eloquence, and in response to one who urged fair play to Cuba: "You are on dangerous ground, sir: in your talk about mere honor, you are likely to forget our business reputation."

How do these various elements unite in the work of government? In the first place, let us look at them as they carry on their proper work of legislation. The making of laws ought to be a very serious occupation, and their object should be the general welfare of the country; but nothing is less serious than the outward semblance of Congress when it is engaged in the task of legislation, and commonly the "general welfare" is as incidental an interest of the ordinary statute as revenue is of a modern tariff bill. In our time, so far as the House of Representatives is concerned, a statute is an edict. The old theory that legislation is the result of discussion, as I have said, is obsolete. This is not to say that there is no longer speech-making and occasionally real debate. Within a few years, votes have been changed even in the House of Representatives, and, what is more extraordinary still, on a contested election case, by the able argument of a member of the majority party in behalf of the sitting member, who was of the minority. But we cannot determine congregated character, any more than individual, by sporadic instances. Debate in the House of Representatives is rare, and, like that on the oleomargarin bill, mainly for home consumption. Legislation is not the formulation of the opinions of the representatives.

THE REED RULES.

THE order of to-day is of course a logical outgrowth. Not many years ago there was, in the House of Representatives, too much of the kind of freedom which our fathers insisted on at the end of the eighteenth century. The basis of that demand for freedom was the assumption that every one having power is bound to become a tyrant. Therefore we tied up the executive so that he had no discretion, while the minority of the legislative branch of the government tied up the majority so that the whole body became afflicted with a sort of creeping paralysis which some twenty years ago naturally culminated in immobility. Then it was that Mr. Thomas B. Reed, the last great gladiator of the floor, took it into his head that the American Congress ought to possess the "go" of the American business man. This was an extreme position, for it did not recognize the enormous value to a democracy of the enforced inactivity of its representatives. Mr. Reed was so occupied by his wrathful efforts to escape the bonds with which Mr. Randall's minority was forever tying up the majority that he forgot, for the moment, the blessings which the country had often derived from the inability of Congress to move in the direction desired by the majority. He poured out his sarcasm freely on the obstinate Mr. Randall and the still more obstinate Mr. Holman, and once, urging a change of the rules which would give the majority the right to accomplish something, said that the whole business of the country was in the power of the minority; that nothing could be done without the consent of members who possessed the power and technical skill of obstruction, or filibustering.

"Why," he said (I write from memory, and recommend that the "Congressional Record" be not consulted for verification), "the gentleman from Pennsylvania, even with the distinguished aid of his friend from Indiana, cannot attend to all the business of the country; you can't pour Niagara through a pipe-stem"—a remark, by the way, which suggests a query. Why should Congress have usurped such a Niagara of jurisdiction? Notwithstanding the removal by the Reed rules of the obstructive valve at the intake, the pipe is no larger, while the flow grows in volume not only as population increases, but as the desire for government aid grows, a growth much more rapid than that measured by the decennial censuses.

Mr. Reed opened a new era, going back to a theory of a century or so ago, whence, however, Congress seems to be progressing toward a real reform, that is, toward the establishment of the responsibility of the majority party. One step more and the country will catch sight of its governors. Mr. Reed found the Speaker sitting at the fountain of all legislation, and therefore of all government; he buttressed him, adding greatly to his strength, giving him, in effect, the power of life and death over bills, and bestowing upon him the right to speak for the House when the question of a quorum to transact business was at issue. Then he constructed a hierarchy, of which the majority members of the Committee on Rules were the center, and to this hierarchy is now confided the control of legislation.

Long ago the work of bill-preparation was placed in the hands of committees. It was very early in the history of the present government that a Committee on Elections was established; and in the Third Congress there followed the Ways and Means Committee, appointed first for the purpose of reporting as to the ways and means to be adopted for the support of the proposed fleet which was to be formed for putting down the Algerine pirates. Very soon, too, came the Committee on Private Claims, fruitful breeder of a now pestilent brood. By virtue of necessity, the necessity being the growth, healthful and unhealthful, of congressional business, the House of Representatives was forced to give over the task of preparing bills to various other committees, which increased in number and gained in power until now they not only prepare the bills, but, as the phrase is, perfect them.

We are in the habit of saying that, in our Congress, no one is charged with the duty of preparing measures, as the government is in the British Parliament. This is in part a mistake. We began very early to leave this matter of preparation to selected bodies, and at the outset both houses founded bills on resolutions which were first discussed in Committee of the Whole. Bills were not introduced then in the Senate until the principle involved was first determined in committee, and in the House they could be introduced only by selected committees to which the subjects had been referred. The individual, however, cannot be kept down in this democracy of ours. Very soon he insisted on his right to draw his own bills, to present them, and to have them printed at the public expense. He knows, nine thousand nine hundred and ninety-nine times out of ten thousand, that his bill will never get any further than a reference to a committee, but he sends copies of the printed bill to his constituents, and they are thus led to believe that their representative is on guard. He

HALF-TONE PLATE ENGRAVED BY R. C. COLLINS.

THE REPORTERS' GALLERY.

will get their post-office for them, and he will see that some federal money shall be spent on the masons, carpenters, and laborers of the district; he will have their stream improved, and the lumber company will do a bigger business and employ more of their fellow-citizens; or he is out trust-hunting, and will bag a few capitalists in the very act of growing richer. It is a great comfort to members to be able to present bills. Besides gratifying constituents, it makes a pleasant break in their regular occupation of running errands, and gives them momentary glimpses of statecraft.

Hundreds and hundreds of bills on the same subject are introduced. This year there was a run on anarchy. Some years ago the minds of congressmen were bent on currency and money subjects. In a few years we shall have a flood of irrigation bills. This frenzy of bill-drawing is not all wasted effort: if the congressman has an idea on a subject which is sure to be considered, the best way for him to get that idea before the country is to put it in a bill. All bills on the subject will go to the committee which is drafting the measure that will be passed upon by the hierarchy, and so his idea will be read and perhaps adopted. Therefore the practice of introducing bills is partly a survival of the older practice of debate. During the first week or ten days of the present session of Congress, more than three thousand bills and resolutions were presented and printed. Before the session is finished there may be thirty times that number, most of them interesting to individual citizens and to localities. A dozen of the subjects embraced in them may affect the general welfare, and of these three or four, outside of the great appropriation bills, will reach the stage of consideration, and may pass one or both of the houses. In nine years the annual cost of legislation has increased from $7,683,514 to $9,972,217. Included in this expenditure is the amount devoted to the Congressional Library, which in 1900 was about $650,000 less than it was in 1892. Therefore the yearly cost of legislation proper, including public printing, was in 1900 about $3,000,000 more than it was in 1892.

METHOD OF LEGISLATION.

THE method of legislation is now to be considered. A Congress never assembled without the avowed consciousness that "something must be done." The trouble is that there are always conflicting somethings, and until the Reed rules were put in operation, there was no one to select those which were essential—in other words, to cut out the work for Congress. There is no government to introduce a bill which shall express the party's policy, and for which the party is willing to stand before the country. Probably the framers of the Constitution believed that the information and advice of the President's message would be accepted and followed, at least by his fellow-partizans. But, in practice, any strong expression of opinion by the President is resented as dictation, his statements of facts are doubted, and his advice is discarded. If he procures what he wants, he makes terms for it; for, in their eagerness to provide against such corruption as that by means of which Walpole controlled the House of Commons, the fathers invented a system of checks and balances which furnished the executive and legislative branches of the government with ample funds for the corruption of each other. President Washington's effort to establish confidence between the two branches of the government, as is known, did not result happily. The "impudence" of the Senate in postponing consideration of his treaty with the Southern

Indians angered him, and we have a record of the impression made upon at least one of the senators by his appearance in the Senate accompanied by the Secretary of War:

"I cannot now be mistaken," wrote the ill-natured Maclay. "The President wishes to tread on the necks of the Senate. Commitment will bring the matter to discussion, at least in committee, *where he is not present.* He wishes us to see with the eyes and hear with the ears of his Secretary only. The Secretary to advance the premises, the President to draw the conclusions, *and to bear down our deliberations with his personal authority and presence.* Form only will be left to us. This will not do with Americans."

Therefore the presence in Congress of the executive and his representatives soon ceased. Hamilton sent in his own funding bill, and Knox a militia bill, but the legislative branch regarded measures prepared by experts and offered publicly as intruders, and looked sourly on them; still there is often manifested a willingness to adopt an executive policy which is presented at the back door and accompanied by a liberal offer of patronage. Mr. Charles A. Dana told a story which illustrates a kind of relation existing between the two "coördinate" powers. He wrote that he was employed by Mr. Lincoln to purchase, with patronage, Democratic votes for the admission of Nevada, the State being needed for the ratification of the Fifteenth Amendment. Mr. Lincoln's death prevented the consummation of the bargain. Any one is at liberty to think, for the sake of all concerned, that Mr. Dana's memory was at fault, but no one who is familiar with Congress will be surprised by the inference that Mr. Dana expected to find his task an easy one.

The effect of patronage on the congressional mind is wonderful, but it is perhaps more wonderful that the fathers did not refuse to give to the dreaded executive so great a corruption fund. One of the most notorious of that noble breed called "watchdogs of the Treasury" had secured a place for his son in one of the scientific bureaus of the government. After that, while he growled at every other appropriation, he was extremely kind to his son's bureau; so, one day, after he had argued in favor of an increase in the expenditures for that service, an inhuman member rose in his place and simply said:

'T is sweet to hear the watch-dog's honest bark
Bay deep-mouthed welcome as he draws near home.

Until Mr. Roosevelt's coming, Mr. Cleveland was the last President to take the public into his confidence, and his victory over the minority of the Senate, which, by obstinate filibustering, by open violent war, and by treachery, sought to prevent the repeal of the purchasing clause of the Sherman Act, suggests that there may be better legislation when the important work of Congress is all performed in the open, and when the country knows definitely which individual or group, or which party, is responsible.

THE CAUCUS AND THE HIERARCHY.

THE executive having failed to make an impression upon Congress by the weight of his authority or by the soundness of his advice, the majority party invented the caucus. It was a Democratic device of the Eighth Congress, and endured as long as party policies were not intersected by sectional or personal interests. When parties began to disintegrate, when Southern Whigs and Northern Whigs looked askance at each other, when there were Breckinridge and Douglas Democrats, when there were gold and silver Democrats, and when the tariff line ran through each party, the caucus became of little value, for congressmen will no more consider the interests of their party when advancement of them would threaten their own political fortunes than they will permit the general welfare to stand in the way of the material interests of their several districts.

The caucus has been followed by the hierarchy or the oligarchy, the origin and power of which I have already explained. There are other institutions than those of Great Britain which develop in the attempts to overcome old evils and to meet new conditions. A few years ago there was no power but the Speaker to determine the measure which the House should consider, and he accomplished all that was possible for him to do by permitting a member to "catch his eye." He could not always do as much as this. On one occasion, for example, Mr. Carlisle had promised to recognize the member having charge of the International Copyright Bill, in order that he might move to suspend the rules for the purpose of passing that measure. The motion was to be made on the last Monday morning of the session on which such motions were permissible. It was an exciting moment, for the representatives of the American Copyright League were in Washington in force; they had been there nearly all winter; knowing that their measure of justice could command about seven eighths of the votes in the House, they were sure that their bill would pass: but once more they were doomed to disappointment, for a man from Illinois, who was recognized first "because his business could be so quickly disposed of," rose, and demanded the reading of a Pacific railroad bill. This consumed the hour devoted to motions to suspend the rules. I believe it was never definitely ascertained whether the Illinoisan's bitterness of soul was caused by the Copyright Bill or by a bill granting a pension to Mrs. Philip Sheridan. If he be still in existence, he is at liberty to take either horn of this dilemma that he prefers. At any rate, he succeeded in postponing enlightenment for a year or more.

When a committee chairman caught the Speaker's eye his troubles began. Every other committee in the House objected to the Speaker's choice, and other bills were offered. The House voted on the question of consideration. Generally there was no choice. If there was, and the bill got in motion before the House, it ran very slowly, and its race lasted a long time. Appropriation bills had the right of way, as a matter of course, but a score or so of committees were meeting behind closed doors, or holding public hearings for the purpose of formulating legislation for the "general welfare," or for the relief or profit of claimants, or of old soldiers not entitled to pensions under the general law, or of inventors who had something to sell the government, or of localities that wanted streams improved,—sometimes at a cost which, as General Grant said, would make macadamizing cheaper,—or new public buildings. And there was, as there is, the District of Columbia, the laws for whose government constitute about ten per cent. of the total legislation of Congress. Of all the legislation thus ground out in the committee-rooms, the only bills which were, and are, perfectly sure to reach the House, besides the appropriation bills, are the River and Harbor Bill, and other measures affecting the personal fortunes of congressmen, because they "do something for the District," or for the "old soldier," or for some still more selfish interest. If legislation of a purely general character reaches the House of Representatives, it does so in response to a loud clamor from the outside which the lawmakers are obliged to heed. Thus legislation advances. Dusty old bills creep out of committee-rooms where they have lain forgotten by the busy men whose chief occupation lies in remembering their constituents. They are brushed up and presented to the country in response to a demand which is always loud and occasionally angry. So it is not true that we never have legislation for the "general welfare." After years of hesitation we obtained a civil-service reform law, an international copyright law, the repeal of the mischief-working silver law, a gold-standard law. After the war with Spain was finished we secured a law which put an end to our eighteenth-century army and gave us a force which is moderately modern.

SECRECY.

THE work of preparing all measures is done in secret, and no one person or leader, and no party, is responsible for what is done or left undone. The country does not know why this item is inserted in an appropriation bill, why that economy has been practised, or what is the reason for some bit of extravagance. Sometimes the committee demonstrates that even it might be enlightened by discussion and criticism, and perhaps the letting in of light would show that advantage might follow if Congress and its committees should leave to the discretion of executive and administrative officers some of the details of expenditure. I have been told of a "breast-high stone wall" at West Point, for example. Years waxed and waned while superintendents pleaded for twenty thousand dollars for the construction of a "breast-high stone wall" on the road leading from the wharf to the plane, the road running along the edge of a precipice. At last Congress moved, and the twenty-thousand-dollar wall was built. Having moved, it was now impossible for it to stop, so it went on year after year appropriating twenty thousand dollars each year for a "breast-high stone wall," until "breast-high stone walls" became a drug at the Military Academy. They ran around the post, and threatened to choke it up. Superintendents begged Congress to shut them off, and finally succeeded.

When we find a special appropriation for five dollars and sixty-six cents for the repair of a harness belonging to the Treasury Department, and when we are told that once the State Department was unable to pay telegraph bills because the money appropriated for that specific object had been exhausted, although there were unexpended balances in other appropriations, we naturally wonder why Congress is so meanly suspicious of the executive that it cannot trust a cabinet officer with discretion to mend his own harnesses, or to use the telegraph and cable as freely as the business of the country demands.

Another illustration of the distrust felt by the legislative branch of the government for the executive has a touch of humor in it, bitter though the experience was for the victim. Congress insists that no money shall be expended, in certain cases, except after advertisement for bids. An officer reached a lake-port late one afternoon with a quantity of public stores. He unloaded them and himself guarded them through the night. The vessel in which they arrived caught fire; the wharf and the stores were threatened. All other resources being exhausted and the danger increasing, the officer found a tug, engaged its services, towed the burning steamboat out into the lake, and saved the public stores. He paid for this tugboat from his own pocket, and when he rendered the bill to the Treasury Department, he was told that he could not be reimbursed for his expenditure, because he had not advertised for bids. Years and years passed, and finally the officer, or his estate, was paid by grace of Congress formulated into a special act. For forty years Congress has been directing the executive department with more and more minuteness as to the expenditure of every dollar.

Woodrow Wilson, nearly twenty years ago, recognized the essential power of committees, saying, in "Congressional Government": "It is now, though a wide departure from the form of things, 'no great departure from the fact' to describe ours as a government by the standing committees of Congress." To-day he could add that it is government by subcommittees of the standing committees, the whole directed by the hierarchy. The subcommittees number from three to five members each, the minority party being represented on each of them. The subcommittee formulates the bills, which are then presented to the full committee, and nearly always, especially the appropriation bills, these bills are accepted by the full committee as they are written. The subcommittees do an immense quantity of work. Their members are industrious, while the members of the Appropriations Committee are intelligent and well equipped. Those of the House of Representatives acquire a tendency to save, but real economy is impossible in a body nearly every one of whose members is eager to secure some government dollars for his own district. It is said that Mr. Cannon has saved the country seventy million dollars since he has been chairman of the Committee on Appropriations. Whether or not this be an accurate or only an approximately accurate estimate of his services, the country surely owes him a debt of gratitude, as it owed one to Mr. Randall and other chairmen and members of this committee. But if this be the saving, think of the magnificence of the loot! The subcommittees are the autocrats at the birth of legislation. When the full committee has occasion to discuss a measure, whether reported by a subcommittee or not, it is often the majority members alone who participate in the debate. This is always done when the question is one of party policy, as tariff bills are. When the majority has reached its conclusions, the minority members are sent for and vote on the measure.

Thus the bill is formulated, and now comes the task of the hierarchy. The hierarchy, as I have said, selects the measures of general importance which are to be presented to the House, determines upon the time which is to be allowed for debate, and fixes the day and hour at which the vote is to be taken. Now we encounter the substitute for the old-fashioned caucus. In this process of selecting bills for consideration the assistants of the hierarchy may be consulted. The hierarchy decides as to what measures shall be heard and passed upon. Thus far it is absolute, or nearly so, because, on the whole, the opinion of the leaders as to what is best for the party is sound; at least, it is usually accepted as sound. Their tenure of power is uncertain, however, because, like the committees and the subcommittees, they work in secret. The public does not know them, and party sentiment therefore cannot sustain them, because it cannot be appealed to in their behalf. They have, for the moment at least, the power of leadership without its responsibility. It would probably surprise the country to know how nearly Congress has become a disciplined body within a few years, and all on account of the spirit of power and of subordination bred of the Reed rules. A few men dictate to it. Two men, for instance, determined that a tariff tax should be imposed on Porto Rico. When the program is made, the majority members of the Committee on Rules call in the minority and inform them of the decree. The minority has long ceased to object; long ago the outcries about tyranny died out, except that perfunctory cry at the beginning of the session. The decree is obeyed, for obstruction is not only difficult, but filibustering has grown unfashionable in both houses. The long struggle against the silver repeal bill was not an unmixed evil: it taught the filibusters a lesson, a lesson which they have learned too well in the Senate, for there many a minority senator now fears to express any opinion whatever, lest he be charged with obstruction.

A STEP TOWARD RESPONSIBILITY.

HERE is a step toward responsible government. When the House and Senate have each a committee, composed of none but members of the majority party, whose business it shall be to select the measures for consideration, who shall be responsible not only for the subjects presented to Congress, but for their purpose and their form, the country will know then, as it does not now, where rests the responsibility for failure or the credit for achievement. Such a reform would not be comprehensive or complete, but it would be a long step forward. It would concentrate responsibility, but no more than power has already been concentrated by necessity arising from existing conditions. The burden of the responsibility is due to those who hold the power as well as to the country. Let us know who frame and direct legislation, and who, therefore, under our system as it has been worked out, govern us. This is a reasonable demand, and its grant is essential, for mysterious and irresponsible power leads either to tyranny or anarchy. We have had a taste of both. Most recently it has been tyranny, but revolt against the hierarchy is always threatened, and revolt would be comparatively easy in the House of Representatives against a power the existence of which is unknown to the public, and which, therefore, cannot defend itself or give reasons for its conduct. At present the revolt of a member is not apparently directed against the party, but it will be recognized as so directed when the majority's full control of legislation is also recognized, and then a revolt for whimsical or personal or purely selfish reasons will be dangerous to the rebel. The party must then abide by the decrees of its chosen hierarchy, and stand or fall on its wisdom and virtue.

CONFERENCE COMMITTEES.

AT the other end of its passage the appropriation bill encounters another arbitrary legislative power—the conference committee. Three members of the Senate and three members of the House, the majority again dividing responsibility with the minority, meet together, theoretically for the purpose of reconciling and composing the differences between the two chambers. Very often they do much more than this: they insert legislation which has not even been considered in either house. A conference committee has been known to increase proposed rates of duty in a tariff bill above the rates determined on either by the Senate or the House. There is nothing more autocratic, and a conference is often concluded on the very last days of the session, when there is no possibility of debating the report. It is at this point, however, that the House Appropriations Committee saves a little of the public money. One of the attributes of the Senate is a large and generous feeling of utter irresponsibility for expenditures. The senators give and take munificently. "If one wants a million-dollar court-house, why, let him have it, if our streams can be deepened, our pools widened, or our fields watered. Are there not millions in the Treasury? And, since the Constitution gives to the House the sole power to originate money bills, our brethren the members can stand the outcry; we spend, and they take the consequences." Therefore the senators largely increase the appropriations in which, in the language of political commerce, there is "pork." And the House conferees must pare down or throw out what, in the same vernacular, are known as the "steals."

It had been a long and weary struggle when, toward four o'clock of the morning of a certain conference, Mr. Cannon said to the conferees of the Senate:

"The House will yield no further; the bill must go without the other amendments of the Senate."

"Well, well," exclaimed the expert senator, rising and buttoning up his coat, "if the House is to domineer, if our propositions are not to be listened to, we might as well report a disagreement. We can't tolerate dictation."

"That is so," said another senator; "we can't yield to a threat, even if we compel an extra session."

And the third senator also murmured of an extra session.

"Shall we call the old bluffers?" whispered Mr. Cannon to his young colleague, who was serving on his first conference committee.

The young colleague assented.

"Well, gentlemen, do as you please. The House will not consent to any further rob-

HALF-TONE PLATE ENGRAVED BY J. W. EVANS.

A LITTLE DISAGREEMENT IN CONFERENCE COMMITTEE—"'WE CAN'T TOLERATE DICTATION.'"

bery. Let there be an extra session, and the Senate will be responsible for it."

So the conferees separated. The senators made doleful speeches about the tyrannical House, even going to the length of declaring that they were in danger of sinking to the level of the British House of Lords; but at length they yielded. Still, as the present evolution is progressing, the time is coming, if it is not already here, when the House will be unable to stand on any point against the Senate.

So we have an irresponsible autocracy at the beginning and at the conclusion of the bill's passage, and most of the members of the House, at all events, are mere recorders of a power undisclosed to the country. The hierarchy always yield, however, to the jealousies and the greed of their majority; that is, they are practical, and select for consideration the measures of whose success they are reasonably sure. Nearly every member of Congress (there are some fine exceptions) thinks first of his own political future. To promote this he seeks appropriations of money that will be expended in his district. Then he considers all general questions from the point of view of the district, or his State, or his section. Only a very few consider, first of all, the general welfare. Therefore the influences which tell most on legislation are selfish. The log-rolling River and Harbor Bill and public-buildings appropriation, pensions, claims, and all legislation with "pork" in it, must be given the right of way after the regular appropriation bills, which themselves contain abundant favors. When general legislation comes up for consideration, local opinion, newspaper opinion, bosses' opinions, the prevailing sentiment of the district, control votes, and all these must be taken into account by the hierarchy. A newspaper correspondent suggests a resolution: the member hastens to offer it. A militia colonel criticizes a regular-army bill: the bill must be changed to suit the militia. A prominent claimant has contributed to a campaign fund: his claim must receive attention, even an unjust decision. The unreasonable, improper, dishonest business goes through partly, at least, because no one can be held responsible for it. Why not let in the light, so that the country may know whom to charge with pernicious measures, with neglect of the public needs, and with undue extravagance, and whom to credit with the sound laws which are passed at every session? Why not work back, then, to legislation by discussion?

Toward the establishment of the right kind of responsibility the House seems to be drifting. It moves slowly, but just now in the right direction. It may not arrive; it may have halted; it may be diverted: but the outlook is that it will never again be without a central authority, that it will not again become an inefficient mob. Whether this be for the better or for

HALF-TONE PLATE ENGRAVED BY R. C. COLLINS.

AN APPEAL IN THE LOBBY.

the worse remains to be seen. What has really happened is this: the hierarchy gives the House an opportunity to do what it desires to do. What remains to be accomplished is the focusing of public opinion on it so that it shall desire to do what it ought.

The Proposed Changes in the National Capitol (1905)

THE PROPOSED CHANGES IN THE NATIONAL CAPITOL

BY CHRISTIAN BRINTON

WITH ILLUSTRATIONS FROM THE PLANS OF MESSRS. CARRÈRE & HASTINGS, CONSULTING ARCHITECTS, NOW FIRST PUBLISHED

OUR most important building, historically and architecturally, is a reflex of the Constitution. It is an embodiment of those principles which from the outset stamped themselves upon the destiny of the nation. Despite differences of policy, despite disaster even, the Capitol illustrates the gradual evolution of a single unifying idea. Threatened more than once with destruction, and on several occasions with changes which would have obliterated its original character, it has yet conformed closer and closer to the aims of its earliest patrons and projectors. In the fullest sense of the term it was, and is, national.

After plans for the city of Washington had been perfected by the expressive and imperious L'Enfant, the next consideration was the construction of what were then called Congress House and the President's House. From the beginning no one knew better than the Father of his Country how much depended upon the completion of the Capitol. In his own wise words he said: "It is the progress of that building that is to inspire or depress public confidence."

Both Washington and Jefferson displayed zealous interest in the various designs submitted, and both agreed on all essential points. What Washington sought was a combination of "grandeur, simplicity, and propriety," and that which appealed most to Jefferson in the plan presented by Thornton was the fact that it seemed "noble, simple, beautiful." The phrase was Miltonic, and the day itself was one of spacious vistas and exalted endeavor. Yet most of these aspiring dreams have been abundantly realized. L'Enfant's city proved a prophetic flash of patriotism, and Thornton's conception of Congress House has always remained a fitting transcription of the noble dignity of the Declaration. The key-note of all that was said or done was, however, that simplicity desired alike by Washington and by Jefferson, that simplicity of which the Capitol is to-day the mute and immemorial witness.

The history of the Capitol, both structural and spiritual, is a history of the preservation and amplification of the same principles which were responsible for its inception. A union of conservatism and sound sense seems from the beginning to have guided the fortunes of the edifice. Virtually all departures from the initial plan have been resented, and substantially everything in the way of legitimate development has been encouraged. At the very outset the jealous and officious Hallett was not permitted materially to alter the sober beauty of Thornton's design, nor has any subsequent meddler exercised a similar privilege. Attempts were made by Latrobe, Bulfinch, and others to institute radical changes, but in each instance the sterling sagacity of Jefferson, Madison, and Monroe prevailed. Its successive archi-

THE CAPITOL IN ITS PRESENT STATE

tects sought to make the Capitol individual; the Presidents and statesmen wisely upheld its general and typical significance.

By 1850, or just a score of years after the completion of the old Capitol, it was decided that the building was inadequate to the increasing needs of Congress. The structure then consisted of the present central portion, capped by a wooden dome, and two wings with smaller domes, the Senate occupying what is now the Supreme Court chamber and the House what is now Statuary Hall. Considering the scope of the projected additions, it was obvious that a crisis in the growth of the Capitol was at hand; and it is due to the good judgment of President Fillmore in appointing Thomas U. Walter as architect that the building emerged not only more commodious than before, but more symmetrical and more imposing. Several schemes were advanced by Walter, the one finally adopted being the logical expedient of placing wings north and south, connected with the main structure by corridors. Each of the wings was embellished with porticos and rows of Corinthian columns, the whole being similar in character to the original architectural unit. Although the older portion of the building was of sandstone, the additions were marble, liberal coatings of white paint being applied to minimize the discrepancy in color.

The corner-stone had barely been laid amid a burst of mid-century eloquence, and work begun on the wings, when it was seen that the dome must inevitably be dwarfed by the proposed extensions. Plans for a new and larger dome were forthwith approved, and the difficult task of substituting the present cast-iron expedient was undertaken. While work was necessarily stopped on the building proper at certain periods during the Civil War, it became an article of faith, almost, with Lincoln to insure the completion of the dome. He felt and fervently believed that "in the progress of this crowning feature of the Capitol all might see typified the continued unity and strength of the United States." Like Washington, he, too, realized that the structure was more than a mere matter of stone and mortar and iron. Before the close of the war, Crawford's by no means divine "Goddess of Freedom" had been firmly implanted on the tholus surmounting the dome, and in 1865 Walter resigned, leaving the building substantially as it remains to-day.

It is little short of amazing that the Capitol, considering its purely natural vicis-

WALTER'S PLAN, WITH THE SLIGHT MODIFICATIONS OF CARRÈRE & HASTINGS, FOR THE EXTENSION OF THE EAST FRONT OF THE CAPITOL

situdes, should produce an impression so consistent and so harmonious. From time to time it has been under the State, War, and Interior departments, and its makers have been many and diverse. Yet somehow it always managed to escape threatened aberrations, and has gradually become the existing sane and inspiring edifice. When Walter retired, after years of admirable service, he realized that while the general effect was in the main satisfactory, there were various shortcomings which his successors would in time see fit to correct. He felt that the dome, which had been built on the old foundations, lacked apparent support when viewed from the plaza, and also that the central eastern motive was unfortunately dominated by each of the new wings. Moved by these considerations as well as by a persistent clamor for even more space, he filed for future reference several alternate sets of plans providing for each contingency. Happily Walter's most pretentious scheme, which consisted in extending the east front two hundred and seventy-five feet, never received serious attention. It is also a matter for congratulation that nothing further was done during succeeding years apart from laying out the grounds and perfecting the approaches, terraces, and promenades. From time to time other propositions for the enlargement of the Capitol were entertained, but always with a certain caution. The building had become in large measure a realized ideal, and each Congress showed less and less inclination to tamper with its structural integrity.

A continued lack of space, the fact that the east front shows undoubted architectural defects, and a natural desire to reface the sandstone portions of the old structure with marble, finally resulted in the appointment of the present Joint Commission of the Senate and the House on the Extension and Completion of the Capitol. At the request of this commission, Messrs. Carrère & Hastings, the consulting architects, recently submitted a report covering the points under consideration; and it is encouraging to learn that all their recommendations have been unanimously approved by the members of the commission. The plans of Messrs. Carrère & Hastings for the construction of office-buildings for the Senate and the House having already been accepted, opportunity is herewith offered for the first time to discuss their scheme in its entirety. Back in the spacious days of the aspiring L'Enfant, and

THE EAST FRONT OF THE NATIONAL CAPITOL AT WASHINGTON

later under the Park Commission's revision of his diagram, it was intended that the east front of the Capitol should form an imposing quadrangle. For a century or more there was scant hope that L'Enfant's quadrangle would be achieved; but eventually, in accordance with his theory, the Library of Congress was placed in the southeast corner of the quadrangle, opposite the Capitol. Following this same plan, the senators and congressmen have now decided to erect two separate office-buildings, the one for the Senate to go on the north and that for the House to go south of the square. These buildings will be on the farther side of avenues, as shown in the plan on page 699, and will be identical except for certain interior arrangements. The equation on the northeast which would naturally balance the Library of Congress has not been provided for as yet, though it will in all probability be a new and much-needed home for the Patent Office.

It is reasonable to infer that, when completed, the quadrangle will form an admirable ensemble. The distribution of the several buildings appears to be excellent, and their proper subordination to the Capitol is amply assured. Although at present the Library asserts an unpropitious independence of conviction, this will be less evident when shared by a companion structure. In their designs for the Senate and House office-buildings, the consulting architects have sought to emphasize rather than to detract from the restful dignity of the Capitol, and a close scrutiny of their drawings seems to imply success. Formerly, when the city was little more than a waste of swamp and scrub-oak, it became necessary for the early commissioners to provide "footways" in order to facilitate communication between the several departments. It is the idea of the existing commission to institute a subway running entirely around the Capitol quadrangle, and accommodating passengers for all present and future points along the line. Senators and congressmen can thus leave the floor and enjoy ready access to their offices and caucus- or committee-rooms, and eager visitors will be speedily shunted from the Capitol to the Library and return.

The incisive Senator Roscoe Conkling more than once remarked that the Capitol was "a dome with a building under it, instead of a building with a dome upon it," and it is mainly this effect which Messrs. Carrère & Hastings seek to correct in their rearrangement of the east front. Unhampered by considerations of space, they are able to approach the problem on strictly architectural grounds. While following in a certain measure the more feasible of Walter's suggestions, they have exercised greater restraint, and have displayed a deeper regard for the accepted appearance of the building. The plan which they favor, and which it is hoped may be adopted, shows as little change as possible in the composition of the façade. In detail their scheme consists in moving the front of the old structure only far enough forward to bring the main wall at its center under the extreme projection of the dome, which now overhangs the wall and seems to repose on the portico. In order to accomplish this, it will be necessary to extend the wall twelve feet ten inches in an easterly direction.

The additional space thus acquired, while it will not be great, will nevertheless prove of advantage. On the main floor, to the east of Statuary Hall, a series of alcoves will be created which can serve for the further storage of documents; and east of the Supreme Court there will be a corresponding series of alcoves for robing-rooms for the judges. In the basement and on the floor above a like increase in space will be afforded,—that in the basement being particularly welcome to the congested Law Library, which is directly under the Supreme Court. This projection of its eastern wall will also give, in the central section of the building on each

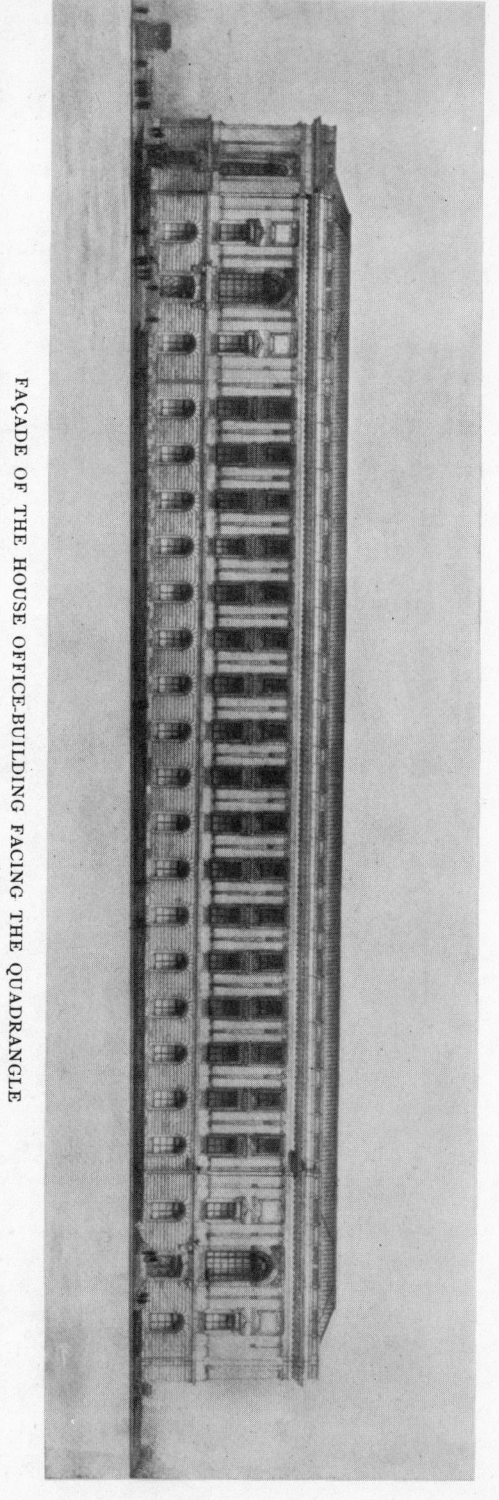

FAÇADE OF THE HOUSE OFFICE-BUILDING FACING THE QUADRANGLE

Drawn by Robert L. Adams and Jules Guérin, after the plans of the consulting architects

PERSPECTIVE VIEW OF THE HOUSE OFFICE-BUILDING

side of the main entrance, two rooms with windows opening on the portico, making, for the three stories, twelve rooms in all. Following Walter's prior suggestion, it is the intention of the consulting architects to add, at the same time, one column on each side of the main pediment, thus broadening the pediment so that it may dominate, instead of being dwarfed by, the pediments of the Senate and House wings.

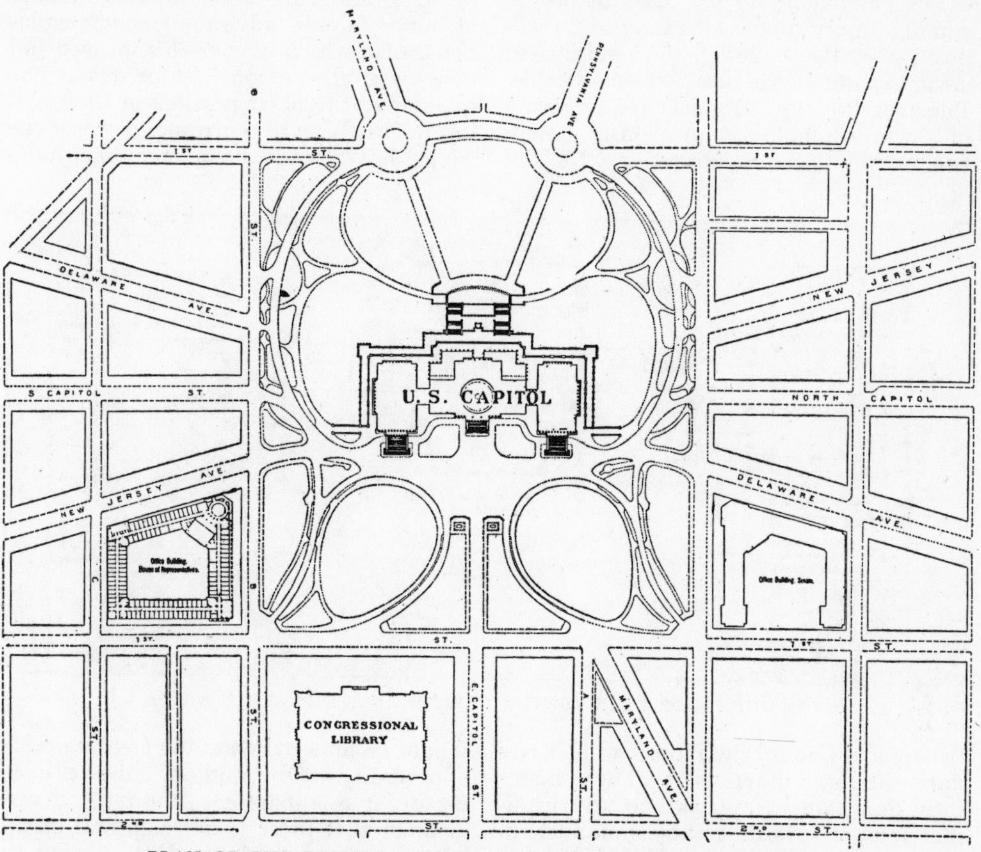

PLAN OF THE CAPITOL QUADRANGLE AND RADIATING STREETS

At the instance of the commission, Messrs. Carrère & Hastings have also prepared a second plan, entitled scheme "B," which is much more ambitious and comprehensive in scope. In scheme "B" the central portion of the building is advanced thirty-two feet and six inches easterly from the walls of the Supreme Court and Statuary Hall, giving, according to the report, fourteen well-lighted rooms on each floor, seven on each side of the main entrance. New sections would be added in order to avoid the recessed courts and to provide for an ample corridor serving the several committee-rooms and connecting the Senate and House wings, the Rotunda, and various important circulations. It is obvious that this latter plan places vastly more space at command; but, owing to the erection of the two separate office-buildings, space is not a primary consideration. The façade would be harmonious and majestic, showing the central portion and wings grouped together with a colonnade running in a broken line along the entire width of the east front. This or any similar innovation must, however, destroy the actual physiognomy of the building. Instead of remaining a unit composed of three distinct parts, it would become a unit of five almost equal parts. The spectator, viewing the mass in perspective from directly in front of either wing, must unquestionably find his vision obscured by the middle section, and would thus lose a desirable and picturesque singleness of impression. It is greatly to the credit of the consulting architects that they do not in any way counsel the adoption of scheme "B," but rather the simple, scrupulous propriety of the plan previously discussed.

There being no possible means of obtaining sufficient space for committee-rooms and offices in the Capitol proper without injury to the character and composition of the building, the decision to erect separate structures was inevitable. Pursuant to the original requirements of the quadrangle, as previously noted, two entirely new buildings, one for the Senate and one for the House, will shortly flank the large inner court. These buildings, duplicate in appearance and in dimensions, will form great colonnades, in each case about five hundred feet long, fronting on the quadrangle. Lower not only in themselves, but being on land ten feet lower than the Capitol, they can hardly fail to enhance the impressive conformity of the general effect. Mr. Carrère for the Senate building, and Mr. Hastings for that of the House, have agreed in choosing the Doric order as being less ornate than the Corinthian, which has been so freely employed in the Capitol both on the first floor and in the dome. The buildings will contain respectively an office for each congressman and two offices for each senator, besides large caucus-chambers, as well as dining-rooms and other agreeable and convenient features.

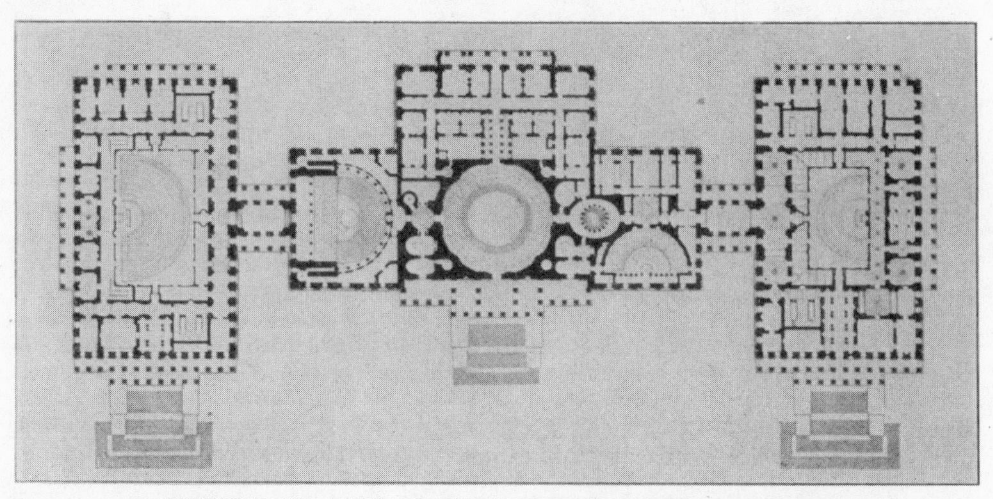

GROUND-FLOOR PLAN OF THE CAPITOL IN ITS PRESENT STATE

Work has already begun on the House office-building, and its progress will be watched with increasing interest, for it marks the first step in the creation of the new Capitol—the Capitol which will not be a single isolated structure, but a composite group of buildings.

In their report to the Joint Commission the consulting architects make a number of minor though advisable recommendations, all of which have been approved and now await the action of Congress. The refacing of the older portions of the Capitol in marble, to correspond with the wings, has already been mentioned, and should be undertaken at the first favorable opportunity. On studying the eastern façade, it is apparent to the most casual amateur that there is no sculptural group in the pediment of the House wing to balance that now adorning the pediment of the Senate wing. This should of course be supplied; and while it must be similar to its predecessor in size, character, and finish, it is to be hoped that it may prove less platitudinous in sentiment. The suggestion for replacing the present blue-stone steps on the west front of the Capitol with steps of white marble is neither costly nor arduous, and would add sensibly to the reposeful uniformity of the approach.

It is not the contention even of enthusiasts that the Capitol is, or ever will be, a complete and perfect whole. There is little hope that it will ever be entirely finished, and still less that it may attain perfection.

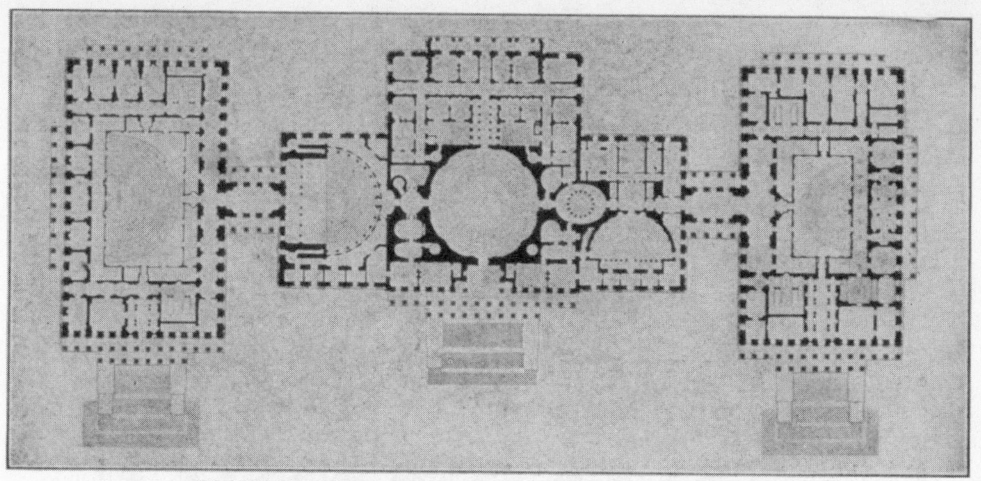

GROUND-FLOOR PLAN OF THE PROPOSED SCHEME "A"

Apropos of the dome, for instance, it may be recalled that the rhetorical and fastidious Ruskin does not admit of iron as a constructive material, and on those grounds inveighed disdainfully against the spire of Rouen Cathedral. Purity and pettishness aside, there are other reasons why the building fails to conform with the essentials of really great architecture. As far as the interior is concerned, the situation is anything but sublime, and it is hence a pleasure to know that Mr. Elliott Woods, superintendent of the Capitol building and grounds, has under advisement a proposition for the rehabilitation of the Rotunda. Yet the faults of the Capitol appear in a measure inevitable to those who know and treasure its history. Looked at broadly, they are not faults, but merely venerable shortcomings incidental to growth and development. Considering the importance of the prospective alterations and extensions, the evolution of the building seems to have entered upon an approximately final stage, and it is gratifying to know that Congress, the superintendent, and the consulting architects realize the dignity and seriousness of the task in hand. Something of the old simplicity should guide and chasten each effort. To this simplicity should also be added a reverence for those traditional ideals and aspirations which are, happily, a country's or an individual's most cherished heritage.

The panorama, once its several features are supplied, will present a majestic and

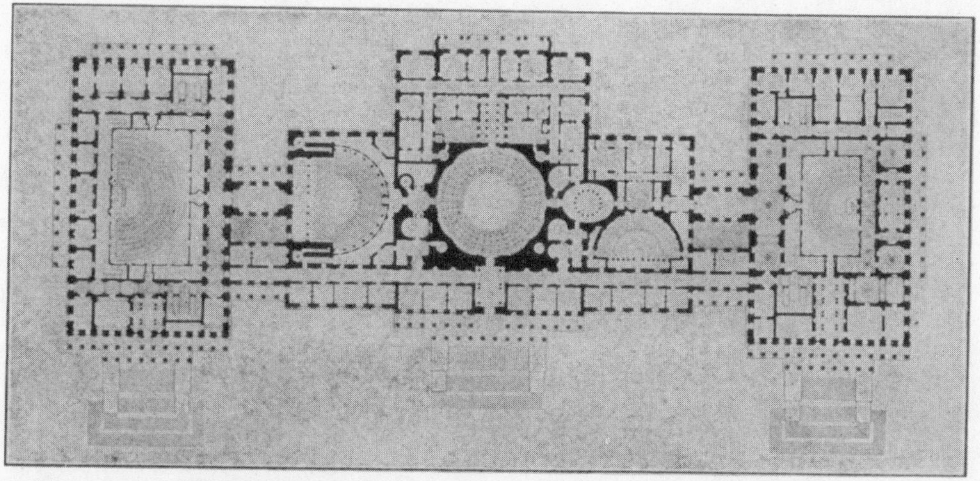

GROUND-FLOOR PLAN OF THE ALTERNATIVE SCHEME "B"

inspiring spectacle. Grouped about the spacious court will be five superb structures,—the Capitol on the west, the Senate and House office buildings to the north and south, and the Congressional Library and its companion on the east. To the average eye the Capitol will offer little change; there will merely be a grateful gain in repose and proportion. It will, as before, continue the focal point, the keynote of the composition. Despite its immensity, there appears to be nothing that is pompous or pretentious in the scheme as at present outlined.

It is but the logical fulfilment of plans, long since formulated, which are the fitting symbol of a subsequent national and territorial expansion.

The Nation's Library (1897)

VIEW FROM THE CAPITOL, SHOWING THE MAIN FRONT OF THE LIBRARY.

THE NATION'S LIBRARY.

BY THE LIBRARIAN.

WITH PICTURES BY E. POTTHAST.

I. THE NEW BUILDING.

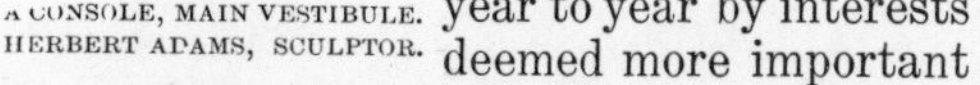

A CONSOLE, MAIN VESTIBULE. HERBERT ADAMS, SCULPTOR.

THE monumental building provided for the extensive collections of the Library of Congress at Washington represents about nine years of construction, besides fourteen years of preliminary agitation and discussion. The act of April 15, 1886, authorizing the erection of a separate library building was the fruit of a public necessity growing out of the rapid increase, beyond all capacity within the Capitol to hold them, of the nation's books. Several proposed measures for this end had been postponed from year to year by interests deemed more important or more pressing, or by differences concerning a proper site, plan, and cost, until the act referred to secured fully two thirds of the votes of both houses of Congress.

The site selected was an ideal one in respect to elevation, salubrity, and dry, solid foundations for a massive edifice of granite. It abuts upon the park of the Capitol, being about 1500 feet distant from that building on the east, and it is surrounded by four streets with ample approaches. The white granite which forms the exterior walls of the building is from quarries in Concord, New Hampshire, and in color is nearly as light as the marble walls of the Capitol. The inner walls, facing the four spacious courts, are in part of a slightly darker granite from Maryland, and partly of white enameled brick resembling porcelain in color, and producing a light and cheerful effect. The dimensions of the library building are 470 by 340 feet, covering about three and a half acres of ground. In style the building belongs to the Italian Renaissance, and four corner pavilions, together with the central front, are moderately projected, completely relieving any monotony incident to so long a façade. The solid and massive granite walls are further relieved by many windows, the casings of which are treated in high relief, and by sixteen ornate pillars and capitals in the central front, with twelve columns in each of the corner pavilions. In the keystones of thirty-three window arches are carved in the granite thirty-three human heads, representing types of various races of men—a unique feature, furnishing an object-lesson in ethnology as well as in decoration. Four colossal figures, each representing Atlas, are carved below the roof on the central pavilion, surmounted by a pediment with sculptured American eagles, and an emblematic group in granite. Three spandrels, carved in granite above the arches of the three main entrance doors, represent Art, Science, and Literature. The whole edifice is surmounted by a carved balustrade which runs around the building. The lower story is of rough-surfaced granite, while the walls of the upper stories are of smooth bush-hammered stone, relieved at the corners of the building by vermiculated work. The height of the walls is 69 feet, and the apex of the dome is 195 feet from the ground. This dome is gilded with a thick coating of gold-leaf, and is surmounted by a lantern the crest of which terminates in a gilded finial representing the ever-burning torch of Science. The galleries of the upper story command a wide and noble view of the Virginia and Maryland heights, the city of Washington, and the river Potomac.

The combined solidity and beauty of the exterior produce an architectural effect which is generally admired. The massive granite approaches, doorway, and staircase with its heavy but finely designed- balustrades, lend dignity to the edifice, instead of detracting from it, as in some notable public buildings. The grounds immediately surrounding it are laid out in a style to correspond with the spacious park of the Capitol, and a beautiful bronze fountain in the central front will contribute a refreshing adjunct to the harmonious effect. In the rear of the library building is located a granite annex with a high tower, providing for all the machinery connected with the heating of the structure—pumps, coal-vaults, steam-boilers, etc. Thus is secured within the library complete immunity from those nuisances of noise, dust, heat, and odors which are the unavoidable consequence when such plants are placed in the basement of any public building.

Entering the building, it is found to be divided into three stories besides the cellar, namely, a ground floor level with the surrounding streets, a first story, or library floor, and a second story, or gallery floor. Passing into the basement under heavy groined arches, the ceilings of which are frescoed in simple designs, we enter one of the four long, spacious corridors which extend all around the building. The feature of all these wide passageways is that they are wainscoted or are lined entirely

BRONZE LAMP-BEARER OF THE GRAND STAIRCASE. PHILIP MARTINY, SCULPTOR.

The arches and the walls above all these polished marble wainscotings are elaborately frescoed in harmonious colors; and when one has circumambulated the great building, he is impressed with the variety and beauty, as well as with the solid proportions, of these basement corridors. The spacious rooms opening from them are to be used for a bookbindery, packing-, receiving-, and shipping-rooms, office-rooms for the heads of the watch and superintendence of the building, and for storage purposes.

CENTRAL PAVILION, SHOWING MAIN ENTRANCE.

with American marbles coming from three different States, and embracing the handsomest colored marbles which this country produces. The western corridor (nearest to the Capitol) is of two shades of mottled blue Vermont marble from quarries at Brandon. The south wing is lined with what we may call Champlain marble, from the Swanton quarries near that lake, a very rich red-and-white stone, most effective to the eye. In the eastern corridor (360 feet in length), a Georgia marble from Pickens County, in black and white veins, has been used with beautiful effect. Finally, the north wing is lined with Tennessee marble of a light chocolate color.

Ascending to the first or library floor, which is also entered from the outside by the granite staircase and bronze doors, the vestibule is reached, through which, decorated elaborately with white marble and gilded ceiling, one enters the foyer, or grand staircase hall. This superb apartment is constructed throughout of the finest Italian marble, highly polished. From its four sides rise lofty rounded columns with Corinthian capitals richly carved, and its heavy but very graceful arches are adorned with marble rosettes, palm-leaves, and foliated designs of exquisite finish and delicacy. The lofty height of this fine entrance-hall, rising 72 feet to the skylight of stained glass, with its ornate vaulted ceiling and grand double staircase, and its white marble balustrades leading up on each side to the galleries above, produces an architectural effect both harmonious and imposing. It has been styled «a vision in polished stone» and «a dream of beauty»; but only readers who have seen it can be expected to appreciate such terms of praise.

Entering through this spacious hall, we pass into the reading-room, or central rotunda, by wide corridors adorned with rich mosaic ceilings. This public reading-room is octagonal in shape, with a diameter of 100 feet, and is lighted from above by eight large semicircular windows 32 feet wide, bearing the arms of all the States and Territories in color. At intervals eight massive pillars rise to the height of 40 feet, their bases being of dark Tennessee marble surmounted by heavy columns of lighter red Numidian marble, and crowned by emblematic statues of heroic size. The wall-space of the reading-room is of yellow Siena marble, with numerous arches and balustrades rising to the height of the upper gallery in a double tier, and having an extremely rich and beautiful effect. There are in all seventy-seven arches, the lower tier being intercalated with pilasters and architraves carved in classic sculpture. All these beautiful architectural effects are embodied in that richest of all known colored marbles which comes from the quarries of the Siena monastery, and their soft, warm, and mellow lights and shades are a pleasure to the eye.

The reading-room is fitted with mahogany desks for about two hundred and fifty readers, allowing each four feet of working-space. In the center, slightly raised above the surrounding floor, are the desks of the superintendent and his assistants, with the card-catalogue of the library in a long series of drawers grouped about the inner circle, while the circular shelves outside the railing provide readers with an assortment of catalogues, bibliographies, and other works of reference to be used freely without the formality of tickets. Within this central desk-space, which commands every part of the reading-room, is an extensive series of pneumatic tubes communicating with the several stack-rooms in which books are stored, and there is to be introduced a system of book-carriers for the speedy service of books to readers from any part of the outlying book repositories.

Opening out from the central reading-room on each side are two extensive iron book-stacks, each of the capacity of about

THE GRAND STAIRCASE HALL, OF CARRARA MARBLE.

800,000 volumes. These stacks are nine stories in height, each tier of shelves being just seven feet high, and each stack rising 65 feet, tier over tier, to the roof. All the floors are of white marble, and every book can be reached by the hand at once. The shelves are made of rolled steel, not solid, but in open bars, very light and firm, and so coated with magnetic oxid as to render them as smooth as glass. The space between the bars secures ventilation for the books, as well as immunity in a good degree from accumulations of dust. They are adjustable by an easy movement to any height for books of various sizes. This shelf system and stacks were designed by Bernard R. Green, engineer in charge during the construction of the building. The book-stacks are lighted by windows of plate-glass without sash, each window being a single plate, and dust-proof, the ventilation of the stack-rooms being from the upper tier of windows, on the down-draft system. Three elevators are provided for the three stack-rooms, and three for public use in other parts of the library building.

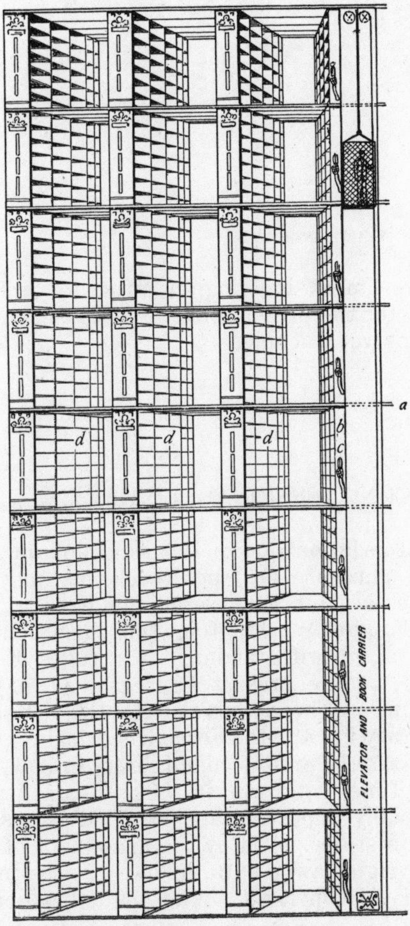

DRAWN BY WELLS M. SAWYER.

A BOOK-STACK.

a, flooring: *b*, pneumatic tube; *c*, carrier; *d*, shelves.

The spacious rooms on the first floor, outside the central reading-room, are designed for the copyright office, or public records, a catalogue-room, a special reading-room for the Senate, and another for the House of Representatives, an apartment for the Toner Library (presented to the Government), committee-rooms, librarian's office, etc. The Smithsonian Scientific Library, long deposited with the Library of Congress, will be placed in the smaller stack-room on the eastern side of the building, which will hold about 100,000 volumes.

The second floor of the building has four spacious open corridors surrounding it, decorated as to walls and ceilings with frescos and mural paintings, and with numerous tablet inscriptions from the great writers of the world. It contains an extensive hall designed for an art gallery, a hall for maps and charts, and three or four spacious exhibition-halls in which choice specimens of early typography, engraving, and Americana will be exhibited in glass cases.

The capacity of those portions of the library building already shelved is ample for about 1,900,000 volumes, there being about forty-four miles of shelves in position. Besidest his, there is space which may ultimately be finished with book-stacks to accommodate about 2,500,000 additional volumes; and the extensive inner courts may still further serve posterity for book storage to the extent of 4,000,000 to 5,000,000 volumes more. When it is considered that the largest existing library numbers less than 2,500,000 volumes, it will be seen how extensive is the provision for future growth for at least a century or two to come.

An underground tunnel between the Capitol and the library building will transmit rapidly any books wanted for congressional use and not found in the reference library at the Capitol.

The floor-area of the library in its first story is about 111,000 square feet, that of the British Museum being a little more than 90,000 square feet, and that of the building for the State, War, and Navy departments 92,000 square feet. The ultimate cost of the entire edifice, including decorations and furnishings, will be about $6,300,000, or a little more than half the cost of the government building last named, and it will be completed within the limit of cost fixed by Congress.

SOUTHWEST PAVILION—THE EXHIBITION-ROOM.

In design and in construction the two great ends of architecture, use and beauty, appear to have been well attained in this government building, a structure erected not for the present generation alone, but for many yet to come.

II. SPECIAL FEATURES OF THE CONGRESSIONAL LIBRARY.

WHAT is the function of a government library? is a question which becomes more than ever pertinent in view of the impending opening at Washington of the noble building to which this article is devoted. That this edifice is a permanent, fire-proof, and fitting home for the nation's books, representing the assiduous gatherings of nearly a hundred years, is already recognized by all. That the mission of the great library which it is to contain is a manifold one, reaching far beyond the limits of its locality and the present age, is perhaps less widely appreciated.

Founded in the year 1800 by the modest appropriation of five thousand dollars «for the purchase of such books as may be necessary for the use of Congress at the said city of Washington,» this collection has grown, notwithstanding the ravages of two fires, to the present aggregate of 740,000 volumes. The acquisition of the Jefferson Library in 1815, the Force Historical Library in 1865, the Smithsonian Library in 1867, and the Toner collection in 1882, all constituted specially important and valuable accessions to its stores. And by the enactment of the copyright law of 1870, followed by the international copyright act of 1891, this library

THE PUBLIC READING-ROOM.

became entitled to receive two copies of all books, periodicals, and other publications claiming the protection of copyright in the United States.

While its primary function has been and still is to furnish the national legislature with all the aids in their far-reaching and responsible duties which a comprehensive library can supply, its more extensive province has made it the conservator of the nation's literature. By the wise legislation of Congress it has been made the one designated legal repository of the entire product of the American press, so far as issued under the government guaranty of copyright. If this salutary and conservative measure had been in force from the beginning of copyright in 1790, instead of being confined to the last twenty-five years, we should now be in possession of an unapproached and unattainable completeness in every department of American books. In the absence of any central place of deposit, the copyright requirements of earlier years were most negligently and imperfectly complied with, and multitudes of books have wholly disappeared, or are found only in second-hand book-shops or in the cabinets of curious collectors. Considered in a scientific view or as absolute knowledge, the loss may not be greatly to be deplored; but, taking a single example, let the reader consider how substantial a benefit it would be to those interested in the profession of education to be assured of finding in a national collection every school- or text-book produced in the United States during the period of a century. Writers for the press may learn as much from the failures of their predecessors as from their successes. And the historian of American literature who would be thoroughly comprehensive cannot overlook the forgotten books read, and perhaps admired, by former generations. Nor can any nation claiming to hold a front rank in civilization shirk the obligation of preserving, in one inclusive and not exclusive collection open to the whole people, all the books which the country produces. From the lack of care in the past to enforce this judicious policy, the National Library of Great Britain has been for years buying up at great cost the dramas, pamphlets, chap-books, and other productions of English literature in past ages, to fill innumerable gaps in its great collection.

Where in America can one find even a respectably full collection of the pamphlet literature of which the country has been so prolific? This class of writings appears foredoomed in each generation to swift and irremediable destruction, unless preserved in public libraries. Yet its great value, as reflecting in condensed and often masterly style the real spirit of the age which produced it, with its controversies, political, religious, and social, and the ideas which moved the public mind, has been recognized by all philosophic historians as incalculable. If all authors of pamphlets would send their productions to the library of the Government, they would not only secure the preservation of their own thought, but would be found to have performed a useful public service. As an instance of the historical value of pamphlet literature, take the Thomason collection of twenty thousand pieces, covering the Cromwellian period in England. Its owner sedulously collected and laid aside every issue of the press from 1649 to 1660; and the collection, after escaping the ravages of fire and of two hostile armies, was finally bought by the king, and afterward presented to the British Museum Library. Carlyle made extensive use of this inestimable collection. In like manner, the great La Bédoyère collection of printed matter relating to the French Revolution, purchased for the National Library of France in 1863, covered exhaustively the issues of the press, including periodicals, for twenty-five years, and its 15,500 volumes were the fruit of fifty years' assiduous research by an enthusiastic and untiring collector. Another devotee to the collection and preservation of historical material, the late Peter Force of Washington, was for forty years engaged in amassing a rich library of manuscripts, newspapers, books, pamphlets, and maps illustrative of American history. He ransacked the bookshops of the cities, imported from abroad, and was a frequent bidder at auctions, where he secured the Duane and the Wolcott collections of pamphlets, representing the carefully preserved and bound gatherings of a Republican and a Federalist during many years of public and political life. The Force collection was fortunately saved from dispersion, and now forms an invaluable part of the Congressional Library.

In another field of library collection, which the Smithsonian Institution may be said to have made its own, consider the value of a complete series of the reports, transactions, and other publications of scientific bodies. Embracing as these do the results of the labors of men of science in every field of thought or investigation, they furnish material of the first importance to the student.

Through its international exchanges the Smithsonian Institution has rendered an inestimable service to the country in assembling at Washington a most extensive collection of these publications, many of which are out of print or rare. They will form a part of the rich stores open to scholars in the new Congressional Library; and as they represent more than two thousand foreign societies and institutions, besides nearly all American ones publishing transactions, they afford a

THE MAIN READING-ROOM GALLERY.

copious repository of scientific information for public use and reference.

That a library is useful and valuable in the direct ratio of its completeness is a postulate that may be termed self-evident, and fairly so. «The true university of these days,» says Thomas Carlyle, «is a collection of books.» While the vast extent of the world's literature may fill the ordinary reader with dismay, it needs only the practised eye and quick discernment of the thorough student to select the more important from the mass, and to extract in each the essential thought or fact from the verbiage that overlays it. The books which it is necessary to know thoroughly may be comprised in a comparatively small compass. The rest are to be preserved in the great literary conservatories—some as memorials of the past, some as chronicles of the times, and not a few as models to be avoided. It is easy to pronounce the great majority of the books in our larger libraries «rubbish,» and to propose, as has frequently been done, to make a bonfire of the trash which the copyright law brings into the government library at Washington. But the grave question confronts us, Where are we to begin? Are there any judgments likely to concur as to what is to be preserved? It is a common experience that the book which was nothing to us at one time came to have a most unexpected value at another. When the priest and the barber, in the immortal romance of Cervantes, sought to purge the library of Don Quixote of the perilous stuff which had bewildered his artless brain, the self-constituted censors were not agreed as to what should be condemned to the flames. Do the learned editors who would like to have the great library «weeded» ever reflect that their own works in great folio might be the first to go out, to make room for smaller books, if not better ones?

THE LIBRARIAN'S OFFICE.

A. R. SPOFFORD.

The ever-widening sphere and influence of the periodical press—one of the great phenomena of modern times—suggest the importance of preserving in our most representative libraries a copious selection from the daily newspapers, and a full collection of the literature of magazines and reviews. While no library, however comprehensive, could possibly store all the periodical publications (now amounting in the United States alone to more than twenty thousand, as against only eight thousand in 1875), it is none the less its proper function to provide full sets of the more important ones. They

THE NORTH CORRIDOR OF THE GRAND STAIRCASE HALL.

afford the completest mirror of the times to be derived from any single source. Taken together, they supply the richest material for the historian and the student of comparative civilization in all its aspects—literary, political, moral, social, religious, and economic. More and more the best thought and the inventive genius of the age become reflected in their pages. No investigator in any department whose aim is full information can afford to neglect this fruitful mine, where his most valuable material will frequently be found; and it is to be considered that unless the representative library preserves them, a very large portion of them will not be preserved in accessible form at all. The destiny of most periodicals is swift destruction. The obvious causes of their rapid disappearance are their great volume, inevitably growing with each year, the difficulty of finding room to store them in our small dwellings, the ravages of fire, and the continual demand of paper for the uses of trade. Add to these the large cost of binding sets of periodicals, and the preference of the majority of families for books, and the reasons why very few private subscribers to periodicals can afford to bind and preserve them are apparent. So much the more important is it that public libraries should not neglect a duty which is due both to their own age and to posterity. These unconsidered trifles of to-day, which are looked upon as not worth space to store or money to bind, are the very things which the man of the future, intent upon the reconstruction of the past, will search for with eagerness. Accordingly, it has been the policy of the library of the United States for nearly thirty years past to preserve and bind up at least two of the daily journals of each State and Territory, and all the magazines and reviews obtainable, with a selection of the weekly press. No department of the library is so widely used, not only for purposes of reference, but of study. When it is considered how far-reaching are the fields embraced in the wide range of these periodicals, literary, religious, scientific, political, technical, philosophical, social, fashionable, medical, legal, educational, agricultural, bibliographical, commercial, financial, historical, mechanical, nautical, military, artistic, musical, dramatic, typographical, sanitary, sporting, economic, and miscellaneous, is it any wonder that specialists and writers for the press seek and find ready aid therein for their many-sided labors?

To the skeptical mind, accustomed to undervalue what does not happen to come within the range of its pet idols or pursuits, the observation of a single day's multifold research in the great library might be in the nature of a revelation. Here one finds an industrious compiler intent upon the history of American duels, for which the many files of Northern and Southern newspapers, reaching back to the beginning of the century, afford copious material. At another table sits a deputation from a department, commissioned to make a record of all notable strikes and labor troubles for a series of years, to be gleaned from the columns of the journals of leading cities. Hither flock the ever-present searchers into family history, laying under contribution all the genealogies and town and county histories which the country has produced. An absorbed reader of French romances sits side by side with a clergyman perusing homilies or endeavoring to elucidate, through a mass of commentators, a special text. Here are to be found ladies in pursuit of costumes of every age; artists turning over the great folio galleries of Europe for models or suggestions; lawyers seeking precedents or leading cases; journalists verifying dates, speeches, conventions, or other forgotten facts; engineers studying the literature of railways or machinery; actors or amateurs in search of plays or works on the dramatic art; physicians looking up biographies of their profession or the history of epidemics; students of heraldry after coats of arms; inventors searching the specifications and drawings of patents; historical students pursuing some special field in American or foreign annals; scientists verifying facts or citations by original authorities; searchers tracing personal residences or deaths in old directories or newspapers; querists seeking for the words of some half-remembered passage in poetry or prose, or the original author of one of the myriad proverbs which float about the world without a father; architects or builders of houses comparing hundreds of designs and models; teachers perusing works on education or comparing text-books new or old; readers absorbing the great poems of the world; writers in pursuit of new or curious themes among books of antiquities or folk-lore; students of all the questions of finance and economic science; naturalists seeking to trace through many volumes descriptions of species; pursuers of military or naval history or science; enthusiasts venturing into the occult domains of spiritualism or thaumaturgy; explorers of voyages and travels in every region of the globe; fair readers, with dreamy eyes, devouring the last psychological novel; devotees of musical art perusing the lives or the scores of great composers; college and high-school students intent upon «booking up» on themes of study or composition or debate; and a host of other seekers after suggestion or information in a library of encyclopedic range.

This collection, extensive as it is, still falls far short of completeness in many important directions. While its quality is by no means commensurate with its quantity, it yet possesses a large share of the standard works i all departments of science and literature. I greatest strength lies in the fields of juri prudence, political science, American an British history, and what are known a Americana. Its deficiencies are most marke in books in foreign languages, and they ar notably great in editions of the classics, i philology, in Oriental literature, and in man of the sciences. With all its manifold defects it may be said that the library, so far a it is the fruit of selection, has been forme with a view to the highest utility, and wit some general unity of plan. Congress ma be expected, now that the expenditure upo the building has ceased, to take a more liberal view of its wants, and to make wis provision for such an increase of its intellectual stores as shall be worthy of th nation and the age. Its new and magnificent building, through the far-sighted liberality of the people's representatives, has

A GLIMPSE OF THE GRAND STAIRCASE HALL.

AN EXHIBITION-HALL, SHOWING A PORTION OF THE FRESCOS BY GARI MELCHERS.

been planned and organized to accommodate ultimately, with every convenience of administration. In the judgment of all who have seen it, its architectural and artistic beauty has been pronounced fully equal to its utility. Its gallery of art will soon be filled with an instructive exhibit of the progress of the arts of design in every form; and it may be hoped that the large-minded policy which has created this noble temple of science, literature, and art will endow it with adequate means of growth, so that its ample shelves may before long be filled with the learning of all lands.

A. R. Spofford.

THE DECORATIONS IN THE NEW CONGRESSIONAL LIBRARY.

THE scene in the new Congressional Library at Washington, when I visited it in the summer of 1896, was interesting and impressive. A guard admitted me at a small door under the imposing terraces and flights of steps which form the approach to the main entrance of the building. I walked through corridor after corridor, ascended broad stairways, and found my way through spacious galleries and vestibules to the great rotunda in the middle of the vast construction. Here was an immense scaffolding rising a hundred feet or more to the base of the dome, and high above that, as I looked up, I saw the iron elliptical truss-work that swung from the platform of the scaffolding to the top of the dome, carrying ladders and landing-places to the crown of the lantern, 160 feet from the floor. Scores of skilled workmen were carving, fitting, and polishing. Some were perched high in the drum of the dome; others were setting mosaics and laying marble floors. In corridors and halls were rolling platforms and bridges full of busy

PAINTED BY KENYON COX. PHOTOGRAPH BY CURTIS & CAMERON.

«SCIENCE» (LUNETTE).

craftsmen painting in fresco on the vaulted ceilings. Four or five artists were at work on their decorative compositions in different parts of the building, and one I found, with his assistant, in the crown of the lantern of the dome. The artists, like the workmen, were in overalls, and the atmosphere of the place seemed impregnated with the spirit of art and labor. It was something as it must have been in Florence or Venice in the Renaissance.

On every side there was evidence that the decorative work had been artistically planned, and that it was being intelligently and durably executed. The interior of the new Congressional Library will be a veritable revelation when the public takes possession of it. It might have been very different if it had not fortunately happened that good brains and good culture were called upon to embellish it. Indeed, they were summoned to set right what had been but badly begun; and we may congratulate ourselves and our legislators that by timely action the country has been spared a gift that might have been an architectural failure, and obtains a great building which, whatever may be its faults of detail, is, taken as a whole, imposing and picturesque. The story of the building of the library is given in a statement prepared by the officials who have been charged by the Government with the duty of bringing the work to completion. By an act of Congress of April 15, 1886, a commission was directed to build a library building after the plans submitted by Messrs. Smithmeyer and Pelz. This commission employed Mr. Smithmeyer, with the title of architect, to supervise and manage, under its direction, the construction of the building. By an act of Congress of October 2, 1888, the act of the 15th of April was repealed, and the chief of engineers of the army, the late General Thomas Lincoln Casey, was placed in charge and directed to prepare plans for a building which should not cost more than $4,000,000. Such plans were accordingly prepared, with estimates, and submitted to Congress at the opening of the session in December, 1888. In the preparation of these plans Mr. Pelz was employed to make the drawings under the direction of General Casey and Mr. Bernard R. Green, who was appointed to the local charge of the work as superintendent and engineer. For the foundation or main lines of the design the building begun under the act of the 15th of April was used. At the same time that General Casey had the plans prepared for the building limited in cost to $4,000,000, he also had prepared a set of plans for a building

PAINTED BY GEORGE W. MAYNARD. PHOTOGRAPH BY CURTIS & CAMERON.

«DISCOVERY» (LUNETTE).

PAINTED BY KENYON COX. PHOTOGRAPH BY CURTIS & CAMERON.

«MATHEMATICS» AND «PHYSICS» (DETAIL).

which would cost about $6,000,000. These plans were evolved from the original general designs by Smithmeyer and Pelz formerly adopted by Congress, but differed from them in numerous important particulars. By an act of March 2, 1889, the design for the $6,000,000 building was adopted by Congress. Mr. Pelz was continued as architect under the direction of the chief of engineers, and construction and detail drawings were prepared. In April, 1892, Mr. Pelz's connection with the work came to an end. Upon the death of General Casey in March, 1896, Mr. Green succeeded to his duties and powers in full. In December, 1892, Edward Pearce Casey, an architect of New York, who had completed his studies at the École des Beaux-Arts in Paris, was employed to prepare the drawings for the interior architecture and scheme of decoration of the building. It is at this point that the interest of American artists was enlisted; and later on commissions were given out, under Mr. Casey's general direction, for mural and sculptural decoration. The amount of work done by Mr. Casey in designing the principal interiors of the library building is enormous. With the exception of the main portions of the mar-

PHOTOGRAPH BY CURTIS & CAMERON.

CEILING. PAINTED BY GEORGE W. MAYNARD.

ble work in the great staircase hall and the rotunda, designs have been made by him for the decoration of the entire interior. He was occupied more than three years with the work, giving all his time to it, and employing, of course, a number of draftsmen to assist him. His decorative schemes show variety of design, fertility of invention, and an excellent sense of the importance of unity in the ensemble. Under his direction all the work not given out to the artists has been intelligently and skilfully carried out by a corps of decorators, headed by Elmer E. Garnsey for the painters, by Albert Weinert for the sculptors and modelers of ornament, and by H. T. Schladermundt for mosaics and for colored glass. Praise for the excellence of the general decorative work in the building is due to the young architect who planned it and presented it in its broad aspect and in its detail forms, so that nothing might be misunderstood, and so that the execution by the hands of the craftsmen should realize his conceptions. The color-schemes chosen by the artists for their compositions will be found to harmonize with this general decoration, each of them, before making his sketches, having taken account of the prevailing general tints, and considered their color-effect as the setting for his work. The greater part of the mural pictures have been executed on canvas in artists' studios in New York, Paris, and other places. These large canvases when completed are removed from their stretchers and sent to Washington. The artist follows, and the pictures are put up under his supervision. The process employed consists in applying a thin bed of composition, of which white lead is the principal ingredient, to the wall or ceiling, and «rolling on» the canvas. In this manner it is fastened smoothly and securely. This process may naturally be most successfully employed where the surface is flat. In France, we are told, painted decoration on canvas has been rolled on concave surfaces by a clever system of goring the canvas, and in one case this was done at Washington. In almost every instance, however, where the surface is concave the painting is done directly on the material of the wall or ceiling itself. Mr. Maynard's ceiling in the southwest pavilion, where the surface is a section of a sphere, and Mr. Blashfield's work in the great rotunda, are cases in point. Both artists executed their designs in place, and spent months, with their assistants, working in the building. So, too, did Mr. Shirlaw, Mr. Barse, and others.

«The Evolution of Civilization» is the subject of the decoration by Edwin Howland Blashfield. It is composed of the collar of the dome in the great central rotunda, and the crown of the lantern. The collar is about 140 feet in circumference, surrounds the eye of the lantern, and is at the height of 125 feet from the pavement of the rotunda. It contains twelve seated colossal figures, each ten feet high. There are twelve cartouches, or tablets, inscribed with the names of the epochs or of the countries which have contributed to the evolution of civilization. These twelve tablets form rhythmical points established between the figures, and under each figure runs a banderole, or streamer, with an inscription referring to the special contribution to civilization of the country or epoch which is represented by the figure above. The wings of all the figures overlap each other and form a dominant factor in the composition, binding together the component parts of the decoration. The figures are divided into four triads. The central figure of each triad is relatively rigid, and the drapery is principally white. The side figures lean toward the central ones, and the drapery is of darker tints. Egypt, with «Written Records» on the tablet, comes first in chronological order. The figure bears the sign of immortality and a tablet inscribed with hieroglyphics. On the throne is shown the cartouche of Mena, the first Egyptian king. Judea (religion) holds stone tablets bearing Hebrew inscriptions. Greece (philosophy) bears a lamp and a scroll. Rome (administration) has a baton of command and a bundle of fasces. Islam (physics) holds a book and a glass retort. The Middle Ages (languages) bears a sword denoting chivalry, a model of a church typifying architecture, and a tiara and keys, symbols of the church. This figure has the features of Miss Mary Anderson. Italy (the fine arts) holds a palette and a statuette of Michelangelo's «David,» and rests her foot on a capital. The features are those of a young lady of New York, a sculptor. Germany (the art of printing) holds a proof-sheet, and beside her figure is a sixteenth-century printing-press. The features are those of General Thomas Lincoln Casey. Spain (discovery) has as accessories the rudder of a ship and a model of a caravel, and the head shows the features of Mr. William Bailey Faxon the painter. England (literature) bears a volume of Shakspere, the page being a transcript of the title-page of the first edition of «A Midsummer Night's Dream.» The head is a portrait of Miss Ellen Terry. France (emancipation) sits upon a cannon and holds out the «Déclaration des Droits de l'Homme.» The features of the figure suggest those of the artist's wife. America (science) is depicted with a dynamo and a book as accessories. The head is that of Abraham Lincoln. The heads of the figures are not intended to be absolute portraiture, but characterizations, the features being used because the artist thought them especially suited to the nation or contribution typified. The dominant colors in Mr. Blashfield's decoration are white (the girdle of wings), bluish green (the background of mosaic patterning), and violet (the banderoles). The drapery of the figures harmonizes with these colors, being gradated from white to violet tints, and the violet hues are shaded into yellow and orange. The composition is light in general tone, and carries with great effectiveness at the distances from which it may be seen either from the floor or from the galleries encircling the rotunda. The collar decoration is inclosed around the eye of the lantern and at the outer edge by heavy gilded moldings in the form of garlands of leaves.

The crown of the lantern, consisting of a circular ceiling, contains three figures. A female figure floating among clouds of white and gray, and lifting up a veil which almost envelops her, is depicted looking upward, and represents Human Understanding looking up from finite achievement, as presented in the decoration of the collar, to what is beyond. Two nude figures of boys float at her sides,

PAINTED BY E. H. BLASHFIELD. PHOTOGRAPH BY CURTIS & CAMERON.

«ITALY» (DETAIL).

one holding a closed book typifying the end of all things, and the other beckoning to the figures below. The drapery of the central figure is blue, darker than the portions of the sky which appear between the clouds, and the color of the veil is orange. The figure is shown as soaring upward and disappearing in the clouds. It is easy to see that Mr. Blashfield's task was a difficult one, considering the places allotted to him for decoration, the necessity of painting for effect at a great distance, and the importance of his color-scheme as the culminating point in the ensemble of the rotunda. At the ground floor the walls and bases of the piers are constructed of brownish-gray Tennessee marble. At the successive stages of the floors rising to the base of the dome the piers and pilasters are of yellow Siena and red and yellow Numidian marble. At the base of the dome, running around the drum, is a sculptured frieze composed of bay-leaf garlands and eagles, with two female figures in the round over each of the eight arches, holding up the garland and supporting escutcheons. These figures are the work of Philip Martiny, while the rest of the sculptured stucco ornament in the rotunda is by Albert Weinert. The vault is paneled in sculptured ornament and rosettes. The latter are gilded, and are relieved against a ground of greenish blue. With all these various elements of material and color Mr. Blashfield's decoration is in harmony, and possesses such individuality of itself that it counts as a dominant note in the whole. His great figures, too, are well

PAINTED BY W. L. DODGE. PHOTOGRAPH BY CURTIS & CAMERON.

«AMBITION» (CEILING).

drawn, and his composition is constructed with a firmness that gives it power while it in no way detracts from its effect, which is intended by its position to be without any heaviness of character.

In a hall about 150 feet long, to be used as a museum, Mr. Kenyon Cox has painted two lunettes of semi-elliptical form. They are at the two ends of the long room, and measure 34 feet 7 inches at the base by 9 feet 7 inches in height at the center. The prevailing color-note in the general decoration of this hall is blue. Mr. Cox's subjects are «Art» and «Science.» Each of his decorative panels is divided into three parts by two pedestals bearing flaming tripods, these pedestals coming directly over the pilasters, which are part of the architectural lines of the room. In the middle part of each lunette is a throne raised on steps; at the sides are balustrades. The panel representing «Art» contains five principal figures typifying the five great arts—poetry, sculpture, painting, architecture, and music. «Poetry» occupies of right the central throne. She is draped in white and pale rose-color, bears the lyre, and looks upward with an expression of inspiration. She is crowned with ivy, and points upward with her right hand. On the steps of her throne are two genii, one with a tablet, suggesting study, the other snapping his fingers and dancing, suggesting the gaiety of poetry. The division to the right of the spectator contains the figures of «Sculpture» and «Painting.» «Sculpture,» in pale yellow, carries a statuette in her hand, which, while an original figure, recalls the style of Michelangelo. «Painting» leans upon the shoulder of «Sculpture» in an affectionate attitude. Her type is that of the Venetian school of the Renaissance, and she is draped, below the waist only, in dusky yellow. In her hand is a palette set with white, red, yellow, and blue. On the left side of the panel are figures of «Architecture» and «Music.» «Architecture» is leaning on a Gothic column, and is simply draped in a robe of the color of terra-cotta, the long lines of which are meant to signify architectural dignity. Beside her is «Music,» in rose-color and violet, with fluttering scarf, playing on the violin, while a winged genius holds before her an open music-book. The scheme of color in this composition, based on rose and yellow, is pale and tawny. The color-scheme of the other lunette, devoted to «Science,» is based on green and blue, but with the use of some warm tints for contrast. In the middle is the figure of «Astronomy,» the greatest of the sciences, leaning over a celestial globe held up by one of her attendant genii, and measuring it with a pair of compasses. She is draped in white and blue, and has a crown of stars on her head. A scarf of pale blue is disposed above her in an arch-like curve. As it was impossible to represent all the sciences in his composition, the

PAINTED BY WALTER SHIRLAW. PHOTOGRAPHED BY G. C. COX.

«GEOLOGY.»

artist has selected typical ones. To the right are «Botany» and «Zoölogy,» the sciences dealing with the vegetable and animal kingdoms. «Botany» is clad in a brocaded gown of green and gold, the forms of the pattern recalling vegetable shapes. In her hand is a small oak-tree. «Zoölogy,» a nude seated figure, points with her right hand to a peacock—introduced because of its decorative beauty, but the eyes in its tail may be thought to symbolize the curiosity of science. To the left of «Astronomy» are «Physics,» in brown and yellow, investigating the laws of weight, and «Mathematics,» type of abstract science. The latter figure is clad in salmon-pink and rich blue, and holds an abacus, while a genius at her knee reckons on his fingers the sum set by the beads. They are arranged to count 1896. While both of Mr. Cox's compositions are painted in an extremely high key, the color is suave. The necessity of raising the tints to a very light value by the use of white has not caused them to become harsh, as sometimes happens with less skilful painters. The quality of the color in this work is notable, and, as in the green robe of «Botany,» remarkably full. The artist's resources as a draftsman are especially well shown in the admirable figure of the boy holding the globe, but the drawing of the figures is erudite throughout the work. The room in which the compositions by Mr. Cox are placed has its counterpart on the other side of the building. This room contains decorations by Gari Melchers. The prevailing color in the general scheme of decoration is red. Mr. Melchers's subjects are «Peace» and «War.» The two lunettes are painted in the sound and competent manner which characterizes the work of this well-known painter, and were executed in Paris.

PAINTED BY ROBERT REID. PHOTOGRAPH BY CURTIS & CAMERON.

«HEARING.»

Two pavilions, octagonal rooms at the corners of the library building, are decorated by George W. Maynard and William L. Dodge. Two others contain ceilings and panels by Robert Dodge and William B. Van Ingen, the decorative schemes for these having been supplied by Mr. Casey and Mr. Garnsey. Mr. Van Ingen's work in the pavilion and elsewhere is notable for striking color quality, possessing some of the characteristics of the La Farge school. Mr. W. L. Dodge's composition has «Ambition» for its subject, and four panels on the walls represent «Science,» «Art,» «Music,» and «Poetry.» They were painted in Paris, and the ceiling was exhibited at the Salon of 1896 before being brought to Washington. There are two groups in the composition of the ceiling, one consisting of a figure typifying «Glory,» holding aloft a crown, and majestically preceding a winged horse, while another figure, symbolizing «Fame,» flies before, holding the bridle of the horse in one hand and a trumpet in the other. The other group, united with the first by a large piece of drapery, consists of a number of figures on a terrace, including one who upsets a flaming brazier at the end of the balustrade, another stretched out dead, others struggling, and a fool with cap and bells. The general aspect of the ceiling is extremely decorative. The decoration of the pavilion containing Mr. Maynard's five works, confided to Mr. Maynard, consists of a general scheme of white and gold, which has been most successfully carried out, and the room shows how satisfactory the result is likely to be when the entire decoration, if practicable, is executed with the coöperation of the artist who paints the decorative pictures. In this case a most harmonious ensemble has been achieved, and the room has an air of perfect completeness. The panels, semi-elliptical in shape, occupying the upper part of the four longer walls of the room, have as their subjects four epochs of America—«Adventure,» «Discovery,» «Conquest,» and «Civilization.» The ceiling depicts the four elements necessary for development—«Fortitude,» «Valor,» «Courage,» and «Achievement.» The figures and accessories in each of the four panels follow a general arrangement common to all, and the color-schemes, while varied, are designed to balance one another. The panel «Adventure» shows a seated female figure with a drawn sword in one hand and a caduceus in the other, symbolizing courage and daring. To her left is a female figure typifying Spanish adventure, with a hatchet and a Peruvian golden image in her hands. The image signifies booty, which was the object of the quests of the first adventurers. On the right of the central figure is a young woman of

PAINTED BY ROBERT REID. PHOTOGRAPH BY CURTIS & CAMERON.

«TOUCH.»

blonde English type, a sword in one hand, and grasping with the other silver pieces of money which fall from a bag. In either corner are the arms of England and Spain. Shields on each side of the principal figure bear the images of Norse ships, and on the background, or field, appear the names of famous adventurers such as Raleigh and Hawkins. The prevailing color is yellow, and the armor of the figures is gold and steel.

In the second panel, «Discovery,» crowned with a laurel wreath of gold, grasps a tiller with her left hand and supports a globe on her knee. On the globe are the outlines of Leonardo da Vinci's map, the first one that is known to have had the name America upon it. On each side of « Discovery » are female figures, one holding a sword, but not in an aggressive position, and a Jacob's-staff, the other a paddle and a chart. In the corners are ornamental figures of mermaids growing out of the border, who hold up corals and pearls. The two shields bear an astrolabe, the primitive quadrant. On the field are the names of great Spanish, French, and English discoverers, but no Portuguese, because their exploits relate to the East Indies, and not to America. The principal colors in this decoration are yellow and blue.

«Conquest» rests her hand on the hilt of a sword, suggesting that her work is done, and her right arm, extended with clenched fist, characterizes her attitude as one of possession and defense. The side figures are in reposeful positions, and bear swords, one entwined with oak, symbolical of the North, the other with palm, symbolical of the South. The arms of Spain and England reappear in the corners, and on the shields are the Pillars of Hercules with the setting sun and the motto «*Ne plus ultra*.» The field shows the names of conquerors such as Pizarro and Standish. The prevailing colors are red and orange. «Civilization» holds an open book on her knees, and bears a torch. One of the two side figures typifying « Manufactures » and « Agriculture » holds a distaff, the other a scythe and a sheaf of wheat. In the corners are mermaids with cotton and Indian corn in their hands, and the device on the shields is a lamp. The field is inscribed with the names of humanitarians and pioneers in civilization, such as Las Casas, Hennepin, Marquette, Penn, and Eliot. The predominant tints in the color-scheme are blue and white. In the circular panel of the ceiling the field is blue, the ornament yellowish white, and the draperies of the figures yellow. « Fortitude,» with flowing robes, supports a column. « Valor » rests her hand on a sword. «Courage,» a strong Amazonian figure, is clad in a lion's skin and carries a shield and a club. «Achievement» points to the symbol of empire, a Roman standard surmounted by an eagle. The four figures, placed at points equidistant on the rim of the circle, are balanced in a symmetrical composition by ornamental designs which fill the intervening spaces and the center.

Besides the work done in this room, Mr. Maynard has painted eight upright panels around the staircase well in the second story of the staircase hall. The panels are three feet by twelve, and the subjects are the virtues — « Justice,» « Fortitude,» « Prudence,» « Temperance,» «Concordia,» « Industry,» «Courage,» and «Patriotism.» The figures are Pompeian in style, floating, and clad in drapery of whitish gray with backgrounds of vermilion. Each panel contains a single figure symbolical of one of the virtues. «Patriotism,» for example, is represented with an eagle on her arm, with wings extended as if having just alighted, and holding a bowl, from which the eagle eats. «Concordia,» the virtue of peace, carries an olive-branch and a cornucopia with wheat falling from its mouth.

Two curtain corridors are decorated by Edward Simmons and Walter McEwen. Nine heroes of ancient history form the subject chosen by Mr. McEwen, who painted his compositions in Paris. Mr. Simmons was given control of the entire decorative scheme in the corridor assigned to him, and has depicted the nine Muses. There is a tympanum at each end of the corridor, and seven others on one side, three over false doors and four over real doors. On the opposite side are windows. Besides the tympana, Mr. Simmons painted figure and ornamental subjects in the panels of the seven small domes of the corridor and in the twenty-eight pendentives. The motives are the attributes of the Muses. The tympana are nine feet long, the upper side consisting of a semicircle described by a radius of four and a half feet. «Calliope,» chief of the Muses, occupies the panel at one end of the corridor, and «Clio» the other. The color-scheme comprehends an arrangement passing from blue in the figure of « Calliope » to orange in that of «Clio.» In the row of seven tympana along the side of the corridor, three of the Muses have their arms extended, and, four between having them disposed otherwise, form a chain of arms uniting the series. The borders of the panels are formed by wreath-like designs in which roses, lilies,

PAINTED BY EDWARD SIMMONS. PHOTOGRAPH BY CURTIS & CAMERON.

MELPOMENE.

poppies, and green foliage are introduced. Grace and dignity are happily combined in these compositions, and Mr. Simmons's authoritative draftsmanship, so well shown in his decorations in the new criminal courts in New York, is here applied with force and distinction. The color-scheme is sufficiently restrained to comport well with the style of his design, while it is not lacking in such animated notes as befit the treatment of some of the details of his theme.

In the vestibule just before entering the great rotunda are five tympana painted by Elihu Vedder. The composition over the door in the middle represents «Government»; those to the right, «Good Administration» and «Peace and Prosperity»; the two on the left, «Corrupt Legislation» and «Anarchy.» Mr. Vedder's capability and good judgment are well shown in these works; for, unlike some of the other rooms given to the artists to decorate, which are fully lighted, this vestibule is somewhat tenebrous. Instead of forcing the color-scheme to a high key, an expedient which might have been adopted by a less experienced painter, Mr. Vedder has treated his compositions in sober, modified tones of an even gamut. They are in absolute harmony with their surroundings, and the restraint in color gives them depth and strength. These finely conceived designs are executed in such a manner that they do not appear as additions to the embellishment of their site, but as a part of the place itself, and nothing better in the way of fitness of placing will be found in the library. For the somewhat larger vestibule immediately preceding the one which contains Mr. Vedder's fine works, John W. Alexander has painted in Paris six tympana depicting «The Evolution of the Book.» His general color-scheme is made up of neutral tints, and the treatment, as may be seen in the illustration «The Story-teller of the Far East,» is extremely simple.

The central pavilion of the building, or the «west main,» as it is called in architectural parlance, contains the grand staircase; and on the second floor of this hall, directly in front of the visitor who mounts the steps to the mezzanine, there is to be a central panel in mosaic representing «Minerva.» The commission to make the design and color cartoon for this was given to Mr. Vedder, and it will be set in place after it has been laid in from the artist's designs. This will be done in Venice. On each side of the grand staircase is a lateral gallery, one of which is decorated by Henry Oliver Walker, and the other by Charles Sprague Pearce. The spaces in each gallery consist of two large tympana and five or six small ones. The ceilings are decorated with conventional designs provided by the artists. Mr. Pearce, whose subjects include «The Family,» «Labor,» and «Recreation,» and who has placed his figures in landscape settings, executed his work at Auvers-sur-Oise, near Paris. Mr. Walker's general theme is «Lyric Poetry.» In one of the large tympana, which is cut out in the middle by the arched top of a blind window or niche, are two female figures symbolizing «Memory» and «Joy.» An ornamental design, with an inscription over the arched space in the center, unites them. In the six small tympana are youthful figures representing concrete personages, such as Endymion, who appears as a nude stripling reclining in a contemplative attitude on a grassy bank, with the crescent moon in the twilight sky. The second large tympanum, which is free in its entire space for decoration, contains Mr. Walker's principal composition. «Lyric Poetry,» draped in rose-color and holding a lyre, occupies the center, with female figures symbolizing «Passion» and «Beauty» on her right hand. On her left are «Pathos,» in blue drapery; «Truth,» a nude figure; and «Devotion,» with robe of dull terra-cotta hue. The figures are placed in a landscape showing the bed of a brook in the middle, with trees and herbage at each side. The general tone of the picture is light, and inclines to gray in the landscape part, with great refinement of treatment in the more positive tints of the draperies. The *mise en scène* is poetic, and the great lines of the composition are graceful and effective. One of the chief qualities in the easel-pictures of the artist is facial expression, and in this composition he has striven to ally this quality with the breadth necessarily requisite in painting so large a canvas. The result is a work of genuine charm.

In the Representatives' Reading-room are two sculptured chimneypieces of Siena marble, in each of which is a mosaic by Frederick Dielman. Like Mr. Vedder's «Minerva,» they were laid in Italy, and are of rectangular shape, three feet six inches in height and seven feet six inches wide. The subject of one of the designs is «History.» A female figure in red and brown occupies the middle of the composition, with «Mythology» on her right and «Tradition» on her left. «Mythology,» in green, yellow, and purple, holds a sphere in her hand, and is intended to symbolize the phenomena of the universe. «Myths are the

PAINTED BY ELIHU VEDDER.

PHOTOGRAPH BY CURTIS & CAMERON.

« GOVERNMENT.»

PAINTED BY J. W. ALEXANDER.

PHOTOGRAPH BY FERDINAND ROUX, PARIS.

«THE EVOLUTION OF THE BOOK: THE STORY-TELLER OF THE FAR EAST.»

earliest recorded utterances of men concerning the visible phenomena of the world into which they were born » is the text illustrated by this figure. « Tradition,» in robes of blue and brown, listens to a nude boy who plays on a lyre and sings the deeds of ancient heroes. In the background behind « History,» a dignified figure with a book in her left hand, is a Greek temple; behind « Mythology » appears one of the Egyptian pyramids; and behind « Tradition » is the Roman Colosseum. The field is a sky of misty blue, and on columns at each side of the throne upon which « History » is seated are inscribed the names of great historians ancient and modern. The subject of the other design is « Law,» represented by a female figure enthroned, with « Peace,» « Truth,» and « Industry » on her right hand, and « Fraud,» « Discord,» and « Violence » on her left. The designs are sufficiently pictorial in character to be effective in that sense, but are composed with a certain formality that lends itself to mosaic treatment. The color-schemes are well balanced, and harmonize with the rich interior in which they are placed, the room being paneled in oak, elaborately carved, and dark in color. The seven main panels in the ceiling of the Representatives' Reading-room were decorated by Carl Gutherz, who took as his subject « The Light of Civilization.»

The figure-pieces in the decoration of the vaults of the four corridors in the second story were painted by Walter Shirlaw, Robert Reid, George R. Barse, Jr., and Frank W. Benson. The corridors are alike in dimensions, but the spaces painted by the artists are different. Mr. Reid, with five octagonal panels in the vaulted ceiling, and four circles on the walls, known as blind bull's-eyes, has for his subjects « The Five Senses » and « Poetry,» « Prose,» « History,» and « Science.» The general decoration of the north corridor, which forms the setting for these works, is similar to the famous designs in the Siena Library, and hence, in its newly painted adaptation, is rather strong and vivid. Mr. Reid has consequently pitched his color-scheme in positive tints of blue, green, red, and yellow. Each of the nine spaces contains a single draped female figure, and the artistic problems, while thus made simple in intention, do not easily admit of satisfactory solution, presupposing, of course, that variety of pose be sought for, and recognizing the inherent difficulty of making a complete and well-balanced composition with one figure in a circular space. The designs show the spaces very well filled, however, and such accessories as are introduced are of the simplest description. The lines of the figures are graceful, and the faces are good expressions of the decorative scheme—to represent each subject by a figure of a young and beautiful woman, to rely in the interpretations on natural beauty without classic convention, and to obtain grace of movement as the chief point in the different arrangements.

Mr. Shirlaw has painted designs in the spandrels between the arches of the west corridor. They consist of female figures, full length, and slightly above life-size. « Chemistry » holds a retort over the burning breath of a serpent coiled about a tripod with an hour-glass upon it. « Astronomy » bears in one hand the globe of Saturn with his rings, and in the other a lens. « Geology,» a strong figure of a type accustomed to labor, holds up a sphere and a piece of mineral, and at her feet are the earth and the moon. « Physics,» a lithe figure in flowing drapery, carries a torch, and symbolizes vital qualities. « Botany,» standing on a lily-pad, holds a water-lily in her hands, and the long stem is entwined about her body. « Zoölogy,» clad in the skin of a wild beast, and with a face expressive of animal quality, holds by his mane a lion at her side. « Mathematics,» a nearly nude figure, has a scroll in her hands on which a formula is written, and at her feet are geometrical solids. The figures are painted in a restrained color-scheme in which purple, blue, tawny-yellow, orange, and greenish hues predominate. They are drawn with special attention to the value of the great lines, and possess a fine statuesque quality.

In the south corridor three octagonal panels in the ceiling and four circular ones on the walls between the windows are painted by Mr. Benson. The subjects for the octagons are « The Three Graces,» and the color-scheme for the whole is a variation of white, blue, and green. Mr. Barse has painted eight upright panels in the spandrels of the east corridor, using as the motives « Epic Poetry,» « Lyric Poetry,» « Comedy,» « Tragedy,» « History,» « Romance,» « Tradition,» and « Fancy.» The decorations consist of a single draped female figure in each panel, painted in positive tints. The backgrounds are light, and the figures, appearing in silhouette, are strongly outlined. Simplicity of treatment, in contrast to the elaborate general decoration of the corridor, characterizes the work.

It is impossible in the space available here to give full descriptions of all the work, and only a small part of it can be reproduced in the illustrations.

PAINTED BY FREDERICK DIELMAN. PHOTOGRAPH BY CURTIS & CAMERON.

«HISTORY.»

Commissions for mural and sculptural decoration in the new Congressional Library were given to some forty American artists. While it will be seen that the decoration undertaken is of considerable magnitude, and far more extensive than has ever before been projected in any public edifice in the United States, no adequate idea of its completeness may be obtained without mention of the large part played by the art of sculpture in the embellishment of the building. The bronze figures in the three niches of the fountain at the main approach to the library were modeled by E. Hinton Perry. In niches in the principal façade are busts of Demosthenes, Dante, and Walter Scott, by Herbert Adams; Emerson, Irving, and Hawthorne, by J. Scott Hartley; and Goethe, Macaulay, and Franklin, by F. Wellington Ruckstuhl. There are six figures in the spandrels over the main entrance by Bela L. Pratt; and there are two sets of bronze doors by the late Olin L. Warner, one of which has been completed since his death by Mr. Adams. The central doors were modeled by Frederick MacMonnies. In the main staircase are lamp-bearers, and sculptures representing America, Europe, Asia, and Africa, by Philip Martiny. In the first great vestibule are ornamental figures of Minerva by Mr. Adams. Spandrels over the door leading into the rotunda bear sculptured designs by Warner, representing students in youth and in old age. In the corner pavilions of the second story are reliefs of the «Four Seasons» by Mr. Pratt. The finely sculptured clock in the rotunda is by John Flanagan.

In the great rotunda, which will be known as the Central Reading-room when the library is occupied, there are eight colossal figures set on pedestals at the top of the piers between the arches. They are «History,» by Daniel C. French; «Art,» by Augustus St. Gaudens; «Poetry,» by J. Q. A. Ward; «Law,» by Paul W. Bartlett; «Philosophy,» by Bela L. Pratt; «Science,» by John Donoghue; «Commerce,» by John Flanagan; and «Religion,» by Theodore Baur. Sixteen bronze figures, slightly over life-size, each on a plinth in the balustrade about forty feet from the floor, and two in each arch, form another important feature of the decoration of the rotunda. Shakspere is by Mr. MacMonnies; Herodotus, by Mr. French; Columbus and Michelangelo, by Mr. Bartlett; and St. Paul, by Mr. Donoghue. Gibbon and Moses are by Charles H. Niehaus; Plato and Bacon, by John J. Boyle. Fulton is by Edward C. Potter; Kent, by George Bissell; and Newton, by C. E. Dallin. Beethoven is by Mr. Baur; Joseph Henry, by Mr. Adams; Solon, by Mr. Ruckstuhl; and Homer, by Louis St. Gaudens. The first thought that must suggest itself when we see this profuse sculptural decoration is surprise that we have so many good sculptors. Even those of us who are aware that great progress has been made by American sculptors in their art of late must be astonished at the resources shown in the work in the library. Taken together with the mural decoration, and seen in its completeness, it will surely produce a strong impression of excellence. A criticism may be recorded here that applies to the work in its ensemble, and not to any particular part. In the sculpture the subjects do not repeat one another, but in the mural decoration there are, if not too many abstract themes, at least too many similar ones. The arts and sciences, for example, have been used pretty frequently in the decoration. The point has no bearing whatever on the merit or effectiveness of the decorations in the artistic sense, but concerns only the whole of the work from the literary point of view. Historical subjects of a certain class would seem to be well fitted for use in the decoration of a library if the abstract themes do not suffice to give variety to an extensive scheme of decoration. The sculpture in the present instance, indeed, has been treated in this way, abstract subjects alternating with such historical ones as Columbus, Shakspere, and Fulton. The importance of the whole work as a step in the onward march of art in the United States must be conceded without discussion. The responsibility of the artists in the matter is not a light one. If the educated public gives as its verdict that the work has been well done, it cannot but have the effect of giving a strong impetus to the rapidly growing conviction that both public and private edifices should be made beautiful as well as convenient. It would seem as if, in the future, the best achievements of American art might be found in the field of decoration. Breadth of scope in subject, and opportunity to work without too much hurrying, are all that are needed to bring out even better evidences than exist in the library at Washington that the American artists of to-day are abundantly equal to the task of decorating American buildings, no matter how great their architectural importance, or how manifold may be the difficulties of the project. The artistic ability has been shown beyond question, and appreciation is a public duty.

William A. Coffin.

The Literary Women of Washington (1898)

THE CHAUTAUQUAN.

SEPTEMBER, 1898.

THE LITERARY WOMEN OF WASHINGTON.

BY ETTA RAMSDELL GOODWIN.

WASHINGTON does not worship genius as it used to in the days when it was young and unsophisticated and when every writer, poet, scientist, and artist was a personage, when to be a statesman was enough without being a millionaire, and when there was no such thing as a "smart set." But even now in its worldly days, while there are other things that weigh heavier in the balance of its favor than merit of intellect, Washington is having the fame of some of its womenkind thrust upon it so persistently by the outside world that it has come to realize that it is time to show pride in the fact that some of the literary work that is attracting the attention of the English reading world is being done, to quote one of the city's own writers, "within sight of the goddess." Taking the representatives of what has been, what is, and what will be, there is enough material to make a literary atmosphere, and mostly woman-made, too.

There is Mrs. Emma D. E. N. Southworth to take us back to the past, for the present generation, with all its aggressiveness, has little to do with the life of this once popular writer. She is seventy years old and feeble, and her life is one of seclusion. She lives where she lived fifty years ago, in Georgetown, on the edge of the bluff overlooking the canal, and with a view of Arlington across the river. Power-houses, electric cars, and what business there is in Georgetown have made confusion about the placid old house, but it has not put on a single touch of newness, there is no visible compromise with the spirit of the times.

JENNIE GOULD LINCOLN.

Leaving what has been for what will be, there is everything to expect from a writer who is still a child, Margaret, the daughter of Mr. and Mrs. Philip Mauro, of Washing-

MOLLY ELLIOT SEAWELL.

ton. She is not yet fourteen but she has been writing for publication since she was nine, when "The Owl" and "The Song of the Winds" appeared. She is a gentle, fascinating creature, seeming younger than she really is, rather delicate looking, and with quantities of pale yellow hair. She has an absorbing fondness for animals and a hearty dislike for mathematics. In her recent poems the child has disappeared and the ripening of unmistakable genius is shown in "My Looking Glass" and in "The Sea Nymph."

Filled with the spirit of the now, the vital present, a splendid company of women is sending out from Washington novels, plays, short stories, historical sketches, poems, and reviews. The play-writing mania is raging. Several Washington women have been the authors of successful plays and nearly all of the writers are trying their hands in that sort of work. Mrs. Frances Hodgson Burnett maintains that "An ecstasy of satisfaction comes to the author with the success of a play that the good fortune of a book does not bring. You can see the success of a play; you have your judges before you; as each line is spoken you can read the verdict in a thousand faces, and if it is favorable, the writer feels such an accumulation of thrills as only a playwright can know." Something beside "thrills" has come to Mrs. Burnett in the profession of play-writing. "Little Lord Fauntleroy" brought her $94,000, "A Lady of Quality" has succeeded, and the author will probably prosper with the dramatization of "His Grace of Osmond," the production of which is causing her stay in England now. As her popularity increases her time in Washington diminishes. It is inconvenient to come; London and New York are business headquarters for her, and her publishers and the theatrical managers will only allow her scraps of time to give to the home life she finds so attractive in

FRANCES HODGSON BURNETT.

Washington. "No one works from will in Washington," she says, "the place is made to rest in." So she keeps her great house on Massachusetts Avenue and it is open for perhaps two months in every year, and her friends, who used to know her when her sons were little boys, the original Lord Fauntleroys, make a queen of her. She is known as the "Mascot." The word has become a verb in her set and success is assured for any enterprise mascotted by Mrs. Burnett. She is a firm believer in her good fairy powers; she is proud of this and of her gift in winning the confidence of children and animals. She says her method in the latter field is successful because she treats both children and animals with respect: "I do not presume to dash into familiarity with little people and with animals. I wait until they have found that I am to be trusted and then they come to me."

Hard mental work has not left marks with Mrs. Burnett, she is as rosy and as young looking as she was fifteen years ago, with the same tawney hair and the same big baby-like eyes. In her house is the luxury that she loves. The hall has settees of English oak, the staircase is tapestry-hung, there are countless old prints and fine etchings, and the hangings are warm in color. Mrs. Burnett's den is in the top of the house, an enchanting place, the pink of the sea-shell in its tints, and books everywhere. She has a house in Portland Place, London, and has just taken a beautiful country seat in Devonshire with over a hundred acres of hunting-grounds, and the house has thirty-two sleeping-rooms. Young Vivian Burnett, who was graduated from Harvard this year, is like his mother in temperament, and inherits considerable talent for play-writing. He wrote "A Fool's Goal" for his college society last year and took the principal part himself.

Now and then in Washington, in the midst of a society which every day is becoming more and more cosmopolitan, one finds a home which preserves what might be called its "southern accent." The atmosphere about such a place is warm with hospitality and the women are apt to be charming. Molly Elliot Seawell, the author of "The Story of Lady Betty Stair" and other delightful stories and several successful plays, has such an establishment. Her high-bred face tells what her tastes are sure to be, and from a look into her attractive house one would know that the fine old mahogany furniture, bookcases full of volumes, many of which are marked with dates a century old, and pieces of china worthy an art-collector's notice, had stories to tell of ancestors who helped to make the history of the country. Miss Seawell's great-grandfather was the father of President John Tyler and was the first governor of Virginia. Thomas Nelson Page and other persons of whom Virginia is proud are related to her. She cannot remember the time when the library of "The Shelter," the old country place in Virginia, was not dearer to her than her playroom. She was a very young girl when she began to write, going into it with an audacity that she speaks of with amusement now.

The off-hand fashion she has of speaking of her work and of herself is one of her most fascinating characteristics. She refuses to be serious with herself. She professed to be overwhelmed with pleasure when she read the other day in a western newspaper, "Miss Seawell is not brilliant but she is industrious." "I have not genius," she has often said. "There is always something uncanny about genius. It is a despot and rules like a despot. Talent is different. One can be the master of one's talents, and all the mere talent in the world does not set one apart from one's fellow creatures as much as a single spark of genius." Concerning her methods of work she says simply: "I work hard and I work systematically. One ought to be as systematic in resting as in working. I am enough of a southern woman to know how to rest I take an hour for it every afternoon, and the servants have orders that I am not to be disturbed unless there is a fire, and then the engines are to be called first." Miss Seawell is uncompromisingly opposed to new-womanism. She agrees with Hannah Moore who declared that "when she was old she had all the liberty she knew what to do with and that when she was young she had a great deal more than was good for her." Miss Seawell never belonged to a club in her life, she does not play golf, she does not ride a bicycle, and she never intends to, and she professes to believe that men are intellectually superior to women. She is prominent in the social life of the city and she finds Washington enchanting, too attractive in one way. She says: "To work here is like trying to work in a summer resort. There is so much that is captivating to encroach upon one's time." The home circle is made complete by the mother of the author and her sister, and every one who knows their Sunday afternoons and their delightful little dinners knows the charm of the family as hostesses. Miss Seawell has been remarkably successful with her plays. "Maid Marian" was played by Rosina Vokes and a dramatization of "The Sprightly Romance of Marsaac," Miss Seawell's three-thousand-dollar prize story, has been brought out recently.

One of the sweetest natures ever known in Washington or anywhere else shows itself in everything that Grace Denio Litchfield writes. It is interesting to know, by the way, that the second word in her name is pronounced with a long *i* and with the accent on the second syllable. To meet this writer before reading her books is to think: "What beauty there must be in any production of hers!" and after the reading her personality still throbs in the memory. In her presence one feels as one might before an ideal father confessor, if the father confessor could be a woman.

GRACE DENIO LITCHFIELD.

HARRIET PRESCOTT SPOFFORD.

She is young and very fair, and in her manner there is a calmness that does not seem to belong to the present, although no one lives more in the full life of the present. The years of physical suffering that were hers gave bravery and no bitterness, and now that happily she no longer calls herself an invalid Washington is able to see something of her. The house Miss Litchfield has built on Massachusetts Avenue is next to the one owned by Mrs. James G. Blaine and occupied by Mrs. Westinghouse. It is of great size and an admirable sort of house, very plain but built to stand for ages and with the back and sides as sightly as the front. In her last book, "In the Crucible," Miss Litchfield has treated Washington life delightfully, and what she thinks of the place itself she tells in its pages: "It is so bright, so clean, so noiseless, so airy, so happy; a city without manufactures or business; a city of luxury, leisure, and delight. Added to these traits is, naturally, its primary attraction as the seat of government. The city's very life is built up around that central fact, yet as the heart of the whirlpool is seemingly the point of greatest quiet, so it is here." The writer could not have described Washington so well if she had not known it well. She says that one of her characteristics as a writer is the inability to write about things of which she has had no experience. The chapter in the same book which tells about the earthquake in Mentone is thrillingly dramatic because she is telling what she was there to see. No writer was ever more modest, and she calls her poems verses.

She began to write when she was a very young girl and much of her work has been done while she was on a bed of illness.

Her first pieces were three poems, which she sent out to three of the leading magazines. They all came back. They were sent out again and to the same set of magazines, but changed about. Again they were returned. The third trial was more successful and two of the poems were accepted. With what they brought the young writer started a little fund to place a memorial window to her mother in Grace Church, Brooklyn, the daughter feeling that the gift had a deeper meaning because "Only what one has earned is one's very own." One fancies that the proceeds of "Criss-Cross," "The Knight of the Black Forest," "Mimosa Leaves," and other books may have been used as unselfishly. Miss Litchfield's sister, Mrs. Lawrence Turnbull, of Baltimore, a woman of geat social prominence, is the author of "Val Maria" and several other books.

Jennie Gould Lincoln, whose first book, "Dorothy's Quest," published when she was a child, would have kept her famous for the twenty years that have passed since, and whose last work, "An Unwilling Maid," has been dramatized and will be presented next season, is the wife of Dr. Lincoln, of Washington. She is a woman successful in a hundred fields. She is a member of the inner circle of the fashionable set in Washington, and for her "Mondays" there is a line of carriages almost as long as if the affairs were official. She is the first woman appealed to when an entertainment for charity is planned, and for the concert for the benefit of the *Maine* sufferers she sold the whole lower floor of the National Theater herself, this being the seventh time she has accomplished this labor for charity. She is musical, she has dramatic talent, and she is an ideal mother, idolizing her daughter, a pretty girl of sixteen, and her big athletic son, who will enter Yale next year. She speaks to her husband when she says in her dedication to "A Genuine Girl," "To you, therefore, whatever there be of merit the lids between, the praise be given and not to me, for you are what I only seem."

Her method of working is astounding. There really is no method in it. She writes no longer than half an hour at a time and sometimes that is snatched while she is dressing for dinner, or after she has her wraps on and is waiting for her carriage, or perhaps in the afternoon of her day at home before visitors arrive. She writes rapidly and seldom corrects what she has written, except sometimes when she has ended a book or story unhappily her husband "begs off" for some of the characters and she treats them more mercifully. She always chooses a title before there is any thought of the story itself. In the same way she sits down and writes a set of headings for chapters, doing it absolutely at random as they suggest themselves. She began to write when she was eight years old but in secret, as her father, Judge Gould, of the Court of Appeals of New York, did not believe in encouraging precocity. But of that father she says: "We were glorious comrades." She has told of Washington life in her novel "Her Washington Season." The scene of "An Unwilling Maid" is laid in the famous Tracy house in Litchfield, Conn., Mrs. Lincoln being a descendant of "Beautiful Sally Tracy." Two years ago Mrs. Lincoln brought out a woman's edition of the Washington *Times*, the only publication of its kind that ever received editorial notice in the New York papers.

Mrs. Harriet Prescott Spofford does not call Washington her headquarters. Newburyport in Massachusetts is home to her now, but fourteen years of her life were passed at the seat of the government and she still comes for two months in the winter to the Sixteenth Street house of her sister, who is the wife of E. A. Moseley, secretary of the Interstate Commerce Commission. She says that it is worth coming from New England to see Washington by moonlight. Much of her writing was done here, although it is to rest that she comes now. When she does work it is often in the midst of her family in a room ringing with conversation. Home life means so much to her that even when she is writing she does not demand seclusion. No more domestic woman ever existed, and no woman ever existed who believed more thoroughly in what are called the rights of women. She says that conversion came to her when, many years ago, she was obliged to endure the sight of the poverty of a woman who, at her marriage, had brought to her busband what was a little fortune, and who on his death saw his property, which had been hers, go to his relatives. They were able to set up a carriage and to live in a good style, while she, poor thing, took in plain sewing. Since that time Mrs. Spofford's ideas about the property rights of women have been rigid.

The strongest treatment of the pathetic side of office life and office seeking in Washington has been the work of Julia Schayer. It has been the theme of many of her stories, and the first book of the author will probably find its plot in the same atmosphere. "The Major's Appointment," perhaps her best piece of work and the one she likes best, is an example of the tragic side Washington life sometimes has, the side that appeals to Mrs. Schayer's talent much more strongly than the frivolous, superficial life of the capital. "Brooks," a story of the civil service, would have been sadder than it is if the writer had not yielded to the wishes of her publishers and changed the ending from the tragedy she had planned into something more happy.

Play-writing has been the work of her life for two years, and surely the drama that will come from her pen will be splendidly intense, well constructed, and artistic. The writer breathes an artistic air. Her daughter, Mrs. Howland, who lives in Paris now, used to be the Leonora Von Stosch whose violin made her famous. Another daughter is an artist and married to a Washington artist, Hobart Nichols. Mrs. Schayer herself gave her young life to music and sings now in an excellent contralto voice. She has a house in the suburbs of Washington, for to be near the country, to have a garden which she can fill with flowers, is happiness for her. Among the interesting things in her drawing-room are the original Gibson illustrations for "The Major's Appointment."

Madeleine Vinton Dahlgren, whose death recently occurred, was well known as the widow of Admiral Dahlgren and as the author of his biography, "A Washington Winter," "The Secret Directory," books on etiquette, and articles against woman suffrage. She was a woman of much prominence in the social life of the capital, but for six months before her death was obliged to narrow her life to what happened within the walls of her own home. She refused all invitations and was almost a recluse, as her illness brought suffering from which she was free for only a small part of each day. She made her summer home at South Mountain, where she was the "Lady Bountiful" of the neighborhood, where she has sixty godchildren, and where she had accumulated about her everything she loved. "For when I love anything very much," she said, "I send it to the country." Mrs. Dahlgren's daughter and her husband, Josiah Pierce, who is a professor in the Catholic University, live with her. Three of her grandsons, the children of Baron von Overbeck, are in Germany, two of them in the army and one an artist.

Caroline Healey Dall has a house in Washington, Mrs. Harriet Riddle Davis, who wrote "Within Sight of the Goddess," is the wife of the United States district attorney and is popular in Washington, and Miss Scidmore often takes some time from the travels that she writes so charmingly about to be in Washington in season.

Centennial of the Nation's Capital (1900)

FROM THE MONUMENT TO THE CAPITOL, ACROSS THE MALL.

THE COSMOPOLITAN.

From every man according to his ability: to every one according to his needs.

DECEMBER, 1900.

CENTENNIAL OF THE NATION'S CAPITAL.

By F. W. Fitzpatrick

PRESIDENT WASHINGTON, in spite of the most violent opposition, selected the present site of the nation's capital in 1790, and Congress soon after passed the necessary legislation to fix it here. Major l'Enfant immediately began the laying out of its streets from his very elaborate plans that so many then pronounced visionary and extravagant. By the summer of 1791 the work was well under way.

That he planned it well is proved by the fact that to-day, a century later, even in the face of our broadened ideas, the exigencies of our times and a phenomenal growth, without any adequate commercial reason therefor, the city is not only substantially but absolutely as he planned it and is one of the finest cities, if indeed not the finest city, in the world.

Daniel Carroll, Dr. David Stuart and Gov. Thomas Johnson were appointed Commissioners to carry out the orders of Congress in establishing the city and its government.

Maryland and Virginia contributed most generously to the erection of buildings and displayed the liveliest interest generally in the welfare of the city that was of their own soil—the District of Columbia, ten miles square, having been ceded by them to the Federal government. At one time, Congress being dilatory in appropriating funds for the continuation of the work, Maryland advanced one hundred thousand dollars to expedite matters.

A good deal of this plot of "ten miles square" was farming-land, belonging principally to David Burns, Daniel Carroll, Samuel Davidson and Notley Young. The land used for streets and parks was "condemned," while that upon which public buildings were located was paid for at the rate of one hundred dollars per acre.

The Capitol was placed on a pretty

AN OLD GEORGETOWN MANSION.

Photograph by Abel.
THE WASHINGTON MONUMENT—"THE GREAT WHITE FINGER SILENTLY POINTING UPWARD."

hilltop and the President's Mansion was set a mile away to the west, in order, some said, that legislators would not visit it too often. By the same token there are times when our Chief Executive must wish it had been placed a thousand miles away. For a time the best residences were there about the Capitol, then speculators got hold of the land, and other matters have operated to the detriment of that section—railway terminals, et cetera—so that now the most fashionable section is north and west of the White House, and in that direction palatial residences are being built well to the very limits of the district line.

Major l'Enfant was never properly compensated for his splendid services. Republics, they say, are ungrateful; this one certainly was in his case. He was buried by private charity in 1825.

There were ups and downs in the fortunes of the city in those early days. Sometimes at the sales of land there were good prices obtained, and then again rumor had it the capital would not be removed to this wilderness. On two occasions, in fact, it was by the merest good luck, once by only two votes, that such legislation was not enacted as would have kept the capital at Philadelphia or removed it to some already settled city. Even among the Cabinet officers there was almost an uprising at the idea of their being banished to such a place of exile, where, as Secretary Wolcott wrote, "people lived in huts and were so poor they lived on fish, or, like the fish, ate each other up."

One wing of the Capitol, and the White House, were built and partially finished inside, and the final transfer of the archives and furniture of state was effected in "one packet-sloop," of the capacity of a good-sized furniture-van, in October, 1800. The officials of the government, fifty-four in all, including President Adams and his Cabinet, followed overland in "coaches, chaises and upon horseback."

Soon after that, Jefferson, who seemed to embody all that was artistic of his time, entered heart and soul into the task of beautifying the city, and through his influence very large sums of money were appropriated for that purpose.

In 1814 the English partially destroyed the Capitol, some of the other public build-

Photograph by Bell.

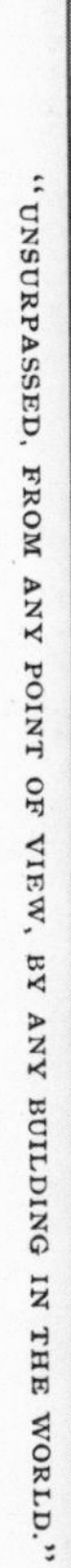

"UNSURPASSED, FROM ANY POINT OF VIEW, BY ANY BUILDING IN THE WORLD."

ings and much private property, doing damage to the amount of a million dollars or more. As soon as the scare was over, the government and the citizens went at the rebuilding of the damaged parts, and the erection of other buildings, with a vim. That fire, and several minor subsequent ones, seemed after all to be beneficent in their results.*

By 1825 there were nearly twenty thousand people here; when the Civil War broke out there were sixty-two thousand, and to-day, including those who reside just outside the ten-mile limit, in office or in business here and to all intents and purposes citizens of Washington, we have a population of three hundred thousand people.

The 12th of December has been decided upon as the time to celebrate the centennial. There will be parades, banquets and speeches galore. Some great projects were suggested as fitting memorials for this occasion. A grand "Centennial Avenue," to be cut off the northern edge of the Mall, from the Capitol to the also proposed Memorial Bridge crossing to Arlington Cemetery, affording continuous sites for the government buildings which the powers that be now scatter rather aimlessly about the city, was one scheme. This scheme was devised by Architect Henry Ives Cobb for the Congressional Committee and Committee of States' Governors. For a long time there has been a clamor to systematize the placing of government structures. Many have been in favor, particularly those with property to sell in that section, of the government's buying the south side of Pennsylvania Avenue—in fact, all of that section south of that avenue and north of the Mall, or park—for sites for these proposed buildings, the Department of Justice, Hall of Records, City Hall, et cetera, and the hundred and one buildings we shall need in the near future. For even to-day, and though there are so many departmental buildings, nearly one-fifth of the United States' business is done in rented quarters. Remember, it is a large

Photograph by Abel. THE LIBRARY OF CONGRESS.

*The valuation of all real and personal property here, that of the United States included, is placed at about five hundred and fifty million dollars. Taxes are levied upon about two hundred and ten million dollars' worth of that, but then Congress appropriates for one-half of most of the street improvements, et cetera.

concern and, of late, growing even beyond the seas.

To the south and west of this new avenue, in that region known to Washingtonians as the "proposed park," would be located the speedway, the polo-ground and areas for baseball and other games, the swimming-pool and -beach—our "outing" grounds so near the city, and the finest that any city possesses—that have been planned by Colonel Bingham under the direction of Congress as part of the work laid out to be done during the centennial year.

This Mall to-day is little frequented. It is almost waste ground in parts. Its northern limit is B Street. Mr. Cobb's proposed centennial avenue cuts off but a strip along that northern edge; this strip would be cut into blocks and upon these would be erected a line of handsome public buildings, and, of course, nothing but public buildings, and upon *our* own ground. To the south there would be no buildings, just a fine stretch of well-kept park. It would be essentially a grand governmental avenue, one of the grandest vistas and the most imposing street one could find in the world.

A grand States Building here, containing offices, exhibition-rooms for state products, post-offices and information bureaus, et cetera, for visitors from each state, and offices and committee-rooms for the delegations to Congress, virtually state legations here, surrounding a large exposition hall that could also be used for conventions, inaugural balls, and other assemblies of masses of people, was another of the most

Photograph by Abel.

PANORAMA OF THE CITY FROM THE NATIONAL CEMETERY, ARLINGTON.

SOUTH FRONT OF THE EXECUTIVE MANSION.

fitting permanent memorials of the occasion that were suggested. The time being so short from the suggesting to the time set for celebration, neither of them has been begun. Time will see both accomplished facts, however.

But, to me, though there is to be no permanent and special memorial completed and dedicated that day, the city itself, our splendid monuments, all about the capital, and all accomplished in the century, are sufficient glory, and will give lasting impressions enough to those who assemble to help us celebrate that occasion and wish us God-speed upon our second century of progress.

The government has built some thirty groups of large buildings here, most of

DOWN THE POTOMAC FROM THE TOP OF THE MONUMENT.

them handsome structures. Neither St. Peter's in Rome, St. Paul's in London, nor any other of the great domed edifices of Europe is to be compared, in dignity, artistic lines or sightliness, with the Capitol. One never tires of it. Grand in the glaring sun, magnificent in a storm, weird and specter-like of a dark night, and a dream of loveliness by moonlight, it stands unsurpassed, from any point of view, by any building in the world. The Treasury and the Patent-Office are also magnificent examples of architecture, and the White House leaves a good taste in one's mouth, so to speak. Foreigners visiting us soon get over the impression they have received from some source or other that we are an inartistic race of shopkeepers. Besides these buildings it has built, the government has bought many others, and rents still others, to house its twenty-five thousand officers and employees.

There are our splendid Library, our museums, a host of fine private buildings, picture-galleries, palatial residences, offices, banks, stores, churches, hospitals, four great universities—all fine buildings. If our city were destroyed we could not replace these buildings for a quarter of a billion of dollars. In what might be called educational institutions, libraries, museums, geological and other bureaus, alone, the government has some forty millions invested.*

Photograph by Abel. IN THE CONGRESSIONAL GARDENS.

No other city on earth has as well-paved streets, two hundred miles of them, broad and kept marvelously clean. We borrowed the "white wings" idea from Colonel Waring's New York cleaners. Upon nearly every block will you see a white-clad figure

* We erect about seven million dollars' worth of buildings a year. Our banking capital is about twenty-five million dollars. Nearly seven thousand of us die in a year—a low death-rate. We have a thousand fewer births—sixty thousand youngsters go to school—and there are some three thousand marriages recorded in the District if not in heaven.

Photograph by Abel. PEACE MONUMENT IN THE CAPITOL GROUNDS.

scraping and sweeping his section all day long. And where will you find as perfect a system of street railways? Mostly underground electric too, one hundred and sixty miles of it within our ten-mile District, and sixty miles of line in outlying districts connecting thereto.

Our electric-light wires, telephone and telegraph lines, are nearly all in conduits underground; there is nothing placed aboveground to mar the beauty of our capital. It is not a manufacturing center —Heaven forbid it may ever be one!—and yet we manufacture nearly fifty million dollars' worth of stuff a year.*

Right in the city there are four thousand six hundred and eighty-nine acres of parks. The Mall, in the very heart of the downtown district, contains nearly one thousand acres, and besides these parks there are some two hundred and twenty little triangles and circles at the bisections of streets and avenues, breathing-places where one may generally also find a fountain, or one of our great "men on horseback" done in bronze. Everywhere there are trees and boulevarded streets. One may truly say it is a great wooded park untouched save for the asphalted streets and the buildings let in *among* the trees, and if you weary of those buildings you have but to stroll across a bridge to Arlington, or on up about Rock Creek Park, where you will be in sylvan surroundings; if then you long for the roar of lions, the noises of the jungle, go a few steps farther to the Zoölogical Park, where your every taste in that direction may be satisfied. If you want the bustle and push of business, saunter down F Street and back by Pennsylvania Avenue to the Treasury at noontime. Or if you wish to be reminded of Paris or Berlin, walk up Connecticut Avenue after four o'clock. There will be

* Apart from fires, I think it generally conceded that Alexander R. Shepherd, "Boss" Shepherd, who was governor of the "territory" for a while in the '70's (from '71 to '74 Congress tried a territorial form of government for the District), did more than any other individual to push the city along to its present high estate. He was cordially hated for his high-handed methods, but we are ready to thank him for it now.

found fair women, handsome men, domestic and foreign, single-eye-glassed, blasé, white-spatted—all kinds; and there are the finest turn-outs, high-stepping thoroughbreds, magnificent carriages, serious and real English coachmen with cockades and liveries their masters are legitimately entitled to sport upon their lackeys. You will also see more automobiles, and the other horseless affairs, there than in any other city, save New York, this side of the Atlantic. Do you want to realize you are in the South? Go up to quaint old Georgetown Heights, where there are the solid old Colonial mansions of long ago and the courtly manners of the same time. Are you lonesome for the brownstone, dingy palaces of New York's Fifth Avenue? Come with me down K Street, Massachusetts Avenue, along Connecticut and up New Hampshire Avenues; there are the great marble and brownstone abodes of the millionaires. What, not dingy enough to resemble New York? Well, that is a fact. We cannot supply that dinginess, however. When you build with white marble here, it will still be white fifty years from now; why, even our black population is growing whiter every generation.

Or, perhaps you are thinking of the West—the newness, daintiness, homelike look, to the houses you've seen in Denver, Portland or Minneapolis? Well, let us take a car out to Chevy Chase. Pretty little cottages with wonderful nooks, turrets and bays, painted most tastily, set down in neatly trimmed lawns that their owners seem to be constantly sprinkling. A facsimile of Minneapolis or I am in my dotage. You will grant we are indeed cosmopolitan. Whatever—nice—you have seen elsewhere, that you will also find here, and with it a thousand things you can find nowhere else.

Photograph by Abel. CORNER OF ENTRANCE-HALL OF THE LIBRARY OF CONGRESS.

Nearly a million people visit us each year. Last year there were nearly enough great conventions, Masons, surgeons, bankers, ladies' A. B. C. D. E. societies, assembled here to give us one for every week in the

FROM THE TOP OF THE MONUMENT TOWARD THE FASHIONABLE QUARTER.

year, and sometimes in batches of twenty-five thousand or more. Some five hundred strangers go up the Monument every day and look down upon us from that dizzy height of five hundred and fifty feet, admiring our charms, artificial and natural.

Statesmen and legislators stay here during their terms of office because they have to, and then remain with us from choice. They not only become attached to the city with its people, but admit, wherever they come from, that there is no place like it. Men of wealth come here to reside after they retire from active business elsewhere, because nowhere else will their wealth procure them the advantages they may here enjoy. Scientists and students flock to us on account of the wonderful opportunities they find here to pursue their various studies. Financiers live here because—well, perhaps chiefly because there is legislation here that might go wrong if not carefully watched; but then, they stay here after that watchful period has passed.

Old men come here to live because they want to or else their wives make them, and young men come for many reasons, not the least of which is that our daughters are so attractive.

THOMAS CIRCLE IN THE NORTHWEST DISTRICT.

PENNSYLVANIA AVENUE ONE HUNDRED YEARS AFTER IT WAS LAID OUT.

Men who have won fame and place, Arctic explorers, scientists, great writers, celebrated artists, the highest in every walk of life, men whose names are known the world over, all you may see if you stay there long enough.

I could spend a great many hours enumerating the beauties of our capital, but I fear it would grow wearisome to you, so let me end this brief exordium by inviting you in the name of the city to come to help us fittingly celebrate the one-hundredth birthday of the nation's capital, Washington. The welcome will be hearty; the visit enjoyable; weather, everything, will be propitious, and the recollections thereof pleasant memories. Hæc olim meminisse juvabit.

PENNSYLVANIA AVENUE AND THE CAPITOL IN 1810.

The White House
(1902)

THERE is no single building, perhaps, in Washington which plays a more important part in the social and political life of the city, or which attracts more attention from the thousands of visitors who come annually to the Nation's capital, than the plain white edifice which stands on Pennsylvania Avenue just west of the Treasury Department, and which is familiarly known to the public as "The White House." It derives its predominant interest not only from its occupation as a private residence by the President of the United States, but also from the historical associations that it recalls and preserves, the uses to which it is put as a great executive office, and the service that it renders as an important center of National life and activity. It is the place where the President transacts his official business; where the diplomatic representatives of foreign powers are received; where the Nation welcomes and entertains its distinguished guests; where large delegations of citizens are constantly presenting themselves with greetings of courtesy or questions of business; where newspaper men from all parts of the country spend hours every day in the collection of news; and where the President, as the head of the Nation, and his wife as "the first lady of the land," must receive and entertain, every year, thousands of American citizens who

THE WHITE HOUSE, FROM THE NORTHEAST

come to Washington as official or unofficial representatives of a great and rapidly growing people.

A building that serves so many purposes, and that is the center of so many social, political, and business interests, must necessarily be an object of National importance; and it ought, manifestly, to be a building adequate in size to meet all possible demands upon it; suitable in plan for the uses to which it is put, and beautiful enough, architecturally, to comport with the wealth, power, and dignity of a great State. That the present structure fails to satisfy most of these requirements is a fact that has long been apparent even to the casual observer. In the year 1800, when the White House was first occupied as a Presidential mansion, the United States had a population of only five and a quarter millions. In the century that has since elapsed we have grown into a Nation of nearly eighty millions, and the social, political, and business interests that center in the Executive Mansion have greatly increased both in complexity and in volume. It is not an exaggeration, perhaps, to say that hundreds of persons go to the White House, socially or on business, now, for every one that visited it a century ago; and yet there has been no enlargement whatever of its capacity or its facilities.

The urgent necessity for some change or extension that shall relieve the congestion and facilitate the transaction of public business in the White House may best be shown, perhaps, by concrete facts and figures.

The clerical work of the Executive office, at the present time, necessitates the employment of a regular force of about twenty men; and for their accommodation—with all their desks, typewriting machines, letter-files, etc.—there are only four rooms, of very moderate size, one of which is used, in part, as a reception and waiting room for persons who desire to see the President or his secretary. Occasionally, when there is a press of Executive business, clerks from the Departments are specially detailed for White House service; and these men have to be crowded into offices already fully occupied by the regular force. Recently Mr. Cortelyou, Secretary to the President, had to put seventeen stenographers, typewriters, and copyists into a room that ought not to have held more than three. As the work of the Executive office is constantly increasing, it will shortly become necessary to strengthen the regular force, either by appointing new clerks or by making permanent the temporary details from the Departments; and then the already congested state of the office rooms will be even more serious and embarrassing than it is now.

THE WHITE HOUSE, FROM THE SOUTH

For the rapidly accumulating files, records, and valuable papers of the Executive Mansion no suitable provision can possibly be made within existing limits of space; and eight tons of such documents have recently been removed from the crowded office rooms and stored either in the basement or in the attic. These parts of the building are not readily accessible, and the sending of clerks up stairs or down stairs after letters and papers is a source of unnecessary inconvenience and delay. The building has no fire-proof vault, and for valuable documents there is no place of deposit other than an old iron safe.

The library accommodations of the White House are almost as unsatisfactory and inadequate as are the office facilities. Secretary Cortelyou, with the assistance of an expert, has recently made an attempt to classify, catalogue, and put in order the somewhat heterogeneous and fortuitously acquired collection of books now at the President's disposal; but the oval room over the south portico is hardly large enough to hold, in convenient arrangement, even the number of volumes that it already contains; and for the new books, charts, reports, and encyclopædias that should be added in order to make anything like a complete, up-to-date reference library, there is no available space.

The room just east of the library, where the President and the members of his Cabinet are accustomed to meet for consultation, is much too small. It ought to be large enough to hold a big globe, books, maps, charts, etc., which are often needed for reference during Cabinet meetings; but at present there is no room for them.

Proposed National Wing. Executive Residence (Present White House). Proposed Official Wing.

MRS. BENJAMIN HARRISON'S PLAN FOR THE EXECUTIVE MANSION, NORTH VIEW

From the copyrighted plan of the architect, F. D. Owen.

Proposed Official Wing. Executive Residence (Present White House). Proposed National Wing.

MRS. HARRISON'S PLAN FOR THE EXECUTIVE MANSION, SOUTH VIEW

From the copyrighted plan of the architect, F. D. Owen.

Better accommodations are urgently required for newspaper men. The White House has become one of the most important news-gathering centers in Washington; and the correspondents and reporters who daily assemble there should have a place of their own, with desks and proper working facilities. At present they are crowded into the eastern end of the upper corridor, which is used, at the same time, as a general waiting-room for persons who desire to see the President or his secretary on business.

This overcrowding of the White House generally, and of the upper part of the official wing in particular, not only involves great inconvenience, but is attended with some risk. The building is now more than a century old; and although it is still strong enough, structurally, to answer all the purposes of a private residence, there is considerable doubt as to the question whether its floors can be trusted to bear the weight that is occasionally put upon them. It is not regarded as perfectly safe now for the President to receive large delegations in the upper part of the building; and Colonel Bingham, Superintendent of Public Buildings and Grounds, told President McKinley that if more than two thousand persons were invited to a single White House reception, he — the President—must assume responsibility for any accident that might occur. Owing to the fact that the offices in the second story are mainly over the large East Room, they have no adequate partition support, and cannot be strengthened by the putting in of underpinning. They are regarded, therefore, as

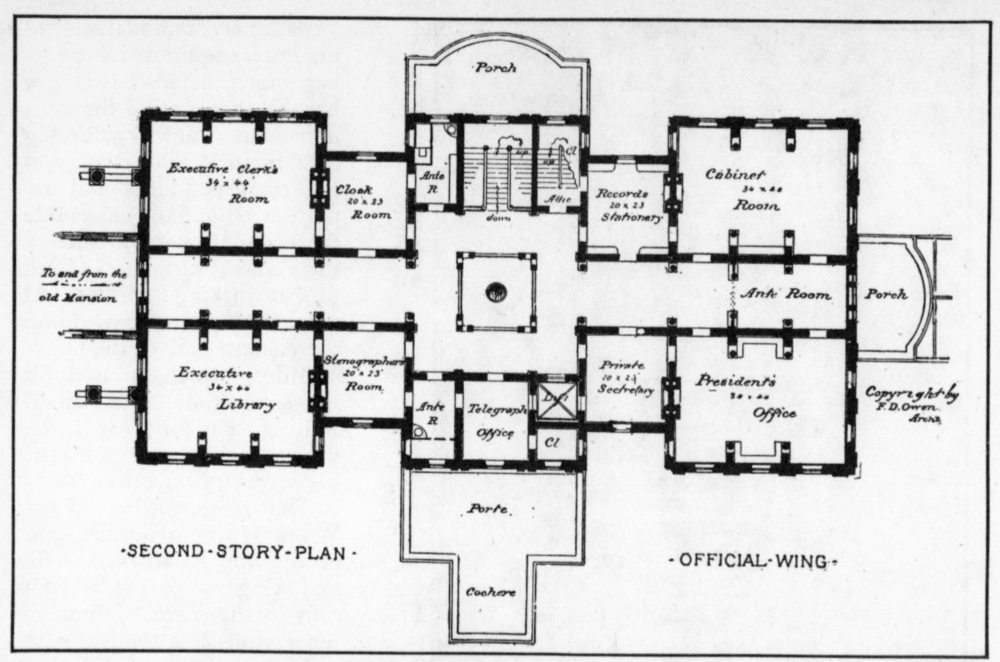

THE SECOND-FLOOR PLAN OF THE PROPOSED OFFICIAL WING

From the copyrighted plan of the architect, F. D. Owen.

somewhat untrustworthy, and nothing but absolute necessity would have compelled the President's secretary to load the floor of one of them with the weight of seventeen men and their desks. The risk had to be taken because the work had to be done; and there was no other place to put the clerks who were doing it.

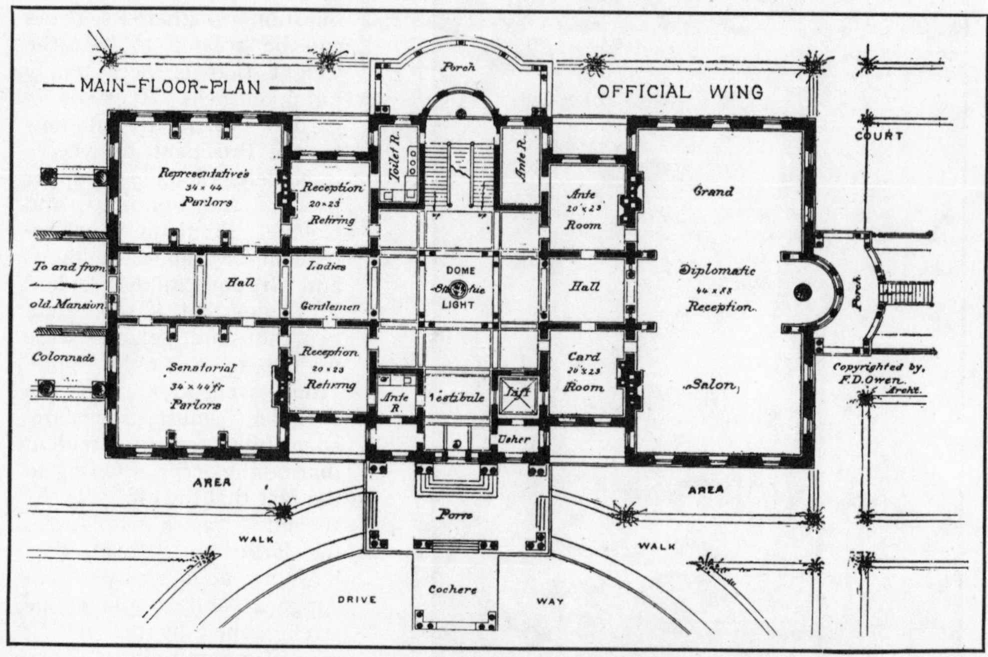

THE FIRST-FLOOR PLAN OF THE PROPOSED OFFICIAL WING

From the copyrighted plan of the architect, F. D. Owen.

It may perhaps be thought that although the official end of the White House is overcrowded, as a result of the great increase in the volume of Executive business, there is ample accommodation in the private part of the building for the President, his family, and their guests; but such is by no means the case. There is no suitable room, on the first floor, for giving important state dinners in the East Room, although the latter is very inconveniently situated with reference to the pantries and the kitchen.

In the second story of the private wing there are only five sleeping-apartments, and it is perfectly obvious that this is a wholly inadequate provision for the President's family and their guests. A few small bedrooms for servants have recently been made by putting up partitions in the attic; but these rooms can be reached only by means of an elevator which must be used also by the President and his family in going to and from the second floor. The dressing-rooms, bath-rooms, pantries, etc., are insufficient in number and inconveniently situated; there is not a single china-closet in the building; the

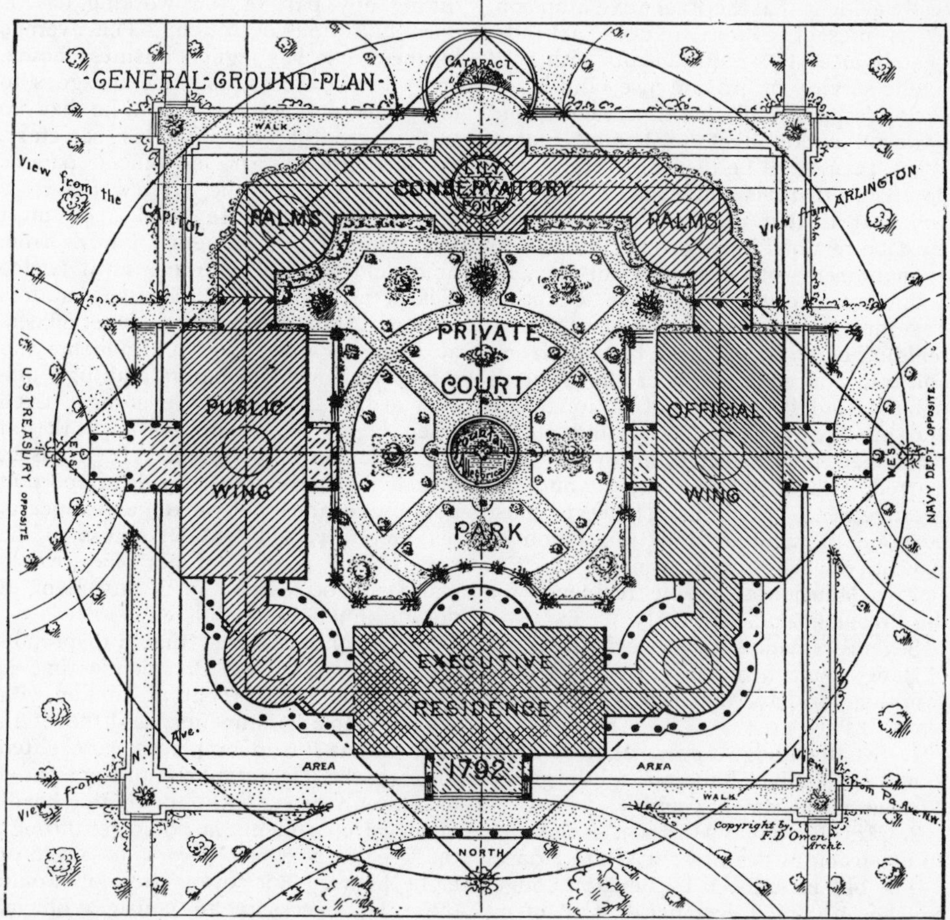

MRS. BENJAMIN HARRISON'S PLAN FOR ENLARGING AND BEAUTIFYING THE WHITE HOUSE AND GROUNDS

From the copyrighted plan of the architect, F. D. Owen.

the great state dinners which must be given at intervals during the winter, and it has been found necessary to use as a dining-room the long corridor that separates the vestibule from the so-called Blue Room. Even this is hardly large enough to accommodate the number of guests that the President would like occasionally to entertain; and the experiment will probably be tried this winter of

servants' quarters would be inaccessible if anything should happen to the elevator; and the only convenient entrance to the private apartments, from the front, is through a door that is used indiscriminately by Congressmen, ambassadors, newspaper men, tourists, sightseers, and the public generally.

Upon this statement of facts it is perfectly evident that the Executive Mansion, in its present condition, does not adequately meet the requirements either of public service or private use, and is not in any respect creditable to a wealthy and powerful nation like the United States. What, then, shall be done with it? Upon one point there is universal agreement; and that is that the old White House must be retained in its present form. As a monument of American history, an architectural ornament to the beautiful city that has grown up about it, and a building closely connected, by association and tradition, with some of the Nation's noblest dead, it is worthy of National care and preservation; and it should not be remodeled, reconstructed, or in any way marred, without the most urgent and imperative need. Something, however, must be done to facilitate the transaction of Executive business, and to make the Executive Mansion a suitable residence for the President and his family.

Several remedies for the existing state of things have been suggested, but only two, thus far, have taken form in definite plans. They are:

1. Senator Lodge's proposition to erect a new Executive building south of the Treasury Department; and

2. Mrs. Benjamin Harrison's plan for an extension of the present White House.

The bill introduced by Senator Lodge, on the 4th of December last, contemplates the erection, just south of the Treasury Department, of an entirely new building, to contain public dining and reception rooms, a Cabinet room, offices for the President and his secretaries, suitable accommodations for newspaper men and executive clerks, and ample storage for all the files, records, papers, and valuable documents that are needed for reference in the daily routine of official work. This plan would relieve the White House from the congestion due to pressure of Executive business, and make it merely a private residence for the President and his family.

At first glance, Senator Lodge's bill would seem to offer a very satisfactory solution of the whole difficulty; but the conditions of the problem are not so simple as they seem, and a plan that involves the separation of the President from his secretary and the records of his office, during any part of the working day, is open to serious objection. The average business man has regular business hours, and when he closes his office and goes to his home, at 4 P.M. or 6 P.M., he has no further use, that day, for his secretary, his stenographer, or his official papers. The President of the United States is not so situated. He works, or must hold himself in readiness for work, from nine o'clock in the morning until twelve o'clock at night. He discusses matters of urgent importance with Cabinet officers at dinner, or listens to the arguments and representations of Senators and high officials at late hours of the evening. Even when he is alone, he often works at his desk until midnight. To transact official business and decide important public questions without the assistance of his secretary, and without access to the papers and records of his office, would manifestly be extremely inconvenient, if not absolutely impossible.

It is doubtless true that a disproportionate amount of the President's time is given to persons who call upon him with reference to appointments; and that if all applications for minor places were sifted through the Departments, and presented to him only at stated hours by the heads of such Departments, he could get through the greater part of his work in seven or eight hours. But even then it would often be necessary to consider official matters and decide public questions in the evening at the White House. In the Garfield administration applications for appointment to office were referred, as far as possible, to the Departments; but the President was compelled, nevertheless, to do a large and important part of his work after 6 P.M.

But this is a statement of only one side of the case. The Executive work of the White House has increased to such an extent in volume and complexity that the President's secretary cannot possibly get

THE WASHINGTON MONUMENT IN MIDWINTER

Photograph by Henry Hoyt Moore. Taken from the southern boundary of the Executive Grounds, on a rainy day in late December.

through his share of it within the hours of a normal working day. Compelled, by virtue of his office, to see almost every one who calls, and to act as a sort of social buffer between the President and the public, he can find little time, during the day, for other work; and the result is that he, too, is often obliged to sit at his desk until midnight, clearing away the accumulation of letters and papers, and attending to matters with regard to which the President has given him verbal orders. In the execution of this work he has occasion almost hourly to go to the President, either with suggestions and reminders or with a request for further instruction.

If, in accordance with Senator Lodge's plan, the Executive offices should be separated from the Executive Mansion, the President could not conveniently get at his secretary when he wanted him in the evening, and would be obliged to send to the Executive building for every letter, paper, or record that he had occasion to examine after office hours. The secretary, on the other hand, while doing evening work in the Executive building, would have to go to the White House every time it became necessary to consult the President or get further instruction, and this would cause great inconvenience and delay. In any time of storm or stress, in case of war, or in the event of trouble in Cuba, Porto Rico, or the Philippines, the President would almost certainly need his secretary, a telegraph operator, and a stenographer at the White House every evening, and this would probably result, eventually, in the establishment of two sets of Executive offices—one at the White House and the other in the new Executive building.

On its domestic side this plan is also open to objection. If the public dining and reception rooms were in the proposed Executive building, the President's wife could not supervise the arrangement of the tables or the decoration of the state apartments without making repeated journeys back and forth between that building and the White House; and in bad weather this might be a hardship as well as an inconvenience. It has been sug-

THE WHITE HOUSE AND GROUNDS FROM THE WASHINGTON MONUMENT
Photograph by Henry Hoyt Moore.

A CROWDED OFFICE IN THE EXECUTIVE MANSION
Photograph by Henry Hoyt Moore.

gested that a tunnel might be constructed between the two buildings, with electric means of intercommunication, so that the President or his wife might go back and forth without ordering a carriage or walking through the streets; but this proposition seems hardly worthy of serious consideration.

In view of the varied and manifold difficulties and inconveniences that would present themselves at the very threshold of a new Executive building, Colonel Bingham, Superintendent of Public Buildings and Grounds, who had had professional training as an engineer officer as well as long experience in the capacity of military attaché at various foreign courts, began several years ago to study the problem with a view to finding some more satisfactory solution. His attention was soon attracted to a plan which was first suggested, in 1889, by Caroline Scott Harrison, wife of President Benjamin Harrison, and which was subsequently worked into shape, under her supervision, by the architect Frederick D. Owen. Careful consideration of this plan led Colonel Bingham to the belief that it was open to fewer objections and combined more advantages than any other that could be—or at least had been—devised. He therefore worked it out in detail and presented it, with a large illustrative model, on the occasion of the centennial celebration of the occupation of Washington as the National capital, about a year ago. In its present form this plan provides for an enlargement of the White House by means of two parallel wings, extending backward from the present building in such a manner as to make, with the latter, three sides of a large square. These wings are to be about equal in size to the structure of which they will form a part, are to correspond with it in style of architecture, and are to be united at the rear by a new conservatory to take the place of the one that now adjoins the White House on the west. The effect of this extension will be to create an imposing architectural quadrangle, with a spacious interior court, like a Spanish patio, where the President's family may take exercise, or enjoy the sunshine and open air, without subjection to public scrutiny, and without danger of being surreptitiously photographed by some enterprising sightseer with a detective camera.

As the proposed extensions are to be made on prolongations of the main corridors of the existing structure, it will not be necessary to touch the latter, even to the extent of closing up a door or a window; and as the wings are to be recessed or thrown back a little from the front line of the main façade, they will accentuate, rather than diminish, the architectural effect of the old historic building.

The conservatory, which is to form the southern side of the proposed quadrangle, will stand on ground that is thirty-two feet lower than the main floor of the old White House, and will therefore offer no obstruction to the view from the windows and present no obstacle to the free entrance of sunshine or air. As the Executive grounds comprise about fourteen acres, there will be plenty of room for the fine architectural quadrangle which the plan contemplates, and its windows will overlook, on the southern side, the eighty-two acres of foliage and lawn in the Presidential park. The lateral extensions will not interfere with the view of the Department Buildings adjacent to the White House, and will present beautiful and harmonious vistas as seen from New York and Pennsylvania Avenues.

Objection to the extension plan may possibly be made on the ground that it is, after all, a makeshift, and that extensions and additions are apt to result in a composite patchwork that has neither dignity nor architectural harmony. As a general proposition this may be true; but it should not be forgotten that the same objection was raised in 1851, when the question under consideration was the proposed extension of the Capitol. The result of Mr. Walters's work in that case was eminently satisfactory; and although the Capitol, in its present form, is a composite structure, made by successive addi-

FROM A SOUTH WINDOW OF THE WHITE HOUSE
Photograph by Henry Hoyt Moore.

tions and extensions, it certainly is not lacking in beauty, dignity, or unity of design. It is a pertinent fact, moreover, that the additions which it is now proposed to make to the work of Mr. Hoban in the White House are, from a structural point of view, exactly like the additions which were actually made to the same architect's work, fifty years ago, in the Capitol; and that they are to be made in precisely the same way—by lateral extensions on the lines of the main corridors, without alteration or reconstruction of the original building.

If the Harrison plan, as worked out in detail by Colonel Bingham and Mr. Owen, were adopted and carried into execution, there would be ample space in the lateral extensions for public dining-rooms and reception-rooms, as well as for a Presidential library, a suitable Cabinet room, Executive offices, accommodations for newspaper men, and plenty of storage for files, records, and valuable documents now exposed to the danger of accidental fire in the White House. Several independent entrances and exits, with cloakrooms, dressing-rooms, and ample carriage facilities, would obviate all of the difficulties now experienced at large evening receptions.

In view of the fact that it may be thought inexpedient to make, at once, the whole of the extension for which the Harrison plan provides, Colonel Bingham has worked out in detail a scheme which will meet the present exigencies of the case, and at the same time admit of future additions in accordance with the original design. This scheme contemplates the erection, at once, of the two curved wings that are to adjoin the old mansion on the east and west, and that are ultimately to serve as great corridors leading from the present building to the two rectangular lateral extensions. These wings, when completed, will afford space for public dining and reception rooms, guest chambers, offices, storerooms, etc., and at the same time will have, architecturally, a finished appearance, and will form, eventually, an integral and essential part of the whole Harrison quadrangle. It is proposed to build these wings on a granite foundation, with walls of concrete and marble inclosing a steel framework. In the western wing there will be, on the first floor, a large state dining-room capable of seating two hundred guests, with suitable provision for kitchen, pantries, serving-rooms, etc., in the basement. Over this room, in the second story, will be six bedrooms, en suite, with four bath-rooms, and also a bright, south-facing apartment that may be used as a boudoir. On the first floor of the eastern wing there will be a large reception-room, intended to supplement the present East Room, and over it, in the second story, the clerical force of the White House will find ample accommodation in six executive offices, with storerooms and closets, while the newspaper men will have a place of their own, properly furnished and fitted up.

The cost of these wings will be, approximately, $1,100,000, and the detailed working plans are so nearly ready that ground might be broken, if necessary, within thirty days. If the execution of the Harrison scheme were intrusted to the officers of the United States Engineer Corps, who have superintended the erection of nearly all the important public buildings in Washington, including the Monument and the Congressional Library, the work might be done economically as well as thoroughly.

With regard to the questions whether or not Mrs. Harrison's plan is preferable to the plan of Senator Lodge, and whether, if the former be adopted, it will not be best to appropriate $5,000,000 and finish it at once, there is room for difference of opinion; but there can be no doubt whatever that some means of relieving the congestion at the White House should be devised at once. The initiative must necessarily be taken by Congress, because the President, although more directly interested than any other single person, cannot insist very strenuously upon an enlargement of the building in which he lives, when that same building, presumably, has answered the needs and served the purposes of all his distinguished predecessors. He should be consulted, of course, and his wishes and preferences should have due weight; but upon Congress, primarily, lies the responsibility of providing for an Executive Mansion that shall meet all social and official requirements, and that shall also be in keeping with the wealth, power, and dignity of a great nation.

Washington in Jackson's Time (1900)

WASHINGTON IN JACKSON'S TIME

WITH GLIMPSES OF HENRY CLAY

FROM THE DIARIES AND FAMILY LETTERS OF MRS. SAMUEL HARRISON SMITH (MARGARET BAYARD)

Edited by Gaillard Hunt from the collection of her grandson, J. Henley Smith

To J. H. Bayard Smith

[January, 1829.]

. . . We talked—my goodness, how we talked, so fast & so loud we could scarcely hear each other. "Tell us all about the gay world," said Mrs. Clifton. "We *poor* people know nothing of it but by rumour." So we told of all the gay & great folks & great parties, & marriages & deaths, funerals & festivals, we knew anything of, while we sat round the table & drank our tea. Scarcely could we get away from these attached friends. But the sun had set & we had other visits to pay. On our way back we stopped to see an old friend Mr. Ingham & his lady, who arrived a few days ago—& then proceeded to Mrs. Clay's, where I reproached myself for not being oftener, considering the present state of affairs. We were conducted up stairs, the door of the little drawing room opened. All was bright with splendid furniture, lamps & blazing fire, but no smiling faces like those we left in the little kitchen mingled their light with the surrounding objects. Mrs. C. was mournfully walking the room & as we entered, held up her finger, to impose silence, & pointed to the sopha. "He sleeps," whispered she. I felt a shock on turning my eyes as she spoke, on the sopha was stretched at full length Mr. Clay face & all, completely cover'd with a dark cloak, which looked like a black pall. We took our chairs, without speaking & sat silent. Our entrance however had awakened him & after a minute or two, he slowly rose & putting the cloak aside reclined in one corner with his feet stretched along the sopha. I had not seen him for three weeks & was shocked at the alteration in his looks. He was much thinner, very pale, his eyes sunk in his head & his countenance sad & melancholy—that countenance generally illumined with the fire of genius & animated by some ardent feeling. His voice was feeble & mournful. I cannot describe dear Bayard what melancholy feelings were excited in my breast. But I had come purposely to try & cheer my excellent friend Mrs. Clay, who I knew was sick & sad, so I resisted my melancholy tho' I could not help continually contrasting the little kitchen & its inmates, with this present scene. There gaiety had been spontaneous, here it was forced. Still I was, if [torn out], at least cheerful & said everything I could think of to amuse my *great friends*, with far less success however, than with my *poor friends*. Gentlemen came in & enquiries were made about the other sick members of the Cabinet. Mr. Rush, who has been alarmingly ill, for a week past, is not it is fear'd yet out of danger. The first symptoms of disease were altogether in the head. Mr. Southard, tho' just out of his room, after three weeks confinement, is appointed acting Secretary of the treasury. He is so feeble that I fear this added labour will produce a relapse. Mr. Clay has not been out for a week & is scarcely able to sit up. Last week Mr. Wirt had two attacks, to which they gave no name, a vertigo, followed by a loss of sense or motion. One attack, he remained three hours, insensible, the gentlemen all agreed, the only chance he had for prolonged life was his relinquishing his practice. During a week or more, Genl Porter, was almost blind from inflamation of the eyes & went to his office with two blisters on, one behind each ear. Mr. Adams always appears in fine spirits, but it is said, is so feeble as to be obliged to relinquish his long walks & to substitute rides on horseback—this, I give from hearsay, for I have not seen him. How strange it is, that every individual of the administration, should be ill. I really feel very anxious about Mr. Rush & Mr. Clay. You, from your connection with his sons, will feel most for Mr. R., & I need not caution you not to mention what I have said, lest you alarm them, as it is probable they are not informed of the worst symptoms. You will know, sooner than I shall, the result of election of Senator. From the last news, I fear Judge Southard will lose his election & Mr. Ewing be chosen.* I shall be sorry. I hoped we should keep this amiable family. The thought of losing so many old & agreeable acquaintances, not to say friends, makes me feel sad,—the time is rapidly approaching. Mrs. Clay's next drawing-room, closes this social scene, intercourse between these families & general society. She says, she shall not go out any more & immediately after next Wednesday, begin to pack up & make preparations for going home. The President in the course of ten days or two weeks is going to leave the President's House & remove to Commodore Porter's House, which he has rented. What a change, what a change will be here in our city. On no former occasion has there been anything like it.

Saturday morning. Susan & I, accompanied by Mrs. Barnet went last evening to Mrs. Lovel's, where we met a much larger company than we expected, but very agreeable. It is a right down snow storm to-day. After closing this letter I shall write a long one to your aunt Boyd. You know I love to write on a stormy day. If the weather does not prevent I expect a small chess party to meet here this evening. Do you not wish you were with us. Good morning dear Bayard. Now you have answered the others my turn comes & I shall look impatiently for a letter.

To Mrs. Kirkpatrick

[WASHINGTON],
January 12, 1829. Monday.

. . . Rank, honors, glory, are such unsubstantial empty things that they can never satisfy the desires that they create. You would not wonder at these reflections, if living as I do in the midst of a defeated & a triumphant party—in the midst of men who have expended health of body & peace of mind, a large portion of their lives, who have watched & worked, toiled & struggled, sacrificed friends & fortune, & domestic comfort, & gained what? Nothing, that I can perceive, but mortification & disappointment, the best part of their lives passed in pursuit of that which in possession was embittered & vexatious, & in the loss leaves nothing behind. Every one of the public men who will retire from office on the fourth of March will return to private life with blasted hopes, injured health, impaired or ruined fortunes, embittered tempers & probably a total inability to enjoy the remnant of their lives. Poor Judge Southard has been very ill, is still confined to his room & looks wretchedly. Mr. Rush totally secludes himself; nobody sees him. Mr. Clay still keeps in the mask of smiles. Genl. Porter less hackneyed & worn out worried or weakened looks & I suppose feels the best of all, but even he, hospitably as he lives & universally as he entertains, must injure his private property. Yet with these examples before their eyes, others eagerly seek for the same places, indulging the same high hopes, which will be followed by like disappointments & vexations. Such are the irresistible allurements of ambition! But, oh what a gloom is cast over the triumph of Genl. Jackson, by the death of a wife fondly & excessively loved! of a wife who, it is said, could control the violence of his temper, sooth the exacerbations of feelings always keenly sensitive & excessively irritable, who heal'd by her kindness wounds inflicted by his violence, & by her universal charity & benevolence conciliated public opinion. It is said that she not only made him a happier, but a better man. I fear not only the domestic circle, but the public will suffer from this restraining & benign influence being withdrawn. Affliction generally softens, but sometimes it sours the human heart,—should it have the latter effect the public councils & affairs will have reason to deplore this awful & sudden event. She died the day before the one on which the festival of triumph was to take place at Nashville,—feasting was turned into mourning, the festival into a funeral, the cannon & drums that were to proclaim the victory of

* Theodore Frelinghuysen was elected. On his retirement from the Navy Department in 1829 Judge Southard became Attorney-General of New Jersey.

political party sounded only to proclaim the victory of death. To die was the common lot, but to die in such peculiar circumstance & at such a moment is an event rare as it is solemn & carries with it such a deep conviction of the impotency of honor & grandeur & power that the impression can not be easily effaced from a reflecting mind. On mine it has made a deep & I hope a salutary one. . . . Strange that a single woman possessed of goodness tho' destitute of talents, could thus influence the destiny of nations! A similar case will occur to your mind perhaps in recollecting the history of Greece. It was Themistocles (I believe) who said, My little son governs his mother, his mother governs me,—I govern Athens, Athens governs Greece, Greece governs the world. So, my boy governs the world! . . . One morning Mrs. McClain of Delaware, who you know is a great favorite of mine, Mrs. Clay, Mrs. Cutts & Mrs. Holly sat a long time with me. Mrs. McC. is so entertaining & agreeable that time literally flies when I am with her. She & Mrs. Porter are extremely alike in character,—gay, frank & intelligent. But Mrs. P. has a warmer heart & no one can know without loving her. I have seen a great deal of her lately & propose passing this evening with her. Every other Monday (which I call her great Monday) she sends out hundreds of invitations, has the band of musick & opens four rooms. The intervening (or as I call it, her little Monday), she sees any friends who choose to go, but without particular invitations. We have been invited to all, but have declined going on the Great Mondays. I promise myself much pleasure this evening.

Last week we were asked for the 2d time to Mrs. Dickens* & as she said it was a small social party I & Susan went, but half, if not all Congress & their wives were there & the people almost a solid mass,—it was with difficulty I secured a comfortable seat in a corner of the room for Susan & myself. For the beginning of the evening we knew not a creature in the room,—they being the strangers & visitors in the city. About 9 o'clock Mr. & Mrs. McClain entered; she spied me, & as glad of a comfortable seat as myself, a vacant chair next me. We laughed & talked so merrily as to attract Mrs. Porter, who with difficulty broke away from the crowd of gentlemen that surrounded her & came to us. She made Susan get up & give her her chair, much to poor Sue's regret who (a most terrible thing to her) had to stand. With the Secretary and Senator's ladies, our corner became the most attractive spot in the room, next to the Pianno, where the Miss Fultons (from New York) were playing & singing in high style —Italian in perfection, Madam Garcia over again. But charming as the musick was, it could not interrupt our conversation. Several gentlemen gathered round the great ladies & the rest of the evening I passed very pleasantly. I knew not who gave most delight Mrs. P. or Mrs. McC. I should call them both Rattles if they were not some thing so much better,—they are charming women. Mrs. P. had asked me to find her a poor girl, who would be willing to go to New York with her as a servant. Last week I was called to visit a family, in the extremity of want & sickness,—6 children, 4 of whom were girls. Their necessities were so far beyond my ability to relieve, that it occurred to me to recommend one of the girls to Mrs. P. & to make known to her the situation of the family. It was dark when I went & bitterly cold. Mrs. P. was going in the evening to Baron Krudener's* Ball, but the moment I described the condition of this family, she called her servant, had bread, candles, &c. put up, tied a handkerchief over her head, put on an old plaid cloak, jumped into our carriage & went with me to see them. The next day when I went to see them, I found on her return home she had sent them a blanket, meat, meal, & other articles. Who that looked at her that evening, gaily dressed, charmed & charming, flattered & caressed, would have imagined her as she had been an hour before, wrapped in an old cloak, seated by the bed-side of a dying woman in a cold, miserable room, surrounded by half naked & starved children? But could they have witnessed the contrast, how would delight & admiration have been converted into love & esteem, or rather the one added to the other. Can you wonder at my loving this woman? Truly, I would rather General Jackson should not come, than that such a woman should go away. There is no one in the city so popular. The New

* Wife of Asbury Dickens.

* Russian minister. 1827 to 1836.

York papers have celebrated her & say she throws Mrs. Clay completely in the shade.

To Mrs. Boyd

Febr. 16, 1829.

. . . I have been a great deal in Mr. Clay's & Southard's family, both ill,—so ill, I do not think either has long to live. Yet, they think not so, & attend to business, tho' they decline all company at home & never go out. I never liked Mr. Clay so well as I do this winter, the coldness & hauteur of his manner has vanished & a softness & tenderness & sadness characterize his manner (to me at least), for I know not how it is in general society—that is extremely attaching & affecting,—at the same time, perfect good humour; no bitterness mingles its gall in the cup of disappointment & I often hear him, when only two or three friends are present, speak of Genl. Jackson & the present state of affairs in a good humour'd sprightly way. He has a cause of domestic affliction in the conduct & situation of his son* a thousand times more affecting than disappointed ambition. We all went to the *last* drawing room,—we did it to show our respect. My heart was heavy, very heavy, that word *Last!* Immense crowds filled the room, crowds of the triumphant party. I could not bear it as well as Mrs. Clay. I staid close to her, knowing she was so sick she could scarcely stand & that both she & Mr. C. for three previous weeks had been made very wretched by their domestic grief,—indeed for two weeks Mr. C. had not been able to sleep without anodynes. I stood behind her & watched the company. She received all with smiling politeness & Mr. C. *looked* gay & was so courteous & gracious, & agreeable, that every one remarked it & remarked he was determined we should regret him. My heart filled to overflowing, as I watched this acting, & to conceal tears which I could not repress, took a seat in a corner by the fire, behind a solid mass of people. Mr. C. saw me, & coming up enquired if Mr. Smith had come. I answered in the negative. "But *you* are," said he taking my hand & looking sadly affectionate. "This is kind, very kind in you, Mrs. Smith." I returned the pressure of his hand, & without reflection said, "If you could see my heart, you would then think so." "Why what ails your heart?" said he, with a look of earnest interrogatory. "Can it be otherwise than sad," I answered, looking at Mrs. Clay, "when I think what a good friend I am about to lose?" For a moment he held my hand pressed in his without speaking, his eyes filled with tears & with an effort he said, "We must not think of this, or talk of such things *now*," & relinquishing my hand, drew out his handkerchief, turned away his head & wiped his eyes, then pushed into the crowd & talked & smiled, as if his heart was light & easy. Alas, I knew, what perhaps no other among these hundreds knew, that anguish, heart-rending anguish, was concealed beneath that smiling, cheerful countenance, & that the animation & spirits which charmed an admiring circle were wholly artificial. Judge Southard has all manner of disappointments to sustain, as well as repeated severe attacks of disease & pain. He had until within a week of the election, every reason to believe he would be chosen Senator, but his friends betrayed him, & one friend, old, tried & who was under great obligations. Oh, ingratitude is sharper than a serpent's teeth. He had just recovered a little strength, when owing to Mr. Rush's extreme illness, he was appointed Secr. of the Treasury pro tem.; scarcely able to discharge his own business the addition was too much for him, & a few nights ago, sitting late & hard at work he was seized with what his Physician called spasms in his stomach,—for six hours he suffered agony, which even opium could not allay, until taken in great quantities. Yesterday, when I saw him, he was sitting up surrounded with papers, his eyes sunk to the very back of his head, the sockets black & hollow, while the eye burnt with unnatural brightness. "Oh do not kill yourself," said I, as I held his burning hand, "put away those papers. You are too ill to attend to business." "I must," replied he, "if I die at my post," & there I verily believe he will die,—he looks awfully. He had his heart set on the exploring voyage & had the preparations for it in such forwardness, that he thought it impossible Congress would prevent it, by refusing the necessary appropriation. But it is said, they will. Hard things are said of him on the floor, motives attributed, which I do not believe ever actuated him. Oh how I pity these public men,

* His eldest son was insane and confined in an asylum.

& as I look at Mr. Clay particularly, how often have I repeated the apostrophe of Cardinal Wolsey, "Oh had I served my God, half so devotedly as I have served my King, I should not now in my old age, thus have been left," etc. Mr. Rush & afterwards Mrs. Rush have been very ill, & are exceedingly depressed,—they have not gone out, or received company this winter. Mr. Wirt, too, has been ill, but is now better. . . . Phillip Barbour was here the day after the General's arrival & warm Jacksonian as he is, I told him his success would cost me too much grief to allow me to participate in the gratulations of the political party to which my husband belonged. "I shall cry more than I shall laugh on the 4th of March," said I. Mrs. Porter is the only one of the administration party, who has been in spirits this winter. It is partly constitutional with her &, I suspect, part policy. It is impossible when one sees her so attentive & even cordial with the Jackson party not to suspect she has some hopes of propitiating them. Yet it may be genuine good humour & good spirits. She is a charming woman, & what is still better, she is a good woman. I have seen a great deal of her, indeed, we are on the terms of old friends & relatives. We have been asked at least once every week to a party there, last week to two,—one a gay company, the other serious, religious folks to meet her Brother Mr. Breckenridge. Oh, what a zealous, saint-like man he is! *he* is indeed a burning & shining light, but he is burning fast away, flesh & blood can not sustain such exhausting & consuming labours. How I wish I could sit under his ministry. How cold & lifeless our Pastor seems, compared to him. Speaking of Mr. Campbell, among other things, all however kind & Christian, he made use of those expressive words, "I wish he was more steeped in the spirit." I had some delightful communion with this apostolic man. Surely he is in all things like the beloved desciple, so full of love. Such a christian would I desire to be, and until I am, until this divine love takes full possession of my soul, I shall never be as happy as I feel I have the capacity of being. It is good to see the world, as I see it. Oh Maria, its splendid out side, its gaiety & glitter, amuse but do not deceive me. How can they, with such striking proofs before me, of the bitterness & heartlessness within. And yet I am amused, and very much interested in the characters & scenes around me, but it is the interest & amusement one finds at the theatre. I look upon life as a stage, & on men & women as mere actors. One drama is just finished, the curtain has dropped, the actors have left the stage & I have followed them behind the scenes, where their masks & dresses are thrown off & I see them as they are, disappointed, exhausted, worn out, retiring with broken fortunes & broken constitutions & hearts rankling with barbed arrows.

Another drama is preparing, new characters, in all the freshness & vigour of unexhausted strength, with the exhileration of hopes undaunted by fear, of spirits intoxicated with success, with the aspirations of towering ambition are coming on the self-same stage. Will public favour cheer their closing, as it inspires the opening scene? Time must show, but most probably, they in their turn will drink the cup of honor to the bottom & find its dregs nauseous & bitter. I hoped this cold morning to have been alone, but one set of ladies have just gone & here stops another carriage. I wish I could be alone one morning. . . .

To Mrs. Boyd, Pine Street, New York

[Spring of 1829.]

. . . Mr. Clay, has this winter, been such an object of interest to me, for to me *intellectual power*, is more fascinating & interesting, than any other human endowment. And never in any individual have I met with so much, as in him. Yes, he has a *natural*, power & force of mind, beyond any I have ever witnessed. In Mr. Jefferson, Madison, Crawford, & other great men I have known, much of their intellectual strength, was derived from education & favoring circumstances, a combination of which carried them forward in the career of greatness & raised them to the elevation they attained. Not so Mr. Clay. Whatever he is, is all his own, inherent power, bestowed by nature & not derivative from cultivation or fortune. He has an elasticity & buoyancy of spirit, that no pressure of external circumstances, can confine or keep down. Nay, occasional depressions seem to give new vigour to this elastic power. For instance his late defeat. So far from disheartening, it has been positively exhilerating in its effects. He began to weary of the measures pursued in the last campaign, it closed, to be sure, in his defeat, but its termination freed him from weights & shackles, which had connections or duties, & like the Lyon, breaking the net, in which he had been entangled, he shakes from him all petty encumbrances & rises in all the majesty of intellectual power & invigorated resolution. He is a very great man. I have seen him, this winter, *as a man*, not a politician or stateman, but studied him, undisguised from any of the trappings of official form & conventional respect. Certainly, one of the most interesting days I have ever passed, was last Sunday. He & Mrs. Clay passed it with us. We had no other company to dinner, & I am certain he enjoyed being thus alone with a family he had known for 18 years, & feeling the triumph of personal regard, over the respect paid to office. He knew that for the last 8 years Mr. Smith had been his political opponent, & felt pleased with finding himself treated with the cordiality of friendship, in such circumstances. Whether it was this, or any other cause, I know not, but whatever the cause might be, the effect was to produce an openness, communicativeness, an affectionateness & warmth & kindness which were irresistibly captivating. We lingered long round the dinner table. He & Mr. S. conversed on past times & characters, long since passed from the scene of action. In the afternoon & evening, Genl. McComb, Mr. Ward, Mr. Lyon (another domesticated beau) & several other gentlemen came in & until past 10 oclock at night the conversation flowed in an unbroken stream & if committed to writing would prove interesting to those yet unborn, for, the topics were national, subjects suited for history. Mr. Clay was the chief speaker. He was animated by his heart as well as genius. Reclining on the sopha, from which he occasionally in the warmth of argument, would rise or stretch out his arm, his attitude as well as countenance would have made a fine picture. But enough of one individual. I will only add, if his health is restored, we will see him more efficiently active than ever. Elizabeth says you wish for a description of the Inauguration, & for some account of the new Cabinet,* of the President & his

Harriet Martineau.

* Martin Van Buren, Secretary of State; Samuel D. Ingham, of Pennsylvania, Secretary of the Treasury; John H. Eaton, of Tennessee, Secretary of War; John Branch, of North Carolina, Secretary of the Navy; John H. Berrien, of Georgia, Attorney-General.

family. On these topics I have but little to say. Bayard will transmit to Sister Jane & she to you, my last long letter to him, containing a full account of that *grand spectacle*, for such it was, without the aid of splendid forms or costumes. Of the Cabinet, I can only say the President's enemies are delighted & his friends grieved. It is supposed wholly inefficient, & even Van Buren, altho' a profound politician is not supposed to be an able statesman, or to possess qualifications for the place assigned him. Yet on him, all rests. Mr. Ingham, is the only member with whom we are personally acquainted,—him we have known long & well. He is a good man, of unimpeachable & unbending integrity. But no one imagines him possessed of that comprehensiveness & grasp of mind, requisite for the duties of his new office. He will be faithful, this, no one doubts. Whether he will be capable, experience only can show. Of the others, we know absolutely nothing, the people know nothing, & of course can feel little confidence. As for the *new Lady*,* Elizabeth enquires of. After a thousand rumours & much tittle-tattle & gosip & prophesyings & apprehensions, public opinion ever just & impartial, seems to have triumphed over personal feelings & intrigues & finally doomed her to continue in her pristine lowly condition. A stand, a *noble* stand, I may say, since it is a stand taken against power & favoritism, has been made by the ladies of Washington, & not even the President's wishes, in favour of his dearest, personal friend, can influence them to violate the respect due to virtue, by visiting one, who has left her strait & narrow path. With the exception of two or three timid & rather

Henry Clay, Secretary of State, 1825–1829.
From the portrait by Edward Dalton Marchant, in the State Department, Washington.

* The famous Peggy O'Neil, daughter of a tavern-keeper in Washington, widow of a paymaster in the navy, and now bride of the Secretary of War, a fine appearing woman, whose reputation had been unfortunately for her made in Washington. Van Buren was the only man who stood by her. She was finally driven out and her husband left the Cabinet.

insignificant personages, who trembled for their husband's offices, not a lady has visited her, & so far from being inducted into the President's house, she is, I am told scarcely noticed by the females of his family. On the Inauguration day, when they went in company with the Vice-President's lady, the lady of the Secretary of the Treasury & those of two distinguished Jacksonian Senators, Hayne & Livingston,* this New Lady never approached the party, either in the Senate chamber, at the President's house, where by the President's express request, they went to receive the company, nor at night at the Inaugural Ball. On these three public occasions she was left alone, & kept at a respectful distance from these virtuous & distinguished women, with the sole exception of a seat at the supper-table, where, however, notwithstanding her proximity, she was not spoken to by them. These are facts you may rely on, not rumours—facts, greatly to the honor of our sex. When you see Miss Morris, she will give you details, which it would not be proper to commit to writing. She & I have become very social & intimate & have seen each other often. I hope she will call on you & talk over Washington affairs. Dear Mrs. Porter, her departure cost me some bitter tears. And so did good Mrs. Clay's. Mrs. Ingham professes a desire to be very social with me, "the oldest friend," as she says her husband has in the city, but a friend of 18 years is a thing I shall never *make* now, it is too late in the day. We visited the President & his family a few days since, in the big house. Mr. Smith introduced us & asked for the General. Our names were sent in & he joined the ladies in the drawing-room.

John Quincy Adams, Secretary of State, 1817–1825.
From the portrait by Jean Baptiste Adolphe Gibert, in the State Department, Washington.

* Robert Y. Hayne, of South Carolina, anything but a Jacksonian when the nullification issue came up, and Edward Livingston, then a Representative from Louisiana, soon to be a Senator, then Secretary of State, and finally minister to France.

I shall like him if ever I know him, I am sure,—so simple, frank, friendly. He looks bowed with grief as well as age & that idea excited my sympathy, his pew in church is behind ours, his manner is humble & reverent & most attentive.

Mrs. Sandford * & I interchanged several visits & she passed an evening with us, but she did not interest me. For your sake, dear Maria, I will visit Mrs. Hamilton, tho' I have resisted many inducements to make ill & I have been a great deal with her. Dear Mrs. Bradley has gone, & she went rejoicing to a better world. Capt. Tingey too. Our first kind friend & acquaintance. Mrs. Clay is as much lost to me as if separated by death, and Mrs. Porter. For ten days I was taken up with sick & dying, & departing friends. The last two weeks have been melancholy weeks to me. Judge Southard continues too ill to move, his little daughter is ill too, their furniture is all sold, & it is

Dr. William Thornton.

After a water-color by himself in the possession of J. Henley Smith, Washington.

Mrs. William Thornton.

After a water-color by Dr. Thornton in the possession of J. Henley Smith, Washington.

new acquaintances. I have too many already. But I shall drop most of them when I return into the country, then I shall regain my freedom, & do as I like. The last six weeks have been far less gay, but much more interesting than the first part of the season. We went less out & had less company at home. Mr. W.'s daily visits, Mr. Wood's & Mr. Lyon's, almost as frequent, & the new books they brought us, fitted up our evenings far more pleasantly than commonplace visitants. Mr. Wood, who is goodness personified, remains, he is our fellow citizen, & we look for his smiling benevolent countenance, daily as the evening returns. Mrs. Thornton has been very melancholy to visit them, but it is a duty I often perform. Mr. Wirt's family go in a few weeks. Mr. Rush, it is said, is to be sent to England by the Canal-company, with a good salary, & the family are in good spirits. Mrs. Calhoun goes home, not to return again, at least for 4 years. Mrs. Ingham will not be back until autumn. All our citizens are trembling for fear of losing offices. Mrs. Seaton is very ill. Gales & Seaton, I fear ruined. In fact, never did I witness such a gloomy time in Washington. I hope things will brighten. My paper is full.

To Mrs. Kirkpatrick

March 11, Sunday [1829].

. . . Thursday morning. I left the rest of this sheet for an account of the inau-

* Wife of Nathan Sanford, of Albany, Senator from New York.

guration. It was not a thing of detail, of a succession of small incidents. No, it was one grand whole, an imposing and majestic spectacle & to a reflective mind one of moral sublimity. Thousands & thousands of people, without distinction of rank, collected in an immense mass round the Capitol, silent, orderly & tranquil, with their eyes fixed on the front of that edifice, waiting the appearance of the President in the portico. The door from the Rotunda opens, preceded by the marshals, surrounded by the Judges of the Supreme Court, the old man with his grey locks, that crown of glory, advances, bows to the people, who greet him with a shout that rends the air, the Cannons, from the heights around, from Alexandria & Fort Warburton, proclaim the oath he has taken & all the hills reverberate the sound. It was grand—it was sublime! An almost breathless silence, succeeded & the multitude was still—listening to catch the sound of his voice, tho' it was so low, as to be heard only by those nearest to him. After reading his speech, the oath was administered to him by the Chief Justice. The Marshal presented the Bible. The President took it from his hands, pressed his lips to it, laid it reverently down, then bowed again to the people—Yes, to the people in all their majesty. And had the spectacle closed here, even Europeans must have acknowledged, that a free people, collected in their might, silent & tranquil, restrained solely by a moral power, without a shadow around of military force, was majesty, rising to sublimity, & far surpassing the majesty of Kings & Princes, surrounded with armies & glittering in gold. But I will not anticipate, but will give you an account of the inauguration in more detail. The whole of the preceding day, immense crowds were coming into the city from all parts, lodgings could not be obtained, & the newcomers had to go to George Town, which soon overflowed & others had to go to Alexandria. I was told the Avenue & adjoining streets were so crowded on Tuesday afternoon that it was difficult to pass.

A national salute was fired early in the morning, & ushered in the 4th of March. By ten oclock the Avenue was crowded with carriages of every description, from the splendid Barronet & coach, down to waggons & carts, filled with women & children, some in finery & some in rags, for it was the peoples President, & all would see him; the men all walked. Julia, Anna Maria & I, (the other girls would not adventure) accompanied by Mr. Wood, set off before 11, & followed the living stream that was pouring along to the Capitol. The terraces, the Balconies, the Porticos, seemed as we approached already filled. We rode round the whole square, taking a view of the animated scene. Then leaving the carriage outside of the palisades, we entered the enclosed grounds, where we were soon joined by John Cranet & another gentleman, which offered each of us a protector. We walked round the terrace several times, every turn meeting new groups of ladies & gentlemen whom we knew. All with smiling faces. The day was warm & delightful, from the South Terrace we had a view of Pennsylvania & Louisiana Avenues, crowded with people hurrying towards the Capitol. It was a most exhilirating scene! Most of the ladies preferred being inside of the Capitol & the eastern portico, damp & cold as it was, had been filled from 9 in the morning by ladies who wished to be near the General when he spoke. Every room was filled & the windows crowded. But as so confined a situation allowed no general view, we would not coop ourselves up, & certainly enjoyed a much finer view of the spectacle, both in its whole & in its details, than those within the walls. We stood on the South steps of the terrace; when the appointed hour came saw the General & his company advancing up the avenue, slow, very slow, so impeded was his march by the crowds thronging around him. Even from a distance, he could be discerned from those who accompanied him, for he only was uncovered, (the Servant in presence of his Sovereign, the People). The south side of the Capitol hill was literally alive with the multitude, who stood ready to receive the hero & the multitude who attended him. "There, there, that is he," exclaimed different voices. "Which?" asked others. "He with the white head," was the reply. "Ah," exclaimed others, "there is the old man & his gray hair, there is the old veteran, there is Jackson." At last he enters the gate at the foot of the hill & turns to the road that leads round to the front of the Capitol. In a moment every one who until then had stood like statues gazing on the scene below them, rushed onward, to right, to left, to be ready to receive

Dear Mrs Smith.

Miss Jeffery & I are sorry that we have not been able to come near your end of the city this long while. Between the attractions of the Capitol & a succession of friendly visitors at home, we are so engaged that we think ourselves in a fair way of forgetting how to put one foot before the other. But you will see us again before we leave the city.

I thank you for the kind

Fac-simile of letter from Miss

him in the front. Our party, of course, were more deliberate, we waited until the multitude had rushed past us & then left the terrace & walked round to the furthest side of the square, where there were no carriages to impede us, & entered it by the gate fronting the Capitol. Here was a clear space, & stationing ourselves on the central gravel walk we stood, so as to have a clear, full view of the whole scene. The Capitol in all its grandeur & beauty. The Portico & grand steps leading to it, were filled with ladies. Scarlet, purple, blue, yellow, white draperies & waving plumes of every kind & colour, among the white marble pillars, had a fine effect. In the centre of the portico was a table covered with scarlet, behind it the closed door leading into the rotunda, below the Capitol & all around, a mass of living beings, not a ragged mob, but well dressed & well behaved respectable & worthy citizens. Mr. Frank Key, whose arm I had, & an old & frequent witness of great spectacles, often exclaimed, as well as myself, a mere novice, "It is beautiful, it is sublime!" The sun had been obscured through the morning by a mist, or haziness. But the concussion in the air, produced by the dis-

method by which you have testified your regard for me. You must feel as strongly as myself how impossible it is for me to appropriate what you say; but the kindness of your feelings is an independent affair; & I thank you for it.

Miss Jeffrey joins me in kind regards to you all. Believe us, dear Madam,

truly yours obliged

Harriet Martineau.

Martineau to Mrs. Smith.

charge of the cannon, dispersed it & the sun shone forth in all his brightness. At the moment the General entered the Portico & advanced to the table, the shout that rent the air, still resounds in my ears. When the speech was over, & the President made his parting bow, the barrier that had separated the people from him was broken down, & they rushed up the steps all eager to shake hands with him. It was with difficulty he made his way through the Capitol & down the hill to the gateway that opens on the avenue. Here for a moment he was stopped. The living mass was impenetrable. After a while a passage was opened & he mounted his horse which had been provided for his return (for he had walked to the Capitol) then such a cortege as followed him! Country men, farmers, gentlemen, mounted & dismounted, boys, women & children, black & white. Carriages, wagons & carts, all pursuing him to the President's house,—this I only heard of for our party went out at the opposite side of the square & went to Col. Benton's lodgings, to visit Mrs. Benton & Mrs. Gilmore. Here was a perfect levee, at least a hundred ladies & gentlemen, all happy & rejoicing,—wine & cake was handed in profusion. We sat with this company & stopped on the summit of the hill until the avenue was comparatively clear, tho' at any other time we should have thought it terribly crowded. Streams of people on foot & of carriages of all kinds, still pouring towards the President's house. We went Home, found your papa & sisters at the Bank,* standing at the upper windows, where they had been seen by the President, who took off his hat to them, which they insisted was better than all we had seen. From the Bank to the President's house for a long while, the crowd rendered a passage for us impossible. Some went into the Cashier's parlour, where we found a number of ladies & gentlemen & had cake & wine in abundance. In about an hour, the pavement was clear enough for us to walk. Your father, Mr. Wood, Mr. Ward, Mr. Lyon, with us, we set off to the President's House, but on a nearer approach found an entrance impossible, the yard & avenue was compact with living matter. The day was delightful, the scene animating, so we walked backward & forward at every turn meeting some new acquaintance & stopping to talk & shake hands. Among others we met Zavr Dickinson with Mr. Frelinghuysen & Dr. Elmendorf, & Mr. Saml. Bradford. We continued promenading here, until near three, returned home unable to stand & threw ourselves on the sopha. Some one came & informed us the crowd before the President's house, was so far lessen'd, that they thought we might enter. This time we effected our purpose. But what a scene did we witness! The *Majesty of the People* had disappeared, & a rabble, a mob, of boys, negros, women, children, scrambling, fighting, romping. What a pity, what a pity! No arrangements had been made, no police officers placed on duty & the whole house had been inundated by the rabble mob. We came too late. The President, after having been *literally* nearly pressed to death & almost suffocated & torn to pieces by the people in their eagerness to shake hands with Old Hickory, had retreated through the back way or south front & had escaped to his lodgings at Gadsby's. Cut glass & china to the amount of several thousand dollars had been broken in the struggle to get the refreshments, punch & other articles had been carried out in tubs & buckets, but had it been in hogsheads it would have been insufficient, ice-creams, & cake & lemonade, for 20,000 people, for it is said that number were there, tho' I think the estimate exaggerated. Ladies fainted, men were seen with bloody noses & such a scene of confusion took place as is impossible to describe, —those who got in could not get out by the door again, but had to scramble out of windows. At one time, the President who had retreated & retreated until he was pressed against the wall, could only be secured by a number of gentlemen forming round him & making a kind of barrier of their own bodies, & the pressure was so great that Col. Bomford who was one at one time, said he was afraid they should have been pushed down, or on the President. It was then the windows were thrown open, & the torrent found an outlet, which otherwise might have proved fatal.

This concourse had not been anticipated & therefore not provided against. Ladies & gentlemen, only had been expected at this Levee, not the people en masse. But it was the People's day, & the People's President & the People would rule. God grant that one day or other, the People, do not put down all rule & rulers. I fear, enlightened Freemen as they are, they will be found, as they have been found in all ages & countries where they get the Power in their hands, that of all tyrants, they are the most ferocious, cruel & despotic. The noisy & disorderly rabble in the President's House brought to my mind descriptions I had read, of the mobs in the Tuilleries & at Versailles. I expect to hear the carpets & furniture are ruined; the streets were muddy, & these guests all went thither on foot.

The rest of the day, overcome with fatigue I lay upon the sopha. The girls went to see Mrs. Clay & Mrs. Southard. Mrs. Rush was at Mrs. C.'s—Mrs. Clay's furniture all sold, the entry full of hay, straw, & packages, & in her little back room, scarcely a chair to sit on & she worn out with fatigue. "This being turned out, is a sad, troublesome thing, is it not?" said Mrs. Rush. "Coming in, is troublesome enough, but *then*, one does not mind the trouble."

After tea, Mr. Ward, Mr. Wood, Mr. Lyon, & Warren Scott, came in & staid until past 11 oclock. Mr. S. & I talked of Brunswick friends & of old times. Col.

* Branch Bank of the United States, corner of Fifteenth Street and Pennsylvania Avenue, of which Mr. Smith was President.

Bomford has been here, just now & given me an account of the Ball, which he says was elegant, splendid & in perfect order. The President & his family were not there. The Vice President & lady & the members of the new cabinet were. Mrs. Bomford was in her grand costume,—scarlet velvet richly trimmed with gold embroidery, the large Ruby, set in diamonds, for which Col. Bomford has refused five thousand dollars, & which I believe you have seen, she wore in her turban. Mr. Baldwin,* notwithstanding his disappointment, for he confidently expected a place in the Cabinet, was, Col. B. says, excessively merry. During all this bustle in the city, Mr. Adams was quietly fixed at Meridian Hill, to which place he & his family had removed some days before. . . .

Everybody is in a state of agitation,—gloomy or glad. A *universal removal* in the departments is apprehended, & many are quaking & trembling, where *all* depend on their places.

The city, so crowded & bustling, by tomorrow will be silent & deserted, for people are crowding away as eagerly as they crowded here. Mrs. Porter goes on Saturday, Mrs. Clay on Monday, Mrs. Wirt & Southard in the course of the week. We are asked to a party at Mrs. Wirt's tonight, but shall not go.

To Mrs. Kirkpatrick

August 29, 1831, SIDNEY.

. . . What does Lyttleton *now* think of Genl. Jackson? The papers do not exaggerate, nay do not detail one half of his imbecilities. He is completely under the government of Mrs. Eaton, one of the most ambitious, violent, malignant, yet silly women you ever heard of. You will soon see the recall of the dutch minister announced. Madm Huygen's spirited conduct in refusing to visit Mrs. E. is undoubtedly the cause. The new Cabinet if they do not yield to the President's will on the point, will, it is supposed, soon be dismissed. Several of them in order to avoid this dilemma, are determined not to keep house or bring on their families. Therefore, not keeping house, they will not give parties & may thus avoid the disgrace of entertaining the favorite. It was hoped, on her husband's going out of office, she would have left the city, *but she will not.* She hopes for a complete triumph & is not satisfied with having the Cabinet broken up & a virtuous & intelligent minister recalled, & many of our best citizens frowned upon by the President. Our society is in a sad state. Intrigues & parasites in favour, divisions & animosity existing. As for ourselves, we keep our of the turmoil, seldom speak & never take any part in this troublesome & shameful state of things. Yet no one can deny, that the P.'s weakness originates in an amiable cause, — his devoted & ardent friendship for Genl. Eaton. . . .

* Henry Baldwin, of Pennsylvania. He was appointed a judge of the Supreme Court in 1830.

To Mrs. Kirkpatrick

Christmas, 1832.

. . . The ambition some felt for its honors exists no longer, & this was one of the strongest stimulants to activity & exertion I ever felt. But a life in Washington cures one of ambition for honors & distinctions, by exhibiting them in all their vanity, instability, & transitoriness, & unveiling at the same time all the pains & some vexations appertaining to them. I wonder if Mr. Clay realizes these things & can learn to be content with the portion he possesses. Were we to have a peep into his bosom what a lesson we should learn. And Mr. Calhoun,* will his high soarings end in disappointment & humiliation or be drowned in blood? However he may now err, he is one of the noblest & most generous spirits I have ever met with. I am certain *he* is deceived himself, & believes he is now fulfilling the duty of a *true patriot.* What a happy nation we were! Alas, & may we not write, *we are?* The impending political storm, as you may easily suppose is almost the exclusive object of interest & conversation. . . .

To Mrs. Kirkpatrick

Wednesday, 12th, 1835, January.

. . . They all paid long visits, & this morning, just this minute, Miss Martineau.† At so early an hour I expected no one & was so engaged in this letter, that I scarcely

* He was in the middle of his efforts to apply the nullification theory.

† Harriet Martineau came over in the summer of 1834, when she was thirty-two years of age and in the zenith of her fame.

raised my head, when the door opened & two plain looking ladies (one of the ladies, was Miss Jeffries, her friend & companion) walked in. They had walked & I had not attended to the ringing of the door bell, not expecting visitors at this hour. "I have come early," said she, "to make sure of finding you at home, & because it is my only disengaged time. I yesterday planned a quiet sitting of two hours with you, but I found it impossible." She is a woman you would love, so plain, unaffected & quiet in her manners & appearance, yet animated in conversation. She brought me a letter of introduction from Mrs. Eckart, & sent it with her card, the day after her arrival, otherwise I do not know whether I should have called on her, under our present plan of domesticity, & the feelings thereby induced, for when one lives out of company one shrinks from it. Accompanied by the girls I called on her, sent in my name. There were three or four other ladies in the room, but her advancing to receive us, was a sufficient indication that she was Miss Martineau. She was sitting in a corner of the sopha, which supported the arm & hand, which held the speaking-tube to her ear, she handed it to me saying, "Do you know the use of this?" I answered affirmatively by an inclination of my head & putting the tube to my lips, soon forgot I held it, & conversed as easily as if not through this, it must be confessed, awkward medium. As I had always understood she was of the Liberal if not radical party, the advocate of the poor & of the working-class, I did not anticipate the reception she has met with from our dignitaries & fashionables. But the English minister was the first to wait on her, introduced her into the Senate, to the President, &c., &c., which at once made her *Ton*. She has literally been overwhelmed with company. I have been told that the day after her arrival near 600 persons called, (an exaggeration I suppose) but the number was immense. Poor I had been planning to show her the same kind of friendly, plain attentions I had done Mrs. Brenton & Miss Sedgwick, & offered to call with the carriage & accompany her to Congress, to make her calls of ceremony, &c., &c. When I found these calls had been dispensed with, & the President's family & Secretaries ladies had first called on her, I told her I did not give nor go to large parties, but should be glad to see her in a social & domestic manner. This I repeated this morning & told her when the hurry of her gay engagements was over, I would ask a quiet day. "Name what day you please after this week, & it shall be reserved for you," replied she. Yesterday she dined at the President's, & in the evening went to a large party. Today she dines at Sir Charles Vaughan's * & in the evening a party at Mrs. Butler's† (the attorney general) two large evening parties to which she had promised to go, violent headaches, induced by the crowds of company during the whole day, obliged her to send an appology. Her health is very delicate. During the last year she has been laboriously employed, to such a degree as to impair her health. Absolute relaxation & change of scene were prescribed, & she thought she could obtain both these remedies by making the tour of U.S. But if followed by such crowds, her aim will be defeated. From her manners & appearance no one would believe it possible she could be so distinguished, celebrated, followed. The drollest part of the whole is, that these crowds, at least in Washington, go to see the lion & nothing else. I have not met with an individual, except Mrs. Seaton & her mother, who have read any of her works, or knew for what she is celebrated. Our most fashionable, exclusive Mrs. Tayloe, said she intended to call, & asked what were the novels she had written & if they were pretty? The gentlemen laugh at a woman's writing on political economy. Not one of them has the least idea of the nature of her works. I tried to explain them to Mr. Frelinghuysen, Clay, Southard & others. But enough of Miss Martineau for the present. If she interests you, tell me so & I will give you what further details. But perhaps like your Bayard you may think it all ridiculous. . . .

To Mrs. Kirkpatrick

Febr. 4th, 1835.

. . . Friday 5th. And now for Miss Martineau, since you desire to hear a little more about her, particularly of the day she passed here. But I really must give you a previous scene which amused me extremely & will not be without some diversion for

* The British minister.

† Benjamin F. Butler, of New York.

you. The day previous to our little dinner party, I sent for Henry Orr, whom I had always employed when I had company & who is the most experienced & fashionable waiter in the city. He is almost white, his manners gentle, serious & respectful, to an uncommon degree & his whole appearance quite gentlemanly. "Henry," said I, when he came, "I am going to have a small dinner party, but though small, I wish it to be peculiarly nice, everything of the best & most fashionable. I wish you to attend, & as it is many years since I have dined in company, you must tell me what dishes will be best. Boulli, I suppose, is not out of fashion?" "No, indeed, Ma'am! A Boulli at the foot of the table is indispensable, no dinner without it." "And at the head?" "After the soup, Ma'am, fish, boil'd fish, & after the Fish, canvas-backs, the Boulli to be removed, & Pheasants." "Stop, stop Henry," cried I, "not so many removes if you please!" "Why, ma'am, you said your company was to be a dozen, & I am only telling you what is absolutely necessary. Yesterday at Mr. Woodbury's there was only 18 in company & there were 30 dishes of meat." "But Henry I am not a Secretary's lady. I want a small, genteel dinner." "Indeed, ma'am, that is all I am telling you, for side dishes you will have a very small ham, a small Turkey, on each side of them partridges, mutton chops, or sweetbreads, a macaroni pie, an oyster pie——" —"That will do, that will do, Henry. Now for vegetables." "Well, ma'am, stew'd celery, spinage, salsify, cauliflower." "Indeed, Henry, you must substitute potatoes, beets, &c." "Why, ma'am, they will not be genteel, but to be sure if you say so, it must be so. Mrs. Forsyth the other day, *would* have a plum-pudding, she will keep to old fashions." "What, Henry, plum-pudding out of fashion?" "La, yes, Ma'am, all kinds of puddings & pies." "Why, what then must I have at the head & foot of the table?" "Forms of ice-cream at the head, & a pyramid of anything, grapes, oranges, or anything handsome at the foot." "And the other dishes?" "Jellies, custards, blanc-mange, cakes, sweetmeats, & sugar-plums." "No nuts, raisons, figs, &c., &c.?" "Oh no, no, ma'am, they are quite vulgar." "Well, well, Henry. My dessert is, I find, all right, & your dinner I suppose with the exception of one or two things. You may order me the pies, partridges & pheasants from the French cook, & Priscilla can do the rest." "Indeed, ma'am, you had best" ——"No more, Henry," interrupted I, "I am not Mrs. Woodbury." "Why to be sure, ma'am, her's was a particular dinner on account of that great English lady's dining with her." "Did Miss M. dine there?" "La, yes, ma'am, & I was quite delighted to see the attention Mr. Clay paid her, for indeed ma'am I consider Mr. Clay the greatest & best man now living, & sure I should know, for I served him long enough. Oh he is kindness through & through & it was but proper, ma'am, that the greatest man, should show attention to the greatest lady. He sat by her at dinner & talked all the time just to her, neither of them eat much. I took particular notice what she eat, so I might know another time what to hand her, for she dines everywhere, ma'am, & I see her taste was very simple. She eat nothing but a little Turkey & a mite of ham, nothing else, ma'am, & Mr. Clay hardly as much, they were so engaged in conversation. I listened whenever I was near & heard them talking about the national debt. Mr. Clay told her our debt was paid off & she told him she hoped their debt would soon be paid off too, & they consulted a great deal about it." "Why is Miss M. such a great woman, Henry?" "Why, they tells me, ma'am, she is the greatest writer in England & her book doing monstrous deal of good." "Well, Henry, it is for this Lady, my dinner is to be, but it is a family dinner, not a ceremonious one. She is to spend the day just in a social friendly way with me." "Why, ma'am, that is just as it should be, as you are a writer too. But indeed, ma'am, if not another besides her was invited, you ought to have a grand dinner. I should like you, ma'am, to do your best. It is a great respect ma'am she shows you & a great kindness you show her, & I dare say, ma'am she'll put you in one of her books, so you should do your very best." But I carried my point in only having 8 dishes of meat, tho' I could not convince Henry, it was more genteel than a grander dinner. He came the next day, & leaving him & the girls as his assistants (for Anna absolutely locked me out of the dining room) I sat as quietly in the front parlour, as if no company was expected. Mrs. Randolph, Mrs. Coolidge (Ellen Randolph that was) James Bayard

& B. K.* were the only additional guests to Miss M. & Miss Jeffrey her companion. About 3, B. K. came. I only was in the parlour, the girls were dressing, presently Ann came down, & told me Miss M. & Miss J. were up stairs in my room. "And you left them there alone?" exclaimed I. "To be sure," answered Ann, with her usual nonchalance. "I have never been introduced to them & they asked me to show them to a chamber." "And you let them go in alone!!" "To be sure." I hastened up stairs & found them combing their hair. They had taken off their bonnets & large capes. "You see," said Miss M. "we have complied with your request & come sociably to pass the day with you. We have been walking all the morning, our lodgings were too distant to return, so we have done as those who have no carriages do in England, when they go to pass a social day." I offered her combs, brushes, etc. But showing me the enormous pockets in her french dress, said they were provided with all that was necessary, & pulled out nice little silk shoes, silk stockings, a scarf for her neck, little lace mits, a gold chain & some other jewellry, & soon without changing her dress was prettily equipped for dinner or evening company. We were all as perfectly at our ease as if old friends. Miss M.'s toilette was soonest completed & sitting down by me on the sopha, & handing me the tube, we had a nice social chat before we went down stairs. I introduced Mr. Smith, my nephews, & son &c. Mr. S. took a seat on the sopha by her, & I on a chair on her other side, to be near to introduce others. It was quite amusing to see Mr. S. He took the tube & at first applied its wrong cup to his lips, but in the warmth of conversation perpetually forgot it, & as he always gesticulates a great deal with his hands he was waving about the cup, quite forgetful of its use, except when I said, as I continually had to do, "Put it to your lips." But Miss M. has admirable tact & filled up the gaps of his part of the conversation, made by the waving of the tube, by her intuitive perception & talked as fluently of Lord Brougham, Lord Durham & other political personages, of whom Mr. S. enquired as if she had heard every word. A little after 4, Mrs. Randolph & Mrs. Coolidge came. I was glad Mrs. R. was so handsomely dressed (in general she disregards her toilette) & looked so dignified & well, for I wished Miss M. to see the daughter of Jefferson to advantage. Mrs. C. looked lovely & elegant. I gave Mrs. R. a seat next Miss M. But she said but little & afterwards told us, the very touch of the Tube, put all her ideas to flight. She went to the contrary extreme of Mr. S., & kept the cup pressed so tightly on her lips, that she could scarcely open them. Mrs. Coolidge managed better, & conversed with perfect ease & great fluency until dinner, which was not served until five oclock, when the curtains being drawn & shutters closed, the candles on the table were lit & made everything look better. Miss M. sat next me, Mrs. R. below her, Miss Jeffries led in by B. K. sat between him & Mr. S., & was, they say, extremely entertaining. J. Bayard sat all the time by Mrs. C., the old friend of his sisters & seemed delighted with her. Dinner went off *very well.* I conversed a great deal with Miss M., as Mrs. R. would not. Our conversation was very interesting & carried on in a tone that all the rest of the company could hear. One fact was new & strange. Speaking of the use of ardent spirits by the poor, she said its high price precluded its use, there were now few gin-shops. Opium had been substituted by the poor for gin, & apothecaries boys kept constantly busy, making up penny & ha-penny worths of opium. It was taken not in sufficient quantities to exhilerate, but only to stupefy & satisfy the cravings of hunger. What a wretched state of society does this imply! Her conversation is rich in most interesting illustrations of manners, facts & opinions & what she said at dinner, if written down would fill 4 or 5 such pages. While at table, a note from Mr. Clay was handed me, so handsomely written & so full of compliments for Miss M. & regrets from being prevented joining our party in the evening, that I handed it to her & she then burst forth in an eloquent eulogium of him. It was near 7 when we returned to the parlour, which was brilliantly lighted, (as I think light a great promoter of social pleasure). Mr. King was lounging in the rocking chair, quite at his ease. He knew Miss M. & instantly sat down on one side of her, I on the other. Mr. King* engaged her in details about the English affairs & great men.

* Bayard Kirkpatrick, her nephew.

* Probably John Pendleton King, Senator from Georgia.

She was copious & interesting in her details. I wish I could relate a hundredth part of what she said, but it is impossible. She pronounced Lord Durham (Mr. Lambton, that was) to be the greatest man now in England. "He will soon be our premier, he will be the savior of England!" said she with enthusiasm. He is her greatest & most intimate personal, as well as political friend. All the other distinguished men passed in review. It was a rich treat to hear her. Her words flow in a continual stream, her voice pleasing, her manners quiet & lady-like, her face full of intelligence, benevolence & animation. She always leans back in the corner of the sopha, seemingly unconscious of the presence of any one except the person she is talking with. Mr. & Mrs. Frelinghuysen & Mrs. Burgess (a most lovely young widow) Mrs. Thornton, Mrs. Bomford & her family, Mr. & Mrs. Calhoun & her 3 young ladies, the Southards, Mr. Palfrey, the unitarian clergyman (ours was asked but did not come) & about a dozen gentlemen, made up the evening party. Mr. Frelinghuysen & Mr. Calhoun both sat & conversed a great deal with Miss M., & most of the company by turns sat a while by her. Mr. Calhoun is one of her greatest admirers, his Mess gave her a dinner, Mrs. Bomford was unexpectedly pleased because unexpectedly she felt herself at ease with Miss M. She is so simple, plain, good natured & unaffected, that I wonder every one does not feel at ease. Ease & animation pervaded the whole of the company, we had some delightful singing from the young ladies, Scotch songs to perfection. It was 11 oclock before the party broke up. Every one gratified at an opportunity of meeting Miss M., in such a quiet, social manner. The next day, by appointment, I accompanied Miss M. & Miss J. to Kalorama. Anna Maria went with us. In a carriage

Andrew Jackson.
From the painting by Sully (1825), in the Corcoran Gallery, Washington.

she needs not her tube, but hears distinctly without it. In a carriage, too, sitting so close one feels so confidential. We rode about from 12 until past three & our conversation would fill several sheets. I enquired about her early life, her motives for embracing literature as a pursuit, the formation of her mind, habits & opinions, all of which she freely gave me the history, & an interesting history it is. "Do tell me," said I, "if praise & celebrity, like everything else do not lose their relish?" "I never," said she, "had much relish for general praise; the approbation of those I love & esteem or respect, I highly value. But newspaper praise or censure, are perfectly indifferent to me. The most valued advantage I have gained is the facility which it gives me to gain access to every person, place or thing I desire, this is truly a great advantage." Speaking of the lionizing of celebrated people, "Well," said she, laughing, "I have escaped that, to my knowledge, I have never been made a show of, or run after as a lion." Of course, I did not undeceive her. I asked her how I should understand an expression she several times used, "Since I have been employed by government." She said, two of the subjects she had illustrated in her stories, had been by the request of Lord Brougham & Lord Durham, who supplied her with the materials, or principles, viz, the Poor-Laws, on Taxation. She was employed by them to write on these two subjects, on which account she & her mother had removed to London, as the transmission of Pamphlets by the mail, became too burthensome, frequently requiring her to send a wheel-barrow to the Post Office. For the last two years she & her mother have resided in London, have a small house adjoining the Park, which is as quiet & pleasant as in the country. Here she had daily intercourse with the members of the Cabinet & leaders of the whig party, particularly the above-named gentlemen. She never makes visits & receives them only at 2 specified hours every day, but while Parliament is sitting, dines out (at night, remember) every day. Once, while at Lord Durham's in the country, at table, a gentleman sitting next her observed, "There is one subject, Miss M., I think your genius admirably calculated to illustrate." "What is that," said she, with eagerness, glad to be instructed. "The Poor Laws" replied he. "Why" exclaimed Lord D., "in what corner of England have you been living, that you do not know, this is the very subject on which she has most ably written." "I did, I candidly own," said Miss M., when she told me this, "I did feel completely mortified." My paper will hold no more. I will soon write again, but as I cannot write all this over & it may amuse Maria, I wish you would send it to her. Oh how tired my head & hands are! The girls are equally so of holding their tongues.

To Mrs. Boyd

Christmas day, 1835.

. . . Poor Mr. Clay, was laughing & talking & joking with some friends when his papers & letters were brought to him; he naturally first opened the letter from home. A friend who was with him, says he started up & then fell, as if shot, & his first words were "Every tie to life is broken!"* He continued that day in almost a state of distraction, but has, I am told, become more composed, though in the deepest affliction. Ann was his pride, as well as his joy & of all his children, his greatest comfort. She was my favorite, so frank, gay, & warm hearted. Her husband was very very rich. Their plantation joined Mr. Clay's & afforded a daily intercourse. Of five daughters, she was the last, & now she is gone, & poor Mrs. Clay, in her declining age is left alone & bereaved of the support & comfort which daughters & only daughters can afford. I now, cannot realize that you or I can ever be so bereaved, we are so far advanced towards our journey's end. . . .

* The story was that he fainted. Ann Brown Clay was his favorite child. Her husband was James Erwine, of New Orleans

A Visit to Washington on the Eve of the Civil War (1905)

A VISIT TO WASHINGTON ON THE EVE OF THE CIVIL WAR

By George P. Fisher

TO all watchful observers of the signs of the times, in the North or the South, the week in which Major Anderson transferred the garrison under his command in Charleston harbor from Fort Moultrie to Fort Sumter was a period of absorbing interest. A portion of that week was spent by me in Washington, naturally a focus of public anxiety and discussion. To several persons in official stations I was indebted for courteous attention and kind services. Two of them whom I met at once were acquaintances of long standing. One of them was Hon. James Humphrey, a representative in Congress from Brooklyn, a Republican in his political relations.

Mr. Humphrey, a son of President Humphrey of Amherst, was a man of talents who united the attainments of a well-trained lawyer with literary taste and culture. A patriot in spirit and conversant with public affairs, his manners and address were so pleasing as to render him a genial companion for all his associates.

Another previous acquaintance was the widely known representative in Congress from Ohio, Samuel Sullivan Cox—yclept sportively "Sunset Cox." I had known him well as a fellow-student, of an older class, in Brown University. In those days his talents won for him much applause as a speaker and debater. He was specially fond of political and historical studies, with an interest likewise in philosophy. He read Locke, and I remember that he relished the writings of Berkeley, especially certain of his colloquies, in which he would read aloud the acute bishop's own rôle of the successful defender of Christian truth, and so vanquish the sceptic, this heretical part being relegated, as in the dialogue, to a younger student. Cox resorted, besides, with zest to a pretty wide range of books, and took pleasure in tolerably successful experiments of his own in authorship and youthful oratory for the magazines and for gatherings of fellow-students. His career later was not a surprise to his college associates. That his preference should be for the legal profession, that he should embark in political controversies, become an aspirant for political office, gain notoriety by conspicuity in Congress, secure diplomatic stations, mingle with his public employments the composition of narratives of experiences of his own and other books of a popular cast, and shine in political life as a humorist and lively jester, was the natural sequel of the characteristics early manifest. Cox owed his advancement to the Democratic party of which he was an adherent. Among certain competing branches of the party, he was a sympathetic supporter of Douglas in his ambition for ascendency in its counsels. As to other lines of policy, whether upheld by Buchanan or other party leaders, he looked on them, for the time at least, with comparative disfavor, which was extended to exertions by such leaders to gain personal control.

Cox met me in Washington with the hearty welcome which he always had ready for his fellow-students of other days. At this time not only were the two parties at variance touching the legislation deemed expedient in dealing with the promoters of secession in the South, but within the bounds of each there were differences respecting the features of policy meriting approval. There was a problem of a personal kind not easy to be solved by Cox, who was not indifferent to the bearing of the course he might take on his own political prospects. He had to settle which of the discordant modes of action was most eligible.

Remembering like services which now and then, when I was in my teens at Brown, I had complied with his request to render him, he now requested me to do him the favor to let him read to me a speech which he had just composed to be delivered in the House of Representatives. He was not careless of the observance of Sunday and apologized for being obliged to borrow time for the prelection of his speech on a Sunday afternoon. When I had patiently listened to its rehearsal, he wanted to get my opinion of it, and I frankly confessed my impression that each of the rival parties would construe it as being on its side. This, he said, was just what he wanted.

Shortly after this conversation—I think it was the next day—I accompanied Cox to make a call on President Buchanan. As we were just about to cross the threshold of the White House my companion said of him—coupling with the mention of him a not flattering epithet, "He has turned out my postmaster twice," referring, as he explained, to a postmaster in Ohio—in Cleveland, if my memory serves me—who belonged to the Douglas branch of the Democracy, but whose appointment Cox had managed to secure and whose removal he warmly resented. We were graciously received by Buchanan, with no apparent lack of cordiality in greeting my guide, who was equally complaisant. The exciting events and controversies of the day became at once the subjects of conversation. Buchanan showed the utmost interest in the recent speech of Pugh, Senator from Ohio, and undivided sympathy with its contents. 'The town is ringing," the President exclaimed, "with Pugh's speech."

That speech, delivered on December 20th, had charged the Republicans with the design to surround the slave States with a cordon of free States so as to compel them to emancipate their slaves; also with the intention to extend the right of suffrage to the blacks and mulattoes. It, moreover, maintained that slavery should be permitted in Territories, and in arsenals and navy yards in the slave States. "Would not the Republicans," inquired Pugh, "feel bound to amend the Constitution so as to abolish slavery in the States?"—an assertion put in the form of an interrogatory. Pugh reiterated in substance Buchanan's declarations in his message against the coercion of a State. He raised his voice in favor of Crittenden's compromise scheme. Of this speech of Pugh, Buchanan spoke with fluent admiration.

Another subject of talk was the late doings in South Carolina. The ordinance of secession had been passed by the convention there on December 20th. On the 22d it appointed commissioners to negotiate with the Government of the United States in order to obtain the delivery of its property within the limits of the State. They started for Washington on Saturday, the 22d. Buchanan was looking for their arrival. He remarked to us that he should present to Congress the communication which he was expecting them to bring. He had foreseen, he said, what would be done up to this point. "I can see no farther," he went on to say; "what is to follow must be left to Providence," glancing upward as he spoke and pointing above to the ceiling, as if to indicate the locality of the Power thus designated.

His plan concerning the commissioners was not carried out. On the evening of the day (December 26th) in which they arrived in Washington, Fort Moultrie was evacuated. Buchanan's only interview with them was on the 28th. He told them that he would receive them as private gentlemen and communicate to Congress any propositions to be made by them. They had refused to make any proposals until Major Anderson should be sent back to Fort Moultrie. Buchanan denied that he had given a pledge to send him back, and refused to accede to their demand.

Leaving the White House, I was conducted next by Cox to the Capitol and to the Vice-President's Room, where I was presented to Mr. Breckinridge. At the date of his election (1856) he was only thirty-five years old, the youngest man that had ever held the office. He was now thirty-nine years of age, while the President was sixty-nine. The Vice-President in his form, his stature, and apparent vigor seemed fully as young as he was. His expressive countenance, the marks of unusual care in his dress, his bearing indicative alike of self-respect and courtesy, would incline one to judge him to be a well-bred man of a resolute spirit. While conversing with us, he walked slowly to and fro in his room. When we had exchanged greetings, Mr. Cox mentioned to him that we had been to the White House, saying, "I wish you were there instead of that ——," giving to the President an appellation the reverse of a compliment. "It matters not," replied Mr. Breckinridge, "who it is that is there. It must be decided whether or not re-enforcements are to be sent to the forts." He emphasized the one alternative which the

Government, whoever might administer it, could not avoid facing. What he meant to insist upon was the futility of trying to shirk this responsibility. He had been chosen Senator from Kentucky in 1860. He had been nominated for the vice-presidency by the anti-Douglas section of the Democracy, and he stood by the slave-holding cause and the Southern Confederacy which it called into being.

Our interview with General Cass had a special interest, owing to the fact of his recent withdrawal from the Cabinet. When, in 1857, he accepted the post of Secretary of State, it was after a long and varied experience in public life. He was seventy-five years old. His loyalty to the Union was sincere, yet free from extreme partisanship, and willing to go far to restore concord. Buchanan in his message at the opening of Congress had taken the ground that there is no legal right of secession and had likewise affirmed that in the Government of the United States there is vested no legal power to prevent it. This mixture, a theory of power on the one hand, and of powerlessness on the other, was not at the moment perceived to be, what it turned out to be, a foretoken of the uncertainty and vacillation shown in his dealing with the revolutionary movement in South Carolina. The treatment of the question whether Major Anderson and his garrison should be, or should not be, re-enforced and furnished with provisions for their need is a record of indecision, the effect of which was to offend all the parties concerned and to divide the Cabinet into contending individuals and small antagonistic groups. In this medley, one person after another resigned his portfolio. In this partial dispersion of discordant counsellors, true to his steady conviction that a State has no right to secede, General Cass, when it was made perfectly clear that Buchanan was resolved to leave the forts of the United States without re-enforcement and not to take the necessary means to compel the collection of duties on imports, notified the President that he should resign, and in his formal resignation, a few days later (December 15th), assigned the reasons for this step.

When we visited him in his dwelling, we found him in very good spirits, seated in a comfortable dressing-gown by a parlor window which looked out in front on the adjacent street. In the most friendly manner, he engaged at once in talk about the current events in which his share had been a *magna pars*. He explained his reasons for giving up his connection with the Cabinet. "I own," he said, "that house," pointing to a dwelling across the street, but noticing that I cast a glance in the direction whither he pointed, he added: "It is *not* mine; it is an illustration. *Suppose* that it *were* mine, and some one should tell me that I could continue to possess it, but that I must put no furniture in it—put nothing in it; that would be the substance of what is said to the Government of the United States concerning its forts by those who refuse to permit soldiers and means for their sustenance to be put in them."

After continuing for a while on this general theme, the conversation turned to the secessionist negation of the existence of an authority in the Federal Government to prevent by force the disruption of the Union. On this topic, Cass made mention, with a smile, of an incident at a late Cabinet meeting. It was a brief passage at arms between himself and Thompson, of Mississippi, the Secretary of the Interior. "Thompson," said General Cass, "said to me: 'Would you coerce a State—coerce Mississippi?' 'No,' I answered, 'but I would coerce *you*, *Jacob Thompson*, if you violated the laws.'" Thus, in a word, Cass set forth a distinction as plain as could be, which a multitude of advocates of the secession doctrine obtusely ignored.

Candid historical students are not surprised that Mr. Buchanan was regarded on all sides, in the earlier period of his administration, with a disrespect mingled with dislike. These sentiments were common to all parties, in the South as well as the North. It is true, however, that fair-minded judges acquit him of a consciously unjust antagonism toward the Northern section and of an equally unmerited favoritism toward the South. Misjudgment growing out of prejudices, not insincere, and however destitute of a sound basis, is not to be confounded with wilful antipathy or the opposite bent of feeling. It is true, moreover, that unprejudiced historical authors give credit to Buchanan for a spirit of patriotism and courageous action in the later period of his administration, when such admirers as Holt and Dix were called to his side and engaged his confidence. It is simply just to praise the support which he gave to Lincoln, when Lincoln assumed the responsibilities of his high office; and in the closing years of Buchanan's life, he was in sympathy with the prosecution of the war.

No one will imagine that the period in the administration of President Buchanan when discontent and derision confronted him on all sides was for the Chief himself a bed of roses. In those days it happened to me, in company with Mr. Humphrey, to pass an evening at the house of Mr. Charles Francis Adams, with Mrs. Adams and one or two other callers. Mr. Adams was absent, being engaged in connection with the House Committee of Thirty-three in quest of a feasible scheme of reconciliation and peace between the two sections. In this undertaking Mr. Adams made his influence felt. One of the members, a Representative from Kentucky, was with us on the evening referred to. He spoke with praise of the service Mr. Adams was rendering. "He reminded me the other evening," said the Kentuckian, "of the old man [John Quincy Adams] *resurrected.*" On our walk to our lodgings, late in the evening, as we passed by the President's house, Mr. Humphrey observed of the master of the silent mansion close by: "When he took up his abode there he felt that he had reached the topmost round of the ladder, but now he would rejoice to be anywhere else."

My acquaintance with Senator Trumbull of Illinois opened to me the privilege of conferring with him freely on political questions. One source of satisfaction in this intercourse was derived from his independence of thought, which, at the same time that he was attached to the Republican party, kept him from being warped by partisan prejudice. I recall a visit to him on a certain evening when Senator Sumner was also present. The prolonged conversation disclosed points of contrast in the mental habit of the two men, coexisting with a considerable measure of harmony of opinion. Sumner had a good deal to say on the legal and moral aspects of fugitive-slave legislation. I do not remember at present special points open to question in his creed, which, on the whole, gave me not so full satisfaction as I had looked for. It was in keeping with characteristics of Sumner that, holding as Webster had formerly held, that the framers of the Constitution intended that not Federal authority, but the States severally and exclusively, should carry out the provision for the rendition of run-away slaves, he still did not, as Webster did, cease to advocate such a construction for the reason that the Supreme Court had decided against this interpretation, but, on the contrary, affirmed in Congress, instead of discarding, the view set aside judicially, and evaded the question put to him by Mason, of Virginia, whether he would *lend support* to the enactments of the *States* to carry out the constitutional guarantee. The warmest admirers of Sumner have pronounced puerile his avowal of the doctrine that the denial of suffrage to the blacks would be a violation of the constitutional guarantee of a Republican government. With an admiration of the varied gifts and virtues of Sumner, they have not hesitated to recognize in him as a marked weakness a vanity showing itself in diverse forms. Versed as he was in so many branches of knowledge, and always a tireless reader in literature—in literature lying even beyond the limits of his own profession, he was not considered by the best trained of his appreciative friends an accurate linguist or thorough in his scholarship in any department of knowledge. His rhetorical habit obliged his hearers and readers to miss in his literary work the charm of simplicity and naturalness. His devoted friend and most competent biographer, Mr. Pierce, points out another trait, that "he never seemed to realize how sharp his blade was," meaning that he carried into debates, even in controversies on theories of prison discipline, a needless severity, a vituperative tone, and disparaging personal references. With all his sincerity and freedom in general from vindictive emotions, a writer far from being unfriendly said of him, that he could not eliminate from a speech the idea that it was an exercise in declamation. It was in him, as it has been in not a few eminent men, a misfortune that he coupled with extraordinary talents a lack of humor.

Senator Trumbull, in the freedom of conversation when he and I were alone together, and knowing that I was with him in valuing Sumner's high abilities and moral worth, frankly, in good humor, adverted to certain minor characteristics not falling under these rubrics. One anecdote I will repeat.

It was a function of the Judiciary Committee of the Senate, of which Senator Trumbull was the chairman, to attend to the furnishing of the old Senate Chamber with busts of eminent judges who had sat on the Supreme bench. In the discharge of this office, Senator Trumbull offered a resolution in the Senate that a bust of the late Chief-Justice Taney should be placed there along with the busts of his predecessors. Immediately, Mr. Sumner warmly objected to this measure on the ground that Taney's decision made in the Dred Scott case—a decision generally obnoxious to people hostile to slavery—was too offensive and infamous to render it fit to grant this honor to its author. Trumbull, in telling this story, smiled as he said that it had seemed to him that, even if Taney might have fallen into a legal error, or been extremely blameworthy, it might still be natural to want to see how he looked! The fire of Mr. Sumner's protest, however, led to a *postponement* of the resolution. Trumbull observed that Sumner speedily went to work to hunt up in the Congressional Library, and to bring from its shelves, book after book on the lives and misconduct of iniquitous judges in the past and to deposit them in a huge pile by his desk in the Senate Chamber, his intention being to draw from these some illustrations of detestable judicial decisions, the authors of which might be seen in the pillory and classed with the judge who presided in the Dred Scott case. After waiting for the objectionable resolution to be called up for action, Mr. Sumner, who had taken time enough to compose an elaborate philippic, inquired of Trumbull when the resolution would be called up anew. To this question an evasive reply was made then and, perhaps, more than once. The upshot of the incident was that no opportunity was given to deliver the harangue which Mr. Sumner had been laboriously getting ready to fortify from the contents of the pile of books at the side of his desk. After the gun had been loaded with so much pains-taking, no chance was afforded to discharge it.

At the outset of Lincoln's administration, the absence of a definite, settled policy and of a concurrence of opinion in the Cabinet as to what was best to be done, left room for Mr. Seward to broach occasionally schemes of an eccentric cast that failed to gain the approval either of the President or of Seward's own colleagues, and to venture on predictions having no probability of fulfilment, being nothing better than a product of optimism. Of the projects of the first class the most extraordinary was the confidential suggestion, in writing, presented to Mr. Lincoln just a month after his inauguration, that the question about slavery should be dropped from discussion, Fort Sumter be evacuated, explanations be called for from four offending European powers, and if not received from two of them, Spain and France, war should be declared against these nations, the end aimed at being to divert the attention of the South and North from their mutual alienation and combine them in a union for the energetic prosecution of a foreign war. Thus domestic strife was to terminate and the belligerent sections of this country be absorbed in their common hostility to a common foe. There was some ingenuity shown in a device of this nature. The difficulty lay in its being totally impracticable.

An instance of the optimistic faith of Mr. Seward at this particular time was furnished in the confident prophecy uttered by him at the dinner of the New England Society in New York on his return from a visit to Auburn. On his arrival in Washington, I went to his office with Mr. Humphrey—who was on terms of frank converse with him—where we passed an evening most agreeably. Present with us on that occasion were Governor Andrew of Massachusetts and Senator Anthony of Rhode Island. It could never be a task to listen to Mr. Seward, although one's pleasure was slightly marred by his nasal tone, consequent on the habit of snuff-taking. Professor Shedd, notwithstanding that he was not a stranger to Mr. Seward, once when talking with him, remarked. "You are suffering, Mr. Seward, from a cold." "But a cold," answered Mr. Seward with a smile, "from which I shall not recover."

On the evening referred to, it was pleasant, I am sure, to all of us, to hear him speak with animation of circumstances in his recent trip. In his speech at the Astor House, he assured the company that the threatening aspect of our relations to the South would be all over in ninety days—a declaration regarded with great surprise when sent abroad in the newspapers, as it immediately was. Mr. Seward told us in a lively way how he tarried a little while in

New York on his way to Auburn, and there happened to meet a friend of his—a gentleman well known and highly respected, whose name he mentioned—who expressed great anxiety at what he regarded as the extremely menacing situation of public affairs. "I assured him," said Mr. Seward, "that there is no such danger as he apprehended, but he reiterated his conviction to the contrary. I tried to disabuse his mind of this mood of feeling, all in vain, and at length said that I wouldn't talk with such a damn fool"—a remark which Mr. Seward repeated, as evidently he had uttered it to his anxious friend, in a good-natured tone.

I was so desirous of ascertaining beyond doubt whether Mr. Seward's optimistic predictions really reflected a firm persuasion in his own mind, that, emboldened by his free and friendly manner, I ventured to ask him if his statement that the clouds that darkened the sky, and inspired the belief that war impended, would vanish so soon—in so short an interval—if this statement was a settled conviction. He answered at once: "Yes; my view is that the excitement in the South was at its height the day after Mr. Lincoln's election. What we have seen since is only the *manifestation* of that feeling, which has itself been constantly lessening." I think that none of us imagined that Mr. Seward doubted in the least his declaration as made at the Astor House dinner and as he reaffirmed it to us—whatever might be our distrust of the soundness of his logic. He had, in fact, in talking with Sumner, set the date as only *sixty* days hence, when "all would be well."

In making the journey shortly after with Governor Andrew and Senator Anthony from Washington to New York, I had the opportunity to learn something of their Washington experiences. They were both men of marked intelligence and geniality of manner. Governor Andrew had conversed with Senator Mason of Virginia, who felt sure that the practice of Massachusetts to pronounce free the slaves brought with the consent of the master within the limits of the State would have to be given up and the law authorizing it would have to be abrogated. To this confident proposition, Governor Andrew replied that slavery was not made illegal in Massachusetts by a *statute*, but by a judicial interpretation of the Bill of Rights. To this Mason rejoined that the *Bill of Rights*, then, would have to be altered. The Governor remarked to me that he did not remind him of the fact, as he might have done, that this Massachusetts Bill of Rights, in its contents, was on the basis of the *Virginia* Bill of Rights, drawn up by the Senator's distinguished grandfather, George Mason, one of the noted leaders of the Revolution.

Senator Anthony had met the diplomatic representative of Bremen, and had been struck with what he had said of the undesirable situation of a small political community, isolated, yet in near local relations with larger States. The lesson drawn by Mr. Anthony was the importance to Rhode Island of keeping up the Federal organization, the Union of the States, threatened with dissolution.

Washington, A City of Pictures (1902)

SCRIBNER'S MAGAZINE

FEBRUARY, 1902

WASHINGTON, A CITY OF PICTURES

By Francis E. Leupp

ILLUSTRATIONS BY JULES GUÉRIN

IT is only since the United States became a nation in the stricter sense that Washington can be said to have become a capital in the broader one. Vaguely forecast in the Constitution as the "seat of government," yet even that distinction marred by frequent threats of removal; satirically described by Moore as the City of Magnificent Distances; despised abroad as a Botany Bay for diplomatists needing discipline, and socially ignored at home as a place where nobody had been born and everybody was a pilgrim; politically ring-ridden, æsthetically neglected, destitute of civic pride, the lot of no town in America seemed less to be envied. But all this was changed by the remodelling of the Union after the Civil War and the troublous period immediately following. Patriotic Americans awoke to the fact that the era of mere federation was over, that they were a nation with a national government, and that the seat of government was a capital with settled claims on their regard and permanent interests, like London and Paris and Berlin. The isolation of Washington for so many years was then proved to have been a blessing in disguise; for it had left the city free from the drawbacks, noisy and noisome, of a centre of trade, and the social soil still in a virgin state, waiting for the seed of letters and art and the humanities generally.

Then began a metamorphosis. In a half-dozen years an overgrown village, characterless and forlorn, was transformed into a real city with an assured cosmopolitan future and the rudiments of a literature of its own. From numberless pens we have had treatments of Washington as an historic city, founded by and named for the greatest of Americans; as an architectural and sculptural museum; as a model municipality, fit subject for every administrative experiment; as a democratic capital without local self-government; as a coming educational centre and a present Mecca of new-made wealth—of Washington in all its phases, in short, except as the picture city of the New World, yet that is the aspect in which it appeals most strongly to its familiars. No other city seems to have made beauty its first thought, and relegated the harder and coarser things of life to a secondary place, as Washington has. No other is so enveloped in an atmosphere of artistic feeling that even the sternest actualities must be studied through this medium. That the atmosphere is real, and not merely an evanescent effect which passes away with the first surprise it excites, cannot be doubted by anyone who has applied the supreme test of long association. Indeed, on one who makes the city his home, the first impression soon settles into a spell, and the spell grows stronger with every year's acquaintance, till no common exorcism can prevail against it. If the strenuous life be here, as we are bound to assume that it is, it does not obtrude itself. The all-pervading spirit of things visible is one of calm, of cheerfulness, of indifference to the flight of time. The present is everywhere dominant, with its most agreeable face to the front. There is nothing to remind one that yesterday had heaped pledges upon to-day, or that to-day is mortgaging the freedom of to-morrow. It is as if a community of 300,000 souls, carved out of the midst of our restless Yankeeland, had shaken off its more serious obligations and voted itself a daily half-holiday.

This suggestion of leisure and recreation is intensified by the width of the highways and the multitude of open spaces, inviting floods of sunshine and pure air. Wherever a street and an avenue intersect, they celebrate their meeting by at least a triangular parklet or two, if not with a more formal circle or square. Grass, trees, and shrubbery revel everywhere in joyous life. Vines spread themselves wantonly over any wall that does not repel their advances, till a commonplace dwelling becomes a castle of living green with arrow-slits and a sally-port. Look in any direction and you have a vista fringed in summer with luxuriant verdure, in winter with a delicate gray lacework of leafless boughs. Statues of the nation's heroes appear at intervals. From this point the fiery Thomas, reining in his steed, stands clear-cut like a big black cameo against a saffron shell of sky ; from that, behold the imperious Scott crossing at a stately walk the arena which bears his name ; yonder, see the sombre McPherson through an opening in the grove where his comrades have left him to receive the salutes of posterity. And following with the eye any radial line toward the place where the river makes its great bend, one sees the Washington Monument standing guard, a hoary sentinel at the city's water-gate.

Would you leave the gayly peopled streets, with their human chatter, for a brief communion with nature ? Here is the Mall, stretching westward like an elongated U from the Capitol to the shores of the Potomac. You could lose yourself in this retreat, so densely is it wooded in spots ; but the keen eye can usually catch a glimmer of light from a public thoroughfare on one side, or on another some dash of color reflected from the rainbow front of the National Museum or the decorous red-brown of the Smithsonian Institution. Possibly your state of mind calls for an atmosphere charged with spiritual prompting ? Go, then, from the centre of the city to its edge, and thread one of the paths in the wood which gives Georgetown College its background. Here will be met, now a black-robed Jesuit father, his chin bent on his breast as he moves along absorbed in his solitary revery, now a brace of neophytes engaged in sober consultation. Is your taste for history, the traditions of patriotic sacrifice and glory ? Over there in the eastern quarter is the Soldiers' Home, a tract of field and forest intermixed, where gray-bearded veterans stroll about and feed the squirrels, or cluster under the trees to fight their battles over and tell stories of comrades who have answered the last roll-call. A cross-road leads to the Zoo, that big, breezy garden of animal exotics, and out again into Rock Creek Park, where a dashing, plashing stream, fed from springs in the Maryland hills, winds through miles of woodland, forcing picturesque little passes for itself, like an Alpine river in miniature.

All these are but glimpses, however. For the broader views seek certain places, and for the best effects seize certain times. So far as I know, one experience of mine in landscape-hunting a dozen years ago remains unique—watching the sunrise from the top of the Washington Monument. It was during a recess in an all-night session of Congress. The journey began at the darkest hour before the dawn, in a weary climb through an echoing dungeon ninety fathoms into the sky, with no guide for my steps but the flicker from a smoke-dimmed lantern, and no company save the spirits of the night, already spreading their wings for flight.

At the top at last ! The winding staircase ends in a square chamber pierced with deep-recessed windows, like the eyes of a giant peering from under glowering brows. Through them may be seen a haze overhanging everything below, thickening in the west and south, where a dense mist marks the tortuous course of the Potomac. The lamps in the city streets

Drawn by Jules Guérin.

A Hoary Sentinel at the City's Water-gate.

Where classic marble façades peep between parted curtains of leaves.

no longer twinkle, but merely lend a yellow radiance to the veil of vapor above them. The only distinct points of light visible are the stars in an inky firmament. Yes, one other: against a background of black in the east glows a flame like a great fixed meteor. Flowing curves which lead down from it, so shadowy as to seem like a phantom etching, suggest a cone-shaped dome. By degrees the contour becomes bolder as the stars go out and the colorless sky takes on a grayish tinge. Then slowly the rosy flush of morning rolls up from the horizon and overcomes the gray; the haze in the foreground melts away; the flame at the top of the dome vanishes like the light of a candle snuffed, and the mass of the Capitol stands forth as a mammoth block of marble on a terraced pedestal of green—the detail of the façade barely visible, but the proud outlines sweeping down and disappearing in a tangle of roofs and foliage.

Faint sounds float skyward from the streets—the first yawns of a waking city. They are presently drowned in echoes which come whirling up the hollow shaft. These repeat the exchange of greetings

Globes of white light suspended here and there among the trees.

between the watchman mounting guard and the colleague whom he is relieving from a night's vigil. The morrow is here, and life is astir again even in the Washington Monument.

Before the witchery of this spectacle has quite released its hold, let me picture another. I have spoken of the way the Monument figures in every view that embraces the river bend. Spread the city out like a fan, and this pile is the pivot which holds the frame together. The visitor who has seen it once has just begun to see it. A smooth-faced obelisk, devoid of ornament, it would appear the stolidest object in the world ; in truth, it is as versatile as the clouds. Every change in your position reveals it in a new phase. Go close to it and look up, and its walls seem to rise infinitely and dissolve into the atmosphere ; stand on the neighboring hills, and you are tempted to throw a stone over its top. Sail down the Potomac, and the slender white shaft is still sending its farewells after you when the city has passed out of sight. It plays chameleon to the weather. It may be

Drawn by Jules Guérin.

This long, narrow tongue of land where

Anacostia Creek joins the Potomac.

Drawn by Jules Guérin.

The quaint old river-front of the White House.

gay one moment and grave the next, like the world. Sometimes in the varying lights it loses its perspective and becomes merely a flat blade struck against space; an hour later, each line and seam is marked with the crispness of chiselled sculpture. On a fair morning it is radiant under the first beams of the rising sun; in the full of the moon it is like a thing from another world—cold, shimmering, unreal. Often in the spring and fall its peak is lost in vapor, and the shaft looks as if it were a tall, thin Ossa penetrating the home of the gods. Again, with its base wrapped in fog and its summit in cloud, it is a symbol of human destiny, emerging from one mystery only to pass after a little into another. Always the same, yet never twice alike, it is to the old Washingtonian a being instinct with life, a personality to be known and loved. It has relatively little to tell the passing stranger, but many confidences for the friend of years.

Statues of the nation's heroes appear at intervals.

It is mid-morning now, but from our outlook on the Capitol terrace we face a thick and troubled sky. The air is murky. Clouds fringed with fine gray fleece, which have been hanging so low as to hide the apex of the monument, are folding back upon themselves in the southern heavens, forming a rampart dark and forbidding. Against this the marble obelisk is projected, having caught and held one ray of pure sunshine which has found an opening and shot through like a search-light. It is plain that an atmospheric battle is at hand. The garrulous city seems struck dumb; the timid trees are shivering with apprehension; the voice of the wind is half sob and half warning. The search-ray vanishes as the door of the cloud fort is closed and the rumbling of the bolts is heard behind it. The landscape in the background is blotted from view by eddies of yellow dust, as if a myriad of horsemen were making a tentative charge. Silent and unmoved the obelisk stands there, a white warrior bidding defiance to the forces of sky and earth. As the subsiding dust marks the retreat of the cavalry, the artillery opens fire. First one masked porthole and then another belches flame, but the sharp crash or dull roar which follows passes quite unnoticed by the champion. Then comes

Drawn by Jules Guérin.

That unbroken mile of avenue.

Drawn by Jules Guérin.

Mount the Capitol terrace at night.

Drawn by Jules Guérin.

The valley of domes and spires.

the rattle of musketry, as a sheet of hail sweeps across the field.

We are not watching a combat, only an assault, for these demonstrations call forth no response. On the champion—taking everything, giving nothing—the only effect they produce is a change of color from snowy white to ashen gray. Even that is but for a moment. As the storm of hail melts into a shower of limpid raindrops to which the relieved trees open their palms, the wind ceases its wailing, and the wall of cloud falls apart to let the sun's rays through once more.

I realize that I have gone rapidly over a wide range. Well, there is no better place to rest than the President's garden on a summer Saturday afternoon, when all the Washington world and its sweetheart turns out to hear the Marine Band play. We can find a cool, soft spot on the side of this grass-tufted hillock to stretch ourselves at full length. Lean on your elbow a moment and look about. To your left is the quaint old river-front of the White House, scenically framed between wings of dark green foliage. Its semi-circular portico, upheld by stately columns, fills the central space, and dense masses of honeysuckle rail in the stone stairways, worn smooth by the tread of the lords and ladies of our republican court for eighty years. To the right, a gentle slope of lawn sweeps away toward the river, but soon loses itself in a labyrinth of shrubbery. Its surface is broken midway by a fountain noiselessly playing, whose spray is blown by the breeze over first one cluster of scarlet cannas and then another. Three-fourths of the horizon is a billowy line of tree-tops; and looming above it, projected against a cloudless southern sky, is seen the upper half of the Monument. The sun has settled far enough to cast long shadows over most of the leaf-walled space and enable the pleasure-seekers to stroll about the greensward without discomfort. The men are clad for the most part in white or in the cooler grays; the women in a multitude of delicate tints which arrange themselves in kaleidoscopic groupings as they stray from place to place.

Where is the city, with its brick and stone and its hard-paved highways, its clang of gongs and clatter of traffic? Surely, a hundred miles away. We cannot see it, for the White House on the one hand and the Monument on the other are the only signs of man's handiwork to remind us that we are not alone with nature; listen as we may, we cannot catch even its distant hum, for between us and it has fallen a curtain of music—one of those untamed Polish dances in which the brasses seem to chase each other across the field, and a night-wind to go howling after the hindmost. Close your eyes. Cannot you see the dainty shapes in lavender and straw-color and white, at which you were looking just now, swaying and swinging and sweeping, this way and that, with the tumultuous rhythm? Are you not watching a village festival in far-off Plotzk?

The dance is ended. You open your eyes for an instant, roused from your day-dream by the clapping of hands; but you close them again and sink back on your grassy couch as the brasses fall to the rear for the encore, and the wood instruments send forth the first melodious bars of the Spring Song. A hush falls upon the whole assemblage. You cannot analyze the sentiment which holds you now, but you are conscious that hundreds of others are feeling what you feel. No wonder the master made this a song without words.

Late October is the season to visit the Old Arsenal, when the grass is at the half-way stage between green and brown, and the yellow leaves strew the ground and play color tricks with the eye that moves from them to other objects. The sunsets are then at their best, and sunset is the hour of hours here.

No spot in all Washington is steeped in more varied associations than this long, narrow tongue of land where Anacostia Creek joins the Potomac. By turns a military post under command of one of Lafayette's lieutenants; the site of the gunshop established by the infant republic; the scene of a disastrous explosion when the British were plying the torch in the War of 1812; a repository for army stores; a penitentiary; the stage on which the last act of the Lincoln tragedy was played; an artillery school; an engineer barrack-ground: here are relics of every occupation, like fossil remains in broken strata, waiting for the historian to dig them out and classify them according to the æon to which each belonged in life. But now the old reservation is well on its way toward a fresh chapter in its career, which will exceed all the rest in dignity and lead, perhaps, to its permanent transformation; for it has been chosen as the home of the new War College, where the international art of meeting force with force will be taught as one teaches a game of chess.

There is a spacious parade, of course, enclosed between footpaths and a carriage drive, and bordered with rows of trees set out with great precision, like troops at drill in open order. The walls of the former prison-yard have been razed, and the two wings of the institution, made over into officers' quarters, in their coats of clean paint wear the air of veterans who are keeping back the signs of age by a careful regard for their health and plenty of cold baths and exercise. Between the two buildings rises a green mound, crowned with a mass of foliage plants and flowers, and in the midst a fountain; here is where the gibbet stood of old, and underneath this sod the bones of many a friendless malefactor have been laid away after he has paid his last debt to justice.

The river side, however, is the one from which to view the sunset. A vine-laden sea-wall, pretty well gone to decay, catches the wash of the vessels which go tacking up the current to reach the shelter of some friendly wharf before night can overtake them. The clouds have deserted the upper heavens and followed the sun down to within a little distance of the sky-line, where they are halted and drawn up to bid the day adieu. The old Lee Mansion, which looked down at us from Arlington Heights an hour ago, has faded from sight. The outline of the crest beyond is softened by a faint purple haze; above this the purple fades into pink, the pink into yellow, the yellow into green, the green into turquoise, and the turquoise into pure sapphire blue. Every gradation of color is reflected in the river, sifted through the embroidery of the trees which line Potomac Island, the redeemed shoal between the Old Arsenal and the Virginia shore. In the northwest the Monument rises out of what seems a plain, so dwarfed are all neighboring objects by its towering height. The sun, even after sinking out of view, continues to mark its descent, dial-fashion, on the shaft, up which creep rapidly the shadows of the hills, absorbing the flush that has suffused its marble face during the last few seconds of farewell.

There is a stir about one of the old bronze cannon on the rise of ground back of us. A bugle-call—a flash—an echo-waking roar—and a dagger of smoke stabs the thin vapors which have already begun to rise from the river. From the staff in the centre of the parade the colors descend like the relieved lookout from a ship's masthead, hand under hand. As the bunting touches the grass, the troops in the several squads, who have been standing like statues at "attention," break ranks and saunter into their barracks. The day is done.

Returning to Capitol Hill for a last look before going to bed, we can do no better than to take a leisurely stroll through a negro quarter which will soon be swept away by the fast advancing tide of improvement. It was forlorn enough in the garish light of noon, but now the dusk has softened everything and laid a poetic touch upon even poverty and dirt. These whitewashed shanties are squatter dwellings which seem to have dropped down at random on the ragged turf. They are a rude patchwork of old bits of board and shingle picked from waste-heaps in the city. With no regularity of structure, and saved from collapse only by many props projecting at uncertain angles, they are nevertheless human homes, with such domestic suggestions as here a pair of bean-vines trained on strings over a doorway, there a protruding elbow of stovepipe shooting up a stream of sparks, and yonder an opening with the light of a candle gleaming through. Had we come here in winter we should have found a sprig of Virginia mistletoe tacked to nearly every lintel, and caught the glow of holly-berries against the single pane which serves for a window.

The city engineers are running a sewer across this malarial flat, and have mounted a zigzag row of ruby lanterns to warn wayfarers away from the open ditch. In front of one of the shanties sit an Uncle and Auntie, all rags and tatters, smoking their pipes demurely beside a little bonfire, while a brawny young son of Ham, half clad and with his black throat and chest exposed, leans against the door-jamb, thrumming a banjo. Around him a dozen solemn-faced pickaninnies are circling in a weird dance, each a law unto himself as to steps and postures, but all keeping perfect time with the well-punctuated jig-tune. It is a bit of the South of forty years ago thrown out on the picket line of to-day.

Climbing the hill, we reach the Library of Congress and mount the staircase to the portico. Night has come on meanwhile, but the moon has not risen. The blackness overhead is pierced with tiny holes through which glow the fires of other worlds ; the blackness below is relieved by globes of white light suspended here and there among the trees like will-o'-the-wisps in a wood, and causing fantastic shadows to chase each other across the ground as the boughs sway with every passing breeze.

Grand and gray, the bulk of the Capitol stands out against a dark expanse. Its base-line, like the hull of an anchored ship, is partly hidden by the surf of foliage between. Studied from here, no obtrusive roof or tower breaks the symmetry of its silhouette. For all that we can see, its nearest neighbors on the other side are the stars. The illumination of the city, however, is reflected against the wall of the western sky-vault, lending to it the faintest hint of ruddy color, and thus accentuating the noble lines of the dome and its massive shoulders.

The Capitol is resting after a period of internal turmoil. Not a window is lighted, not even a watchman is visible. The mantle of sleep is over everything. But somewhere up in the sky, though we cannot see her, we know that "the great bronze Freedom" still

> Peers eastward, as divining
> The new day from the old.

It will be observed that Washington offers its wealth to the picture-seeker only by a frequent shifting of the point of view. Its beauties are many, but lack continuity. Owing to the accidental character of the city's development hitherto, they are still amid incongruous surroundings, and so scattered that one must learn by patient experiment where to go in search of them. The topography is full of wonderful possibilities, some of which have been improved, though here and there a vista with a perfect foreground calls for the free use of the axe and battering-ram to clear the middle distance, and another with a beginning of great promise ends ingloriously. It is to the task of assembling the unrelated fragments and adjusting them to each other in a harmonious whole, that the new Park Commission, consisting of Messrs. Burnham, McKim, and Olmsted, with Augustus St. Gaudens as advising sculptor, has just addressed itself.

No city in the world is so bountifully supplied with parks and breathing-places, but they need a common key and a consecutive interpretation. These the Commission hopes to give them before proceeding to its larger scheme, which embraces novel enterprises in landscape engineering and architectural assimilation. The single feat of connecting by a generous driveway the several scenic beauties, and thus reducing them to a system, would be worthy of the highest artistic endeavor. If no more than the plans already in hand are carried out, the visitor may be borne through grassy fields and virgin forests ; along a river's edge bristling with masts ; past corners where classic marble façades peep between parted curtains of leaves ; down into gorges ploughed by foaming streams, and up over panoramic hill-tops ; across spider-web bridges and viaducts of massive masonry : and all within an hour's walk of the heart of a teeming city—a heart that throbs with the concentrated life of 70,000,000 people.

Whether from the heights of Arlington on a fair spring morning we survey the valley of domes and spires, or mount the Capitol terrace at night and sweep with our glance that unbroken mile of avenue which impresses even the Parisian fresh from his boulevards, whether we assist at the dedication of a new monument to heroism or watch the devotees of pleasure taking their way homeward from an official ball, it is always the picturesque

Washington which first reveals itself to us. Our capital has its practical side, its sordid side, even its repulsive side, but these do not appear till we have broken the spell of that first impression. And why should not the spell work deeper than the surface? If nature and art, joined hand in hand, exert the ennobling influence with which we credit them, is it too much to hope that in course of time, when the renaissance now in prospect shall have reached its full fruition, the face of the City Beautiful may become but the mirror of its soul?

Envoys at Washington (1901)

THE COSMOPOLITAN.

From every man according to his ability: to every one according to his needs.

MAY, 1901.

A GROUP OF DIPLOMATS LEAVING SECRETARY HAY'S HOUSE. COUNT G. DE LICHTERVELDE, BELGIAN MINISTER, TURNING TO ADDRESS A FRIEND.

ENVOYS AT WASHINGTON.

BY WALDON FAWCETT.

THE nearest approach to the pomp and pageantry of a royal court, with its attendant emblems of heraldry and insignia of rank, its gorgeous, stately ceremonials and the dazzling splendor of the raiment of its devotees, which the American continent has known since the days of Montezuma, is to be found in the assemblages of the Diplomatic Corps at Washington. These levees — invariably half social, half official, for the representatives of royalty never wholly unbend—easily constitute the most attractive of all the spectacular features of life in the nation's most beautiful city. In glitter and sparkle and color, the pictures presented are well-nigh the peer of any afforded by the capitals of Europe or the Orient, and even in the settings—the ball-rooms and banquet-halls—the seat of government need not blush for its possessions.

Uncle Sam now has diplomatic relations with fully three dozen countries, which are represented at the American capital by six Embassies and thirty Legations. Composing these various transplanted households are more than two hundred persons,

BARON HENGELMÜLLER, AUSTRO-HUNGARIAN MINISTER.

ALI FERROUH BEY, TURKISH MINISTER.

natives of every land and clime, and constituting the most interesting "foreign colony" to be found on this hemisphere. To look after the business of the Embassies alone, and provide the proper social environment for these official habitations, more individuals are now required than were to be found in the entire Diplomatic Corps at the City of Magnificent Distances a few years ago. In addition to the Ambassador, who is, of course, intrusted with the entire direction of the affairs of the Embassy, there are Secretaries, Naval Attachés, Military Attachés, and mayhap interpreters, forming a staff which in the case of some Embassies, such as the British and the Chinese Legations, includes about a dozen persons.

The diplomatic contingent at Washington has been growing larger year by year, and the increase has been particularly marked since the consequences of the Spanish-American war forcibly installed the United States in the position of a world-power. More than that, a broader importance and deeper significance have been imparted to this congress of nations at Miss Columbia's Court by an action taken by Congress some years ago. It may be explained that in the management of international problems of statecraft Ambassadors and Ministers Plenipotentiary bear much the same relation to each other as do Senators and Representatives in the deliberations of the American legislative body. The Ambassadors are the bright particular stars of the diplomatic firmament. Not only do they enjoy higher rank than their confrères, and the presumption of representing more directly the authority of their sovereign or government, but, through the possession of greater discretionary privileges, they are enabled to handle the matters which come within their jurisdiction with less delay for instructions from officials at home.

In conformity with one of the strict rules of diplomatic usage, however, no nation sends an Ambassador to a country which has not delegated in exchange an official of equally high diplomatic rank, and so the intensely democratic convictions of the American lawmakers restricted Uncle Sam's

BARON DE FAVA, ITALIAN AMBASSADOR.

official guests, for more than a century, to envoys of lesser rank. Since the passage of the law making it possible to raise representatives of the United States from the rank of Minister to that of Ambassador, the most powerful nations on the globe—Great Britain, France, Russia, Germany, Italy and Mexico—have demonstrated their respect for the Republic by sending to Washington ambassadorial appointees. Adding dignity to the personnel of this cosmopolitan gathering on American soil, has also contributed to its splendor and impressiveness. In the corps, as at present constituted, are many men of world-wide reputation —statesmen whose names stand for some of the most brilliant diplomatic triumphs known to modern times.

COUNT CASSINI, RUSSIAN AMBASSADOR.

In spite of the fact that the light of publicity beats so fiercely around these bearers of the greetings of kingdoms and empires to the land of freedom, they in reality live to a considerable extent in a realm of mystery, and to penetrate this realm seems to be one of the dearest ambitions of a considerable portion of American citizens. If one would gain tangible evidence of how potent is the attraction exerted by these distinguished foreigners, with their suggestion of strange peoples and unheard-of customs, he has only to note the eager interest manifested by the vast crowds of spectators, representing every state in the Union, who throng every formal function at Washington where a glimpse may be caught of this contingent of gaily attired dignitaries.

VISCOUNT DE SANTO THYRSO, PORTUGUESE MINISTER, AND THE VISCOUNTESS.

There are only a few occasions each year, however, when the general public may feast its eyes upon this brave show of fur and tinsel. The New Year's reception at the White House, and the special reception which the President tenders annually to the Diplomatic Corps, bring out the showiest court costumes in the wardrobes of the distinguished foreigners; as does also some special event, now and

LORD PAUNCEFOTE ABOUT TO CALL ON THE SECRETARY OF STATE.

then, such as the inauguration of the Chief Executive, a memorial service in honor of some departed monarch, or a wedding in which the chief participants are members of the diplomatic circle.

The costumes in which the representatives of the governments of the world come to pay their respects to the highest official in the United States, are in most marked contrast to the habiliments of America's envoys in the throne-rooms of Europe. In the early years of the century, Uncle Sam's diplomatic Ministers were authorized to wear on state occasions one of two kinds of uniform, each including a coat of blue, lined with silk, both coat and cape being heavily loaded with embroidery. For half a century, however, our emissaries at the courts of the world have been restricted to "the simple dress of an American citizen," now and then modified in detail, as by the introduction of knee-breeches or a dress-sword.

In the official plumage of the diplomats gathered at the American capital, on the other hand, there is embodied every hue known to nature. Many Attachés are officers in the military or naval service of their respective countries, and appear in the brilliant uniforms of the various branches of such service. The fashion-plates of diplomatic court-dress embrace everything from splendid uniforms of glowing crimson and snowy white to others gleaming with gold embroideries on black, set off in many instances by the fur trimmings of the hussar capes and a wealth of dec-

SIN TEH MOO, KOREAN CHARGÉ D'AFFAIRES.

SEÑOR DON CARLOS MORLA VICUÑA,
CHILIAN MINISTER.

orations, while prominent by contrast are the red fezes of the Turkish Minister and the members of his staff, and the rich Oriental silks of the Chinese Legationers.

A titled visitor who is eagerly sought out by the eyes of the spectators at every diplomatic function is Lord Pauncefote, the British Ambassador to the United States. This interest is perhaps due in part to his position as Dean of the Diplomatic Corps. The coterie of diplomats, constituting a body by itself, is governed by laws of its own making, and custom has decreed that length of service shall fix the Deanship. If all the foreign representatives at Washington still ranked as Ministers, it is possible that Lord Pauncefote would not hold the coveted post; but since seniority among the Ministers does not count where there are Ambassadors, and Lord Pauncefote was the first Ambassador appointed to this country, he stands as arbiter in all the delicate questions of precedence which arise from time to time within the Corps. Modern times have known no handsomer costume than the regulation gold-embroidered dress-uniform of the British diplomat, and the regular ornamentation is augmented, in the case of the uniform which Lord Pauncefote has worn upon most state occasions of recent years, by numerous insignia of his rank.

The court-dress of many of the diplomats bears a slight resemblance to the Knights Templar uniform so familiar in this country, but is much more elaborate in every way. A majority of the Latin-American governments have within the

WU TING FANG, CHINESE MINISTER.

past year or two adopted a universal design for diplomatic dress—a uniform resplendent in red and gold. One of the most striking uniforms ever seen in Washington is that worn on state occasions by Baron Hengelmüller, the Minister from Austro-Hungary. It consists of deep-red trousers, high black boots, and a black velvet cloak splendidly ornamented.

GEN. ISAAC KHAN, PERSIAN MINISTER.

Count Cassini, the Russian Ambassador, is a diplomat who has during his long career performed many notable services for his government, and the testimonials of appreciation which have come to him in the form of decorations have made of the front of his court-coat literally a mass of gold and jewels that sparkles with every move. The members of the Russian Embassy are notable for the sumptuousness of their uniforms, and this made all the more noticeable the mark of respect which they showed when, at the memorial services in honor of Queen Victoria, they appeared in plain black, with astrakan-trimmed chapeaux with black feather tufts. It may be noted, also, that on occasions such as the one mentioned all the foreign diplomats have the hilts of their swords intertwined with black crape.

The representatives of our sister republic, France, are provided with far more imposing court-dress than are the officials in the diplomatic service of the United States. In addition, the French Ambassador, Monsieur Cambon, and all the members of his staff who served in Washington during the Spanish-American war, are adorned with the superb decoration of the Order of Isabella, presented by the Queen Regent of Spain in acknowledgment of their good offices in effecting peace.

Dazzling as are the uniforms of the Europeans, and the diplomats from South and Central America, however, they are outshone in a measure by the elaborate attire of the courtiers from the Orient. At the head of this contingent stands Wu Ting Fang, the famous Chinese Minister. His favorite garment for state ceremonials is a dress of purple silk, trimmed with white fur, over which he wears a heavy silken, fur-trimmed cloak. His costume represents the acme of magnificence in one direction, just as Lord Pauncefote's coat of scarlet, with gold collar, frogs and slashes, does in another. A distinguishing characteristic of Minister Wu's costume is an immense diamond which he wears in the front of his silk turban. The able representative of the Celestial Empire tells most humorously of his fright when on one occasion he missed the precious stone, only to discover after a terrified search that he had reversed his turban in donning it. The members of the Chinese Legation are the only servitors of the nations at Washington who do not carry the regulation dress-sword.

DR. EDUARDO WILDE, ARGENTINE MINISTER, HIS WIFE, AND HER BROTHER, SECOND SECRETARY OF THE LEGATION.

The uniforms of Minister Takahira of Japan and his Secretaries and Attachés, although the embodiment of gorgeousness, more nearly conform to Continental fashion; and so also does the attire of the Koreans, although it has

MINISTER TAKAHIRA OF JAPAN, AND THE FIRST SECRETARY.

been but a few years since the latter were pointed out to spectators at White House receptions as the most picturesque figures in the human medley. The Siamese diplomats have, to a considerable extent, taken the place in the panorama vacated by the Koreans, and their trappings more than compensate the sight-seer for the suddenly acquired modesty in dress on the part of their neighbors in the Far East. The Siamese Minister, Phya Prasiddhi, one of the new arrivals at Washington, is of the most unostentatious appearance when clad in the prescribed garb of American society, but on state occasions he blooms, like a suddenly unfolded flower, in robes of the richest brocaded satins and a silken scarf of wonderful hues.

The closing months of the century brought the Siamese envoy a rival for the position of the most elaborately dressed diplomat, in the person of Gen. Isaac Khan, the new Persian Minister. In this connection it may be recalled that the former Persian envoy, the first representative whom the Shah ever sent to Washington, was virtually driven away by the funny pictures whereby the American newspapers portrayed his fantastic costumes. The new-comer is evidently not so sensitive, and moreover he is more likely to excite admiration than amusement, for the new uniform which was made for him in Paris just before his departure for his present post of duty is quite the most gorgeous outfit that has been seen on this side of the Atlantic.

The unique feature of the apparel of Ali Ferrouh Bey, the Turkish Minister, and the members of his suite, is found, of course, in the omnipresent red fez, which these diplomats wear even in church. The masculine contingent from the Turkish Legation was compelled to divide interest at the White House reception which ushered in the century, with the only lady

HERR VON HOLLEBEN, GERMAN AMBASSADOR, AND COUNTESS QUADT.

1. SHEN TUNG, OF THE CHINESE LEGATION. 2. CONSTANTIN BRUN, DANISH MINISTER. 3. LIEUTENANT SHROEN, GERMAN ATTACHÉ. 4. SEÑOR DON JUAN RIANO, SPANISH FIRST SECRETARY. 5. BARON FERSEN, RUSSIAN ATTACHÉ.

who ever accompanied the representatives of the Sultan on such an occasion. The Minister could not be accompanied by his wife or sister, who are strict Mohammedans and take no part in the social life of the capital, but Mme. Sidky Bey, the wife of the Second Secretary, was present with her husband, and her quaint gown attracted no end of attention.

The gowns of the feminine members of the diplomatic households are so similar in general appearance to those of the fashionably dressed American women that they are rather outshone, in so far as popular interest is concerned, by the costumes in which their liege lords appear on state occasions. The one notable exception is found in the case of Madame Wu, the wife of the Chinese Minister. Madame Wu is the possessor of some of the handsomest jewels in the United States, and these, with her close-fitting velvet head-dress, are alone sufficient to rivet feminine interest. The head-dress is fastened by three ornaments, the settings of which are respectively: an enormous pearl, a large solitaire diamond, and a ruby surrounded by a number of large, brilliant diamonds. Among the Chinese woman's other treasures are ear-rings and a necklace of diamonds, and several clusters of pearls. Madame Wu is also the possessor of a collection of surplice-like overdresses, for wear over her short skirts—garments of the richest brocade, which are the envy of nearly all the members of the gentler sex among the lookers-on at the pageantry of official life.

But it must not be supposed that all the gaiety of dress among the diplomats is restricted to formal functions. Many of these temporary sojourners from other climes appear now and then in golf costumes that are amazing to behold. The French Ambassador, the Danish Minister, and many of the Attachés of the British, German and other Legations, are enthusiastic golfers, and although Minister Wu may occasionally be seen trudging around

COUNT QUADT, FIRST SECRETARY OF THE GERMAN EMBASSY.

the links in a flowing robe, the counterpart of which, for vividness of tint, could scarcely be seen on the comic-opera stage, he hardly presents so striking an appearance as some of the younger diplomats with their fearful and wonderful plaids and checks.

SEÑOR CALVO, COSTA RICAN MINISTER, TALKING WITH MR. J. N. LEGER, MINISTER FROM HAYTI.

The provision of the elaborate costumes necessitated by his official duties is the severest strain upon the pocketbook of a young man in the diplomatic service, and unfortunately he cannot emulate the example of some of the junior naval officers and arrange joint ownership in some of the trappings of his station. Doubtless the younger members of the Diplomatic Corps find many compensations in the adulation which is bestowed upon them. No other class of men in official life at Washington is so sought after by the hostesses of society, and owing to the proverbial feminine fondness for gold braid and bright buttons, even the officers of the American army and navy often fail to defeat these foreigners in a tourney for the favor of the beauties of the American Court.

During the past decade, many members of the Diplomatic Corps have married American girls. This is, however, seriously discouraged in the case of the Ministers by their respective governments, who contend that an envoy, having to reside, as occasion may demand, in any part of the world, should be wedded to one of his own countrywomen. Of course, this has not prevented a number of Ministerial representatives from marrying daugh-

COUNT CASSINI, RUSSIAN AMBASSADOR, STEPPING FROM HIS CARRIAGE.

SEÑOR DON MANUEL DE AZPIROZ, MEXICAN AMBASSADOR.

ters of Uncle Sam, although in almost every case the action has been closely followed by transfer to some other post. With the Secretaries and Attachés the case is different, the governments seldom, if ever, interposing objection, and a large number of international marriages of this kind have been solemnized in the United States.

SIN TEH MOO, KOREAN CHARGÉ D'AFFAIRES.

The wives of diplomats at Washington are entirely exempt from giving public receptions, which custom has prescribed as one of the duties of the ladies of the Cabinet and the wives of United States Senators, but nevertheless many of them, actuated by a fine sense of courtesy, have frequently given charming public entertainments. There have been numerous regrettable features connected with some of these functions at the diplomatic homes. Curiosity to catch a glimpse of the treasures of these transplanted homes has naturally attracted immense crowds, and in some cases the hospitality of the foreign Embassies and Legations has been grievously intruded upon.

Minister Wu had perhaps the most distressing experience. When the affable Chinaman first took up his residence in Washington, he held a grand reception, but the swarming crowds trampled upon his lawn and carried off his bric-à-brac, and now nothing could induce him to repeat the experience. Countess Cassini, who presides over the household of the Russian Embassy, was lately obliged to request the publication of a notice to the effect that her receptions were designed for her friends. At the Mexican Embassy, on one occasion, a mother took her brood of dirty children into the great ball-room, and after seating them on a divan done in French upholstery, proceeded to the dining-room and helped herself to enough cake to satisfy the ravenous youngsters. It is hardly to be wondered at, therefore, that to give a public entertainment is not regarded as a pleasure by the foreign Embassies, and the decline of this form of function has been very rapid.

I. CONSTANTIN BRUN, DANISH MINISTER. 2. MR. DE WOLLANT, RUSSIAN FIRST SECRETARY. 3. MR. CRACKANTHORPE, THIRD SECRETARY OF THE BRITISH LEGATION. 4. MR. NORMAN, SECOND SECRETARY OF THE BRITISH LEGATION.

The diplomats at Washington are great dinner-givers. Some of the most brilliant assemblages at the capital are to be found at their tables. On the other hand, there are diplomatic repasts to which all the envoys and their wives are invited which are rather dull affairs, nor is this strange when it is taken into consideration that a guest may sometimes be assigned to take down to dinner a lady with whom he has no language in common.

The members of the foreign colony are most punctilious in the observance of all the details of official etiquette. Although three days is allowed by the dictum of officialdom for the return of a first call, Ambassadors and Ministers usually return a call immediately, taking this promptitude as the most delicate possible expression of their appreciation of the visit. Not infrequently a caller at an Embassy or a Legation will find the card of the person called upon when he returns to his own home at the end of the afternoon round of visits.

SEÑOR DON MANUEL DE AZPIROZ, MEXICAN AMBASSADOR.

A grave pitfall to be eschewed by every new-comer in Washington society is found in the intricacies of social precedence based on official rank. Paltry and incredible as it may seem, grave international complications have on more than one occasion been threatened because ignorant hostesses at the national capital unwittingly assigned envoys to seats at dinner lower than their rank should have permitted.

In the social scale the President is followed by the Vice-President, and then come the Ambassadors, who, being presumed to represent the persons of their sovereigns, are disposed to yield precedence only to members of the royal family of the court or the sons and brothers of crowned heads. Even this point caused some merry complications a few years since. Lord Pauncefote claimed that his position entitled him to take precedence of every person save the President, and it was not until the venerable diplomat received a special hint from the Foreign Office at London that he consented to call on the Vice-President.

LORD PAUNCEFOTE, BRITISH AMBASSADOR, LEAVING THE RESIDENCE OF THE SECRETARY OF STATE, WITH HIS DAUGHTER.

cedence at festivities at which diplomats are hosts, but when an outsider entertains the Corps the event is usually preceded by an interchange of correspondence equal in volume to that of a big business firm, before all the guests are assigned to positions compatible with their dignity.

Finally, nations, like small boys, occasionally get in quarrels, and during these "don't speak" periods the greatest care must be exercised to prevent embarrassing occurrences at social functions at the capital. Then, too, there are Powers that have long-standing feuds which their representatives seek to perpetuate. A case in point is that of Austria and Mexico. The former government did not until a few weeks ago recognize the existence of the latter nation, and several times the Secretary of State or the Dean of the Diplomatic Corps was called upon to devise ways whereby the envoy of one country might be honored without giving offense to the other.

Following the Ambassadors, in the official list in use at the White House, comes the Secretary of State, although when the Ambassadors give functions at which he is a guest the Premier ranks even the Dean of the Diplomatic Corps. After the Secretary of State, when the regular order is observed, come the Envoys Extraordinary and Ministers Plenipotentiary and Chargés d'Affaires. It is not expected that the President shall ever call at any of the Embassies or Legations, although in the case of one or two Chief Executives this rule has not been rigidly adhered to.

Probably the diplomats are really seen to best advantage at the annual balls or receptions which some of the Embassies and Legations give in honor of their sovereigns. The greatest of these functions in recent years have been the balls given by the British Ambassador on each recurring anniversary of the Queen's birthday. Of course, there are never any tangles over problems of pre-

SEÑOR DON JUAN CUESTAS, MINISTER FROM URUGUAY, AND DON TOMAS HOWARD Y ARRIEN, FIRST SECRETARY.

The new Post Office.
United States Treasury. Capitol. New District Building. Department of Justice. New National Museum.
South end of White House. Pennsylvania Avenue. Sherman Statue. Department of Commerce

The three new buildings as seen from the roof

in obtaining suitable facilities and accommodations for their respective shares of the Federal service, and are fain, it is reported, to resort to the deprecable method of logrolling in order to gratify their legitimate desires. Washington, one feels in Washington, is the spoiled child of the republic.

The reason is not far to seek:

> "The cities are full of pride,
> Challenging each to each—
> This from her mountain-side,
> That from her burthened beach."

If the representative in Congress of a city cannot perform the Herculean feat of obtaining an appropriation for its embellishment equal to its own appreciation of its own deserts, it at least behooves him to prevent its rival city from obtaining more. The competition is thus keen. But Washington is *hors concours*. The rivalry is at bottom commercial, and Washington has no commercial pretensions. It is still strictly a political capital, with the social attractiveness for residence or for sojourn which that position gives. Alone among American cities, unless you choose to call Newport a city, it must live on its beauty, like Paris. More exclusively than Paris, for Paris is, incidentally to its political position, the first commercial city of France. Washington is analogous rather to Versailles, except that it is the plaything not of a monarch but of a nation, which here delights to celebrate itself, and which celebrates itself on so much larger a scale than that on which Louis XIV celebrated himself by how much the national resources of the United States are beyond the dreams of Colbert. They are lavished upon the capital. "The District" is the Danæ upon which Uncle Sam descends in showers of gold. It is only

SCRIBNER'S MAGAZINE

FEBRUARY, 1912

THE NEW WASHINGTON

By Montgomery Schuyler

ILLUSTRATIONS FROM DRAWINGS BY E. C. PEIXOTTO, AND PHOTOGRAPHS

THE authorization of three new department buildings, designed to be seen together, and accordingly harmonized in their architecture, is the longest single step thus far taken in the evolution of a Virginian village into a city worthy to be the capital and show-place of the second in population and the first in wealth of modern nations. (One excepts from the comparison, for different but obvious reasons, the British and the Chinese "Empires.")

He who visits Washington now after ten years, who has not seen it, say, since just after the war with Spain, finds so great a transformation that he is fain to take his bearings anew from the ancient landmarks and is relieved to find the Capitol and the Monument still predominant. Even after five years one finds the new monuments, architectural and sculptural, vying in interest with the old. But the decade is a more eligible period than the lustrum, for the purpose of comparison, because it is ten years since the Senate authorized its district committee to employ experts "for the improvement of the park system of the District of Columbia," and it is from that authorization that we may date the beginning of the New Washington.

A chief element of one's wonder is the costliness of the new erections. Probably the first thought of the average American, visiting or revisiting Washington, is that of Mrs. Carlyle's domestic at the sight of the engraving of the Sistine Madonna: "Lor', mum, how expensive!" The expenditure on all these new expanses of hewn granite or elaborated marble has been not only ungrudging but lavish. The three new department buildings which form the immediate occasion of these remarks are estimated to cost eight millions, and the official explanation of the project accurately sets forth that its costliness is not its chief distinction, since that sum has been "not infrequently exceeded by single Federal or State buildings." It is worth noting that the cost of the Library of Congress, completed in 1897, the chief national monument erected between the civil and the Spanish wars, and a marvel of economical administration in the building, was six millions. That was the last important building projected and erected in disregard of the original plan of Washington, the last before the revision and extension of that plan so as to bring it down to date and adapt it to the probable growth of the capital for still another century. It is the last likely to be so erected. The marble palaces that have been built since are all contributions to the execution of that plan—the monumental Union Station, the House office building, the Senate office building, the new National Museum, the municipal building of the District of Columbia, and the two wings along the southern building line of the Mall with the gulf between yawning for a supplementary appropriation to erect the central pavilion which is to unite them and to complete the building of the Department of Agriculture. If our republic is by no means like Cicero's in "hating private luxury," it resembles it at least in "loving public magnificence." One wonders at the ungrudging liberality with which the capital has been amplified and adorned by a legislature from which other cities find some difficulty

The New Washington (1912)

and Labor. Department of State. Washington Monument.

of the present State, War, and Navy Building.

Washington upon which these pecuniary refreshments fall with anything approaching this profusion. And one may say of the burghers of Washington, disfranchisement and all, as Virgil said of his farmers, that they would be too lucky if they only knew their own good. As it is, some of them are so ill-advised as to agitate for the commercial "booming" of the capital by the encouragement of manufactures. That would be a suicidal operation. In the first place, manufactories are unsightly and incompatible with "the city beautiful," which the whole country by its representatives in Congress assembled has shown and is showing its determination to make of the capital. From any point of view from which the city can fairly be seen as a whole, from the Potomac, say, or from the portico of Arlington House, the chimney shafts of such factories as now exist are unsightly and incongruous with the main purport and expression of the unique municipality, even the chimney shaft of so unquestionably necessary and pertinent an appanage of a political and uncommercial capital as that of the Bureau of Engraving and Printing. As Mr. Muirhead puts it, in his "America: The Land of Contrasts":

"The absence of the wealth-suggesting but artistically somewhat sordid accompaniments of a busy industrialism contributes to Washington's position as one of the most singularly handsome cities on the globe."

In the second place, the encouragement of manufactures or of any "business" beyond what is strictly incidental and accessory to the primary purpose of the place tends to deliver Washington to the competition from which it is the very condition of its prosperity and one may say the very reason of its being that it shall be delivered. It is only while Washington sits apart and aloof from the general industrial movement that no effective voice will be raised against the extraordinary privileges and immunities which are bestowed upon it in consequence of its detachment. The golden shower amounts to a mean annual rainfall of between five and six millions. The real entry of Washington into the interurban competition would startlingly reduce this precipitation and substitute aridity. The Washington "base-ball team," one of the "circenses" of the District of which the Congress, excepting in the individual capacities of its members as sympathetic playgoers, has nothing to do with defraying the expense, probably deems itself the victim of a cruel fate, but might be actuated by high policy, in maintaining a modest last or penultimate position in the competition of its respective "league." And yet it appears that there are business men in Washington who even claim the praise of public spirit in demanding that the capital shall enter the industrial competition. The story might be commended to them of that French Theodore Hook who interrupted a singer of the music-hall, successively announcing his desire to be a butterfly and his desire to be an angel, by asking him "Which?" and sternly adding: "You cannot cumulate; you must choose." The true function of the capital in respect of the other cities of the country is that of a "counsel of perfection," the furnishing of a model of municipal planning and municipal administration which will be no less useful and exemplary to the cities engaged in the industrial competition from which it is exempted because the conditions of their existence put the complete attainment of it by them out of the question.

This function Washington is coming more and more perfectly to perform, and has extraordinary and even unique advantages for performing. The first of them is, of course, the priceless advantage of having been from the first intelligently planned with prevision of its special municipal destinies. Philadelphia had, indeed, been "regularly laid out" before Washington was thought of, and by its founder. But a British tourist, John Davis by name, who visited Washington for the inauguration of Jefferson, and when there was little, indeed, of Washington to be seen, except on paper, was appreciative enough to note:

Tomb of Major L'Enfant at Arlington.
W. W. Bosworth, architect.

"From the Capitol, the President's house, and some of the important areas are to be diagonal streets, which will prevent the monotony that characterizes Philadelphia. We here perceive the superiority of taste in a travelled Frenchman over a home-bred Englishman. Penn was the founder of Philadelphia; the plan of Washington was framed by Major L'Enfant."

Washington, it is true, found Pierre L'Enfant "of an untoward disposition," but this may have been only on account of the engineer's stickling, to what the great man

Drawn by E. C. Peixotto.

Detail of the east colonnade of the Treasury Building.

Robert Mills, architect.

Portico of the Patent Office.
Robert Mills, architect.

thought an unreasonable degree, for his own notions of a capital city, although he was the only person in the councils of the new "Federal City" who had any detailed and specific notion of what a capital city was. If it be only just now that he has been appropriately commemorated by the tomb at Arlington, it is only just now, one may say, that the city of his design has earned the right to commemorate him by the execution of his design. No commemoration could be more appropriate than the erection of the engineer's tomb directly in front of the Arlington House which George Washington Parke Custis built at the beginning of the nineteenth century at the precise spot which commands the most effective bird's-eye view of the city, barring the top of the Monument and of the Capitol, and enables the best appreciation of the engineer's work. Thanks to that work it is that Washington has never had and never will have to be Haussmannized to fulfil its destiny. L'Enfant's plan fell, indeed, into neglect, fell into oblivion. From 1830 to 1900, one may say, the gist and essence of it had faded from all minds. To be sure, the Shepherd administration, of mixed memory, had recurred to the original map for the making of the streets and the embellishment by planting of the squares and circles and polygons accruing from the intersections of the original plan. These were the services for which that administration is entitled to be remembered, along with the undeniable set-offs, insomuch that it would take a very rigid and uncompromising moralist to regard the statue of Shepherd in front of the new District with the impulse of inconoclasm only. For all other purposes than those of sewering, paving, grading, and guttering, the plan vividly summarized by Mr. Muirhead as " a wheel laid upon a gridiron" (in fact, there are three superposed "wheels") had lapsed, in a single generation, from the memories of men.

And yet how effectual were these humble reclamations. Recall Dickens's account of Washington in 1842, John Tyler *consule:*

"Plough up all the roads; plant a great deal of coarse turf in every place where it ought not to be; erect three handsome buildings in stone and marble, anywhere, but the more entirely out of everybody's way the better; call one the Post Office, one the Patent Office, and one the Treasury, . . . leave a brickfield without the bricks in all central places where a street may naturally be expected; and that's Washington. . . . It is sometimes called the City of Magnificent Distances, but it might with greater propriety be termed the City of Magnificent Intentions; for it is only on taking a bird's-eye view of it from the top of the Capitol that one can at all comprehend the vast designs of its projector, an aspiring Frenchman."

The aspect of the city was essentially the same to and through the Civil War. During the war, indeed, the cupola of the Capitol was completed by the erection of the crowning figure of Freedom above the metallic simulation of lithic forms. That soaring bubble makes its unfailing effect in any distant view. But close at hand, it has the overpowering effect of an extinguisher upon the structure beneath. Particularly upon the east front, for in the view from the west the terrace added by Fred. Law Olmsted finds an excellent æsthetic function in dissembling the architectural baselessness of the crowning dome. But on the eastward front it is so plain that the dome rather crushes than crowns the substructure that the projection of the centre, for which Thomas U. Walter, the author of the dome, made a design, is still an urgent architectural need of the edifice.

The Washington that Dickens saw was the Washington that another British tourist saw twenty years later, Sir William Russell, not yet "Sir," when he came out to do the war for the *London Times* and to receive his American nickname. Revisiting it twenty years still later, in the early eighties, he was

Order of the old General Post Office.

Robert Mills, architect.

astonished to find it "by far the handsomest of American cities." And yet, during this interval there had been no addition to the architectural attractions of the capital. Nobody, then or since, counted among those attractions Mr. Mullett's State, War, and Navy Building, or General Meigs's Pension Building, of which it is traditionally reported that General Sheridan bitterly complained to its author that he had made it fireproof. The conversion of the Virginian village into the handsomest of American cities had been effected solely by the labors of the "Boss," whom one cannot too seriously blame old Washingtonians for delighting to honor.

Original design for the Washington Monument.
Robert Mills, architect.

L'Enfant himself had laid it down: "Lines or avenues of direct communication have been devised to connect the separate and most distant objects with the principal, and to preserve through the whole a reciprocity of sight." The three "principal objects" of the plan were the Capitol, the President's house, and the Washington Monument, at that time expected to take the form of an equestrian statue. The avenue which was intended to preserve "reciprocity of sight" between the first and second was Pennsylvania Avenue; between the first and third was the broad stretch of the Mall, bordered with trees and buildings; between the second and third the President's garden, or, as we say now, the White House grounds. The last alone has been maintained. The first was destroyed in the thirties, according to tradition, by the emphatic walking-stick of "Old Hickory," planted by his own hand at the spot he had determined for the cornerstone of the Treasury. The testimony of the architect of that building, Robert Mills, was explicit that the site was the President's personal selection. The selection showed how, within ten years after L'Enfant's death, a primary purpose of his plan had either been completely ignored or completely forgotten, probably the latter. In any case, the blunder is irretrievable. Pennsylvania Avenue is permanently deflected around the huge obstacle to "reciprocity of sight" between the White House and the Capitol. Equally forgotten or ignored, throughout the whole of the nineteenth century, was the primary purpose of the Mall, projected as a majestic and monumental promenade, or parade, between the Capitol and the Monument, a cisatlantic Champs Elysées on a much larger than the transatlantic scale, for L'Enfant's "Grand Avenue" is twice as long as the parked part of the Parisian promenade and four hundred feet wider. Washingtonians kept on calling it "the Reservation" without

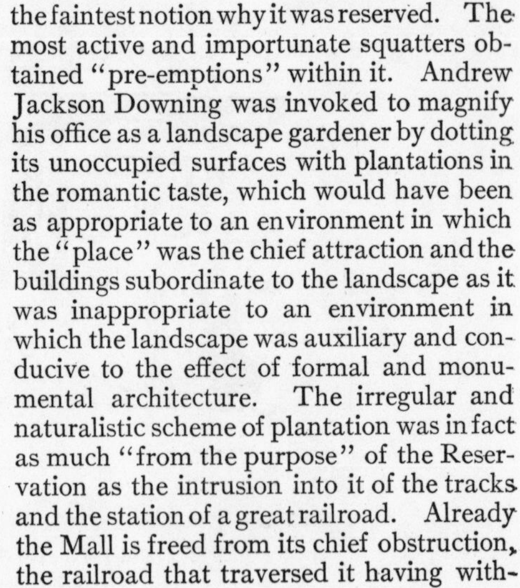

the faintest notion why it was reserved. The most active and importunate squatters obtained "pre-emptions" within it. Andrew Jackson Downing was invoked to magnify his office as a landscape gardener by dotting its unoccupied surfaces with plantations in the romantic taste, which would have been as appropriate to an environment in which the "place" was the chief attraction and the buildings subordinate to the landscape as it was inappropriate to an environment in which the landscape was auxiliary and conducive to the effect of formal and monumental architecture. The irregular and naturalistic scheme of plantation was in fact as much "from the purpose" of the Reservation as the intrusion into it of the tracks and the station of a great railroad. Already the Mall is freed from its chief obstruction, the railroad that traversed it having withdrawn to find much more suitable and dignified accommodation elsewhere, while the unfinished buildings of the Department of Agriculture and the new National Museum, on opposite sides of it, exemplify its intended use, which will be even more imposingly exemplified by the main front of the new Department of State. The three new buildings will also find one of their main uses in redeeming the triangle of which the base is the line that has been chosen for the three façades, and of which the Mall and Pennsylvania Avenue are the other two sides. In the contemplation of the commission of 1901, this triangle was destined to the buildings intended to supply the local needs of the District. Of these, the "District Building" is already in being, and is imposing by its extent and its material, a fresh and glittering white marble, if not altogether by its architecture. It is in sooth a very busy and eventful front, in which the visitor accustomed to the tamer and more reposeful aspect of the older public buildings will be apt to find that there is altogether too much going on. He will be apt to prefer the unbroken colonnade of the side to the colonnade of the front, interrupted by the three projected pavilions, which are one, if not two, too many for its extent. Even in the side he will be apt to resent the competition which is set up by the attempt to make the intercolumniations as interesting as the colonnade, and will be likely to hold that this elaboration justifies the architect of the old department buildings in relying for his effect exclusively upon his colonnades, and treating his windows as necessary evils, as mere unmodelled and unadorned rectangular holes.

We come here upon the question of the style, the "Official Style," of Washington. This may fairly be said to have been fixed not by the Georgian version of Palladian architecture, which we call "Colonial," and in which the Capitol and the White House are composed, but by the style which succeeded it, the "Greek Revival" of England, the "Style Empire" of France, which was founded on the publications of the "Antiquities of Athens." Of this style Latrobe, the second architect of the Capitol, showed knowledge, proposing, in fact, a

The Union Trust Company Building.
Wood, Donn & Deming, architects.

Photograph by Harris & Ewing.

The Masonic Temple.
Wood, Donn & Deming, architects.

New Senate Office Building, showing Union Station at foot of street.
John M. Carrère, consulting architect.

little Greek temple as the entrance to the west front, a proposition which we may be thankful was not executed. But it became really fruitful only in the hands of Latrobe's pupil, Robert Mills. He was the architect, in the late thirties, of the three original department buildings. He designed the Patent Office in the Doric of the Parthenon, the colonnade of the Treasury in the Ionic of the Erechtheum, but in the Corinthian of the General Post Office he divagated from the choragic monument of Lysicrates, the only Grecian example of Corinthian then accessible, to the examples of the Italian Renaissance. One may admire Greek architecture more than any of its derivatives, and still maintain that he was in the right in his divagation, seeing that in the engaged Corinthian order of the Post Office he attained much of the effect of the colonnade or the portico, without the necessary interference with the practical uses of a modern building which the projecting and umbrageous colonnade entails. The fact remains that Mills's Greek buildings and not his Italian building set the pattern for subsequent public architecture in Washington, and it is they which have been reverted to by the designers of the three new department buildings now authorized. The architect who brought about that result is surely entitled to a memorial in the city which he embellished. The memorial which would do most to appease his manes is, doubtless, the completion of his Washington Monument according to his design. Twice did he attempt to adorn and enliven the base of an Egyptian obelisk with Grecian architecture, once in the Bunker Hill Monument, of which he complained that the decorative architecture, omitted in execution, was essential to the effect of his design, and again, upon a much larger scale, in this Washington Monument, and was both times baffled. In Washington he might reasonably have expected that his design would be fully executed, seeing that a picture of the entire design was the basis of the appeal in which the erection of the Monument was "earnestly recommended to the favor of our countrymen," during Taylor's brief administration, by the President and Vice-President, by all the surviving ex-Presidents and ex-Vice-Presidents, and by those citizens whose names commanded the largest measure of public confidence. Without doubt the omission was a misfortune for the Monument, since the crystalline shaft, so impressive from a distance, has now nothing to repay a closer inspection. Mills, in one respect, has suffered more grievously than L'Enfant from the neglect of posterity, since the commission which rescued and extended L'Enfant's design not only did nothing for the execution of the most conspicuous of Mills's designs, but suggested another site and another plan for the patriotic Pantheon for which the peristyle of the Washington Monument purported to provide. The completion of the Monument, according to the intention of its architect, would without question be one of the notable embellishments of the Mall, when "reciprocity of sight" between the Capitol and the Monument is fully established, would be a pious recognition of services to the capital of a Washingtonian so well worthy of memory. Dumas puts into the mouth of his historical favorite, that French Alcibiades, Nicolas Fouquet, in relation to the château of Vaux le Vicomte, which excited the envy and emulation of Louis XIV, and which furnished quite its quota of hints to the Washington commissioners of 1901, words which are as applicable to the builders of Washington: "Vaux is not mine: it belongs to Levau and Le Nôtre and Le Brun," the three being respectively the architect, the landscape gardener, and the decorator of the more than royal residence. That an

Entrance of the New Union Station.

D. H. Burnham, architect.

Photograph by Harris & Ewing.

Corcoran Gallery of Art.

Ernest Flagg, architect.

Photograph by Harris & Ewing.

Carnegie Library.

Ackerman & Ross, architects.

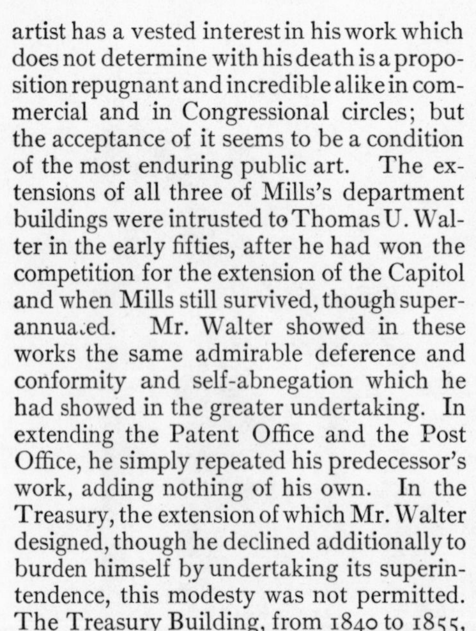

artist has a vested interest in his work which does not determine with his death is a proposition repugnant and incredible alike in commercial and in Congressional circles; but the acceptance of it seems to be a condition of the most enduring public art. The extensions of all three of Mills's department buildings were intrusted to Thomas U. Walter in the early fifties, after he had won the competition for the extension of the Capitol and when Mills still survived, though superannuated. Mr. Walter showed in these works the same admirable deference and conformity and self-abnegation which he had showed in the greater undertaking. In extending the Patent Office and the Post Office, he simply repeated his predecessor's work, adding nothing of his own. In the Treasury, the extension of which Mr. Walter designed, though he declined additionally to burden himself by undertaking its superintendence, this modesty was not permitted. The Treasury Building, from 1840 to 1855, consisted only of the shallow east wing, fronted by the Ionic colonnade which, like the painted stone centre of the Capitol, attested that it was built in the day of pecuniary small things, the columns being laid up in successive drums of sandstone. It is only within these last years that these have been superseded by monoliths of granite in conformity to the later work. What Walter did was to enclose the colonnade between powerful, pedimented pavilions containing an engaged order, "distyle in antis," of the same scale as the colonnade, to the great architectural advantage of the colonnade, and to omit the order on the other three fronts, excepting in a projecting portico at the centre and an engaged order at the ends, to the great practical advantage of the building as a place to do work in. It was not until the seventies that a violent departure was made from the examples of Mills and from the public architecture of the capital, in the design of the State, War, and Navy Building. Irretrievably misplaced as the Treasury Building had been by the ignorant

Photograph by Harris & Ewing.

The old State, War, and Navy Building.

A. B. Mullett, architect.

Photograph by Harris & Ewing.

The new District Building

Cope & Stewardson, architects.

Photograph by Harris & Ewing.

The Army War College.

Charles F. McKim, architect.

Photograph by Harris & Ewing.

The new National Museum.

Hornblower & Marshall, architects.

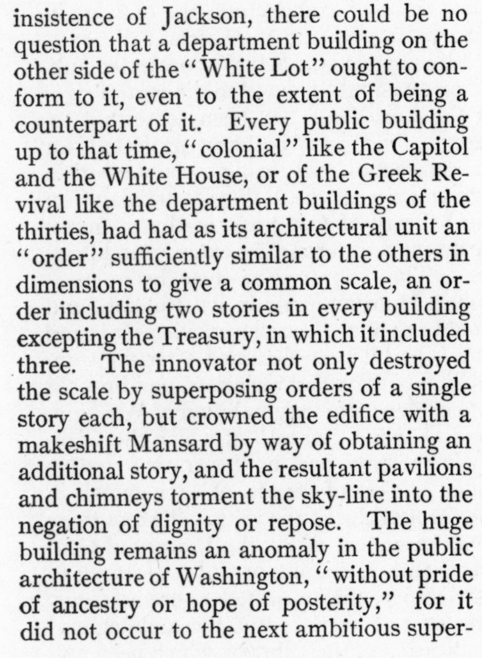

insistence of Jackson, there could be no question that a department building on the other side of the "White Lot" ought to conform to it, even to the extent of being a counterpart of it. Every public building up to that time, "colonial" like the Capitol and the White House, or of the Greek Revival like the department buildings of the thirties, had had as its architectural unit an "order" sufficiently similar to the others in dimensions to give a common scale, an order including two stories in every building excepting the Treasury, in which it included three. The innovator not only destroyed the scale by superposing orders of a single story each, but crowned the edifice with a makeshift Mansard by way of obtaining an additional story, and the resultant pavilions and chimneys torment the sky-line into the negation of dignity or repose. The huge building remains an anomaly in the public architecture of Washington, "without pride of ancestry or hope of posterity," for it did not occur to the next ambitious supervising architect, the designer of the new Post Office in the early nineties, to imitate it. He initiated another departure, this time in the Richardsonian Romanesque that then prevailed, to the current forms of which he brought nothing of his own. There is nothing in this to encourage imitation. Its sterility is the encouraging fact about it; its sterility and the circumstance that, standing where it does in "The Avenue," it compromises nothing but itself, and might be taken for one of the freaks of the private building of Washington more readily than for an example of the public architecture.

It is no wonder that these two horrible and Helotic examples of the danger of nonconformity should have sufficed for the succeeding architectural authorities, in those better days of our public architecture which are commonly dated from the "Tarsney act," allowing competitions for Federal buildings, but which really began with the appointment of a cultivated and competent

Photograph by Harris & Ewing.

The Memorial Continental Hall.

Edward Pearce Casey, architect.

Photograph by Harris & Ewing.

International Bureau of American Republics.

Kelsey & Cret, architects.

practitioner, in 1896, to be supervising architect of the Treasury, followed, in 1897, by the appointment of another architect of the same qualifications, who is in office still. One may be ever so firmly impressed with the inadequacy of classic architecture to general modern uses. He may hold ever so firmly that Greek architecture is a perfect and admirable style in which to build Greek temples, but not really available for any other use. He may insist upon the necessity of a manner of building which has a less meagre repertory both of "motives" and of details, which is more flexible and more variously and specifically expressive, and which gives more scope for the individuality and invention for which Greek architecture gives none at all. He may even both understand and sympathize with what Ruskin meant when he wrote:

"The choice of Classical or Gothic, using the latter term in its broadest sense, may be questionable when it regards some single and considerable public building; but I cannot conceive it questionable, for an instant, when it regards modern uses in general: I cannot conceive any architect insane enough to project the vulgarization of Greek architecture."

He may deplore the extension of the public architecture of Washington for any more practical purpose than the "court of honor" of a world's fair. And yet he may be compelled to admit that, for the public architecture of Washington, the case is closed, the capital is committed, and there is nothing for it but a reversion to the "official style." This is the view which the projectors of the competition for the three new buildings took, and which the successful competitors have adopted. They have welcomed the monotony which they have doubtless incurred as a refuge from the miscellany they have doubtless avoided. There is nothing in the architecture of the new buildings which smacks in the least of modernity, even of the modernity of the Beaux Arts, unless haply the interpolated attic or superpolated pediment of the Ionic Department of Justice be held to be a modern gloss, or the Roman instead of Athenian Doric of the Department of Commerce and Labor. The motive of the southern front of the Department of State is in effect the motive of the southern front of the Treasury, with the substitution of Corinthian for Ionic. It is all the architecture of the thirties and the fifties, and would have no disturbing novelties for Mills or Walter, for that matter none for Pericles or Phidias. But, doubtless, the better part has been chosen. Doubtless there are, along with the monotony, the essentials of dignity and repose which more animation and variety would have been in danger of impairing. Doubtless the new buildings carry on, in an imposing manner, on an imposing scale, and in an imposing material, almost compulsorily white marble, the tradition of the public architecture of Washington, which is, in sooth, in civil architecture, the only tradition we can be said to possess.

Elsewhere, in the actual or projected public or quasipublic new buildings, the rigor of the precedents has been somewhat relaxed. The new building projected for the Supreme Court, being a counterpart in size and site of the Italian Renaissance of the Library of Congress, is almost necessarily its counterpart in exterior architecture. The Library, as has been mentioned, is an anomaly in its situation, and would not have been placed where it is and as it is had it been designed after the commission of 1901 had reclaimed and brought into evidence the original plan of Washington. For the "wheel" of which the Capitol is the hub had no fewer than twelve radial spokes of streets, of each of which the Capitol closed the vista. Two of these spokes were cut off by the Library of Congress, and, in the interest of conformity to that edifice, the projected Supreme Court cuts off two more. But the architectural duplication of the Library, which need not, of course, exclude such improvements in detail, and even, within limits, of composition and arrangement as the designer may see his way to, will form a noteworthy addition to the attractions of Capitol Hill. The Senate and House office buildings, virtually identical in their architecture, are entirely conformable to the Capitol, if they have not much individual interest of their own. Another recent building which undoubtedly has such an interest is the Union Station, and this is sufficiently conformable, though neither its conformity nor its interest depends upon the order, which is here a negligible and omissible detail. The power of the design resides in the simplicity and the largeness of its exterior and interior

Portico of the new Department of Justice.
Donn Barber, architect.

disposition, the arch being substituted for the column as the unit of the architecture, and the arcade for the colonnade as the means of emphasizing the horizontal expanse. This is the contribution to the execution of the plan of ten years ago, made by one of the architectural members of the commission. The Lincoln Monument, reserved to the other, the lamented Charles F. McKim, and represented in his sketch as an extreme example of classicality, being in fact the periptery of a Greek temple without the cella, is still, one learns, on the knees of the gods. Meanwhile, the only executed work of the architect at the capital is the War College, which the casual visitor is liable to miss altogether, unless he be well enough advised to make his pilgrimage to Mount Vernon by the river. It is in the main an unpretentious and businesslike building of humble brickwork, which is classicized and architecturalized by a central feature at each end and on each side, an arched aperture enclosing a colossal order. The single and lonely statue in front of it indicates the War College as the most appropriate place which could be found in the capital of the American Republic for

The new Department of State Building.

Arnold W. Brunner, architect.

the imperial and somewhat elephantine gift of a statue of Frederick the Great.

The public buildings, other than Federal, which have been erected to the westward of the White House are attractive additions to the New Washington. The situation, purpose, and ownership of these dispensed the architects, it should seem, from adhesion to the official style imposed upon the government. Not all of the architects have lived up to their privileges. One is moved particularly to congratulate the architect of the Corcoran Art Gallery on his success in showing that the classical effect can be attained, the effect of "magnitude, uniformity, and succession," in an "astylar" front which does not contain a single classical member, even while condoling with him on the imposed necessity of annexing the curvilinear and excrescential structure which so evidently does not "belong." The Memorial Continental Hall, which we owe to the piety of the Daughters of the American Revolution, was plainly indicated as "Colonial," and the indication might with advantage have been even more strictly followed. Similarly, the Bureau of American Republics offered an opportunity of paying a graceful tribute to our Southern little sisters of "Latin" traditions by a much stronger suggestion than the exterior architecture offers of the Spanish Renaissance of the sixteenth century, though to be sure this "leading" has been followed in the interior patio, and to a very attractive result. But of all three buildings it may fairly be said that they execute variations upon the "style officiel" within permissible limits, and that the variety they attain is not gained at the expense of any quality more important than variety.

With much of the recent commercial building of Washington one has to quarrel upon the ground that it is too strictly in the "style officiel," that it comes altogether too closely into competition with the edifices which are national possessions. Directly envisaging the north front of the Treasury, for example, are two banks in granite, with "orders" effectively of the scale of that monument, designed with academic accuracy and scholarly sensibility and which one would be glad to meet almost anywhere else, but cannot help wishing away from where they are. Just to the north, again, is an office building in white marble of which the order outscales that of the public buildings, old or new, since it includes five complete stories against their maximum of three. This strikes one as a kind of architectural lèse majesté, that the commercial hustler should thus domineer over the official edifices. It is related of a certain pope of the Renaissance that he enjoined architects and owners, on pain of the major excommunication, or equivalent penalty, from presuming to put a pediment on any building but a church. There were popes of the period whose deliverances ex cathedra on questions of taste are accepted by posterity as at least as infallible as their deliverances on questions of "faith and morals," and many moderns visiting Washington will sympathize with the prohibition and wish that it might be extended to the use of the colossal order by private and unauthorized persons, intent only on their singular lucre and profit. One would at any rate like to see the commercial competition with the official architecture prevented by a permanent injunction against using both the style and the material of the public monuments. White marble and the colossal order might very well be reserved for public uses. The Masonic Temple, besides being in truth a quasi-public building, evades competition by its humble material, which is only baked clay, and escapes censure by the singular suitability to its site of the motive of its truncated end. Likewise the New Willard, both by its detail and by its renunciation of marble or granite in favor of a modest limestone. The architect of the Hibbs Building is entitled to congratulation for showing that an effective commercial front may be attained without the use of an order, and that of the pretty little office alongside, although his front is garnished with an order, for employing "such a little one" as by no means to challenge the government architecture on its own ground. But upon the whole, the recent commercial architecture of Washington shows that there are not one but many architects "insane enough to project the vulgarization of Greek architecture," many of the mind of Clough:

> "I from no building, gay or solemn,
> Can spare the shapely Grecian column."

The architectural Bacon would surely "note no deficience" of Grecian columns if another were never to be set up in Washington. The three Grecian orders are already worked nearly to the limit of their capacity and are likely to be overworked, and the monotony which is the defect of their quality to degenerate into tiresomeness, in the official employment in which no eligible substitute for them has been suggested. It were greatly to be wished, in the interest of the New Washington, that they might be confined to that employment, if necessary, by some secular proceeding analogous to the papal injunction.

At this suggestion, naturally, all Anglo-Saxondom will be up in arms. The right of a man to do as he will with his own, so commonly held to be the palladium of our liberties, is assumed to be invaded if he be not permitted, in his office building, department store, or what not, to copy or caricature the public monuments. This impatience of restraint is often said to be an expression of "democracy." It is not so. It is the voice of an exclusively Anglo-Saxon individualism. Building restrictions are quite as rigid in Paris under the republic as they were under the monarchy or the empire. When the question is of the beauty of a capital which largely lives by its beauty, collectivism must prevail over individualism, and, after a civic education of some three centuries, this is recognized by the Parisian, and the necessary sacrifices of his individual preferences are cheerfully incurred. Why should it not be equally recognized by the Washingtonian? The beauty of the capital is a national object, but it is still more a local object. If Washington were to relapse to the condition described by Dickens, the first sufferers would be the business men of the District, who would also presumably be the first protestants against any curtailment of their right to build as they like. "The condition of our nature is such that we buy our blessings at a price." The Washingtonians can no more than other people eat their cake and have it. To have as a municipal partner an uncle of boundless resources and boundless liberality to divide your bills and even to advance your share of them, is a happiness that is worth paying for in some renunciation of your own devices and desires. Washington pays for it even to the extent of disfranchisement. It has its reward in being better governed than any American municipality of which the inhabitants govern themselves. Of what other municipality is the local taxpayer so sure of receiving a dollar's worth for his dollar? In fact, the Columbian taxpayer receives, through the liberality of his uncle, two dollars' worth. The budget of the District is highly satisfactory, the debt, in part a legacy from the days of the questionable Boss, is in process of steady extinction at the rate of a million a year. Largely, thanks, no doubt, to the moderation and forbearance of the benevolent uncle who is a principal creditor, and still more largely to his own contributions, the current revenues considerably exceed the current expenses. In return, the District does fulfil its function of a model for other municipalities in all points of municipal housekeeping. It is thirty years since the experiments of "Captain Greene, of the Engineers," now General Greene, upon street pavements inured to the benefit not only of Washington but of all the cities, for not one has failed in some measure to profit by them. The "engineer commissioner" of the District government has ever since worthily represented the corps to which the country owes so much, in peace and in war. The present engineer commissioner has made the liberality of the general government the basis for an argument that taxpayers who contribute so largely to the prosperity of the District are entitled to something more for their money than mere maintenance, that they are entitled to see monumental betterments in progress. He accordingly has urged an annual appropriation "for permanent works of improvement," beginning in 1913 with $1,230,000, and increasing annually thereafter by not less than $100,000. The proposed use of the appropriations is the execution of such large designs as the reclamation of the Anicostia Flats and their conversion into a public park, the extension of the improvement of the Rock Creek Valley, the improvement of the harbor front by means of public wharves, and the completion of the park system—all works of embellishment as well as of utility. To these might be added the provision of such a special or supplementary supply of water as will enable the execution of the design of the commission of 1901 for a profuse use of that element for decorative purposes. The work which should answer that requirement would have no historical parallel since the aqueduct of Marly.

But it is upon the private still more than the public building that the general aspect of any city must depend, and the engineer commissioner has sought for the passage of a law that would mark a long stride in the direction of a collective control of individual rights. This will authorize the commissioners to designate such streets as may seem to them fit as "Class A" streets, preferring them for improvement in their discretion, and imposing "such requirements as to height of buildings, materials of construction, and architectural design as shall secure, in the judgment of such commissioners, the beautiful and harmonious appearance, as viewed from the public streets, of all structures to be erected or altered on the land to which such restrictions shall apply." The proviso is that the owners of nine-tenths of the property concerned shall convey to the commissioners the easements which will enable the enforcement of the special restrictions, taking compensation for the easements less deductions for the benefits. It is left to the discretion of the commissioners whether the "submerged tenth" shall be excepted from their operations of embellishment or included in them after proceedings for condemnation; all in complete disregard of the palladium of our liberties, the right of the individual to do as he likes with his own—the grand old principle that the Anglo-Saxon's house is his castle for offensive as well as for defensive purposes.

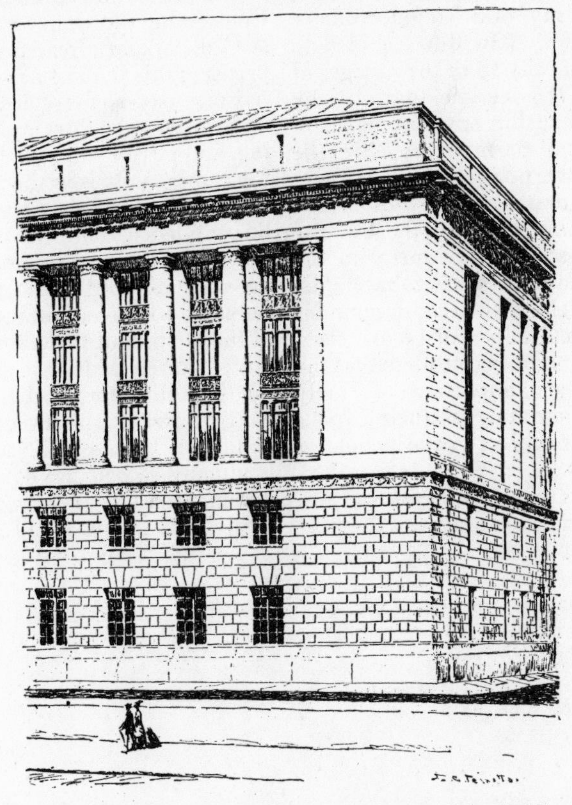

South-west corner of the Department of Commerce and Labor Building

York & Sawyer, architects.

The enactment into law of this project would probably mark the greatest triumph of collectivism, as applied to civic æsthetics, in the legislation of any Anglo-Saxon community. It would be an effective set-off to Matthew Arnold's famous example of the triumph of individualism in the establishment of a truss-factory on "the finest site in Europe." Washington also has had its triumphs of individualism. Some fifteen years ago a private owner, doing as he liked with his own, erected a stark twelve-story apartment house in a quiet residential region—"N.-W." It was consolatory to remark that the erection, at a time when a twelve-story building meant a good deal more than it would mean now, aroused a sense of pain and outrage by no means confined to Washington itself, and a general hope was expressed that if this malefaction could not be undone, at least some means might be found of preventing its repetition. The means have been found. Under the complicated and minute building regulations of the District another "Cairo" would apparently be impossible. Even here, however, one must note the curious Anglo-Saxon prejudice according to which it is necessary to allege some pretext of sanitation or safety from fire in order to prohibit an outrageous erection. But what real necessity is there for thus whipping the cosmetic devil around the utilitarian stump? Why resort to any subterfuge? An offender against the auditory or the olfactory nerves of his neighbors can be called to account. Why not an offender against their optical sensibilities? Why should a racket or a stench be justiciable and an eyesore not? Why, in a word, should not the official guardians of the "beauty and harmony" of the capital be clothed with the powers necessary to perform their function, with the powers, say, of a Roman ædile or of a French prefect, and thus enabled to protect the community from the ravages of individualism? It is certain that only by the lodgement of such a power somewhere can beautiful and harmonious cities be made, and that the power would be more safely lodged with the authorities of the District of Columbia than with those of any city dependent for its government on the suffrages of all its adult male inhabitants. Practically, the right of eminent domain inherent in the community can be exercised whenever the community considers that the object is of sufficient importance. Surely the beauty and harmony of their capital should be such an object to the people of the United States.

This view seems to be making its way into the minds of the representatives of the people in Congress assembled. It is noteworthy and encouraging that, after many years, an "art commission" has been authorized and appointed for the Federal building of the capital, including the surviving architect-member of the commission of 1901. Considering the Congressional, which is to say the popular, dread and distrust of "expertise," this is a signal victory for "collectivism." It is true that the powers of this body seem to be thus far limited to answering, and possibly to asking, questions. But the camel's nose is in the tent. If the commission continues to commend itself to public confidence, there is every reason to hope that its powers will be enlarged to include a permanent and salutary check upon the public if not also upon the private building of the District of Columbia. With the enlarged powers which are also to be expected for the authorities of the District, it is not wildly unreasonable even to hope that the end of the twentieth century may see what is already recognized as "the handsomest city in America," recognized as the handsomest city in the world.

The Hibbs Building (J. H. De Sibour, architect) and its little neighbor (Paul J. Pelz, architect).

The Capital of Our Democracy (1902)

HALF-TONE PLATE ENGRAVED BY R. C. COLLINS.

"ALL AMERICA ON AN EVEN FOOTING."

THE CAPITAL OF OUR DEMOCRACY.

BY HENRY LOOMIS NELSON.

WITH PICTURES BY CHARLOTTE HARDING.

HOW is one to describe the distinguishing trait of a city, and especially of an American city? It is a sufficiently difficult task in the Old World, where traits have run down from generation to generation through many centuries, and have had time to set. Even there, however, a city must be picked to pieces if one is to reach a satisfactory conclusion as to its potent characteristic, an analysis likely to lead to much confusion. There are the St. Antoine quarter, and the Faubourg St. Germain, and the Boulevard St. Michel, and the Boulevard Montmartre, and the Boulevard Bois de Boulogne, and the Avenue Malesherbes. There are Lombard street, and Park Lane, and St. John's Wood, and Chelsea. And as it is thus with the most finished of man's municipal products, how much more difficult is it to find the current of potency in the rushing tides of a city which has not yet settled down to its distinct and separate self! How can Boston, for example, be differentiated from other American cities? Has it a dominant current? In one quarter of the city it is borne in upon the wayfarer that such a current is to be found in the Harvard nobility, or, as it was recently expressed by a scion of one of the university's old families, writing of another scion, who was dead, the "nobility of Massachusetts." The perfect specimen of this nobility is as fine in character and tone as any in the world, as fine as England's best, but intensely American and a trifle self-conscious. "We have had a charming morning, sir," said a candidate for governor of the State, who was attempting to fulfil his promise to his party leaders and to win the friendship of a strong and influential man of the people who had complained of the candidate's haughty bearing—"a charming morning together, and hereafter, if I fail to recognize you when we meet in the street, I beg you to attribute my apparent lapse in courtesy to my near-sightedness, and not to my consciousness of the difference in our social positions." Naturally, when we are among such an insistent aristocracy, the whole town takes its tone from the pure blue of its, at least present, status.

One does not go down to India Wharf for the purpose of tracing its origin. However, when one does find one's way to the shipping, the leather, and the wool and cotton parts of the town, one discovers a stream as puissant and even as domineering in its way as that which becomes the social back-water in the neighborhood of the State-house. In the end we are likely to be confused between the phenomena of the wharves and Quincy market and those of Beacon street, so that we cannot definitely say, at last, whether Boston is chiefly commercial or ancestral, busy or fashionable or intellectual, whether

HALF-TONE PLATE ENGRAVED BY H. C. MERRILL.

A PUBLIC RECEPTION AT THE WHITE HOUSE.

the Harvard "eleven" or the Boston "nine" stands on the pinnacle of the city's greatness. Eventually we shall conclude that neither one nor the other, neither nobility nor trade, is the sole element of Boston's atmosphere; the finer elements are mixed with commerce in such considerable proportions that the intellectual and the spiritual may also thrive; but we shall, furthermore, see that the various social strata are definitely marked and easily distinguishable. Here we have an American city, somewhat self-conscious and self-centered, like the nobility of Massachusetts, but American emphatically—the New England Boston. Of all the cities of the country, this is the one which most nearly has been built by the transplanted English race, and developed by it in the spirit of English custom and tradition. An American city it is, but it is not America. Its most glittering life is not democratic, although highly satisfactory to its participants and gratifying to the stranger.

It is more American, however, than New York, perhaps, for not so many of its people pass their days in making money that they may pass their evenings and their next days in spending it in the public gaze. It possesses an atmosphere of homes to which its people retire after business hours, and where they may sometimes be found during business hours. Most Bostonians have the domestic traits of the middle-class English—traits which have stamped themselves with much distinctness upon all that part of the country which lies outside of our cosmopolis, and even there—in the Ninth Ward especially—they may also be found in their pristine virtue.

These remarks about Boston are intended as an introduction to a short study of Washington. One can speak of the New England capital as an American city; but Washington is the city of America. One is a bit of America, with its local eccentricities and its racial virtues—a city to be proud of: the other is all America; and if the traditional book-writing foreigner wishes to study us as we are, and has not time to study us thoroughly, let him try to catch glimpses of us in Washington. There, at least, he will find the life of the country gathered into a municipal lake of no great dimensions, but fed from nearly all our national, though not always native, sources; as the streams flow into the pond they mingle with a fair degree of amiability, although one may nevertheless discern, on the surface, proofs and indications of the variety in their origins.

Notwithstanding the fact that Washington may be called the city of America, it differs materially from every other American city. Leaving out of consideration, for the moment, the political activities of the capital and of the men who go there for the purpose of engaging in them, politics being, of course, the reason for the city's existence, Washington is busy with nothing that absorbs the minds and occupies the energies of the typical American city. It has so little commerce that that little is an unknown quantity. No one born in it, and having his way to make in the world, finds an opportunity for beginning a business career in his native city. The lazy life along the river-front is about the same to-day that it was twenty-five years ago. The same grass continues to push up between the same large cobblestones in the streets of the port of Georgetown. Even the retail shops are only recently shaking off a rusticity which, a few years ago, made Baltimore the shopping district of the more particular dames of the capital.

HALF-TONE PLATE ENGRAVED BY R. C. COLLINS.

"A SPORT AMONG HER KIND."

Mark the tone of the American city typified in Boston, and note the difference between it and Washington. The basis of our ordinary city life is commerce. The day is active with the work of money-getting; but with the end of it, and the return of evening, trade nearly ceases, dribbling out through the retail quarters, and the Americans go home. With most of them, happily, trade is carried on for the comforts and delights of life, although it is inevitable, in an energetic and commercial age and among an enterprising people, that many, and they are, unhappily, an increasing number, should live for the delights of trade. But, in general, at the end of the American day the office and counting-rooms are closed, the lamps are lighted, and the head of the family dozes comfortably over the evening newspaper in the presence of a delighted family, or of that portion of it which is not seeking joys outside; or he is himself enjoying his family and his friends. He is content among his own people, although he realizes the existence of a local nobility,—not American merely, simply human,—curiously composed and still more curiously recruited. Usually it and its serious absorbing play amuse him. Sometimes they are forced upon his overstrung nerves by wife and daughters. Occasionally an under-educated and wasteful son reminds him that none of his own fruitful games of chance demand so much capital as the useless enterprises of the idle. Sometimes he meets the candidate for governor, and is angry because, say what the candidate may, the plain citizen believes that consciousness of social rank makes its victim blinder than the most serious case of myopia. On the whole, however, he is much prouder of the importance he has earned than the ordinary descendant in this country can possibly be of his ancestor. The life of the real American city is summed up usually in a phrase which most honest people like to avoid, so soiled by cant is it, but which is expressive.

Outside of business the life of the American is a "home life," and in this phrase are included his social ceremonies and functions as well as his domestic intimacies and repose.

The life of our cities, which is not characteristically American, but simply human, has been well described, by one of the cleverest of American social philosophers, as simian. The local aristocracy puts up its bar, and no one can get over it except by jumping. Commerce and gainful professions, however, are the bases of the busy aristocracy as they are of our peaceful "home life," and therefore the dynamos and motors, the boilers and engines, the wires and wheels, of our prosperity and happiness, our work and our play, our comforts and our luxuries, are pretty prominent in all our American cities.

If Washington is not like the typical American city, how, then, can it be the city of America, the one city above all others in the land where the stranger can most satisfactorily study the national traits? If its people are not bubbling over with boiling energy; if it is not shaken with the national moral fever and ague, one day burning with the heat of a "boom," and another day shaking with the chill of a panic; if most of its men are not struggling for money all day, and rushing home to slippers and rest at evening; if the wives and daughters of many of the more successful of these hunters for wealth are not vain seekers after social distinction; if the idle American nobility is not dominating in its society, as it is in our other American cities—why is life in Washington characteristically American? Because it is all America on an even footing, and all America in repose, with time to be idle. It is America not engaged in making its living or its fortune.

This is, in a way, the city of successful America—of America that has arrived. It is American fruitage, not the richest and best, doubtless, but its average flavor is much finer than that of the cities and towns and rural neighborhoods where the successes have been wrought. The men who go to Washington are fair specimens sorted from the products of the whole country. Their wives are sometimes their equals and often their superiors. As to their daughter, she will be an extraordinary American girl, a sport among her kind, who, if she be caught young enough, will not take full advantage of all the opportunities she desires, will not speedily acquire, for example, if she have the taste, all the graciousness or the ungraciousness, all the civilities or all the impertinences, all the charms or all the folly and boorishness, of what we vaguely call society.

HALF-TONE PLATE ENGRAVED BY T. SCHUSSLER.

A COUNTRY WOMAN.

HALF-TONE PLATE ENGRAVED BY S. DAVIS.

"JUST AS SHE HAS SEEN HER CARELESS HUSBAND WEAR HIS OVERCOAT."

How quickly these American buds born and reared in soils remote from the haunts of society learn the ways of the town, as they used to say in Jane Austen's time! Does Washington forget, I wonder, that chit of a Western girl, a girl from the real West, daughter of a man thrown hastily and unexpectedly into the Senate? She was as fresh and hardy as the breezes and firs of her mountains, and all her notions of etiquette and self-composure among the great were to be found in the social code of the mining-camps. But in a year, native wit and keenness and some judicious novel-reading aiding her, she became as sophisticated as a lady of the republican court need be.

Hurrying into the drawing-room of the wife of a cabinet officer rather late, unknown and apologetic, she was received by the woman of the house with a rudeness that is sometimes witnessed in Washington—generally characterizing the women whose husbands have lifted them up, and who consequently have not been obliged to fit themselves into their environment, to mold their tempers and talents to the sinuosities of society.

"It is very disagreeable to be obliged to waste every Wednesday afternoon receiving everybody who has a mind to come," said the grand dame.

"Oh, but fancy, Mrs. X——, how much pleasure your polite hospitality gives every one who is obliged to come," chirped the young thing, blowing swiftly and quietly out of the room as she had blown in.

There was the young matron, a year off the plantation, too, who learned so quickly the devious ways of *les femmes rangées*.

"Do you not know the lady on my left?" dashed the man who took her in to dinner.

Now, the young matron was smarting under the loss of a cook who, in the language of the law of labor, had been persuaded.

HALF TONE PLATE ENGRAVED BY S. M. NORTHCOTE.

"A SOILED NEGRO WAITER WHO BRUSHES THE CRUMBS . . . WITH THE FLAT OF ONE HAND."

"I know who she is," she replied. "She called on my cook the other day, and my cook returned the call."

The young American, girl or boy, is apt enough at all the daily doings of society; their influence counts for something, too, especially where riding horses, chasing paper, driving golf- or tennis-balls, or dancing are the joys of the hour. There is, on account of them, a certain raciness and flavor of individuality in Washington that, for pure liberty, can be compared only with the conduct and speech of the most self-selected and unrefined society of the metropolis, while, for other qualities, it is as free from taint as the primmest of New England "sugar eats." But these youngsters were to have been anticipated in the abodes of gaiety; the marvel is that so many of them settle down to five-o'clock-tea tastes, to intellectual pursuits, to evenings at the Naval Observatory, to eager discussions with the learned scientists of the Museum of Natural History and the Smithsonian and the Geological Survey. I do not refer now to the learned lady who read the proof-sheets of a great history as her maid did her hair in the morning, but to the young woman who came from a wheat-farm and married an entomologist in order that she might help him in his in-

HALF-TONE PLATE ENGRAVED BY C. W. CHADWICK.

"A FINER TASTE IN DRESS."

HALF-TONE PLATE ENGRAVED BY C. SCHWARZBURGER.

"EVEN A CONGRESSMAN IS DEAR TO HER."

vestigations, and to the other young woman, fresh from a salt fishing-town, who took lessons in constitutional law at the Columbian Law School in order that she might be a worthier companion for her coming husband, whose practice, at that time, was largely in dispossession proceedings for the collection of arrears of rent.

A characteristic which one encounters in Washington, say in a hotel parlor after dinner, is decidedly and delightfully American. It is the unconsciousness, on the part of those who are never called into the inner social circle, of the existence of the inner social circle. The good people do not know that there are any social strata—that, for example, there breathes any man or woman who would not be delighted to receive the wife of any ex-President or of the congressman from Tombstone.

HALF-TONE PLATE ENGRAVED BY J. TINKEY.

"HONEST WOMEN WEAR DELAINES."

To their minds, fed on the Declaration of Independence, the whole of officialdom, at least, are created equal. Surroundings are accidental. The woman who has her own house is fortunate, but the boarding-house parlor is on the same plane.

"I went in and sat with the President and his lady last evening," said the wife of a congressman who had just come on from a little manufacturing town. She was addressing a woman from her own State, the wife of a senator, a perennial senator, whose twelve years at the capital had made his wife an old Washingtonian.

"Yes? How charming! Take your knitting?" asked the adept.

"No; but I might as well. We sat around the grate in the library and had cider. Don't you like her?"

"I never met her."

"Never met her?"

"No. She does n't know any of my friends; no one knows her. She lived in a boarding-house, I believe, when her husband was in Congress. Why should I bother about her?"

"Ma'am," replied the other, rising in freeborn majesty—"ma'am, I 'm shocked that any American woman can speak thus of her

HALF-TONE PLATE ENGRAVED BY R. C. COLLINS.

"AFTER DINNER."

President's wife. Not bother about her, indeed—the first lady of the land!"

Here spoke the native woman who, some day, will learn that the adept's disdain resulted from the failure of her husband to secure from the despised President the cabinet office at which he aimed. The fault of the capital is perhaps a trifle too much adulation of well-placed women for personal and social qualities which they do not possess, and for the attainment of which their placing occurred a little too late in life. We will not call this tendency snobbish; it is rather the expression of a sublime faith in the democracy which selects, and the dazzlement wrought upon the ingenuous by gilded heights, even if it be the gilding of the setting sun.

When the new congressman's wife takes possession of her hotel sitting-room and bedroom she is at home. When she makes her first appearance at a White House reception, she is sure that she belongs to the court circle. If she be a city woman who has suffered at home from a consciousness that her social rank was not equal to her own merits or her husband's success in the world, she now keenly enjoys the sense of having jumped the barrier which has heretofore prevented the realization of her ambition. She even looks forward to a triumphant return to her old home, to a time when dinner-gowns will be one of her husband's problems, and when she will no longer be publicly advertised as out of society by the announcements of the society reporters that she is in. If she be a country woman, one who has been bred in real equality with her neighbors, it is impossible to disturb the placid serenity of her mind. She is very likely to be one of the finest types of American womanhood. Her house has been an open one; all the good women of the neighborhood have been her associates. The only difference between her and her acquaintances has been that of worldly circumstance. The wife of the honest mechanic or laborer is welcome to her tea-table if she is outwardly respectable, and especially if she is a member of her own church. She has her intimates, naturally,

HALF-TONE PLATE ENGRAVED BY W. G. WATT.

"WHEN THEY ACCOMPLISH SILK PURSES, THEIR WIVES ARE ENTITLED TO BROCADES."

HALF-TONE PLATE ENGRAVED BY J. W. EVANS.

"THEY TALK . . . ABOUT THE CLOTHES WORN BY THE GRAND DAMES OF THE REPUBLIC."

who can afford to dress as well as she does, and she would not for the world embarrass a poor neighbor who has only a mohair dress by bidding her come, to her shame, among the silks and satins. I have heard of a woman like this who shocked the wife of the commanding officer of a military post by going directly from her husband's quarters to make a ceremonious call on the wife of the commissary sergeant, who dwelt in the quarters set apart for non-commissioned officers.

When such a woman reaches Washington, her husband having recently been chosen a member of Congress, or maybe appointed head of a bureau, no one, to her thinking, is her social superior; and her mind is as simple, straightforward, and unclouded with doubts as to her own place in the world as it is as to the place of her old schoolmate who married the leading "hack gentleman" of the village. She realizes, of course, that Martha's husband is not so important a figure as her own husband, the lawyer and politician, and that Martha cannot wear such fine clothes as she possesses, and, therefore, cannot go where good clothes are essential to an easy mind and easy manners; but, notwithstanding this difference between her old friend and herself, one is just as good as the other, and no one has the right to look down upon either. Not that she is so lacking in acumen that she misses the distinction between individuals. She knows that this woman has more intellect, or more cultivation, or more manner, or greater beauty, or a finer taste in dress, or a keener moral sense, or more lovable qualities, than that one; and she is quite well aware that a reception at the White House, especially one that is made brilliant by uniforms, is a much finer function than any strawberry festival that was ever held by the First Congregational Society.

She knows good clothes, too, when she sees them, and she enjoys them as women have enjoyed them ever since the evolution of the ball-dress began with the elementary fig-leaf; although she is apt to fear, at first sight of a ball-dress, that the process of development has not yet gone far enough. In a word, she likes the pageant, and she feels that she is just as much a part of the show as the wife of the dean of the diplomatic corps, or the Austrian hussar who wears over his shoulder a brilliant jacket into the sleeves of which he never thrusts his arms, carrying it just as she has seen her careless husband wear his overcoat. A thousand details of splendor and luxury please her in this new life, and she would certainly have Martha there to see it all and to enjoy it with her, were it not for her old friend's foolish persistency in being ashamed of her unfashionable clothes. In her second session she will have Martha's girls at Washington, and she will enjoy being a chaperon for the first time in her amiable and worthy exis-

HALF-TONE PLATE ENGRAVED BY WILLIAM MILLER.

"MEN OF MARK IN THEIR COMMUNITIES."

tence. A chaperon! She had never heard of the institution when she left her rural home, but she comes to approve of it in time, and to insist upon it, in her talk at all events; for among her old neighbors her new knowledge is the cachet of her new life and her richer experience. And how soon the young women will bloom and fill with fragrance an atmosphere far above the head of their kindly friend, the friend of their mother, to whose big house, at the end of the village street, they used to go for sweets and other hospitality, and whom they have always called "aunt," the kindly term for one from whom children are supposed to have expectations. They will learn to meet the demands of polite intercourse, but she never. If she live in Washington for twenty years she will still be frank and truthful. It was she who wrote on the back of the card of a senator's wife who had called at a boarding-house on her and other "congressional ladies": "I have got a headache; Mrs. Brown is in the bath-tub; and Mrs. Smith is dead." It was she, too, who glided up to the daughter of a Secretary of State, who was pouring tea in her own house, and said, with her sweetest smile: "I really forget, miss, whether your father is on the Republican or Democratic side of the house." "Oh," was the quick reply, "my father is not in Congress; he is only in one of the departments." And the poor woman was so sorry that she had injured the feelings of the young girl, such a nice young girl, too, that she talked about it for a week. The longer she dwells in Washington, the greater will be the liking felt for her by those whose intimacies have generally been with the sophisticated; but she will always wear "high-necked" gowns to dinner, although, in time, she will realize that the other women at the feast are not necessarily indecent.

The hotel in Washington introduces many an American woman into the vestibule of social life. There used to be boarding-houses in Washington, but they changed their names, when they began to be patronized by congressmen, and now call themselves hotels. In many instances it is an easy change to make, for it may be effected by a sign at the portal, a transfer of the dining-room from the basement to the parlor, a few round tables in place of one long one, and a soiled negro waiter who brushes the crumbs from the table with the flat of one hand into the palm of the other, instead of a colored waitress who shakes them from the cloth after the meal is finished. If the former boarding-house keeper and present hotel proprietor desires to furnish corn-bread to Southern patrons she calls her inn "The Calhoun"; if she prefers to cook buckwheat-cakes for New-Englanders she calls it "The Webster." Thus are the traditions of great statesmen preserved at the nation's capital. But these small inns are not the centers of the gay life which is so dear to the hearts of the women who long for social delights. The large hotels that have old names and parlors furnished in the richest hotel manner are the true abodes of kindergarten fashion. The

HALF-TONE PLATE ENGRAVED BY G. M. LEWIS.

"SPEND THEIR DAYS IN THE SENATE GALLERY."

old boarding-house, indeed, was a more "social place," to quote an eminent feminine authority, than the new small hotel, for the old-fashioned boarding-house had at least a parlor, where there was conversation after dinner, and where a lady, so inclined, might give a tea, at which, as a matter of course, the landlady and her daughter always assisted, and to which all the other "lady guests, and as many of the gentlemen as were gallant," were cordially invited.

The life of a Washington hotel of the first social importance is marvelous to fresh eyes from the country. There, in the dining-room, one meets the American statesman and his family—that is, the general run of them. No one will be inclined to sneer at the inexperienced person who enters the great apartment for the first time, at the dinner-hour, with a feeling of awe, if he has had the good fortune to do so himself in his youth and before his ideals were shattered. The writer distinctly remembers the reverence with which he regarded his two accidental commensals at a little round table in the Riggs House dining-room on his first visit to Washington. The future Speaker of the House of Representatives, who lived at the hotel, stopped to greet them on his way out of the room, and they actually called him John, while he asked them to visit him at his rooms, and assured them that they need not go through the formality of sending up their cards. I have always understood, since that impressive moment, why the American woman, on her introduction to this company of the great and its families, believes that she then sees about her all the splendor of intellect and all the grace and courtliness that her country, and therefore the world, can display. She has the deepest admiration for the men who carry on the government, for her husband and his comrades who work our institutions; but she has no knowledge of the institutions themselves, and very little regard for some of them, while she has long outgrown the old notion about republican simplicity.

It is perfectly clear to her that anything that is good ought also to be splendid. It is in the established order of things that women dress themselves according to their condition in life. Honest women wear de-

HALF-TONE PLATE ENGRAVED BY J. TINKEY.

"SHE MAY GO TO WASHINGTON WITH THE HEARTY AND FRANK OUTSPOKENNESS OF THE CHURCH FAIR,

HALF-TONE PLATE ENGRAVED BY J. W. EVANS.

"EVENING AFTER EVENING AT THE THEATER."

laines so long as their husbands have delaine purses, but when they accomplish silk purses, their wives are entitled to brocades. The republic, to her mind, is not what it was when simplicity was a virtue, and why not live up to the new conditions? She would have our ambassadors and ministers in uniform; she would order army officers to wear their gold lace at all times; she would fill the White House with flunkies. To her the President, no matter what his politics or hers, is an object of adoration and adulation. He cannot be so awkward that he does not shine in her eyes as the prince of fine gentlemen, and his wife is always the "first lady of the land," be she a "home body" or a dowdy, or, in reality, a woman of commanding talent, as she more than once has been. Even a congressman is dear to her, and she will quote as a statesman a representative who is an accidental bit of political flotsam teetering on the shore of success, seeing little difference between him and the venerable senator who has risen to leadership by sheer force of ability and character; for is not a congressman one of the nation's chosen? A fine trait, perhaps, this adoration and adulation of the nation's servants! Some day, when the broader-minded, deeper-thinking woman begins to show signs of losing that blind faith in public mankind which is now so amiably accepted by the lords and masters, these latter will awaken to the value of genuine feminine respect, and then we private citizens may have occasion to be grateful for the trait which now often amuses us, because the dread of losing it will then inspire the politician to endeavor to deserve what is now so freely and generously given. Perhaps the

HALF-TONE PLATE ENGRAVED BY C. W. CHADWICK.

AND QUIT IT WITH THE PURR OF THE DINNER-PARTY."

safety and preservation of our best traditions lie in the mistaken notion, entertained by good women, that most public men are loyal to the pure republic. Perhaps when the ideals of the republic are seen in all their beauty and comprehended by women, the men will understand that they must return to their loyalty or forfeit the homage of the fireside which, where it is deserved, broadens into respect. But the stamp of our times is certainly not knowledge of our political institutions, and the women who control and embellish the official society of Washington would set up a regal establishment at once, even if Congress could not be prevailed upon to appropriate more than enough for the purchase of cotton-velvet robes for the monarch, and silver-gilt coronets for the "ladies of the cabinet." And this they would do, not for vainglory, but that the republic might be as grand as its equals.

When Washington society is looked at from the point of view of the hotels, where a good deal of greatness "and wife" make their home, it seems, at first glance, to be as imitative as that of our new American nobility. It is very far, however, from being imitative in essence; it is not simian; it is wholesomely democratic. The atmosphere of the hotel dining-room, or of the parlor in the hour of "social reunion" after dinner, is not, to be sure, pleasing to the fastidious. The dinner is sometimes good and sometimes a colored rustic's attempt to compose French dishes and sauces. The waiter is so friendly that you feel that he either ought to take a chair at the table and laugh at your jokes at his ease, or that he ought to remove his alpaca jacket, one sleeve of which is nearly torn out at the socket with too much reaching in front of you, and join you after the meal in the parlor. You feel also that if the gowns of the women are of the right material, the sleeves are too long and the collars too high, while the frock- and sack-coats of the men are distinctly malapropos, and the mussed white neckties which some of them have worn all day add nothing to the ceremonial side of the feast. You will not like the haste in which the dinner is eaten, the evidence proffered by the statesman's wandering eyes that the presence of a stranger in the room is of more interest to him than the conversation of his wife and daughters and their women friends. A little observation will teach you, however, that the women of the average "congressional family" have little conversation which they deem worthy of their statesman's ears. Their words are for one another, and if you ever "get to know them," as their saying runs, you will find that it is not about their servants that they talk, as in commercial centers, but about the clothes worn by the grand dames of the republic.

HALF-TONE PLATE ENGRAVED BY S. DAVIS.

THEIR DAUGHTERS.

When you go into the "social hall" after dinner you will meet a number of women whose minds are wrapped up in what they call "society." Some of them are the wives of congressmen. Some are the wives or widows and the daughters of private citizens. Some devote their winters to the capital because it is the center of interest to them; these spend their days in the Senate gallery, and their evenings in the elucidation of public questions. Nearly always you will find delegations—delegations of teachers or of temperance women or suffragists; women who are here to persuade Congress to do something for a "good brother" or a "good cause." It will always be a company of the

American womanhood that is obvious in every town and village—the sewing-circle, book-club, tea-drinking, and platform womanhood. With the congressman's wife will be the sweet girls whom she is chaperoning with that conscientiousness and wearying labor which prove her not to be of the hardy, pleasure-seeking, usual variety—in short, a mere amateur chaperon. What "society" means to most of them is a pageant in which they are both observers and participants. They look on and they embellish.

"I 'm a very social person," said an excellent matron to the writer. "I like to go. But the judge don't care for it. He says to me, 'You do the social, and I 'll do the business.' So he goes out with his friends, and I always have some charming girls; perfect beauties I 've got now—did you see them, sir?" (They always say "sir.") "Yes, indeed, very pretty; gone out now to the theater with a middle-aged young man about thirty-five. He is their chaperon to-night. I would n't dream of letting them go out without a chaperon, so I asked him to chaperon them. He is engaged, you know."

In such a woman is often the crude beginning of a career. What tact and graceful kindliness democracy instils into its women! It was different at the courts of the great kings, for there the tasks of the women were rendered simple by simplicity of morals and manners; they had nothing to contend against but polished and cynical brutality. Here our women have to strive against some of that also, for dead fish float on the surface of every society; but there is something besides: ineffably bad manners occasionally, native unrestrained ugliness, coarseness, vulgarity; yet at times they encounter honest and lovable awkwardness, the native soil of a precious marble which it half conceals.

"Madame," said an old diplomat at his own table, "I have some bonbons here from Paris. They have medallions of the potentates of the world, and I have had your ruler's face stamped on one of them. Is it not a good likeness?" And he handed a chocolate to the woman on his right, who, for reasons of her husband's, did not like the new President.

"We have no rulers in this country," said the gracious guest, throwing the chocolate under the table.

The host's attention had been attracted elsewhere, and he did not see the insult, but he was made aware of something by the silence which followed. However, before he could know what had happened, a young woman's voice said to the butler: "Won't you find that bonbon which Mrs. C—— dropped? I want to look at it."

One day a delighted and awkward new statesman was taking tea at the house of a clever woman, and was suddenly plunged into terror, agony, and shame by the annihilation of the delicate and costly Sèvres cup from which he had been drinking; but before his palate was dry or his tongue responsive to his scared mind, the hostess broke its mate, saying to the servant as she did so: "Never put these cups on the table again, Smith; they 're too brittle for use."

In its earlier stages feminine intercourse means a gathering for mutual observation and personal gossip; in its earlier stages in Washington it means public receptions at the White House, calls at the houses of "cabinet ladies" and "senatorial ladies" on Wednesdays and Thursdays, one or two grand receptions by the "congressional ladies" of each prominent hotel, and evening after evening at the theater. At a public reception at the White House one sees what the wife of the new congressman means when she speaks of the "society of the capital"; one discovers what the court circle of a democracy really is; and if one penetrates beyond and into more eclectic circles, one may discover, further, what may be effected in society by the saving grace of common sense, and, occasionally, what spiritual wreckage may be wrought by untamable brutality.

It was not for mere background that the typical American city was sketched at the beginning of this article. The American city owns its class distinctions, and the line is drawn sharply. Whatever may be the test in other places, however, the chief test of social acceptability at Washington is success in some kind of intellectual effort. This does not appear from the brief outline of the hotel life which I have just given, but it is, nevertheless, the truth. The men who go to Washington, to Congress especially, are men of mark in their communities. They are not the average men of the country; they are the men whom the average man regards as superior. They may be intriguers, or political sharpers and charlatans, or the tools of unscrupulous party leaders or statesmen. Whatever they are, they are superior to most of their neighbors, and have so stamped themselves upon the communities in which they dwell that they have been preferred to their opponents. Their eminence may be bad or good; their service may be that of the subtle and cunning tool of the strong-minded

HALF-TONE PLATE ENGRAVED BY F. H. WELLINGTON.

"HER FIRST APPEARANCE AT A WHITE HOUSE RECEPTION."

leader, it may be the conscientious labor of the drudge, or it may be the brilliant career of a statesman; essentially it is the possession of some degree and of some kind of intellect which carries a man to Congress. Even the men who are said to be in public life because they are rich, with the exception of an infinitesimal number of inheritors of wealth, are men necessarily of mental capacity. Going to Washington, the seal of officialism is set upon them, and the society of Washington is at their command, and at the command of their wives and daughters, if they possess either wealth or talents. They can have anything they are willing to pay for, either in costly entertainments or by lending an intellectual or eccentric tone to society. There is no one to repel their pushing efforts; there is no one to frown openly upon them; there are scores eager to listen if they have wit or wisdom; and while there are some sneerers and critics, covert and open, there are, even behind their backs, whole armies of lauders of the millionaire who might knock at the doors of Boston in vain, and who would find difficulty in New York.

Here are democratic social conditions. Some of them are offensive and some are discouraging; but the outcome of a study of them is a large measure of hopefulness. The woman who insisted on safeguarding her young charges with a middle-aged young man chaperon carries the awkward stiffness, the unconsciousness of conventions and their value, the palsied tongue, or the bumptiousness and coltishness of the village picnic into the drawing-room of the White House. This is the complexion of nine tenths of the company at one of the President's public gatherings; it is the complexion of the Washington society which encounters you; but not that of the society which may discover you, and which is largely recruited from the general body with which it is almost constantly in contact, as well as from the leisurely rich of the rest of the country who are ambitious for something else than sport.

In the hotel parlor, where one studies the American citizeness on her first contact with life at the republican court, one is very likely to find the woman who is destined to step from the lowest moving circle to the next, and on and on until she reaches that small and stationary center where the polite arts are understood and practised most politely. Washington and the official position of her husband give her the opportunity she needs. She may go to Washington with the hearty and frank outspokenness of the church fair, and quit it with the purr of the dinner-party. An intelligent woman has told me that very clever American women who have entered Washington gowned in brocades put together at home have been known even to learn how to dress. It is often a question of first hotels, for there are hotels at Washington which differ from the social kindergartens I have described—hotels which may be set down as the grammar and high schools, connecting-links between the infant schools and the private houses where most of the graduates and the professors dwell. In a hotel where foreign fashion puts up on its flying visits to Washington, or where some domestic fashion finds it economical to dwell, according to my authority, a clever American woman, by close observation, may learn what is correct, and in time may come to prefer the creations of a French artiste, or her American imitator, to the wild and untutored vagaries of some village Paquin born to make others blush at what they see.

The most difficult person to manage, as I am told by this same informant, is the wife of a senator who arrives at Washington with fixed dressmaking notions of her own. Such a woman's theories of costume usually favor a modification of the Greek pallium, or the mingling of discordant and mutually abusive colors, occasionally "hand-painted" after her own designs, or the employment of soft stuffs which cling to a form whose gracefulness would better be left to the imagination. If the senator be rich, however, and hospitable, especially if the task of arranging his entertainments and inviting his guests be left to a trained and ever-ready old resident, the wife's insistence on yelling and fighting colors, or even on classical enigmas, will in time be counted as eccentricities of genius. Sometimes influential dependents will seriously sustain them, and they will thus become the microbes of an epidemic of bad taste.

The impression made by an official function is that of an assemblage of incongruous persons; but this is as it must be, and as it ought to be, at the capital of a democracy. It is rather the fashion to say that a representative and his family count for nothing in the life of the place; this depends on him and the family. It is true that most of the men of place tuck themselves and their wives away in obscure corners, and yawn through the dreary years of their official existence. To such as these Washington offers nothing of intellectual profit or pleasure, not so much as is offered by the home village or by the remote farm neighborhood; for not even a picnic happens along at Washington to break the monotony of days, each one of which is as wearing to the obscure "congressional lady" as is the laborless Sunday, with its burden of black clothes and walking-stick, to the New England village shopkeeper. The man, too, grows weary and discouraged as he dozes in the House or writes letters to constituents who, in the pauses between requests for office, demand of him why he has not kept his hustings promise and shaken with speech the empires of the world and their tools of Wall street. These are of the class whose mental and moral faculties are benumbed by Washington. No one who has not lived in the city and studied its denizens can imagine the terrible deadliness of much more than half its political life. It is a slouch to the Capitol in the morning, with overcoat hanging listlessly from the shoulders; a long yawn that lasts to the adjournment in the afternoon; a slouch back at the end of the legislative day to a bored wife gazing at nothing out of the window, with no relief in mind except, perhaps, a possible gossip with some other congressman's bored wife.

The melancholy truth is borne in upon many a new congressman that his public place, which raises him in public estimation at home, seems to do nothing for him in Washington. But, after all, a democracy can give him only a fair opportunity; the rest depends upon himself. And as it is with him in his sphere, so it is with his wife in hers. In the apparently incongruous assemblage at the White House, not only the woman of social instincts and capacity, but the woman of social desires also, finds her opportunity. The democracy is on its vantage-ground at its own capital. Where the plain woman from the village or the farm mingles with the smart people from the smart sets of the cities, with the representatives of foreign powers, with the professional men, civil and military and scientific, she stands or falls on her merits. Sometimes she passes on her demerits, but, say what the old residents and the inner circles may to the contrary, an election to the House of Representatives gives to the fortunate man a *prima facie* right to respect and consideration. The doors of society that were once difficult to force are now open to him and his wife if either one of them is clever or wise or the possessor of any social talent; if he is powerful and influential; if he has made his mark or promises to make it; if she is beautiful or musical, or is the sweet reflection of the man who has made his impression.

There is nothing so beautiful in democracy as the friendliness of its opportunities. The human plant appears in its soil and pushes up into its ether. It may be that no one knows whence came the seed, nor what may be the quality of the parent plant. The unknown stalk grows and brings forth its leaves and blooms. The fruit may be poison or delicious and wholesome food. In some way or other its merits are accounted for. It is at least accepted at its material worth. But there is only one place in the country where, if it have the proper qualities, it may surely be planted among the hothouse and exotic flowers, only one pleasure-garden where its new blossom can certainly find a place among the blossoms that have long been known and classified in the social herbarium. There are more splendid opportunities offered by democracy, but none so dear to some hearts.

There is a large hospitality in Washington for the successful public man. There is also the same, perhaps even a larger, certainly an increasing, hospitality for rich public men. There is very little literature in Washington—so little that there are no literary standards; books that are unheard of elsewhere one finds talked about at the capital. Sometimes they are written by geniuses who have married public men. There is a little struggling art, but rich Washingtonians bring their pictures with them, or go to New York to buy them, as New-Yorkers used to go to Paris. But power counts, and power is respected. Even place alone, as I have already said, adds new graces to its occupant. In the groups and circles which make up the many-hued life of the city, one will find the rich seeker after pleasures, with his country club, his horses, and his fox; the amateur politician, often a woman, who wonders, as she regards her own parlor, why people say that a salon is impossible; some men and women who are among the most interesting in the country; some diplomats, among them, to quote a sometime English secretary, men and women who are entirely worthy of respect; some satellites, male and female, of those of the foreigners who do not even respect themselves; some pure and unselfish men who have devoted precious lives to the public service for an inadequate return; some birds of prey who find the vestibules of the hotels the most profitable social centers; women without social ambitions, but with social cares; women of social ambitions and much social experience; women with ambition but without experience. And all these meet more or less frequently in the public assemblies, and the spirit of democracy has its way with all of them. None, except those who cultivate the foreigners only, escapes it. In the ebb and flow of the classes which would be sharply divided from one another in the typical American city, the flood picks up individuals from the unaccustomed mass, and carries them into quiet social pools, where they are shaped, in a measure, to the requirements of conventions, but where they also shape a little that with which they are brought in contact. Democracy is an elevator as well as a leveler, and it is here that the task of elevation and leveling goes on most actively and most obviously. On one side it is a refining process; on the other, it is a liberalizing process. Politeness, wide sympathy, adaptability, self-assurance, are not bad acquisitions for the awkward man or woman who comes to the capital tongue-tied, shy, unresponsive, uncompanionable, but with ability and character, or with lighter intellectual and moral virtues. On the other hand, the capital does something for the selfish, self-centered, egotistic, impertinent member of a self-constituted caste if it informs him of the worth of the larger humanity which has heretofore lain beyond his ken, and whose simple and rich virtues may perhaps, unhappily for him, continue to lie there.

Much outward seeming patriotism has been bred by the Spanish War: it is not always an admirable patriotism; it is sometimes due to the showing of force which we have made, and which appears to give us a place among the gory nations of the earth; it is often boastful, offensive, self-assertive jingoism. But democracy will eventually leaven it, as it has leavened other ill conditions; and even as it is, it is much more agreeable than the poor little feeling, once pretty general, that we are not as the foreigners are, because we lack gold lace, large armies, and traditional diplomacy. Nothing essentially unsound or mean can long survive in a democracy; there is too much soundness at the heart.

In the capital of democracy one may see its vices also: rudeness that will not be refined; refinement that is soiled by contact with rudeness; the greed of the boor; the suffering of the gentleman who must come in contact with the boor. But hope is born in the hearts of all who see the chosen of our countrymen and our countrywomen—far below the very best as they frequently are—take advantage of the opportunities of the motley society into which they are plunged, and out of their experience gain in grace and character. It is difficult to recruit a society which yachts and races horses; it is much more difficult to recruit one resting upon grandfathers; still more to add to the numbers of those who have a high and liberal cultivation in arts and letters and science. It is comparatively easy to find accessions in Washington to a society which is near the heart of politics, in which all Americans are interested. Sometimes the social triumph of a public man or his wife ends with their departure from the capital; sometimes it is so well founded that it continues in remote places where there are branch lodges of the American nobility. Occasionally a rich politician who failed as simple millionaire to make his way among the elect storms successfully at the gates of New York and Newport, even of Beverly Farms, through a triumphant career at Washington.

Washington in the Hands of the British (1906)

WASHINGTON IN THE HANDS OF THE BRITISH

FROM THE DIARIES AND FAMILY LETTERS OF MRS. SAMUEL HARRISON SMITH (MARGARET BAYARD)

Edited by Gaillard Hunt from the collection of her grandson, J. Henley Smith

To Mrs. Kirkpatrick

Tuesday, July 20, 1813.

. . . I every day from the time I received Maria's, intended writing to press you to come on & pass a few weeks or more with us & to bring Fanny & Elizabeth. I believed such a jaunt might be highly serviceable to you all. But it is now out of the question & will be so while the British are such near neighbours & continue to menace us. Until the late alarm I have never been able to realize our being in a state of war; but now when such active preparations are made, when so many of our citizens & particular acquaintance have marched to meet the enemy, I not only believe but feel the unhappy state of our country. Mr. Seaton & Mr. Gales* are both with our troops at Warburton, & Mrs. Seaton & Miss Gales' anxiety naturally excite ours. It is generally believed impossible for the English to reach the city, not so much from our force at Warburton, tho' that is very large, as from the natural impediments; the river being very difficult of navigation. Every precaution has been taken to ensure the safety of the city. Fort Warburton is in a state of perfect defence & our troops are each day augmented by hundreds & thousands from the adjoining country who come pouring in. The presence of Genl. Armstrong & Col. Monroe animates & invigorates our soldiers. And our little army is full of ardour & enthusiasm. Mr. Gales & Seaton have each been up to look after the paper & give a most interesting & animating picture of the scene. There is so little apprehension of danger in the city, that not a single removal of person or goods has taken place,—a number of our friends have desired leave to send their trunks here & a number have determined to come themselves, should the British effect a passage by the fort, so you see we are esteemed quite out of danger. As for our enemy *at home* I have no doubt that they will if possible join the British; here we are, I believe firmly in no danger, as the aim of these in the country would be as quickly as possible to join those in the city & the few scatter'd s———s about our neighbourhood, could not muster force enough to venture on an attack.* We have however counted on the possibility of danger & Mr. S. has procured pistols &c. &c. sufficient for our defence, & we make use of every precaution which we should use were we certain of what we now only reckon a possibility. In the city & George town the gentlemen who by their age or other circumstances are exempted from service, have formed volunteer companies

* They were brothers-in-law and edited the *National Intelligencer* from 1812 to 1860, when Gales died. Gales acquired the paper from Mr. Smith in 1810.

* Wherever there were slaves there was terror of their insurrection.

both of horse & foot, who nightly patrol the streets. The members of congress have determined to join the citizens, in case of an attack & there are many old experienced officers amongst them. The affair of Hampton,* which I disbelieved until the publication in the Intelligencer, inspires us with a terror we should not otherwise have felt. There were 300 French men at that attack & it was chiefly these wretches who perpetrated these horrors. Their intention was to desert to our side & they march'd near to our militia with a view to surrender, but were fired on & so obliged to fight in their own defence,—20 did desert & are now at the fort. The French prisoners taken from the English jails, will it is supposed, & the Irish likewise all desert the moment they are landed. Mrs. Seaton behaves with admirable self command, I quite admire her composure & serenity, as I am certain loving as she loves her amiable husband, it must require great effort. We one & all resist the intrusion of useless anxiety & alarm. We go on regularly with our every day occupations. I spend the morning in my family affairs & school. Ann sits with our guests & after dinner we all assemble & while the rest sew, Miss Gales reads some amusing book. If we did not resolutely adhere to this plan of occupation our fancy would augment our fears & we should be sad enough. As it is we are quite animated, each strengthens the resolution of the other & since we have been so well provided with fire arms, my apprehensions have quite ceased. *For those whom I fear'd are easily intimidated.* Mr. Smith has this morning gone in to the Bank, & Mrs. Seaton & Miss Gales, to see Mr. Seaton who has come up to arrange the paper. If Susan is with you, read or show her this letter as you think proper, or if at Princeton & you think it may allay her anxiety, please to send it. Ann is quite a Heroine. She makes no protestations but her cheerfulness & freedom from unnecessary alarm shows that she is not easily intimidated. She is a dear good girl. I love her every day more & more. And if danger comes, I shall not think of or risque more for my children than her. We expect Mrs. Clay, her sister Mrs. Brown, Mrs. Catting & many others to come to us in case of a serious alarm. At present all the members & citizens say it is impossible for the enemy to ascend the river, and our home enemy will not assail us, if they do not arrive. . . .

M. H. S.

To Mrs. Kirkpatrick

August [1814], BROOKVILLE [MD.].

On Sunday we received information that the British had debark'd at Benedict. They seem'd in no haste to approach the city, but gave us time to collect our troops. The alarm was such that on Monday a general removal from the city & George Town took place. Very few women or children remain'd in the city on Tuesday evening, altho' the accounts then received were that the enemy were retreating. Our troops were eager for an attack & such was the cheerful alacrity they display'd, that a universal confidence reign'd among the citizens & people. Few doubted our conquering. On Tuesday we sent off to a private farm house all our linen, clothing & other movable property, in the afternoon Dr. Bradley's family came from the city & took tea with us,—the Dr. said several citizens from the camp brought information of the enemy's remaining quiet at N. Malborough, but that 3 of the volunteer companies, . . . ,* Davidsons & Peters were order'd to attack the Pickets & draw the B—— on to a general engagement. This was the last news; until we were roused on Tuesday night by a loud knocking,—on the opening of the door, Willie Bradley called to us, "The enemy are advancing, our own troops are giving way on all sides & are retreating to the city. Go, for Gods sake go." † He spoke in a voice of agony, & then flew to his horse & was out of sight in a moment. We immediately rose, the carriage & horses were soon ready, we loaded a wagon with what goods remained & about 3 o'clock left our house with all our servants, the women we sent to some private farm houses at a safe distance, while we pursued our course. I felt no alarm or agitation, as I knew the danger was not near. I even felt no distress at the idea of forsaking our home. I could not realize the possibility of the B. gaining possession of the city, or of our army being defeated. We travel'd very slowly & as it

* The village of Hampton, Va., was sacked June 25, 1813, by the British and given over to pillage and rapine by Cockburn's orders.

* Illegible

† The battle took place August 24.

was dark I walk'd part of the way. Ann was equally composed. At sunrise we stop'd to breakfast at Miss Carrol's & then pursued our journey. The girls were quite delighted with our flight, novelty has such charms at their age, that even the exchange of comfort & peace, for suffering & distress, has its charms. Even for myself, I felt animated, invigorated, willing to encounter any hardship, calmly to meet any danger, patiently to bear any difficulty. I suffer'd considerably pain during the ride, & fear'd every moment being taken ill, but happily I was not, & we all reach'd this place at one oclock in perfect health. We received a most kind reception from Mrs. Bently, & excellent accomodations. The appearance of this village is romantic & beautiful, it is situated in a little valley totally embosom'd in woody hills, with a stream flowing at the bottom on which are mills. In this secluded spot one might hope the noise, or rumour of war would never reach. Here all seems security & peace! Happy people may you never be obliged to fly from this peaceful spot, which now affords so hospitable a shelter to our poor citizens!

Thursday morning. This morning on awakening we were greeted with the sad news, that our city was taken, the bridges & public buildings burnt, our troops flying in every direction. Our little army totally dispersed. Good God, what will be the event! This moment a troop of horse have enter'd, they were on the field of battle, but not engag'd. Major Ridgely * their commander, disapproving Genl. Winder's order, refused to obey, left the army & is taking his troops home. E. Riggs, who was likewise there has given us a sad detail. He was in Loughbourough's, who with ten men form'd a reconnoitering party, & Riggs was employed in carrying messages from Winder. His account was that the first skirmish was near Malborough, where Peters, Davidson's & Strul's (?) companies were ordered to attack the enemies picquets, but on finding how inefficient their force were, order'd to retreat, which they did in great disorder. Winder finding the enemy marching on the Bladensburg turnpike, forsook the posts he had taken & march'd towards the city, where they station'd themselves on the hills near Bladensburg bridge. The enemy march on in solid column & attack'd with coolness, & order. The 5th regiment from Baltimore commenced the attack & stood their ground firmly, but for a short time only, they were almost destroy'd & our whole troops gave way & began a disordered retreat. The President who was on the ground, escap'd & has gone into Virginia. *Winder* with all the men he can collect are at the court house. He has directed our poor broken militia to make the best of their way to Baltimore. Every hour the poor wearied & terrified creatures are passing by the door. Mrs. Bently kindly invites them in to rest & refresh. Major Ridgely's troop of horse all breakfasted in town, that not a man was left to breakfast in the tavern. Ann & I hasten'd to assist Mrs. B. in getting their breakfast,—and Julia & Susan wanted to do something, help'd to set the table, &c.

Noon. We were much alarm'd by Mr. Milligan, who called & told Mr. Smith, Genl Winder had ordered him to come here for an express, that Montgomery C. H. was burnt by the British, who were then on their march for Frederick. But a person who knew him assured us he was crazy, his account afterwards proved untrue, as a great many have passed since. Our men look pale & feeble but more with affright than fatigue,—they had thrown away their muskets & blankets.

Just as we were going to dinner, a tremendous gust arose, it has broken the trees very much, in the midst of it, a wagon came to the door with a family going they knew not whither. Poor wanderers. Oh how changed are my feelings, my confidence in our troops is gone, they may again be rallied, but it will require a long apprenticeship to make them good soldiers. Oh my sister how gloomy is the scene. I do not suppose Government will ever return to Washington. All those whose property was invested in that place, will be reduced to poverty. Mr. Smith had invested a large portion of his in bridge stock,—both the bridges are destroy'd,—it serves to beguile the time to write, so my dear sister I will write a kind of journal to you, & send it when I can. I wish you to keep it. If better times come, it will serve to remind me of these.

Thursday evening. Our anxiety has been kept alive the whole day. Our poor men are coming in some two or three, sometimes

* One of the Maryland militia officers.

a dozen at a time, just now another troop of horse have come in, they have not been in the engagement, as they did not arrive until a retreat had been order'd. Mr. Carr one of the clerks of the Bank was here just now & has given us the most correct account we have yet had. Our position was a bad one, so placed that neither the artillery or cavalry could act. Barney* took a position on a hill, the enemy had to pass & as they ascended rak'd them prodigiously but they never halted one moment, but marched on in solid mass, disregarding the dead bodies that fell before them. Barney & his men did not leave their cannons until they were within 5 yrds, then spik'd them & retreated,—Barney badly wounded. They [the enemy] never left the turnpike but enter'd the city after our retreating army. They first march'd to the navy yard which is wholly consumed; then to Capitol Hill. They had great difficulty in firing the capitol, several houses on the hill were burnt by cinders from the Capitol, but none by design, the President's house, the Potomac bridge, & all the other public buildings. Mr. Lee went to their camp at Malborough (as a citizen unmolested) conversed with the officers, several of whom he had known in London. They told him that resistance would be vain; that instead of 7000, they wished we had 40,000 militia, as it would make the greater confusion. They bade Mr. Lee tell the citizens that private property would not be injured, if the houses were not deserted, or private persons molested, that they intended to destroy the public buildings & shipping, & then to march to Baltimore on one side while Lord Hill with his fleet would attack it by water. I left our house with reluctance, but when I urged Mr. Smith to let me remain to protect the house, he would not hear of it, his duty called him away, & my situation being so critical, he said no consideration would induce him to leave me, for altho' the troops when under their officers might behave well, yet small parties or drunken soldiers might alarm or injure me in my present situation. And Ann declared she would not leave me if she were to die by my side. I had therefore to yield. I am afraid the consequence of leaving the house empty will be its destruction. Our house in the city too is unprotected & contains our most valuable furniture. In a week more & we may be penniless! for I count little on the continuance of Mr. S.'s salary. God only knows when the executive government will again be organized. But I can say with truth, the individual loss of property, has not given me a moment's uneasiness. But the state of our country, has wrung tears of anguish from me. I trust it will only be momentary. We are naturally a brave people & it was not so much fear, as prudence which caused our retreat. Too late they discovered the disspreparation of our troops. The enemy were 3 to 1. Their army composed of conquering veterans, ours of young mechanics & farmers, many of whom had never before carried a musket. But we shall learn the dreadful, horrid trade of war. And they will make us a martial people, for never, never will Americans give up their liberty. But before that time comes, what sufferings, what reverses, what distress must be suffer'd. Already, in one night, have hundreds of our citizens been reduced from affluence to poverty, for it is not to be expected W—— will ever again be the seat of Govt. Last night the woods round the city & G. T—— were filled with women & children & old men & our flying troops. One poor woman, after wandering all night, found at day light she wander'd 10 miles,—a lady in our neighbourhood, the wife of one of Mr. S.'s clerks, went out of her senses, her son was in the army. Mrs. Genl. Mason,* that lovely woman whom you knew, is likewise laying dangerously ill. Her husband was in the engagement & her anxiety has render'd a common fever dangerous. I am going tomorrow to see her.

Night, 10 oclock. The streets of this quiet village, which never before witnessed confusion, is now fill'd with carriages bringing out citizens, & Baggage waggons & troops. Mrs. Bently's house is now crowded, she has been the whole evening sitting at the supper table, giving refreshment to soldiers & travellers. I suppose every house in the village is equally full. I never saw more benevolent people. "It is against our principles," said she this morning, "to have anything to do with war, but we receive & relieve all who come to us." The whole

* Captain Joshua Barney, U.S.N., was the only man who reaped glory in this, the greatest disgrace to American arms.

* Wife of Armistead Thomson Mason, then colonel of a cavalry regiment. He was killed in a duel by his brother-in-law, John M. McCarty. They fought with muskets at six paces on the famous Bladensburg duelling ground.

The President's house, Washington, after the conflagration of August 24, 1814.

settlement are quakers. The table is just spread for the 4th or 5th time, more wanderers having just enter'd.

I know not when you will get this letter. I suppose the mail will be impeded. How is Maria,—is N. Y. menaced. My health is improved, thank a kind Providence, the event so dreaded has not taken place & I now begin to think I shall continue well.

I have not yet read this letter. I know not what I have written. I thought you would be anxious for intelligence, for tho' you were no friend to Washington, yet the recent event is interesting to the nation. The enemy are in the centre of union!

I will now bid you good night,—let Maria & Susan Smith know we are safe. Susan particularly,—she will be miserable.

Farewell, dearest sister. God grant this letter may contain more news, than I may ever have occasion to write again.

Farewell,

To Mrs. Kirkpatrick

BROOKVILLE [August, 1814].

Saturday morning. On Thursday evening I closed my letter to you. The next morning soon after breakfast I went to see Mrs. Mason. She had found refuge in a farm house, with a poor but respectable family, about 4 miles from this place. She had her 3 eldest daughters with her & 2 servant maids. She was very ill, of a highly inflamatory billious fever. When I enter'd her chamber her spirits were much affected. She was too ill to talk, but when I offered to stay, gladly accepted the offer. She felt cheerless & desponding, had no confidence in her young physician or servants, who indeed seem'd very ignorant. She thought herself in danger, if not of her life, yet of derangement of mind, so continued & violent was the pain in her head. I immediately took on the functions of a nurse & being much accustomed to her disease, I soon succeeded in procuring her entire relief from the pain of her head, & other alarming symptoms. I did not leave her a moment during the day & sat up part of the night. Dr. Worthington, her physician arrived. He distress'd me excessively by his conversation. He exulted in the defeat of our army in the capture of our city. "Did I not tell this," said he, "I suppose, Mrs. Smith, your wise men will now believe a standing army a necessary thing & a navy in the bargain." "If they do" (I answer'd)

View of the east front of the President's house, with the addition of the north and south porticos.
From a drawing made in 1807 by B. H. Latrobe, surveyor of the public buildings, Washington.

"they will certainly aim at establishing them, for however mistaken in judgement, be assured sir, in all their measures, the administration have honestly & sincerely endeavour'd to promote the welfare of their country. It was believed, & all history has proved it to be so, that a standing army is an instrument of despotism; but if our liberties cannot be preserved without; the lesser evil will be chosen,—the risk run." "I do not allow," said he, "a standing army to be the instrument of despotism, but I allow it to be inseparable from a monarchy." "I am not competent to discuss such questions, Sir, but I beg at such a moment as this, you will not thus seem to rejoice at what every friend of his country must mourn over." The tears started in my eyes, & seeing my distress silenced him at the time, tho' every now & then his evident satisfaction broke forth. Surely it is not possible that such is the disposition of all the federal party, no, no, few I hope could speak as he did. On Saturday morning Genl. Mason arrived, this was joyful tidings for his poor wife. I left them together & did not see the Genl until breakfast. He appeared excessively harrass'd. He & Mr. Rush had never left the President since our disgraceful retreat. He had crossed over with him into Virginia, where he had collected troops & 2000 brave fellows then following his steps to our poor city, commanded by Genl. Hungerford a revolutionary officer. Wherever they pass'd, they as well as our flying forces were received with the most affectionate kindness, not only at large houses but at every hovel; the women came out with milk, bread, spirits, or something to offer the weary soldiers & to press them to rest & refresh. Everywhere he met indignation at the invading force & an alacrity to march against them, but the most prominent sentiment was mortification at the precipitate retreat of our army. The President & himself had arrived the night before & staid at Mrs. Bently's where we were. Mrs. Mason begged him not to stay one moment on her account, but urged him to depart that he might to the utmost serve his country. After breakfast he return'd to Brookville, soon after Mr. Smith sent for me & I was obliged to leave this amiable woman. She parted with me with reluctance as I was the only one near her who had any experience in her disease. When I arrived to-day at Brookville, the President & his suite had gone. The girls were very sorry I had been absent, as the scene in B. had been novel & interesting. Just at bed time the Presd. had ar-

The Capitol after the conflagration of August 24, 1814.

rived & all hands went to work to prepare supper & lodgings for him, his companions & guards,—beds were spread in the parlour, the house was filled & guards placed round the house during the night. A large troop of horse likewise arrived & encamp'd for the night, beside the mill-wall in a beautiful little plain, so embosom'd in woods & hills. The tents were scatter'd along the riverlet & the fires they kindled on the ground & the lights within the tents had a beautiful appearance. All the villagers, gentlemen & ladies, young & old, throng'd to see the President. He was tranquil as usual, & tho' much distressed by the dreadful event, which had taken place not dispirited. He advised Mr. Smith to return to the city, whither he was himself going. Mr. Monroe & some other gentlemen join'd him & about noon he set off for our suffering city. The rest of the day we pass'd tranquilly. It is now night, all around is quiet. All the inhabitants of this peaceful village sleep in peace. How silent! How serene! the moonlight gilds the romantic landscape that spreads around me. Oh my God, what a contrast is this repose of nature, to the turbulence of society. How much more dreadful is the war of man with man, than the strife of elements. On Thursday the hurricane which blew down houses, tore up trees & spread terror around, pass'd in a few minutes & nature recovered her tranquility. But oh my country, when will the destroying tempest which is now ravaging & destroying thy property & happiness, when will that be hushed to peace! At this moment, escaped from danger, I, & my family, all I hold most dear, are safe. But when I think of my good fellow citizens, when I think of our poor soldiers, flying on every part, sinking under fatigue & pain & hunger, dying alone & unknown, scattered in woods & fields—when I think of these horrors, I can hardly enjoy my own security.

Tuesday 30. Here we are, once more restored to our home. How shall I be sufficiently thankful for the mercies I have experienced. Once more the precious objects of my affection are gathered round me under our own roof. But how long shall I enjoy this blessing! The blast has pass'd by, without devastating this spot. But the storm is not yet over, dark, gloomy, lowering is the prospect, & far more dreadful scenes may be impending. Never did I feel so affected, so hopeless & sunk, as I did yesterday in the city. Oh my sister, what a sight! But to resume my journal. On Sunday morning we left Brookeville. Our ride was pleasant. All the way we were conjecturing how we should find our dwelling. We saw no vestige of the late scene till we approach'd the gate that open'd into our farm, then in the woods we saw a cannon whose carriage was broken, near the ruins of our cottage. On descending the hill, at the foot of a tree we saw a soldier sleeping on his arms,—leaving the woods we saw four or 5 others crossing the field & picking apples. When we reach'd the yard, a soldier with his musket was standing by the gate & asked permission to get a drink. These men were only passing over the farm. We found the house just as we had left it, & the vestige of no enemy, but the hurricane of Thursday which had blown down fences & trees. Julia & Ann cook'd us up a little dinner & in the afternoon we rode to the city. We pass'd several dead horses. The poor capitol! nothing but its blacken'd wall remain'd! 4 or 5 houses in the neighbourhood were likewise in ruins. Some men had got within these houses & fired on the English as they were quietly marching into the city, they killed 4 men & Genl. Rosse's horse. I imagine Genl. R. thought that his life was particularly aim'd at, for while his troops remained in the city he never made his appearance, altho' Cockburn & the other officers often rode through the avenue. It was on account of this outrage that these houses were burnt. We afterwards look'd at the other public buildings, but none were so thoroughly destroy'd as the House of Representatives & the President's House. Those beautiful pillars in that R—— Hall were crack'd & broken, the roof, that noble dome, painted & carved with such beauty & skill, lay in ashes in the cellars beneath the smouldering ruins, were yet smoking. In the P. H. not an inch, but its crack'd & blacken'd walls remain'd. That scene, which when I last visited it, was so splendid, throng'd with the great, the gay, the ambitious placemen, & patriotic Heros was now nothing but ashes, & was it these ashes, now trodden under foot by the rabble, which once possess'd the power to inflate pride, to gratify vanity. Did we ever honour the inhabitants of this ruin the more for their splendid habitation,—was this an object of desire, ambition, envy? Alas, yes, and this is human grandeur! How fragile, how transitory! Who would have thought that this mass so solid, so magnificent, so grand, which seem'd built for generations to come, should by the hands of a few men & in the space of a few hours, be thus irreparably destroy'd. Oh vanity of human hopes! After this melancholy survey, Mr. Smith went to see the President, who was at Mr. Cutts' (his brother in law) where we found Mrs. Madison & her sister Mrs. Cutts. Mrs. M. seem'd much depress'd, she could scarcely speak without tears. She told me she had remained in the city till a few hours before the English enter'd. She was so confident of Victory that she was calmly listening to the roar of cannon, & watching the rockets in the air, when she perceived our troops rushing into the city, with the haste & dismay of a routed force. The friends with her then hurried her away, (her carriage being previously ready) & she with many other families, among whom was Mrs. Thornton & Mrs. Cutting with her, retreated with the flying army. In George town they perceived some men before them carrying off the picture of Genl Washington (the large one by Stewart) which with the plate, was all that was saved out of the President's house. Mrs. M. lost all her own property. The wine, of which there was a great quantity, was consumed by our own soldiers. Mrs. M. slept that night in the encampment, a guard being placed round her tent, the next day she cross'd into Virginia where she remained until Sunday, when she return'd to meet her husband. Men, soldiers, expresses were round the house, the President was in a room with his cabinet, from whence he issued his orders. The English frigates were laying before Alexandria & as it was supposed only waiting for a wind to come up to the city. The belief was that about 700 or more sailors were to be let loose in the city for plunder, dreadful idea. A universal despondency seem'd to pervade the people,—we every where met them in scatter'd groups, relating or listening to their fears. We drank tea at Mrs. Thornton's, who described to us the manner in which they conflagrated the President's H & other buildings,—50 men, sailors & marines, were marched by an officer, silently thro' the avenue, each carrying a long pole to which was fixed a ball about the circumference of a large plate, —when arrived at the building, each man was station'd at a window, with his pole & machine of wild-fire against it, at the word of command, at the same instant the windows were broken & this wild-fire thrown in, so that an instantaneous conflagration took place & the whole building was wrapt in flames & smoke. The spectators stood in awful silence, the city was light & the heavens redden'd with the blaze! The day before Cockburn paid this house a visit & these will answer as a memento. I must take something too, & looking round, he seized an old hat a *chapeau de bras* of the President's, and a cushion off Mrs. M.'s chair, declaring these should be his trophies, adding pleasantries too vulgar for me to repeat. When he went to burn Mr. Gale's office, whom he called his "dear Josey";

Mrs. James Madison.

From the steel engraving by J. F. E. Prudhomme, after the portrait by J. Wood.

forced a young gentleman of our acquaintance to go with him,—on entering the dining room they found the table spread for dinner, left precipitately by Mrs. M.,—he insisted on young Weightman's sitting down & drinking Jemmy's health, which was the only epithet he used whenever he spoke of the President. After looking round, he told Mr. W. to take something to remember this day. Mr. W. wished for some valuable article. No, no said he, *that* I must give to the flames, but here, handing him some ornaments off the mantel-piece, Mrs. Brush, Mrs. Stelle & a few citizens remonstrated with him, assuring him that it would occasion the loss of all the buildings in the row. "Well," said he, "good people I do not wish to injure you, but I am really afraid my friend Josey will be affronted with me, if after burning Jemmy's palace, I do not pay him the same compliment,—so my lads, take your axes, pull down the house, & burn the papers in the street." This was accordingly done. He told Mrs. Brush & several others, that no houses should be injur'd but such as were shut &

deserted. Mr. Cutting & Mrs. B. saved ours by opening the windows. Cockburn often rode down the avenue, on an old white mare with a long main & tail & followed by its fold to the dismay of the spectators. He, & all his officers & soldiers were perfectly polite to the citizens. He bade them complain of any soldier that committed the least disorder & had several severely punished, for very slight offences. All provisions were paid for. He stop'd at a door, at which a young lady was standing & enter'd into familiar conversation. "Now did you expect to see me such a clever fellow," said he, "were you not prepared to see a savage, a ferocious creature, such as Josey represented me? But you see I am quite harmless, don't be afraid, I will take better care of you than Jemmy did!" Such was his manner,—that of a common sailor, not of a dignified commander. He however deserves praise & commendation for his own good conduct & the discipline of his sailors & Marines, for these were the destroying agents. The land troops & officers were scarcely seen while in the city, but kept close qrs at the navy yard. Cockburn had ordered Col. Wharton's & Capt. Tingey's houses (both public property) and the barracks & arsenal to be burnt, but on a remonstrance from the citizens, & an assurance the fire would destroy private property he desisted, "I want to injure no citizen," said he, " & so your Barracks may stand." I must praise his moderation, indeed his conduct was such as to disarm the prejudices that existed. During the stay of their troops in the city, it was so still you might have heard a pin drop on the pavement. The negroes all hid themselves & instead of a mutinous spirit, have never evinced so much attachment to the whites & such dread of the enemy. I could fill sheets with similar anecdotes, but the above

James Madison.
From a picture by Gilbert Stuart in the possession of T. Jefferson Coolidge.

Montpelier.
Madison's home near Richmond, Virginia.

will give you an idea of Cockburn. They left the city precipitately, from the idea that Winder was collecting his forces & would by going round them, cut off their retreat to their ships. And this could have been done, & our poor soldiers were willing & able for any enterprise, but their commanders,—Ah their commanders, Armstrong & Winder—on their shoulders lies the blame of our disastrous flight & defeat. Our men were all eager to fight & were marching on with a certainty of victory, more than 2000 had not fired their muskets, when Armstrong & Winder gave the order for a retreat, & to enforce that order added terror to authority! The English officers have told some of our citizens that they could not have stood more than 10 minutes longer, that they had march'd that day 13 miles, & were exhausted with thirst, heat & fatigue. It is said 2 Irish regiments wish'd to be taken & were on the point of joining us when the retreat commenced. I have conversed with many of our officers & men. All agree in this statement, that the troops wish'd to fight, & were full of spirit & courage. The English expected great resistance. Yesterday when in the city I conversed with a great many citizens, they were all desponding, dishearten'd. The President is determined on making a resistance in case the enemy return. But our citizens sent a deputation begging him not to attempt it, as it would be ineffectual, & would only be making them & the roofs that shelter'd them a sacrifice. "They now," they said, "had neither honor or property to loose. All they valued was gone." The President's orders, however, were enforced & all day yesterday while I was in the city I saw them collecting. Troops are order'd from all around, & 3000 are expected tonight. Alexandria has surrender'd its town with all their flour & merchandize & the frigates are now laying before that town, loading the Alexandria shipping with the goods of the citizens. What will be our fate I know not. The citizens who remain'd are now moving out, & all seem more alarm'd than before. I brought Eliza Doyne (that was) out with me. Mrs. Brush is coming out this evening & has sent out all her furniture. I prefer offering our house as an asylum to the poor than the rich. There is dreadful individual suffering,—one of Mr. S.'s clerk's was here this morning, his house & furniture were all burnt, even his clothing & he & his family are reduced to penury. Hundreds, I may say thousands of our flying troops pass'd thro our farm after the engagement. The

English got within half a mile of us & have plunder'd our neighbours on the adjoining farms,—the intervening wood hid us from them. On their retreat through Bladensburg they have done a great deal of injury, destroying furniture, carrying off cattle, &c. The consternation around us is general. The despondancy still greater. But *I* look forward with hope, our troops are again collecting & altho' the poor citizens are disheartend'd by the fate of their city, the rest of the army are still willing to fight. Universal execration follows Armstrong, who it is believed never wished to defend the city & I was assured that had he pass'd thro' the city the day after the engagement, he would have been torn to pieces. The district certainly was not in a state of preparation, whether from want of ability or want of inclination on the part of the administration we can not know. The city was capable of defence & ought to have been defended. But we will retrieve, yes I trust we will retrieve our character & restore our capital. Oh that I a feeble woman could do something! This is not the first capital of a great empire, that has been invaded & conflagrated; Rome was reduced still lower by the Goths of old, than we are, & when its senate proposed removing the seat of government, they were answer'd, Romans would never be driven from their homes, Rome should never be destroy'd. May a Roman spirit animate our people, & the Roman example be followed by the Americans. Meanwhile, you will ask for some domestic details. We are in that state of confusion, which with our clothes & furniture all removed you may imagine. Mrs. Brush & Mrs. Grammar (E. Doyne) are added to our family. Every hour brings a different rumour; we know not what to believe & scarcely what to hope. We are determined however not again to quit the house, but to run all risques here, as we find our enemy not so ferocious as we expected & that property is much endanger'd by quitting it. I shall persuade Ann to go to Brookville & take the children, if more alarming intelligence arrives. I am now so harden'd to fatigue & alarm, that I do not fear my health will suffer. The same external symtoms continue & I am astonished I am not much weakened by so long a continuation. But I am not [torn out] no depression, but feel wound up to be [torn out]. I trust when the hour of alarm or trial comes I shall be enabled to support it. Ann is as composed & easy as if all was peace. She is all that is kind & attentive to me & the

Mrs. James Madison.

After a water-color by Dr. William Thornton.

children, & in the absence of our servants, she & Julia do everything. Do not be so anxious about us my dearest sister. The back is fitted to the burden. As yet, my strength has not been tryed. I trust not in myself,—the firm, the innate, the deep felt conviction that every thing is over ruled by a great & a good God, reconciles me to every event. The late astonishing events in Europe, & the dreadful ones here, seems to have so sunk all human grandeur, all human concerns in my estimation, & human life appears so short, so very short, that instead of anxiety, I feel almost indifference. All will soon be past, whether life is spent in suffering or enjoyment, is of little moment, so that it is well spent,—we cannot suffer long. External circumstances are of little consequence, so that in all we do our duty. Such are my reflections; & my whole effort now, is not to escape from suffering & danger, but to be active in the performance of the duties they bring with them. Please to send my letter to Maria. I cannot write over,—dear, dear sister adieu. Do not be anxious about me—I am not uneasy myself.

To Mrs. Kirkpatrick

SIDNEY, Sept. 11 [1814].

. . . The affairs of our country grow more & more gloomy; last night the perusual of the paper made me quite melancholy, at Plattsburgh, N. London, N. Haven, all was consternation & alarm, families removing their property, & many, I suppose, as in this place wandering from their homes, without knowing where to find a shelter. All around our neighborhood was fill'd; those who could not get into houses encamp'd in the woods. In our old church there were 9 families. At Mrs. Fries 5 families with 18 children with scarcely anything to eat. Every day we are hearing of new instances of the cruelty of the soldiery & individual suffering. It has been the poor who have been the principle sufferers. At Bladensburgh which was inhabited chiefly by poor persons, the gentlemen having large houses & farms around the houses are much damaged by cannon ball &c.—many of them occupied by the British wounded & our wounded men. (The army left all of their wounded for us to take care of)—The poor owners thus excluded, their gardens, corn fields & enclosures laid waste; their horses all taken. In the army's march from Benedict they made tents & beds of all the green corn, for which purpose they cut down whole fields. I am told this country (from Benedict to Washington) is totally laid waste; you can scarcely get anything for man or horse to eat. They strip'd the people of their clothing, taking women's & even children's clothes. All this was done by the straggling parties of soldiers who robb'd only the poor. At Bladensburg, Malboro' & Wood Yard, the officers had guards placed around the houses of many considerable & wealthy persons & obtruded no further than to go to lodge, breakfast or dine with the gentlemen, except where they found houses empty & deserted, in which case they generally destroyed them. We ran a great risque in deserting ours. We are again establish'd & I now think nothing (excepting an army of Cossacks) shall induce me again to leave it. The battle was very near to us. In the next farm, there was skirmishing, & 10 dead bodies were found (of the enemy) some only 4 or 5 days ago. A poor old lady, one of our nearest neighbors, heard the bullets rattling around her house & has found a good many in the yard. I say I will remain, tho' all who did, say nothing would induce them to again go through such scenes. I have heard of two persons, I knew, who have lost their senses, & several I have seen are very much alter'd in their looks. Mrs. Bradley is the only one who would go thro' the same scenes again —she is generally timid, but she says when the hour of trial came, courage came with it. Several hundred of our flying troups were at her house, she dress'd their wounds & gave them meat & drink. I am persuaded the enemy lost many more than was at first supposed, as bodies are daily found, unburied, under bushes, in gulleys. Alas poor wretches, how many anxious hearts in England may be looking for your return! The wounded & prisoners who remain, all express themselves delighted with this country, many who have been in France & Spain, say they never saw so beautiful or so rich a country & wonder how so happy a people could go to war. It is supposed between 4 or 500 blacks have either [obliterated] taken. They have behaved well, been quiet, & [obliterated] in general appear to dread the enemy as much as we do. Thus we are spared one evil & the one I had most dread of. Muskets, cartridge boxes, were found by 100's & in possession of the blacks, who have all cheerfully given them up, to the persons sent to look for & collect them. Our black men found 3 on our farm, which they immediately gave up. Citizens have returned & are slowly & despondently resuming business, but society & individuals have received a shock it will require a long time to recover from. I now begin to feel a little composed & able to resume my ordinary employments. Mr. Smith has lost considerably by the destruction of the Bridges, in both of which he had invested a large sum. We shall make some change in our living, so as to reduce our expenditures. We have given up our house in the city, as it was much wanted & we shall not go there next winter. Excuse me for writing on one subject only. It is the only one of which we talk or think. But our country, our poor country. It seems surrounded. No place seems safe. I will not begin on another sheet, but conclude this with begging you my dear sister to write as soon as you can. All our family are perfectly well. Matty as well as ever she was in her life, she was quite safe during the alarm, in an obscure farm I had sent her to.

*To Saml. Harrison Smith**

LONE HOUSE-BY THE WAY SIDE [1815].

What a novel letter I could write you if I but had the time & if the passing stage will not take me up, I shall have time enough, for here I must stay till they do, if its all day & night too. A few miles this side of Chester, our stage broke, but the mud was so deep, the gentlemen would not let me get out, we all sat on the upper side, (one of the braces was broke & the carriage rested on the axel) & were drag'd thro' the mud to this house, about two miles off. It was ten o'clock & the people all abed & it was a long time before we could waken them. At last the door was open'd by a nice good looking old quaker lady, with fear & trembling however. There were no men & no assistance of any kind—the moon was just down & the night so foggy that the driver said it would be very dark. I therefore begged the old lady to keep me all night. The gentlemen said they could get on the horses or walk & as they were anxious to get on, they bade me farewell & commended me to the lady's care. It was eleven o'clock before they got off, the stage supported by an old rail. I then begged my good quaker, to take me to the kitchen fire, as I was very cold & wet. My feet had been wet all day, & getting in & out of the stages in the rain, for it had rain'd hard all day, had wet my clothes. Two sweet looking young women got up & soon made a fine fire. I got into the chimney corner, for the chimney was like old Mrs. Tracy's, undress'd & dried & warm'd myself. I ask'd them if it would not be too much trouble, if they could give me something for supper. They said they really had nothing at all in the house, they didnt often accommodate people, it being a house just for the market folks to stop at. I told them a bowl of tea, with brown sugar would do, for I felt chilly & weary. They put on the tea kettle, & on my asking for an egg, found *one*. They seem'd curious about me, & when I told them that I came from *Washington*, I became an object of curiosity to them & they asked me a hundred questions,—particularly about its being taken by the British, & about slaves. While my kettle was boiling, I sat in one corner & the old lady in the other corner of the chimney. She was a pale, delicate looking woman, with an uncommonly sweet face. She regretted much having no better accomodation, but I told her truly it was more agreeable than a public house, that I could feel as if she was my mother, at least take as good care of me & that her daughters were just the age of mine. Here I must say, a few tears would in spite of me break from my full heart, at the thought of *home* dear home—dangers being now over my courage was over too. The dear old lady was so kind. In a few moments I went on with my history of the taking & burning of Washington, which all listen'd eagerly to, while we sat cowering over the fire. I related all the little anecdotes I could remember, our fears at Sidney, & when they heard that I could fire a pistol & had slept with a loaded pistol under my head, & Ann with a pen-knife in her bosom, they were lost in astonishment & look'd on me as something wonderful. The simplicity of the good folks amused me & their extreme interest excited me to tell them all about Ross Cockburn &c &c I could recollect & like the old soldier I sat

* Mrs. Smith was on her way to Philadelphia to visit her brother. Andrew Bayard, President of the Commercial Bank of Philadelphia. She finished the letter in Philadelphia.

by the "fire & show'd how fields were won" —lost I mean— Whenever I was about to pause, they begg'd me to go on. My little table was put in the corner by me, my bowl of tea & *one* egg & two crackers. I was wrapped in my flannel gown, & my clothes hung round the stove to dry. The sheets for my bed were hung on a chair before the blaze, & if I had indeed been her daughter she could not have been more careful of me, but there was a sick child upstairs whom they had to watch by. I therefore summon'd up courage to go to bed alone (the only thing I dreaded) they took me thro' five or six doors, into another house which had been built in addition to this. I requested the candle might be left. In vain I tried to sleep. It was raining & blowing, the windows & doors rattling. I became every moment more nervous, something in the room, threw a shadow on the wall exactly like a coffin—that night week dear Elizabeth had died—her image, almost herself was by me, the candle was almost out, I trembled so the bedstead shook under me. I felt almost sure if left in the dark I should fall into some kind of fit, at last I jump'd up & without waiting to put on my flannel gown, I took my almost expiring candle, determined to find my way to the kitchen, & if I could not find another candle, to sit in the chimney corner all night. I open'd the door of a chamber next me, hoping some one of the family might be there, but I saw a bedstead, the idea that some one might have just died there struck me. I dared not look farther, but found my way down stairs into a large empty room, with four doors, I opened the one nearest to me, the wind rushed in & blew out my candle. I then groped all round the room. Two doors were bolted, at last I found one that yielded to my hand, I open'd it, but knew not where I was & was afraid of falling down steps. I thought it best to return to my chamber, tho' with a horror I cannot describe—then I thought I would sit down in the empty room on the floor. The windows shook with the storm, as if they would have fallen in—the wind blew most violently & some open door was creaking & slaming. I shook, so I could scarcely stand & was quite unable to find the door at the foot of the stairs. At last, some one called out—Who's there? I answer'd & the old woman came to me with a light, & look'd quite frightened to see me there. She took me in the kitchen,—the fire was still burning, & they had been making up bread, &c. I told them I felt unwell & had come down for another candle—they mixed me a glass of toddy, as they saw me shaking as if I had an ague. After I got warm'd I began one of the stories that had interested them so much & was very eloquent indeed, in hopes of beguiling them to sit up an hour or two with me, but they were too sleepy, for even my most wonderful stories to keep them awake. At last finding neither Cochburn's murders, nor negro conspiricies, nor Georgia negro buyers could keep their eyes open, I again ask'd for a bed fellow & said I felt so lonely I could not sleep. But the daughter could not be spared, & I again return'd with a whole candle & crept into bed, where the kind girl tucked me in. But it was in vain, I repeated poetry & exerted my reason. I whose courage had that morning been so admired & extoll'd by my fellow travellers, when in danger of losing my life, was now ill with imaginary terrors. After about an hour, I heard doors opening & shutting, then foot steps ascending the stairs—then some one at my door, who whispered, "Are you awake?" To which I gladly answered "Yes," for even the entrance of robbers would have been welcome. But it was my good old lady, who feeling uneasy, had made her youngest daughter, a little girl the size of Anna Maria get up & brought her to me as a bed fellow. The moment I felt *warm* flesh & blood near me & her little arm round me my trembling & shiverings ceased & soon I drop't into a sweet sleep, from which I was awaken'd by a bright sun, shining in my windows. My pretty bed fellow assisted to dress me & when I went down in the sitting room, I found a fine looking grey-headed old man that put me in mind of Mr. K. He was the father of the family, & I had again in answer to his questions to relate my dangers & hair breadth escapes. A little breakfast table was set for me, & when done they cut this sheet of paper out of a book for me & with an old stub of a pen, I am sitting by the stove to write. No stage has yet pass'd. I think it probable the roads were so dangerous near the Susquehanah & so deep elsewhere, something may have happen'd & that they will not be along till in the evening or night, like us. I can find no book in the house, so for my own amusement as well as yours will write on, if it is all day & by way of making it answer for a chapter in the great work, will go into details in the novel style—this will be killing two birds with one stone.

Now to begin my journal. Like all other times of war & peace, it affords little to say. My ride to Baltimore was as pleasant as on a summer's day, my companion a very agreeable man who knew everybody I knew in New York, & we talked of all the old acquaintance of twenty & 30 years back—he told me who he was, his business & family. I told him who I was, my husband's business & our family & before we reached Baltimore felt like old acquaintance. When the stage stopp'd we were taken into the stage office & found on enquiry, not a single passenger was going on to Philad. Mr. Dey, said if I would wait he would go to the other stage office & enquire. There were a parcel of men standing round, but no one offer'd me a chair. I asked one of them to carry my letter into Mr. Williamson. Soon after the bar keeper, came & asked me to walk into a parlour, where a very genteel young man, came & in the most respectful way, enquir'd what he could do for my accomodation, stating his father was very ill, but he would execute any commands I might give him. When he understood my wishes, he begg'd me to walk in a better parlour up stairs, while he would go to the other stage office & learn what passengers there were, begging me to feel quite at home & order what I pleased. He soon return'd, likewise Mr. Dey, with information there were two gentlemen going on to Philad. I then ordered a slight dinner, while Mr. D. went to take my seat & speak to the gentlemen & Mr.——

The stage stopp'd & I left off. In the stage were very clever people, but you may judge of the state of the roads, when I was four hours coming 15 miles. At four o'clock I got safely here, but alas not to find all as happy as I had hoped, the whole family were in the greatest anxiety as Sally was very ill. I did not see sister or Elizabeth until this morning, her life was in danger I believe for some hours, at one, the child was born—it was six months, it is still alive but no probability of its living. I hope Sally is out of danger, but poor sister & brother are very, very anxious. In this state of the family I feel in the way, 'tho' all are kind enough to persuade me to stay longer, I think it best to go tomorrow. Brother would have gone with me, had not this event occur'd. Oh how frail is the tenure of human felicity. This happy family may soon be plunged into the greatest grief. Mrs. Bayard, Caroline, Susan & Mrs. Hodge * & several other friends came in to see me & have been again this morning. I can scarcely steal time for a few lines, & am writing with them all around me. All are unsettled, going & coming from Sally's. I feel anxious but shall go tomorrow. I am perfectly well, all the better for the exposure & adventures I have met with. I meant to give you an account of the passage of the Susquehannah, & the rest of my journey, but now I feel in no spirits to write it. All our friends & connections of all the different families are in deep mourning. I do not want the girls to get any, but it might be as well to lay aside their gay ribbons. Things seem very different here & at Sidney—they have just come in to say Sally is much better & has fallen asleep. This is very favorable. I wrote those few lines from Elketon under the impression the mail to Washington would be missing, but it was the northern mail which was deranged. I cannot write more now, for every moment some one is coming in. Heaven bless you all.

M. H. Smith.

I cannot even read over what I have written.

* Mrs. Smith's mother, Col. Bayard's first wife (he was married three times), was Margaret Hodge.

Washington: A Predestined Capital (1901)

WASHINGTON: A PREDESTINED CAPITAL

By Anne Hollingsworth Wharton

Author of "Through Colonial Doorways," "Colonial Days and Dames," etc.

IN Boston it is said that the winding streets which so perplex strangers were made to follow the cow-paths of more primitive days. Wandering through the wide-spread thoroughfares of Washington, losing one's self in a labyrinth of streets and avenues to awaken in a circle, one might almost believe that the intricacies of these streets and avenues had been laid out upon the circuitous windings of an old Indian trail. This theory, however, falls to the ground before the many documents which prove that the plan of the city of Washington, mysterious as it is beautiful, is the result of a most carefully defined system of streets, avenues, and circles.

Washington, as it stands to-day, with more than a hundred years upon its head, is simply a development of the plan made by the French engineer, Major L'Enfant, whose scheme for beautifying the nation's capital has been followed by his successors.

Even if we may not trace the footprints of the native tribes of the forest in the intricate streets of the capital, it is interesting to know that the broad plain which General Washington chose for the site of the Federal City was once the capital of the powerful Algonquin Nation. Here the villages of a number of tribes were built, and near Capitol Hill, where the laws are made for the guidance of a great nation, the smoke of Indian camp-fires ascended towards the blue vault that now arches one of the most beautiful of modern cities.

General Washington, we are told by Martin, probably knew that the ten-mile square had once been the capital of an Indian nation, and although this may have appeared to him an interesting coincidence, his choice of the site of the new city was guided by considerations more practical. Jefferson and Madison were closely associated with Washington in this important selection, and numerous letters still preserved in the Department of State prove how earnestly and conscientiously they all considered this subject.

"In 1800 we are to go to the Indian place with the long name on the Potomac," wrote the Secretary of the Treasury one hundred years ago. Mr. Wolcott evidently referred to the mouth of the Conococheague, in Washington County, Maryland. The President had full power to locate the capital anywhere upon the Potomac between the mouth of the Conococheague and the Eastern Branch. That he should have chosen the V-shaped plateau lying between the Potomac and its chief tributary is not only a proof of Washington's foresight and sagacity, but of his thorough acquaintance with the territory. On this broad plain he had hunted, fished, and carried the surveyor's chain in his youth, and here he had encamped with General Braddock before the ill-fated western expedition.

The original boundaries of the "Territory of Columbia," as defined in the official proclamation, included a ten-mile square, starting at Jones's Point, the upper cape of Hunting Creek, in Virginia, the two lines beginning at an angle of forty-five degrees, and after running far asunder uniting in a terminal point at the junction of the Potomac and the Eastern Branch.

The choice made by the President and his advisers having been abundantly justified by the experience of a hundred years, the story of how this choice was finally accepted by Congress may be of some interest to-day. Various reasons have been given to explain why Philadelphia was not made the capital, among these the frequent and violent epidemics of yellow-fever in the Quaker City. In point of fact, the most severe and prolonged outbreaks of fever occurred when Congress was in session in Philadelphia, after the whole question of the residence had been finally settled, and the bill in favor of the banks of the Potomac passed.

❧

According to Mr. Jefferson's statement in his "Anas," the site of the capital was not really decided in Congress, but over the Virginia statesman's dinner-table. It may have been to this dinner that Senator Maclay referred when he wrote in his New York diary, July 20, 1790, as if carefully washing his hands of it, "There was a dinner this day which I had no notice of and never thought of such a thing."

Mr. Jefferson, now Secretary of State, had recently returned from abroad. Colonel Hamilton met him in front of the President's house, and as the two walked up and down the street together, Hamilton explained to Jefferson the strained relations between the North and South. If, he argued, the North accepted the bill for the assumption of the domestic debt and secured the residence of the capital for a Northern city, Mr. Hamilton clearly saw dangers and difficulties ahead, even an early secession of the Southern States, while, on the other hand, if the war-debt of twenty millions were not assumed by the General Government there was a danger of the Eastern or creditor States seceding from the federation. Plainly a compromise was necessary, in the opinion of the wise and far-seeing Hamilton. Mr. Jefferson pleaded ignorance of the matter, as he had been abroad. He would, he said, be pleased if Colonel Hamilton would dine with him the next day, meet a few Virginians, and discuss the question calmly over Madeira and punch. Like many other important matters, the site of the capital was decided over a glass of wine, and before the guests quitted the table the bargain was concluded, and in this case a fair bargain, and one that the nation has never had reason to regret, for those who met over Mr. Jefferson's table were actuated by no motives of self-interest or greed of gain, but by such only as had in view the good of the country.

Alexander White and Richard Bland Lee bound themselves to vote for assumption, while Alexander Hamilton and Robert Morris undertook to carry through a bill fixing the seat of Congress in Philadelphia for ten years, and after that time permanently upon the banks of the Potomac.

This clause fixing a ten-years residence in Philadelphia was inserted in order to mollify the Pennsylvania Senators, who had had every reason to expect the capital to be located in their State. Indeed, a bill had passed both houses in September, 1789, locating the capital in a ten-mile square of the quaint old village of Germantown. That this old German settlement should have been thus distinguished was no more remarkable than that Trenton, Harrisburg, Wright's Ferry, Lancaster, and various other unimportant inland towns should have been seriously considered as sites for the capital city.

❧

The Board of Commissioners appointed to attend to all practical details connected with the establishment of the seat of government were Governor Thomas Johnson, of Maryland, who had served under Washington in the long war, the Honorable Daniel Carroll, who owned much of the property included within the limits of the projected city, and Dr. David Stuart, of Virginia, who was an old and trusted friend of the President. Dr. Stuart was connected with Washington's family by marriage, having become the second husband of pretty Eleanor Custis, the widow of Mrs. Washington's son, John Custis.

In his diary Washington recorded several meetings with the Commissioners during his brief holiday trips to Mount Vernon. On the 28th of March, 1791, he wrote that he found the interests of the landholders about Georgetown and those about Carrollsburgh so much at variance that they might prove injurious to the best interests of the public. After a meeting at his lodgings with the adverse parties, and a dinner with the Commissioners at General Forrest's, the President wrote more cheerfully of the prospect of an adjustment between the landholders.

General Uriah Forrest, the owner of Rosedale, was a friend of Washington. The house in which the President dined with General Forrest and the Commissioners is still standing upon Georgetown Heights. It is occupied by the descendants of General Forrest, who take pleasure in showing the broad piazza where the President and the Commissioners sat discussing preliminaries, while in imagination they beheld the well-wooded and well-watered plain before them transformed into the beautiful city of their dreams.

The principal landowners in the ten-mile square were Daniel Carroll, Samuel Davidson, Notley Young, and David Burns. Thomas Beale, Robert Peter, James Lingan, Benjamin Stoddert, and others owned land within the limits of the new city. Mr. Carroll owned a large patrimonial estate along the Eastern Branch, including the site of the Capitol. This property failed to appreciate in value, while the land of David Burns near the White House soon became valuable. The canny Scotchman may have realized that his property would rise in value more rapidly than the more eastern lots. For this reason, or because of a certain native tenacity and obstinacy, he gave President Washington more trouble than any of the other landholders, and frequent visits were made by the President to the little cottage of Davy Burns, which stood for so many years at the foot of Seventeenth Street.

❦

By the end of February, 1791, Burns and all the other landowners had come to terms, and on September 18, 1793, the President took part as a Mason in the ceremonies of laying the corner-stone of the Capitol. This was done amid discharges of artillery, addresses, and prayers. The plate, with its offering of corn, wine, and oil, was placed upon the corner-stone by the President, while an ox weighing five hundred pounds was barbecued and partaken of by the company.

By the time the corner-stone of the Capitol was laid, Major L'Enfant had quarrelled with the Commissioners in general and with Mr. Carroll in particular. The latter's new house on New Jersey Avenue, he had pulled down because the situation did not suit him.

Major L'Enfant was succeeded by Andrew Ellicott, who had been his assistant. He closely followed the original design of the French engineer, and it is indisputable that to L'Enfant belongs the glory and honor of having first outlined upon paper the city of Washington as it now stands. The design of L'Enfant is still preserved among important manuscripts in Washington. It was the overbearing Frenchman's refusal to hand over his plan to the Commissioners, even when requested to do so by Washington himself, that finally led to his dismissal. He declined a handsome sum of money sent him by the Government as compensation for his services, and refused a building-lot placed at his disposal. After executing some designs for public buildings in Philadelphia, he retired to Green Hill, near Bladensburg, the seat of his friend, Dudley Digges. Here Major L'Enfant spent the last years of his life, and here he died and was buried.

That General Washington's estimate of L'Enfant's abilities and limitations was a fair one is proved by the fact that when, in 1812, the engineer was appointed to superintend the construction of Fort Washington, he again quarrelled with his associates and was obliged to relinquish his position.

❦

Although Washington was a new city, existing chiefly upon paper when the Government was removed thither in 1800, it was fortunate in being near several old towns. Georgetown and Alexandria were both places of some importance in the trade of the Colonies, and both boasted a social life of more or less distinction, according to the value placed upon education, refinement, and the graces of life. In Alexandria was Christ Church, built prior to 1765, and attended by the planters and their families from the neighboring countryside, while near by—religious and social duties seeming to go hand in hand, as in old England—was the famous inn where many noted guests were entertained. Alexandria boasted its Dancing Assembly, and here balls were given in Colonial and Revolutionary days. The long hall is still shown, now divided into several rooms, where Washington and Lafayette entered into the gayeties of the hour.

Georgetown, which was separated from the Federal City by the picturesque and beautiful Rock Creek that now flows through one of the city parks, was the centre of much gayety and genuine Southern hospitality. Here stood Union Tavern, a fashionable inn, where General Washington so often recorded that he met the Potomac Company and afterwards dined. At this old-time hostelry were entertained such guests from abroad as Louis Philippe, Talleyrand, the eccentric French traveller Volney, Lafayette, Jerome Bonaparte, and Baron von Humboldt. Of this latter German nobleman Mrs. Madison wrote in 1804: "He is the most polite, modest, well-informed, and interesting traveller we have ever met, and is much pleased with America. I hope one day you will become acquainted with our Baron Humboldt. . . . He had with him a train of philosophers who, though clever and entertaining, did not compare to the Baron."

Mr. Thomas Peter, who married Mrs. Washington's granddaughter,

Martha Custis, was living in one of the few houses in the Federal City in the latter years of the century, for General Washington recorded in his diary in January, 1798, that he "lodged at Mr. T. Peters." A few years later Mr. Peter built his handsome house, Tudor Place, on Georgetown Heights, which stands to-day seemingly untouched by the hand of time.

The home of Francis Scott Key, author of "The Star-Spangled Banner," was at Georgetown; here also lived the Fitzgeralds, Alexanders, Mackalls, Masons, and many other old Virginia families.

General Mason, in addition to his Georgetown residence, had a beautiful home on Analostan Island in the Potomac, and a country-seat, "Clermont," in Fairfax County, Virginia. Mrs. Benjamin Stoddert, in writing of Mrs. Mason in 1760, said: "She is a charming woman—not so much in her face as in her whole deportment—her face tho' quite pretty enough, for she has charming eyes and fine teeth—and plays delightfully and sings really sweetly—her face as I before began to say is not as pretty as I expected, but she has sufficient reason to be satisfied with it. I know I should if I had such a one—her sister I imagine is more a beauty to please the Ladies than Mrs. Mason is, for Miss Murray looks all *amiability,* very pretty too."

Mrs. Mason's sister, Miss Murray, whom Mrs. Stoddert also found so charming, afterwards married the Honorable Richard Rush, of Philadelphia.

Mr. J. Harrison Smith, founder, first editor, and proprietor of the *National Intelligencer,* owned a country-seat called "Sydney," in Georgetown. This house, which was the gathering-place for distinguished men from near and far, and the scene of many animated political and legislative discussions, is still standing within the grounds of the Catholic University. Georgetown was an early stronghold of Catholicism in America, and the college founded there by Bishop John Carroll, in 1789, was the first Catholic educational institution of any size established in the United States.

The old town also boasted a young ladies' school of some prominence, to which Mrs. Stoddert refers in her family letters. Major Benjamin Stoddert was appointed first Secretary of the Navy by John Adams, there having been no separate Naval Bureau until his administration. In consequence of his official duties Mr. Stoddert removed with his family from his home in Georgetown to Philadelphia in 1798. While living in the capital, Mrs. Stoddert wrote many charming letters to her family, inserting vivid and spicy descriptions of the gayeties that surrounded her, of the fashions and beauties of the day, of birth-night balls, levees at Mrs. Adams's and Lady Liston's, and of brilliant sumptuous entertainments at Mrs. Bingham's. In one of her letters to her niece, Miss Eliza Gantt, of Graden, Maryland, Mrs. Stoddert, after retailing a piece of gossip connected with "an elopement in high life," quotes Mr. Stoddert as saying that "large towns are terrible places for young females," adding, "and I am sure I can find nothing in this to make an old female wish to remain in it one moment longer than necessity obliges."

❧

When the seat of government was removed from Philadelphia to Washington the Stodderts were fortunate in being able to go to their own home in Georgetown, as Mr. Stoddert had built himself a house at the corner of Prospect and Federal Streets. A number of the government officials rented houses or boarded in this old town, which boasted about three hundred and fifty houses and a population of three thousand souls.

When President Adams arrived at the capital in June, 1800, he seems to have lodged in Georgetown, as the White House was not yet habitable, nor was it completed the following November, when Congress first met in the Federal City, as appears from the mingling of elegance and discomfort so graphically pictured in Mrs. Adams's letters.

Mr. Abraham Bradley, Assistant Postmaster-General, wrote that he had secured a large three-story house for Mr. Habersham, the Postmaster-General, within a few rods of Blodget's Hotel. This inn, which was doubtless named after Mr. Samuel Blodget, of Philadelphia, who had invested largely in Washington lots, was situated midway between the Capitol and the White House. It was also spoken of as the Great Hotel. Dr. Samuel Busey, who has made careful and accurate researches into the early life in Washington, locates the house engaged by Mr. Bradley for the Postmaster-General near the corner of Ninth and E Streets, Northwest. Blodget's Hotel occupied the site of the south wing of the present Post-Office Department.

Many fanciful tales with regard to the removal of the government have been repeated until they have gained credence. One story to the effect that the treasure of the United States was brought to Washington in one two-horse wagon is readily disproved by the fact that all the government effects, including books, papers, and moneys, were conveyed in vessels. Christopher Hines, in giving his recollections of this time, says that these vessels landed and discharged their cargoes at Lear's Wharf, and that their contents were then carted away to the War and Treasury offices, the only two government buildings erected at that time. Mr. Hines says that many of the boxes were marked with the name of Joseph Nourse, who was then Register of the Treasury, and that as wagons were scarce in Washington one cart was employed to remove the contents of the ships. This fact may have given rise to the one-wagon story, as it is not stated how many trips the single cart made from the wharf to the government offices. Another statement, that "a single packet ship" brought all the government furniture and archives to Washington, is also disproved by Mr. Hines's recollections, in which he speaks of several vessels being used in the transfer. It also appears from the records of the Treasury Department that the expense of the removal amounted to forty thousand dollars, which was a rather large sum for a moving that could be accommodated in one wagon or ship.

All the outlay of government officials, incident to a change of residence, as well as the expenses of the journey, was defrayed by the Treasury, as appears from the records of this department, to which bills for removal and incidental expenses were presented by Charles Lee, the Attorney-General, Samuel Meredith, Treasurer of the United States, Benjamin Stoddert, and other officials. One John Little, a clerk in the Register's Office, sent in a bill for moving expenses, which is a triumph in the art of itemizing. In this bill, after giving various items for carriage hire, travelling expenses, and board, Mr. Little states that "during the hurry attending a removal many incidental expenses occurred of which he kept no account," adding, "the damage occasioned by the removal of my furniture was considerable, which with cooperage, porterage from my house in Philadelphia to the wharf, and other necessary expenses not enumerated, would upon a moderate computation, amount to $80.00."

❦

The best descriptions of the condition of the Federal City when Congress met there in November, 1800, are to be found in the letters and diaries of the time. Congress assembled in a small wing of the unfinished Capitol, and the government officials who could not find accommodations at Blodget's Hotel, or in the two rows of new houses called the "Six and Seven Buildings," on Pennsylvania Avenue between Nineteenth and Twenty-second Streets, were obliged to find lodgings in Georgetown, between which place and the Capitol stretched three miles of bad road. A number of houses and several farm-houses were scattered over the "ten-mile square," and a little hamlet of shanties occupied Greenleaf's Point; but Mr. John Cotton Smith says that the only really comfortable houses within the city limits were those of Daniel Carroll and Notley Young, which were surrounded by gardens. Mr. Smith, who was a member of Congress from Connecticut, says that the Connecticut members lodged with a Mr. Peacock on New Jersey Avenue, in company with Senators Chipman and Paine, of Vermont, "all in pairs" except Speaker Sedgewick, who was allowed a room to himself, adding, "to my excellent friend Davenport and myself was allowed a spacious and decently furnished apartment, with separate beds, on the lower floor."

A little later the Reverend Manasseh Cutler wrote to his daughter of being pleasantly "paired" with the Honorable Nathan Read in a fine room at Mr. King's, east of the Capitol. Here they were comfortably situated and most agreeably entertained in the evenings by the host's daughter, Miss Anna, who played for them on "an excellent Forte Piano," and indulged them in such songs as "The Way-Worn Traveller," "The Twins of Latma," or "Selim's Complaint," while on a Sunday she varied the programme by treating the company to "Old Hundred," "Denmark," and "St. Martin's," in which General Ebenezer Mattson, Mr. Elias Perkins, and the other guests joined with great spirit.

Mr. Wolcott wrote to his wife that he had been obliged to take lodgings more than half a mile from his office in the Treasury Department, and so situated he finds himself better off than many of his associates.

With all the inconveniences incident to life in the new capital, it is not strange that the Adams administration was not marked by much gayety in social life. Mrs. Adams told her daughter that the ladies clamored for a drawing-room, which was held on New Year's Day, 1801, in the still unfinished White House. Mrs. Benjamin Stoddert wrote to her niece of dining at the President's and having a dozen or fourteen to dine with her. Although Mrs. Stoddert seems to have entertained numerous guests herself, which necessitated constant recourse to the pages of Mrs. Glass, she says that there was not half the gayety in Georgetown that she had expected to see follow the advent of Congress.

Mr. Adams's four years of office ended in March, 1801, and the elderly couple, who had spent only a few months in the White House, returned with their Lares and Penates to Braintree, Massachusetts, reflecting, and with some justice, perhaps, upon the ingratitude of republics.

During Mr. Jefferson's administration life in the Executive Mansion was conducted with generous hospitality, but with extreme simplicity. It was not until the inauguration of Mr. Madison, in 1809, that the Graces took up their abode in the White House. Under the gentle sway of Mrs. Madison, whose social tact and charm reached the dignity of a talent, and during the reign of Mrs. John Quincy Adams, who was so cultivated that she drew around her the most brilliant men and women of her time, a new era was inaugurated in the social life of the capital.